Dear you,
your second
hard back ART BRUT book
you are not doing too
badly. 'BLUG' means
'plough' in German dialogue
and is a reference to
Franz Kernbeis - one
of the Gugging artists.
Love,
me
xxx

blug

gugging
- ein ort der kunst

gugging
- grounds for art

Johann Feilacher

Christian Brandstätter Verlag
2006

Inhalt / directory

Johann Feilacher

blug – der pflug oder eine logische folge

Als ich nach Gugging kam, hatte Dr. Leo Navratil schon etwa 20 Jahre mit seinen talentierten Patienten gezeichnet - mit ihnen sein eigenes Leben gestaltet und begonnen, ihnen ein neues Verständnis in der Öffentlichkeit zu geben. Das Zentrum für Kunst-Psychotherapie war zwei Jahre alt und Navratil suchte einen späteren Nachfolger, damit seine Bemühungen nicht früher oder später der Vergessenheit anheim fallen, sondern weitergeführt werden sollten. Die Errungenschaften sollten weitergehen, die Künstler weiter gefördert werden.

Auf den ersten Blick war es ein Haus voller interessanter Persönlichkeiten mit unterschiedlichen und bemerkenswerten Talenten. Ein Ort, an dem es noch viele Aufgaben gab. Ich erhielt die Möglichkeit, mich diesen Aufgaben zu widmen. 23 Jahre später ist es immer noch so. Nach dieser zweiten Periode Guggings, zwanzig Jahre nach dem Ausscheiden Navratils, ist ein neuerlicher Meilenstein in der Geschichte dieses Ortes erreicht worden, der ein Verschwinden des Projektes aus der Geschichte unwahrscheinlich macht. Ein eigenes Museum für die Künstler aus Gugging ist nicht nur ein Meilenstein für Gugging, sondern auch für die österreichische Kunstgeschichte und die Art Brut allgemein. Ein Ort, an dem sich die Art Brut mit allen anderen Kunstrichtungen treffen, einander ergänzen und auch messen wird können. Es ist eine Stiftungssammlung vorhanden, die wesentliche Werke von Kunst aus Gugging schon beinhaltet und noch unbeschränkt erweitert werden kann. Dieses *Art/Brut Center* will aber keine zweite *Collection de l'art brut* in Lausanne werden, sondern ein Ort, an dem auch Künstler aktiv tätig sein sollen und junge und ältere Talente sich aus aller Welt treffen können. Der Schrägstrich zwischen *Art* und *Brut* soll die Öffnung auch für die Kommunikation mit anderen Richtungen der Kunst aufzeigen: ein Treffpunkt für Diskussion und Diskurs, auch

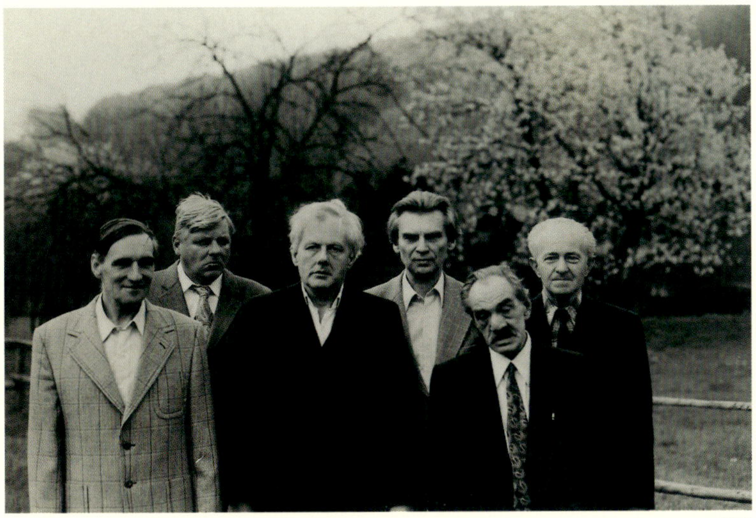

1970

hauser, mach, reck, navratil, herbeck, tschirtner

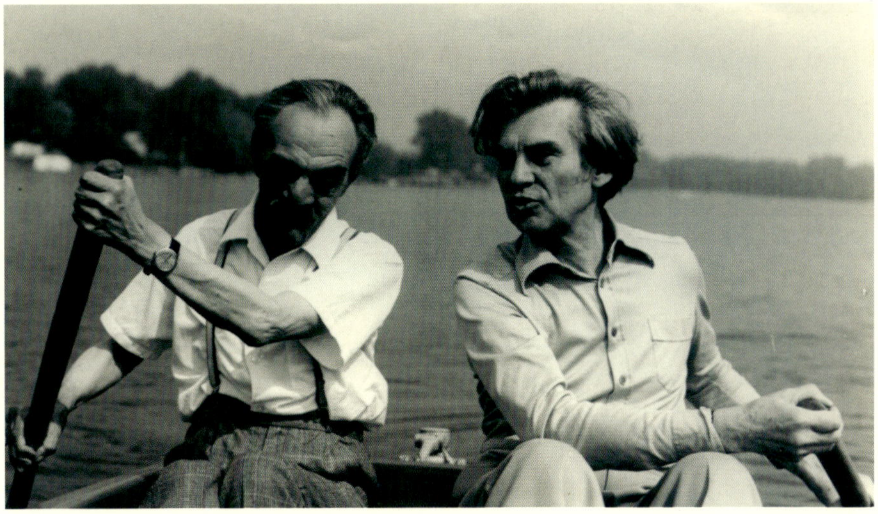

1968

herbeck, navratil

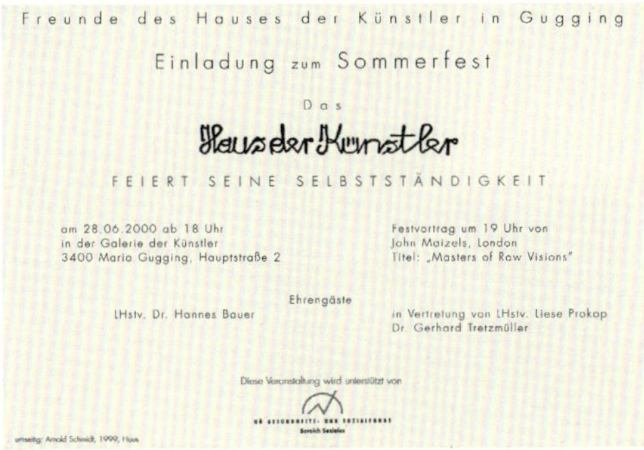

Freunde des Hauses der Künstler in Gugging

Einladung zum Sommerfest

Das

Haus der Künstler

FEIERT SEINE SELBSTSTÄNDIGKEIT

am 28.06.2000 ab 18 Uhr
in der Galerie der Künstler
3400 Maria Gugging, Hauptstraße 2

Festvortrag um 19 Uhr von
John Maizels, London
Titel: „Masters of Raw Visions"

Ehrengäste

LHstv. Dr. Hannes Bauer

in Vertretung von LHstv. Liese Prokop
Dr. Gerhard Tretzmüller

Diese Veranstaltung wird unterstützt von

umseitig: Arnold Schmidt, 1999, Haus

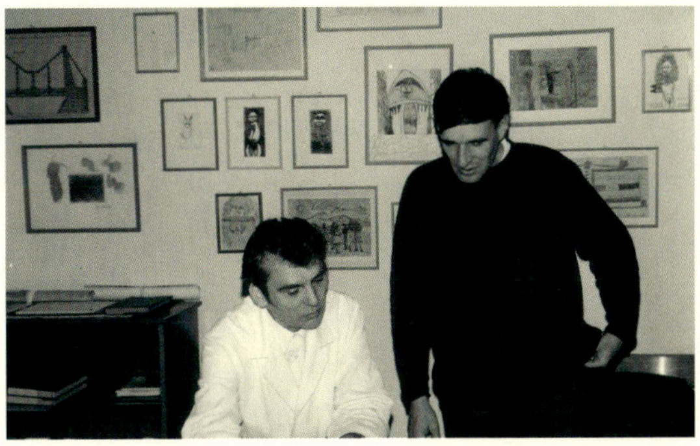

1970

navratil, hauser

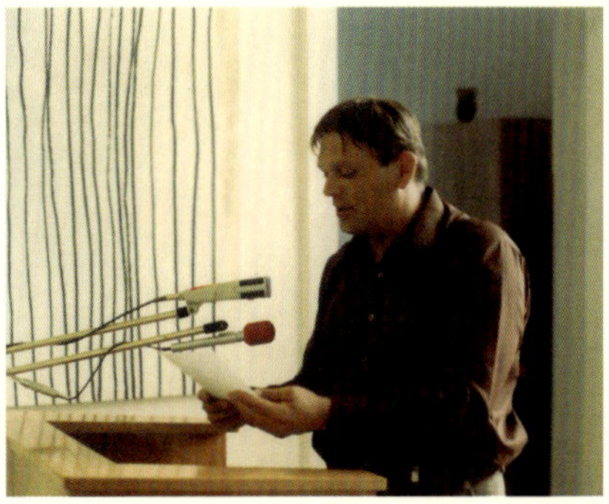

1982

garber

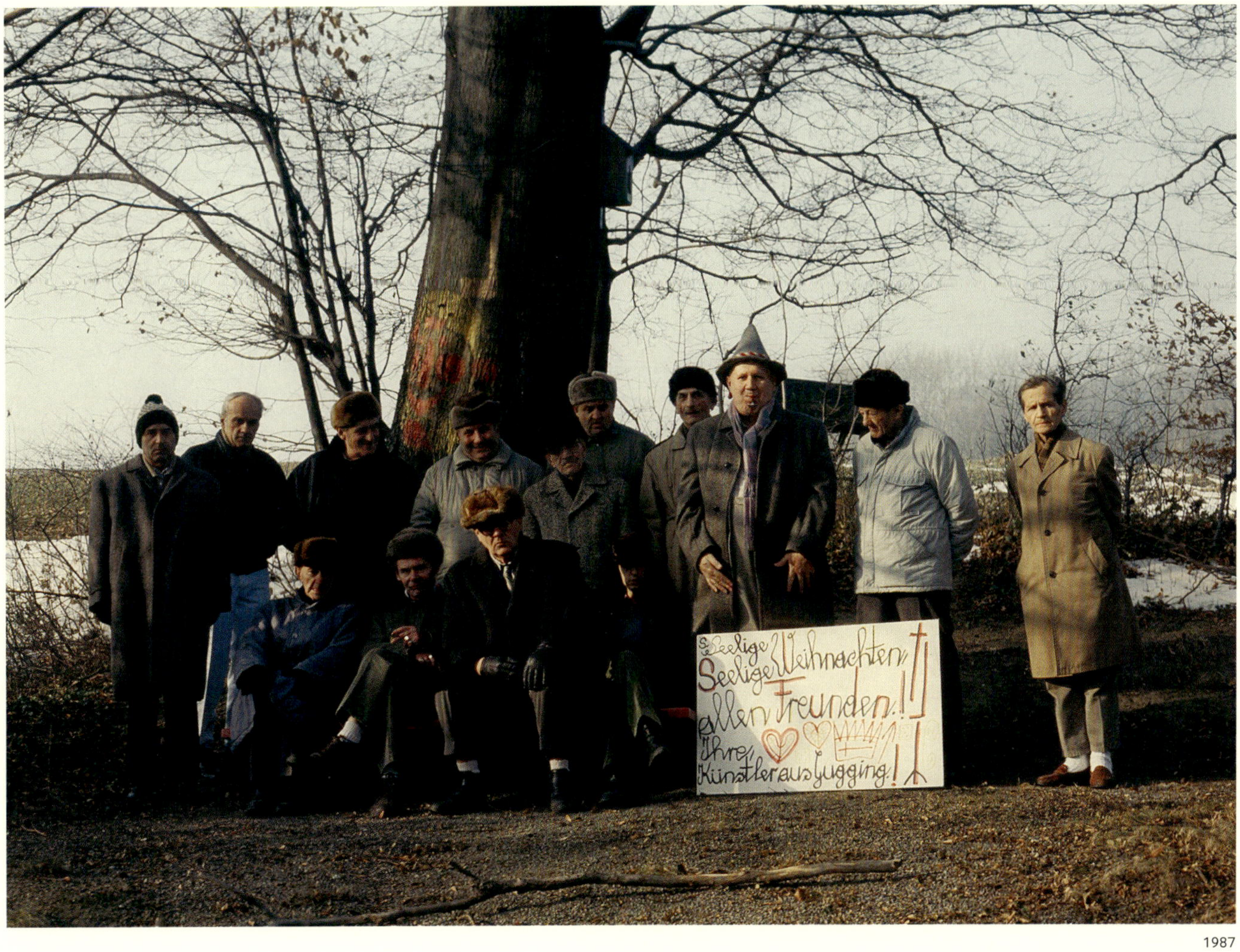

1987

foto für weihnachtskarte / photo for christmas card

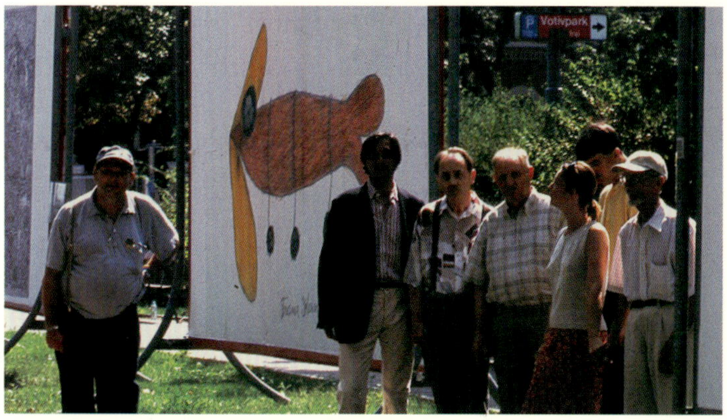

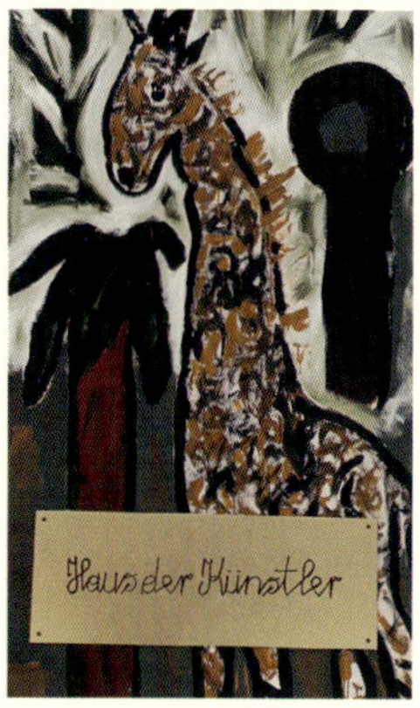

2003
summerstage wien / vienna

1988

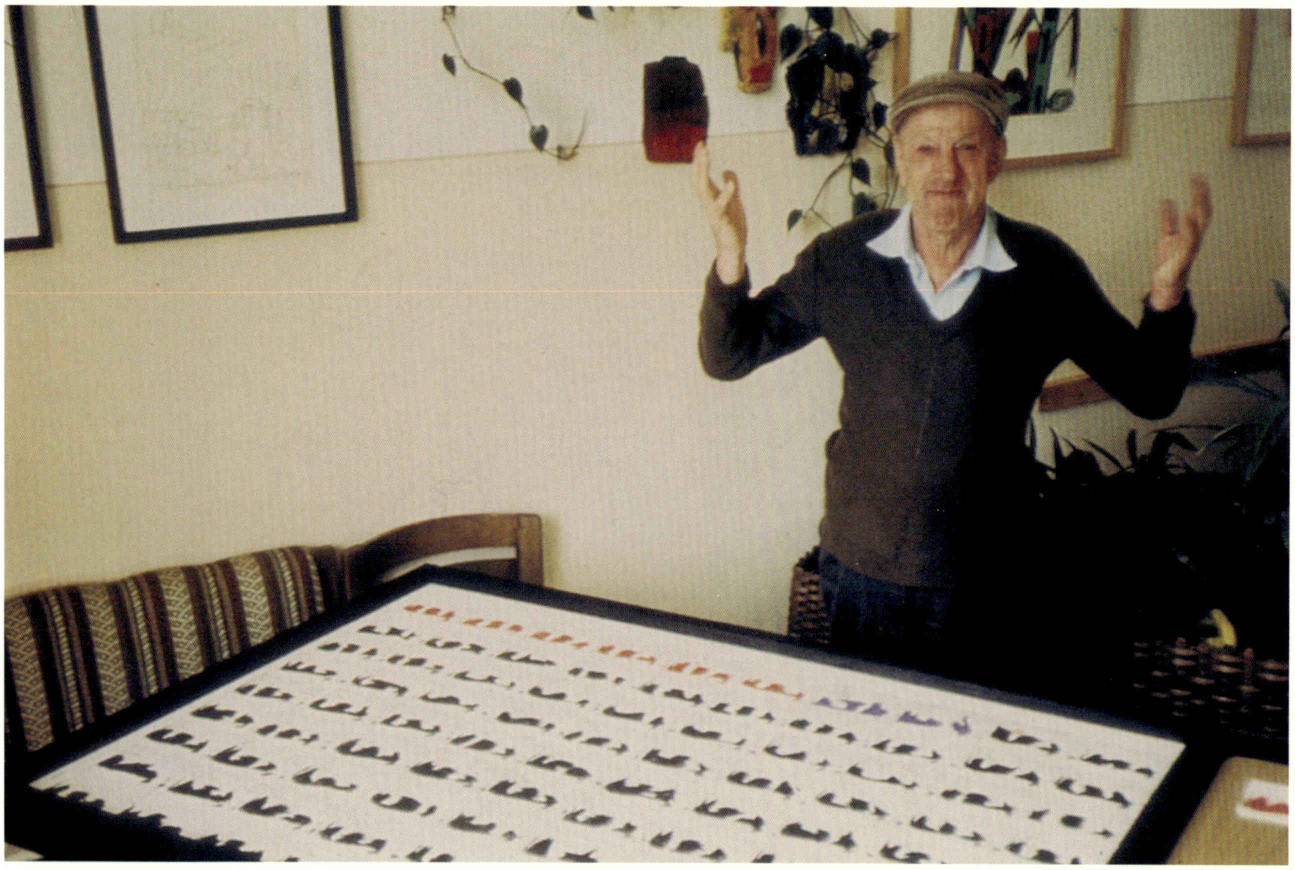

1983
kamlander

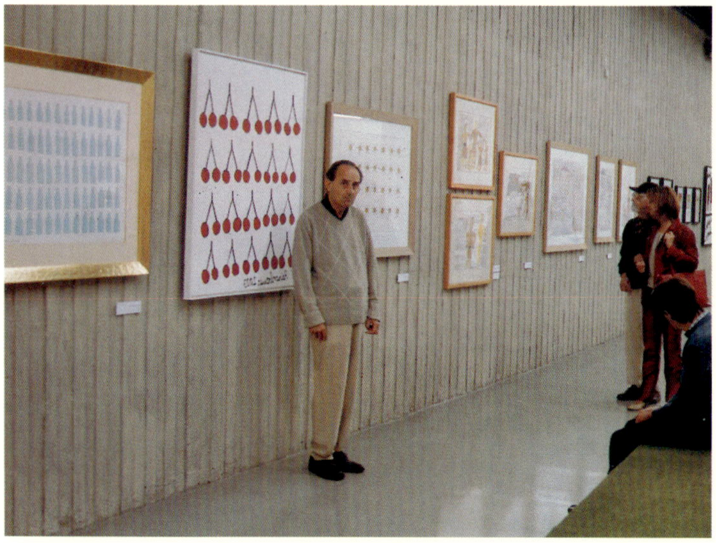

2005, Bratislava
heinrich reisenbauer, slowakische nationalgalerie / slovak national gallery

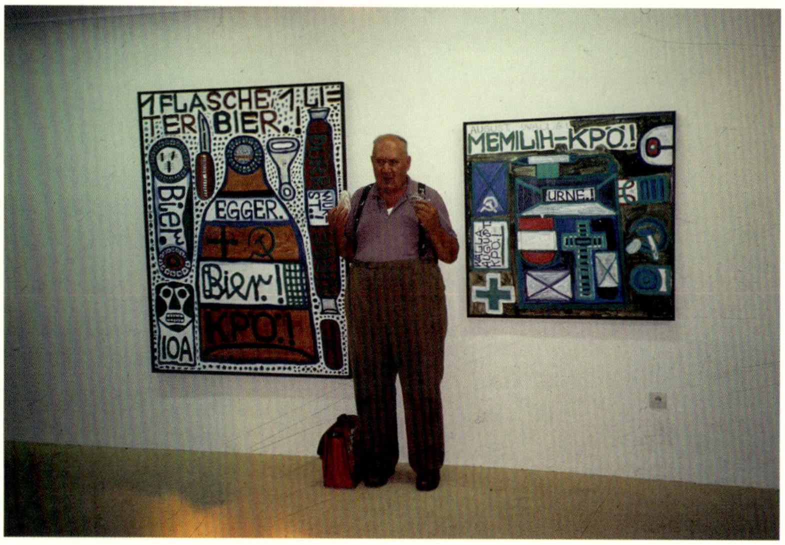

1993, Salzburg
august walla
galerie altnöder

Johann Feilacher

blug, the plow or a logical next step

When I first came to Gugging in 1983, Dr. Leo Navratil had been drawing with his talented patients for about 20 years. He had created a life with them and had started to raise a new public awareness for their art. At that point, the *Center for Art-Psychotherapy* was two years old and Dr. Navratil was looking for a possible successor. He did not want his efforts to fade into oblivion over the course of time, but to be continued. His achievements should endure, and the Gugging Artists were to be supported in the future.

At first sight, the Center was a building full of interesting personalities, each with unique outstanding talents. It was a place where much work still needed to be done. I was given the opportunity to dedicate myself to that work. Twenty-three years later, this is still the case. After this second period in the life of the Gugging project, twenty years after Dr. Navratil resigned, we have reached another milestone that makes it highly unlikely that the project will fade from memory. The *Art/Brut Center* with a museum dedicated to the Gugging Artists, is not only a milestone for Gugging itself, but for Austrian art history and for Art Brut in general. The museum will be a place where Art Brut can intersect with all other artistic styles and where it can complement them by showing that it measures up to them. Our foundation has started a collection that includes the most important works by Gugging Artists. There are no limits to its expansion. The *Art/Brut Center* does not want to become a second *Collection de l'art brut* like the one in Lausanne, but instead be a place where artists can be actively engaged and younger as well as older talents from all over the world can meet. The slash between *Art* and *Brut* signalizes that Gugging is open to communication with other artistic directions. The museum will be a forum for discussion and discourse that wants to present starkly opposed works and increase their acceptance in the public eye.

Gegensätzliches soll hier vereint gezeigt und akzeptiert werden.

Auch der Weg dieser zweiten Periode Guggings war nicht immer ganz einfach. Die Bewohner des Hauses hatten schon Anerkennung als Künstler gefunden, sie begannen damit auch schon vereinzelt Geld zu verdienen. Der Weg in Richtung einer künstlerischen und sozialen Integration war angezeigt. Aber es gab noch einige Schritte zu bewältigen, um wirklich in diesem Metier akzeptiert zu werden: nicht nur als *Künstlerpatienten*, sondern als Künstler - ohne Vorbehalte und psychopathologische Assoziationen. Sie hatten ein Recht auf volle Anerkennung, sowohl ihrer Kunst, als auch als Menschen. Nicht soziale Almosen für ihre grandiosen Werke, sondern Gleichstellung mit allen anderen Künstlern sollen angestrebt werden; das heißt: gleiche Anerkennung für gleich gute Kunst und letztlich auch die Chance auf gleiche pekuniäre Bewertung.

Das *Zentrum für Kunst-Psychotherapie* war für mich ein Haus in dem primär Künstler lebten, also erhielt es dementsprechend auch gleich 1986 den Namen *Haus der Künstler*. Direktor Dr. Marksteiner war damit einverstanden. Die Möglichkeiten im Haus waren schon 1981 gegenüber den Zuständen im vorherigen *Pavillon 2* wesentlich verbessert worden. Aber sie konnten noch weiter optimiert werden, es musste mehr Platz für die einzelnen Bewohner geschaffen werden, indem man frei gewordene Plätze nicht nachbesetzte. Ausstellungen und Publikationen führten zu weiterer Bekanntheit, sogar in den USA und Japan. Durch größere Formate der Kunstwerke und die Ansammlung von vielen Graphiken und Malereien wurde der Platz im Haus immer enger. August Walla malte 3 mal 6 Meter große Bilder im ehemaligen Kohlenkeller, sonst war nirgends Platz in dieser Dimension.

Für eine weitere Förderung mussten Mitstreiter gefunden werden, da die Möglichkeiten der Klinik in diesem Bereich erschöpft waren. Es wurde ein Förderverein gegründet, der wegen seiner Gemeinnützigkeit die Möglichkeit bot, temporär geförderte Mitarbeiterinnen und Mitarbeiter anzustellen. Die anstehenden Aufgaben konnten alleine nicht mehr bewältigt werden.

Die Künstler sollten eine neue, gehobenere gesellschaftliche Positionen bekommen. Drei Jahre dauerte die Ausarbeitung und Überprüfung eines Vertrages zur Gründung einer Kommanditerwerbsgesellschaft, die sie zu Besitzern einer privaten Gesellschaft und damit einer eigenen wirtschaftlichen Vertretung machte. Damit war der Grundstein für die eigene (nicht subventionierte) Galerie geschaffen. Zuerst blieb dies jedoch noch der kleine Verkaufsraum im Untergeschoss des Hauses, den es schon lange gab.

Als im Nebengebäude Räume leer wurden, war dies eine Chance, unsere Möglichkeiten zu erweitern, zumindest ein Lager zu bekommen. Zwei Jahre später wurde das ganze Gebäude frei. Es war klar, dass diese Möglichkeit genützt werden musste. Das Gebäude war riesig, es hatte 3500 Quadratmeter benutzbare Fläche.

Es war immer knapp an Geld und die Energiekosten waren hoch, da das ganze Gebäude im Winter nicht zu kalt werden durfte. Wenn Wasserleitungen eingefroren wären, wäre es zerstört worden. Kostenlos arbeitende Mitarbeiter, unter ihnen etwa Florian Reese und Dieter de Vlieghere verbrachten unzählige Arbeitsstunden mit uns, um in Eigenregie Räume zu restaurieren und wie eine Galerie herzurichten: eine eigene Galerie, in der die Werke der Künstler aus Gugging präsentiert werden konnten - mit genügend Raum zur Verfügung für Lager und Ateliers.

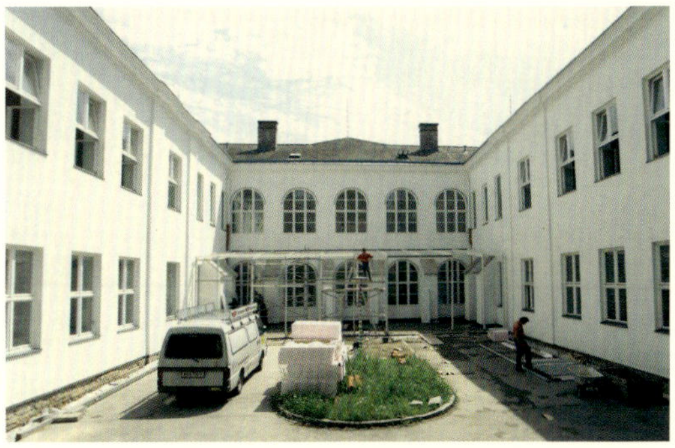

2006
Museumsgebäude / museumbuilding

The path of this second period in Gugging's life was not always an easy one. The residents of the building had already found artistic recognition. Some of them had even started to earn an income from their art. A path towards artistic and social integration was emerging. Some further steps needed to be taken, however, to ensure that the artists would be fully accepted in the art world without reservations and psychopathological associations. They had a right to be regarded as genuine artists, not just *as artistic patients.* Their artwork deserved to be fully recognized and they merited full acceptance as human beings. The artists didn't want social alms for their superb works, but longed instead to be put on a par with all other artists. Since their work was equally strong as other artists', it finally also deserved to receive the same financial evaluation.

From the beginning, I considered the *Center for Art-Psychotherapy* as a place inhabited primarily by artists. That is why it was given the name *House of Artists* in 1986, a decision that was fully supported by Director Marksteiner. As early as 1981, the facilities had been considerably improved from their previous existence at *Pavillon 2*. There was room for further improvement, however. By turning down new applicants, we created more space for our residents. Exhibitions and publications raised the artists' profile, even in the United States and Japan. As the artists started using larger formats and producing an increasing amount of graphic art and paintings, space became more and more restricted. August Walla even had to resort to the coal cellar to paint his three-by-six meter canvas. Otherwise, there wouldn't have been any room for this format.

After all hospital funds had been exhausted, we had to look for comrades-in-arms to raise additional funds. A non-profit development association was founded, which was able to employ temporary workers on a permanent basis. After all, just one person could no longer fulfill the tasks at hand.

The artists were ultimately to attain a better position in society. It took three years to draft and revise a contract to found a limited commercial partnership that would make the artists co-owners of a private company and turn them into independent economic agents. This was the cornerstone for their own non-subsidized gallery. At first, it was located in a small sales room on the first floor of the building, which had been used for this purpose for a long time.

When rooms in the adjacent building became available, we had a chance to expand and at least acquire storage space. Two years later, the entire building became available. It was clear that we had to seize this opportunity. The building was huge, providing us with 3,500 square meters of space. Resources were, however, always scarce. Energy costs ran high because we couldn't let the building get too cold in the winter. If our water pipes had frozen, the building would have been destroyed. Colleagues such as Florian Reese and Dieter de Vlieghere donated many hours of unremunerated work to restore the rooms with us and to turn them into an independent gallery for the Gugging Artists, which was to provide enough space for both storage and studios.

The artists' work became increasingly popular once we were able to present it better in this new space. Nina Katschnig, who had been employed to serve our project by a public program for recent university graduates, became a full-fledged staff member of the gallery. Gertrude Hacker took charge of all administrative tasks for both the gallery and the association.

We started to think about creating a collection for the Foundation of Gugging

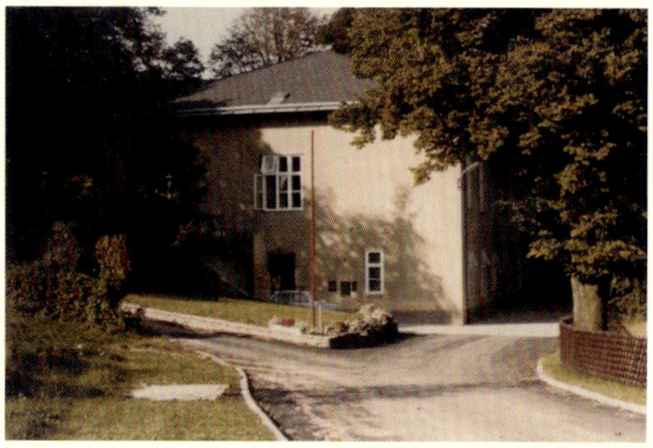

1980

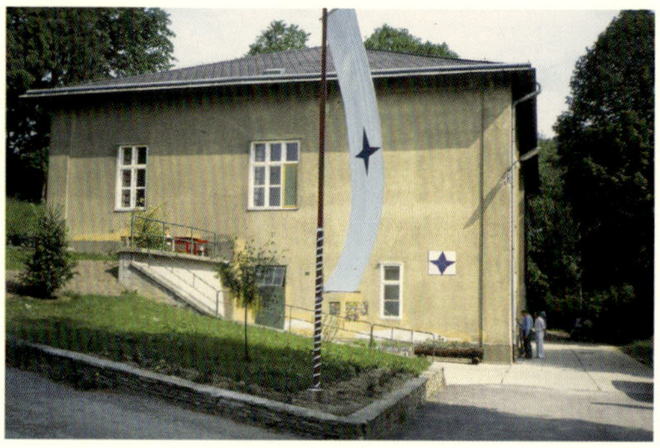

1981

Die Werke der Künstler fanden Anklang und konnten am eigenen Ort erstmalig besser präsentiert werden. Mag. Nina Katschnig, die bis zu diesem Zeitpunkt durch das Akademikertraining gefördert worden war, konnte nun aus eigenen Mitteln in der Galerie angestellt werden, Frau Gertrude Hacker für die Sekretariatsarbeiten sowohl für den Verein als auch die Galerie.

Die Idee einer Stiftungssammlung kam auf, damit Werke der Künstler nicht in alle Winde verstreut werden, sondern zur gemeinsamen Präsentation auch an Ort und Stelle bleiben können. Trotz Beratung durch den wohl hierorts besten Stiftungsrechtsexperten, Dr. Franz Helbich, dauerte es sieben weitere Jahre, bis diese Stiftung in die Realität umgesetzt werden konnte.

Der Weg der Selbstständigkeit sollte aber auch auf das Haus der Künstler übergreifen, und nach langen Verhandlungen mit Mitgliedern der niederösterreichischen Landesregierung, konnten diese für die Idee einer eigenen, selbstständigen Sozialhilfeeinrichtung gewonnen werden. Im Jahr 2000 war es soweit. Der Sprung in die Freiheit war getan und das Risiko der Eigenständigkeit konnte bis heute problemlos bewältigt werden.

Das Gebäude, in dem die Galerie untergebracht war, lag größtenteils brach. Es war natürlich verführerisch, diesen Raum auch gezielt zu nützen. *Die logische Folge* war die Idee eines eigenen Museums für Gugginger Künstler: ein Haus, in dem ihre Werke der großen internationalen Öffentlichkeit gezeigt werden konnten; ein Museum für Art Brut, aber nicht nur dafür, sondern eines, in dem man Vergleiche anstellen konnte zwischen Kunst jeder Stilrichtung mit Art Brut. Um zu zeigen, dass es sich nicht um irgendeine *psychopathologische*, sondern einfach um Kunst handelt, die jedem Vergleich mit anderen Kunstwerken standhält und die meisten sogar an Originalität übertrifft. Die großen und eher konservativen Museen zeigen Art Brut noch immer nicht, da noch vieles unter diesem Namen angepriesen wird, das den Titel *Art* eigentlich nicht verdient. Dieses neue Museum sollte ein Qualitätssiegel für die ausgestellten Künstler werden, so wie das MOMA New York für die Klassische Moderne eines darstellt.

Es war zu dieser Zeit kein Geld für ein Museum aufzutreiben, daher war ein Arbeitsprojekt mit Arbeitslosen die erste Möglichkeit, um mit dem Umbau zu beginnen. Es vergingen viereinhalb Jahre, bis in langsamer Kleinarbeit die erste Etage des hundert Jahre lang von Hausarbeitern zerbauten Gebäudes - neu hergerichtet und dem neuen Zweck angepasst - eröffnet werden konnte. Alle Mitarbeitenden hatten sich dafür verausgabt und in allen Bereichen mitgeholfen. Unzählige unbezahlte Überstunden wurden von ihnen geleistet. Nina Katschnig, Florian Reese, Kazimierz Parucki seien stellvertretend für alle genannt, die sich verdient machten. Aber es zahlte sich aus. Das Ergebnis, von dem vorher keiner geglaubt hatte, dass es zu erreichen wäre, überzeugte alle Besucher. Und die Künstler aus Gugging nahmen sofort Besitz von ihren neuen Räumen, nutzten die Ateliers oder kamen oft auch nur, um sich zu unterhalten, nutzten die neuen Räume als Kommunikationstreffpunkte.

Mit geringen Mitteln angefangen, erhielten wir nun von der niederösterreichischen Landesregierung nach der Fertigstellung der ersten Etage mit Galerie und Ateliers das Geld zur Restaurierung des zweiten Stockwerkes für das Museum. Auch das Bundeskanzleramt beteiligte sich und wir genießen nun die Unterstützung von Bund und Land. Die museale Architektur sollte ästhetisch und praktisch entsprechen, ohne die Grundsubstanz zu stören. Die Mittel reichten aus, um sehr sparsam, aber mit allen notwendigen

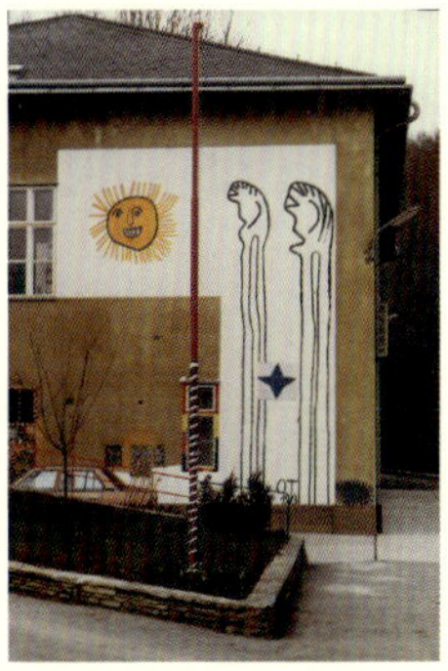

1983

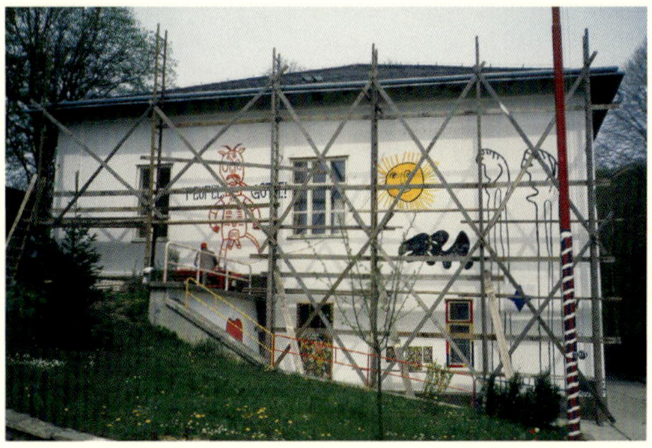

1984

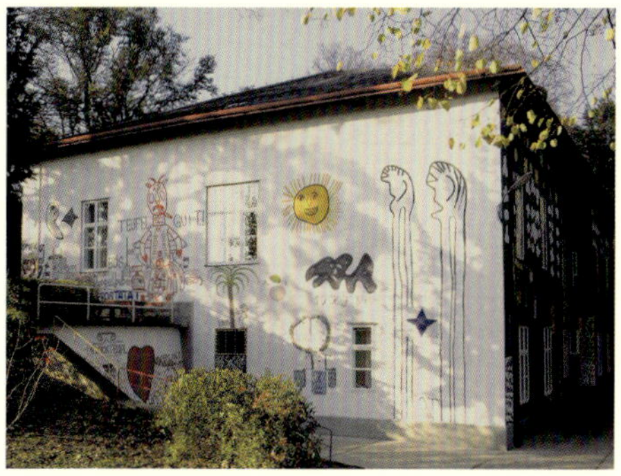

1995
Haus der Künstler / house of artists

Artists so that their work would not be dispersed into the four winds, but could remain on site and be jointly presented. In spite of the fact that the best local foundation expert, Dr. Franz Helbrich, lent us his invaluable advice, it took another seven years until the foundation became a reality.

The House of Artists was to follow an independent path, as well. After long negotiations with members of the government of Lower Austria, we were able to solicit support for an independent social aid organization. In the year 2000, the big moment came when freedom was finally achieved. We have been able to handle the risk of independence without a problem to this day.

The building in which the gallery was housed lay mostly idle. Of course, it was tempting to find a targeted use for its rooms. *A logical next step* was to establish a museum for Gugging Artists in which their work could be shown to a wide international public. It was to be a museum for Art Brut, but not only for that. It was also to be a place where comparisons between other styles and Art Brut could be drawn. We wanted to show that Art Brut was not just a *psychopathological* type of art, but that it could stand up to other styles and surpass most of them in its ingenuousness. The big and rather conservative museums still do not show Art Brut because many undeserving works bear this label. Our new museum is meant to serve as a seal of quality for all the artists it represents, just like MOMA New York is a hallmark of classical modernism.

In the mid to late 1990s, we were not able to raise the necessary funds to renovate the future museum. That is why we started reconstruction with a team of unemployed people. Four and a half years went by during which the first floor of the building was painstakingly adapted to its new purpose after having been subjected to ill-informed improvements for one hundred years. All staff members gave their utmost to help the project along. They donated innumerable hours of unpaid overtime to this project. I would just like to mention Nina Katschnig, Florian Reese, and Kazimierz Parucki to stand in for all those who helped us with this project. Their efforts really paid off. Even though nobody believed that we would reach our goal, we certainly have been able to convince our visitors with the results. The Gugging Artists immediately took possession of their new space and started using their studios. Sometimes, they would just drop in for a chat and use the new space to engage in conversation.

We started out with little means, but after finishing the gallery and studios on the first floor, we obtained funds from the Lower Austrian government to restore the second floor to establish our museum. The Federal Chancellery also became involved. We now receive support from both the federal and the provincial governments. The museum's architecture is designed to live up to high aesthetic and practical standards without damaging the building's substance. Our limited means were sufficient to open the museum and comply with all necessary safety and fire regulations. We had to cut back in many areas, but our preliminary solutions can always be expanded and completed at a later point in time.

The *Private Foundation of Gugging Artists* came into being one year ago and presently includes 230 works donated by the artists. The Lower Austrian government made the necessary budget available for the association to be founded. Additional private donations brought the number of works in the collection up to 600 originals and etchings. I am sure that many people will follow this example, with collectors entrusting their treasures to our museum.

Erfordernissen wie Sicherheit, Brandschutz usw. das Museum zu eröffnen. Bei vielem musste gespart werden, aber die vorerst einfachen Lösungen können später jederzeit erweitert und vervollständigt werden.

Die *Privatstiftung - Künstler aus Gugging* wurde vor einem Jahr realisiert und beinhaltet derzeit 230 von den Künstlern gestiftete Werke, das notwendige Gründungsbudget stellte die niederösterreichische Landesregierung dem Verein zur Verfügung. Private Schenkungen erhöhten die Anzahl der Werke der Sammlung nun auf rund 600 Originale und Radierungen. Ich bin sicher, dass dieses Beispiel noch viele Nachfolger finden wird und viele Sammler einige ihrer Schätze dem Haus anvertrauen werden.

Die Eröffnungsausstellung und dieses Buch heißen *Blug* und wurde einem Werk von FRANZ KERNBEIS entnommen. Ein Neologismus, der den Titeln früherer Publikationen *Sonneastro*, *Carom!* und *Guggging* konsequent nachfolgt. *Blug* bedeutet Pflug und kann symbolisch dafür verwendet werden, dass der Acker bestellt wurde, um dieses Museum zu ermöglichen. Die Künstler schufen einmalige Zeichnungen, Graphiken, Malereien und Objekte, die eine dauernde öffentliche Präsentation verdienen, und die Öffentlichkeit hat ein Recht auf den Genuss möglichst vieler Werke der Gugginger Künstler.

The opening exhibition and this catalogue are titled *Blug*, an invented term borrowed from a work by FRANZ KERNBEIS. This neologism logically follows titles of earlier publications such as *Sonneastro*, *Carom!* and *Guggging*. With *Blug*, KERNBEIS meant to denote a plow. And, in fact, a field has been plowed for this museum to become a reality. Our artists have created outstanding drawings, graphic works, paintings, and objects that deserve to be shown on a permanent basis. The public has a right to enjoy as many works by Gugging Artists as possible.

Franz Kernbeis, Blug / Plow
2001, 23 x 62,2 cm, Bleistift, Farbstifte /
pencil, color pencil

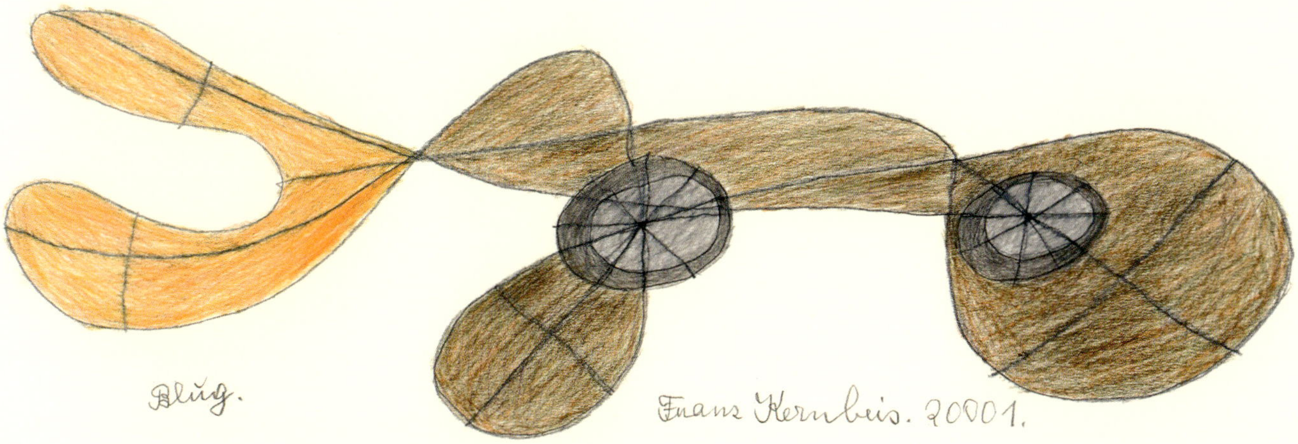

Helmut Zambo

braucht gugging ein eigenes museum? oder

die bedeutung der stiftung und des museums

Im Sommer 2006 schließt sich der Kreis zum *Art/Brut Center Gugging* mit der feierlichen Eröffnung des Museums für die *Privatstiftung Künstler aus Gugging*. Ein krönender Abschluss des Projekts, das 1960 begonnen hat. Die Künstler aus Gugging freuen sich und sind stolz. Das können auch das Land Niederösterreich und die Republik Österreich sein. Warum eigentlich?

Gibt es nicht bereits ein *Musée de l'art brut* in Lausanne? Die Sammlung Prinzhorn in Heidelberg oder private Initiativen wie die Sammlung ABCD in Frankreich und *Outsider Art*-Messen, unzählige Museums- und Galerieausstellungen, bedeutende Privatsammlungen wie die von Arnulf Rainer, kürzlich gezeigt im *Maison Rouge* in Paris.

All diese Gegebenheiten und Veranstaltungen sind wichtig, weil sie nicht nur das Verständnis für die Kunst, die fast immer außerhalb eines *normalen* sozialen Umfelds entsteht, fördert, sondern auch klarmacht, wie bedeutend diese Arbeiten im Kontext einer zeitgenössischen Kunst sind. Aber es bleibt Stückwerk. Gugging heute dagegen ist als eine Art Gesamtkunstwerk zu sehen, einzigartig in der Welt. Was aber macht Gugging so einzigartig?

Angefangen hat es 1960. Wie in vielen psychiatrischen Kliniken, aufgrund von wissenschaftlichem Interesse oder zur Unterstützung therapeutischer Maßnahmen. Es wurde gezeichnet. Leo Navratil erkannte jedoch bald mit Hilfe bedeutender Künstler, dass das, was in Gugging entstand und sich entwickelte, viel mehr war als Äußerungen *kranker Seelen*. Es war Kunst. Mancher Patient blieb Patient, trotz interessanter bildnerischer Dokumente, einige aber wurden Künstler. Mit einem überzeugenden, eigenständigen und unverwechselbaren Werk, das auch – von Experten kritisch betrachtet – standhielt und manchen Arbeiten anerkannter Künstler nicht

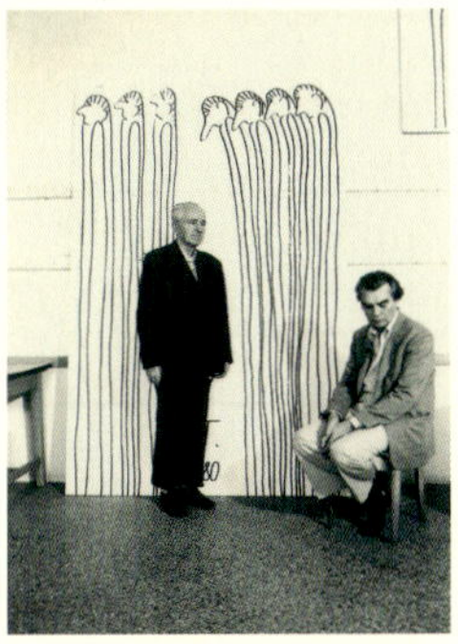

© h. bütler 1980
tschirtner, navratil

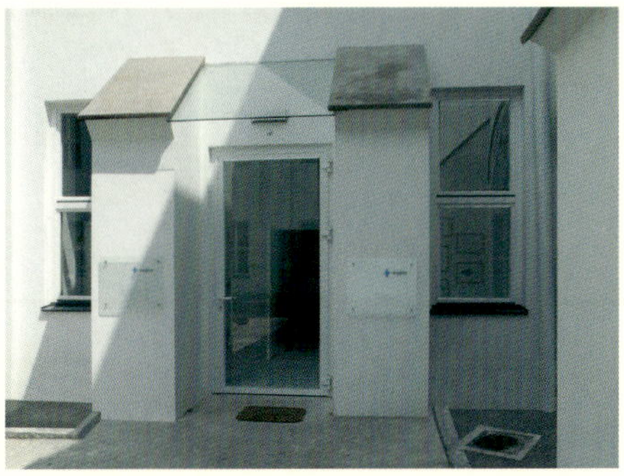

2005
eingang der galerie / entrace of the gallery

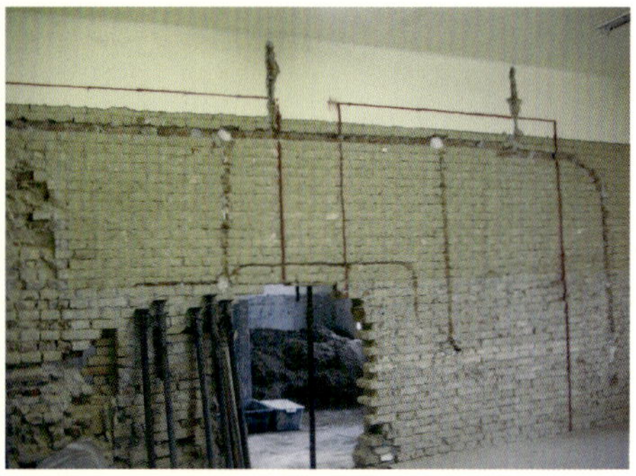

2001
under construction

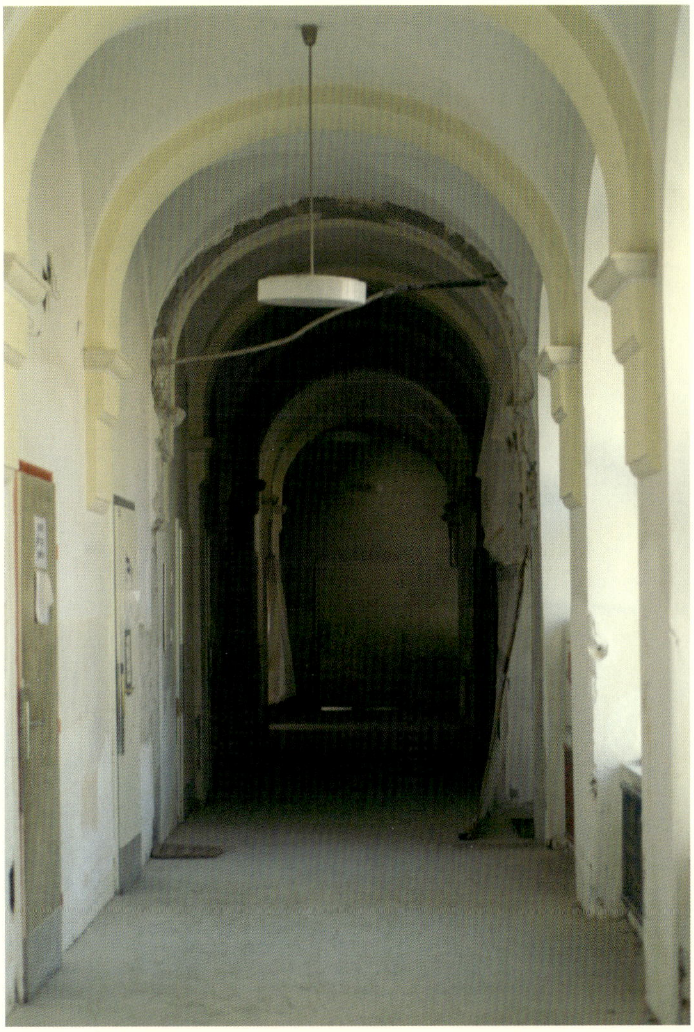

2003
eingang im erdgeschoß /entrance first floor

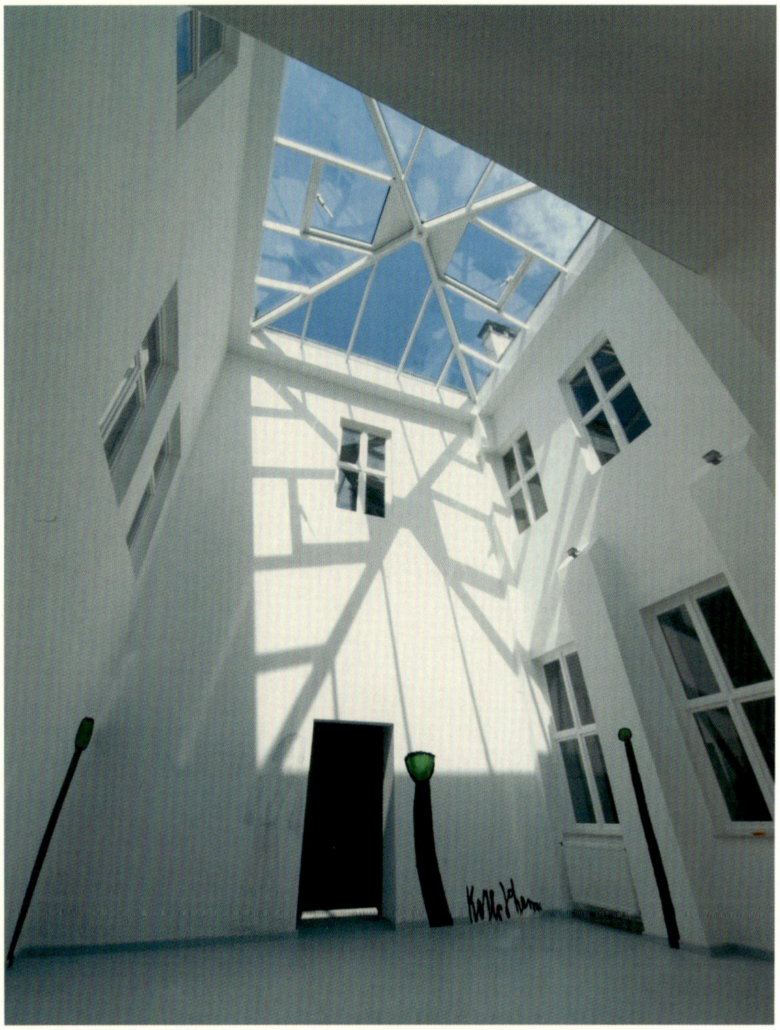

2005
lichthof / halation

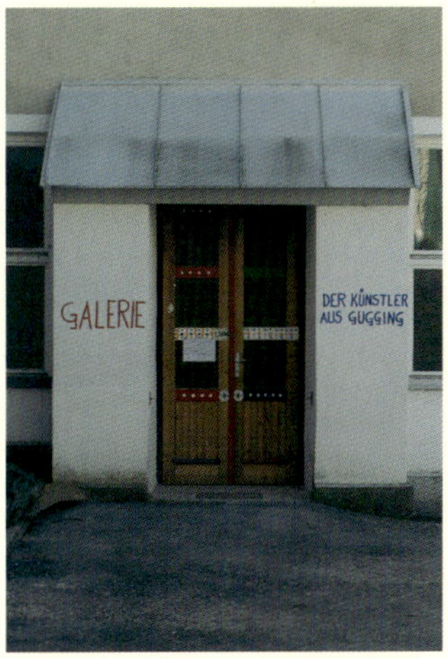

2001
früherer eingang / former entrance

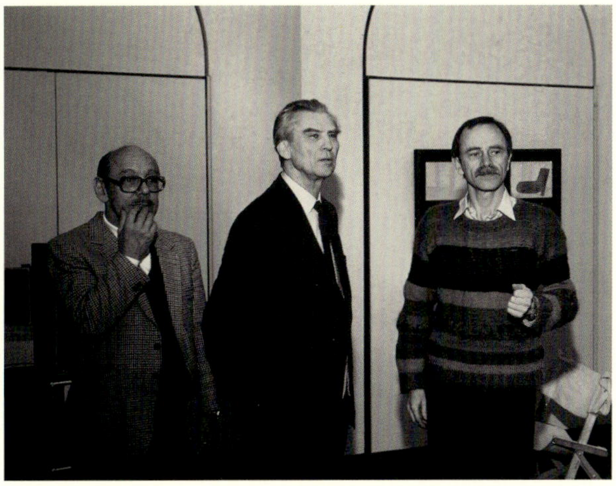

1983
bader, navratil, thevoz

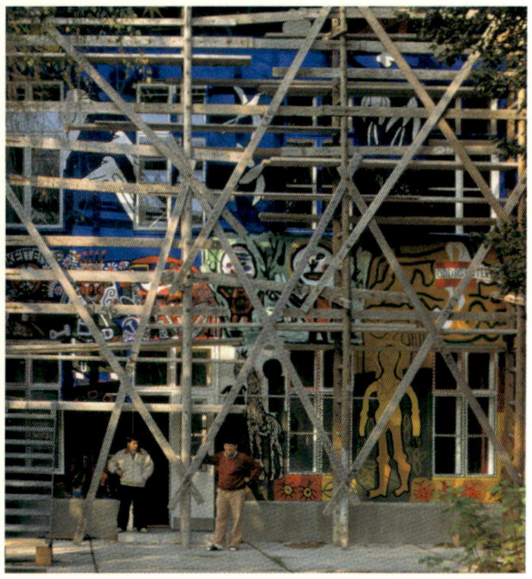

1988
gerüst haus der künstler / scafold house of artists

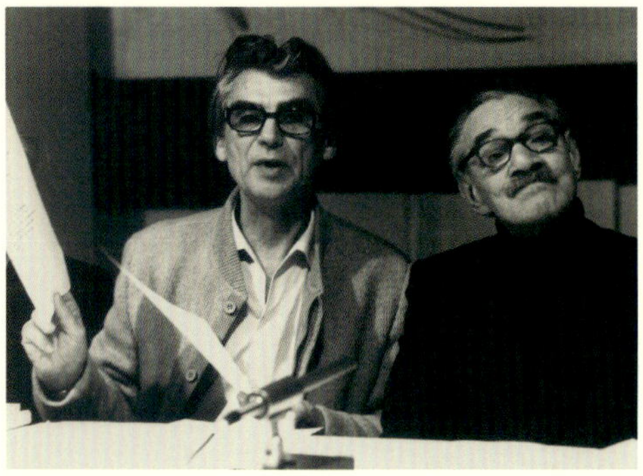

1975
navratil, herbeck

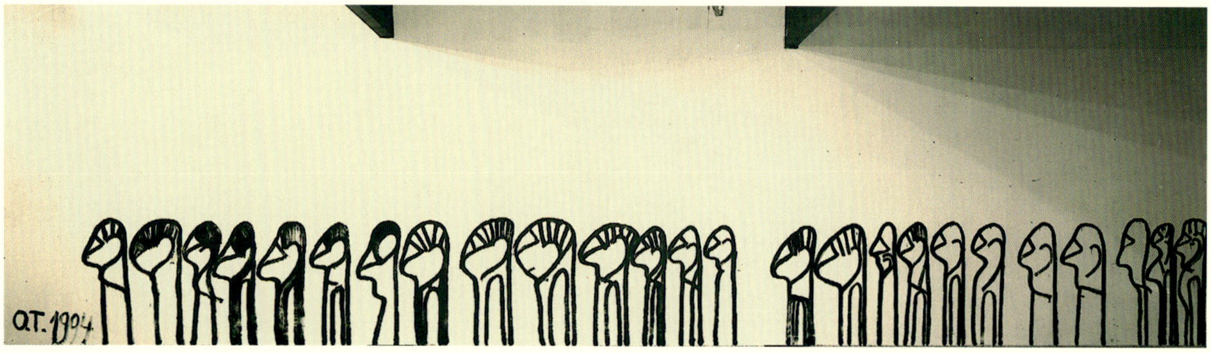

1994, Graz
steirischer herbst kunstfestival / art festival

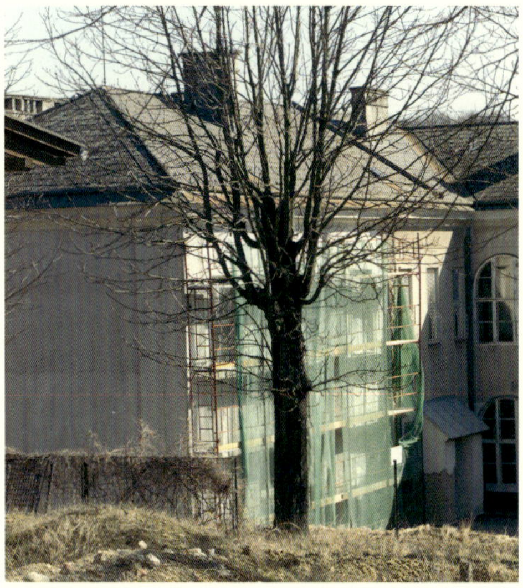

2001
fassadenrestaurierung / restoring the facade

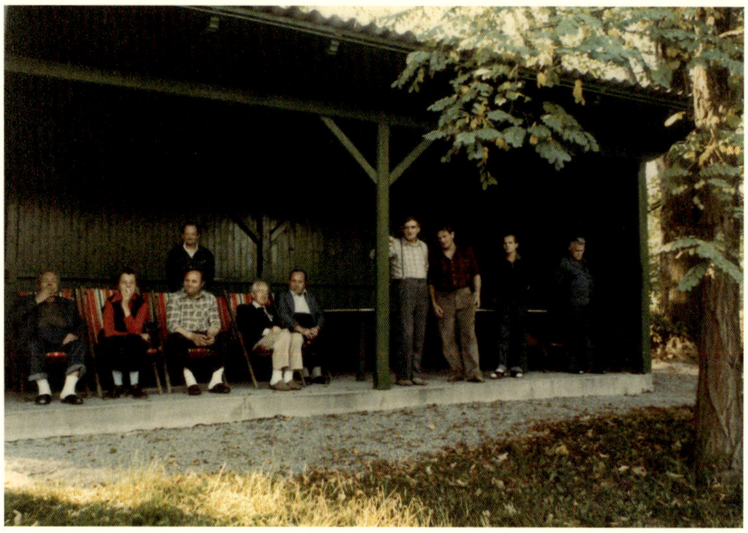

1981
gartenhaus / garden hut

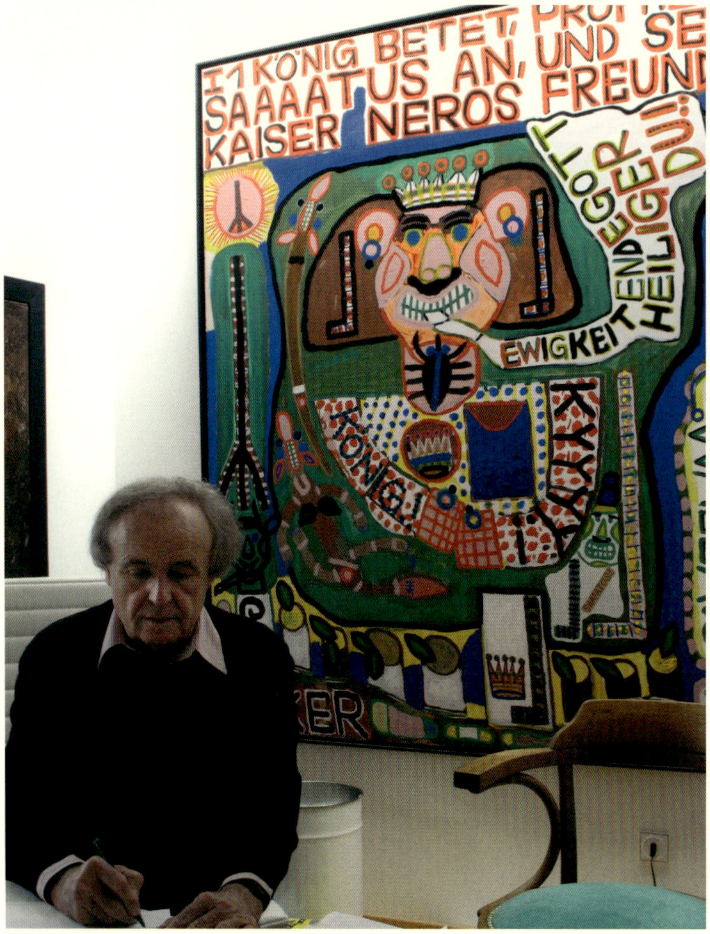

2006
zambo
sammler / collector

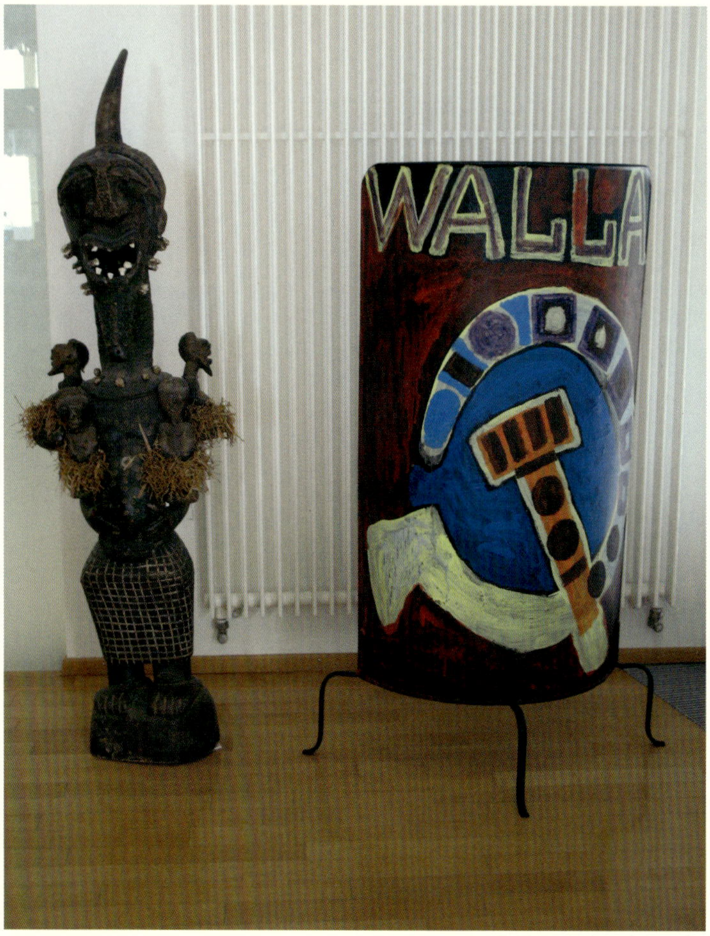

2006, Badenweiler
zambo
sammlung / collection

Helmut Zambo

does gugging need a museum of its own? or

the significance of the foundation and the museum

In summer 2006, *Art/Brut Center Gugging* will come full circle when it celebrates the official opening of the museum for the *Foundation of Gugging Artists*. It is the crowning conclusion of a project that started in 1960. The Gugging artists are pleased and proud. The State of Lower Austria and the Republic of Austria can be proud, too. But why?

Isn't there already the *Musée de l'art brut* in Lausanne? Then there are the Prinzhorn collection in Heidelberg and private initiatives like the *ABCD* collection in France. There are *Outsider Art* fairs, countless museum and gallery exhibitions, and important private collections such as the Arnulf Rainer's, which was recently shown at the *Maison Rouge* in Paris.

All of these venues and events are important. They not only promote an understanding for a genre of art that is nearly always produced outside of a *normal* social environment, but they also make it clear how significant these works are in the context of contemporary art. Nonetheless, their focus remains specialized. Gugging today, on the other hand, can be viewed as a kind of Gesamtkunstwerk, a synthesis of the arts that is unique in the world. But what makes Gugging so unique?

It all started in 1960. Like in many psychiatric clinics, due to scientific interest or to support therapeutic measures, patients were encouraged to draw. With the assistance of leading artists, however, Leo Navratil soon recognized that what was being created at Gugging, and what was evolving there, was far more than the expression of *sick souls*. It was art. Some patients remained patients, despite interesting visual documents, but some of them became artists. Their oeuvre was convincing, original, and unmistakable. It could withstand the critical eye of experts and not

nur Paroli bieten konnte, sondern häufig sogar den Rang ablief.

Konsequenterweise bekamen die Künstler 1981 mit dem *Zentrum für Kunst-Psychotherapie* ein eigenes Haus, 1986 von Johann Feilacher in das *Haus der Künstler* umbenannt. Die Talentiertesten konnten dort unter wesentlich verbesserten Bedingungen leben und arbeiten. Daran hat sich bis heute nichts geändert. Das wäre schon einzigartig genug. Hervorragende Talente, als Patienten und Künstler optimal versorgt und betreut. Aber nicht genug für den jungen Nachfolger Leo Navratils, Johann Feilacher.

Er setzte einerseits das Lebenswerk seines Vorgängers fort, entwickelte es aber auch andererseits weiter, indem er experimentierfreudiger war als sein Vorgänger. Es war nicht mehr von Patienten die Rede, sondern von Künstlern, deren Arbeiten auch dann hohe Qualität zeigten, wenn sie nicht *zustandsgebunden*, sondern in einem normalen täglichen Lebensablauf entstanden. Einschränkend muss eingeräumt werden, dass die wichtigsten Zeichnungen JOHANN HAUSERS in den psychischen Ausnahmezuständen entstanden sind. Aber auch sein Alltagswerk besitzt hohe künstlerische Aussagekraft von musealer Qualität.

Unter Feilachers Regie wurde experimentiert mit neuen Formaten, Techniken, freizügigen Tages- und Arbeitsabläufen sowie mit Überraschungen, für die nicht nur HAUSER, sondern auch seine Kollegen WALLA, TSCHIRTNER, KERNBEIS, KOLLER, FISCHER, GARBER und SCHÖPKE sorgten. Die Arbeiten bekamen zum Teil vollkommen neue Inhalte und nahmen an Umfang und Qualität zu, so dass man für die Künstler nach einer eigenen permanenten Ausstellungsmöglichkeit suchte.

Aus diesem Bestreben entstand 1997 die *Galerie der Künstler aus Gugging* mit Einzelausstellungen, Dauerpräsentationen, erweitert durch eine Reihe sonstiger Veranstaltungen wie Lesungen, Diskussionen, geselligem Miteinander zwischen den Künstlern und Museumsmitarbeitern, Sammlern, Galeristen und anderen Interessierten. Begleitet von regelmäßiger Pressearbeit und Publikationen, die nicht nur das Interesse an den Gugginger Aktivitäten wach hielten, sondern auch etliche Ausstellungsmöglichkeiten im Ausland schufen. Diese wirklich überzeugende Arbeit wurde und wird von einem kleinen Team von Enthusiasten geleistet, mit meist geradezu lächerlich geringen finanziellen Mitteln.

Eine Privatstiftung nach österreichischem Recht wurde 2005 gegründet mit dem Zweck, die bildende Kunst unter Konzentration auf die Werke der Künstler aus Gugging zu fördern. Stifter sind die Künstler aus Gugging und der *Verein Freunde des Hauses der Künstler aus Gugging*. Die Stiftung verfolgt ausschließlich und unmittelbar gemeinnützige Zwecke, im Sinne der österreichischen Bundesabgabenordnung, und kooperiert eng mit den kulturellen Einrichtungen des Landes Niederösterreich.

Ein offenes Atelier wurde neben der neu eröffneten Galerie eingerichtet, in dem auch andere *Grenzgänger* der Kunst arbeiten können, ohne dabei auf Dauer hospitalisiert zu sein, sozusagen als willkommene Gäste der Gugginger Künstler.

Eine Jahrhundertwende-Villa wurde aus eigenen Mitteln und mit finanzieller Unterstützung durch das Bundeskanzleramt renoviert und wird seit Ende 2005 als Haus für Veranstaltungen genutzt mit einem Platzangebot für 140 Besucher, mit Künstlergarderoben, einer Bühne, Erfrischungsräumen etc.

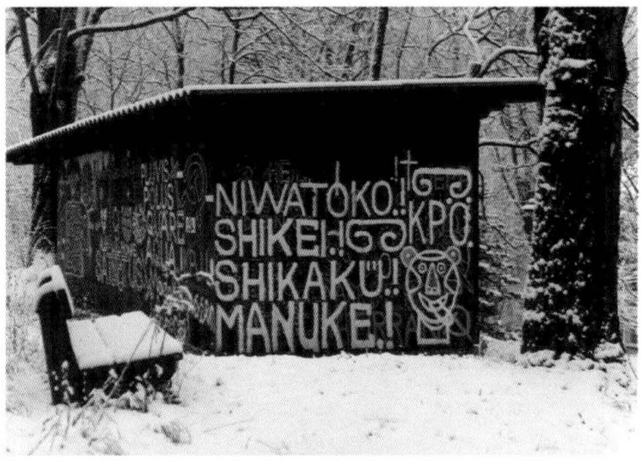

1995
Gartenhaus / garden hut

only defied some of the work of recognized artists, but often even outclassed it.

As a logical development, the artists received their own facility in 1981. Originally called the *Center for Art-Psychotherapie*, Johann Feilacher renamed it the *House of Artists* in 1986. The most talented among the artists could live and work there under considerably improved conditions. This is still the case to this day. The house alone would already be remarkable as a place where exceptionally talented people are optimally cared for and supported as patients and artists. But it wasn't enough for Leo Navratil's young successor Johann Feilacher.

He continued Navratil's lifework, and at the same time he took it further thanks to his greater willingness to experiment than his predecessor. Instead of referring to the residents as patients, they were now called artists. Their works exhibited the same high quality when they were produced in the course of normal, everyday living rather than in situationally dependent settings. It should be noted, however, that Johann Hauser's most important drawings were produced in exceptional psychological states. But his everyday work also has a high degree of artistic expressiveness that is of museum quality.

Under Feilacher's guidance, they experimented with new formats, techniques, tolerant daily schedules and work routines, and the surprises produced by HAUSER and his colleagues WALLA, TSCHIRTNER, KERNBEIS, KOLLER, FISCHER, GARBER, and SCHÖPKE. Some of the work incorporated entirely new content, and as the scope and quality increased, it became apparent that it was time to look for a permanent exhibition facility of their own.

This aspiration led to the founding of the *Gallery of the Gugging Artists* in 1997. It featured solo shows and permanent exhibitions and was supplemented with a number of other events such as readings, discussions, and informal get-togethers with the artists and museum staff, collectors, gallerists, and the interested public. It was supported by ongoing public relations and regular publications that not only kept the interest in the activities at Gugging alive, but also created a number of opportunities for exhibition abroad. This truly remarkable work was contributed by a small team of enthusiasts with funding that was usually ludicrously low.

A private foundation was founded under Austrian law in 2005 for the purpose of promoting visual art with an emphasis on the work of the Gugging artists. The benefactors are the Gugging artists and the association *Freunde des Hauses der Künstler aus Gugging*. The foundation exclusively and directly pursues nonprofit objectives within the meaning of the Austrian Fiscal Code and cooperates closely with the cultural agencies of the State of Lower Austria.

An open studio was set up next to the newly opened gallery where other *outsiders* could produce art without being hospitalized on a long-term basis, but rather as welcome guests of the Gugging artists.

A villa from the turn of the century was renovated with the foundation's own funds and with financial support of the Federal Chancellory. It has been used as a facility for events since late 2005 and offers enough space for 140 visitors, a stage, dressing rooms, refreshment rooms, and more.

- Ein Haus der Künstler
- Eine Galerie für die Künstler
- Ein offenes Atelier für Gäste
- Eine Villa für Veranstaltungen
  und jetzt im Sommer dieses Jahres die Eröffnung des Gugginger Museums
- 3500 Quadratmeter für die Kunst

3500 Quadratmeter für die hochgesteckten Ziele in der Betreuung der Künstler, von Museen, Sammlern, Journalisten, Studenten, Kunsthändlern.

3500 m² für eine Sammlung der Art Brut von höchstem Anspruch, in der die besten Arbeiten der Gugginger Künstler, aber auch anderer renommierter ausländischer Vertreter dieser Kunstrichtung zu sehen sein werden. Ermöglicht durch Stiftungen, Ankäufe, Leihgaben und Geschenke. Das *Art/Brut Center Gugging* , geografisch und landschaftlich bevorzugt gelegen, in unmittelbarer Nähe der 1000 Jahre alten Babenberger Gründung Klosterneuburg mit seinem wunderbaren Stift und kirchlichen Kunstschätzen, auf der Kulturachse Wien – Krems – St. Pölten.

Es wird eine Bibliothek geben, Studien-, Lese- und Aufenthaltsräume für Besucher sowie ein kleines Cafe-Restaurant. Ein attraktiver Ort für alle Kunstliebhaber, der durch die geplante Gründung einer europäischen Eliteuniversität auf dem Gugginger Gelände noch mehr an Bedeutung gewinnen kann. Ein Angebot, mit dem das *Art/Brut Center Gugging* die Schlüsselposition weltweit im Art-Brut-Bereich besitzt. Heute schon ein Stück lebendige Kulturgeschichte und hoffentlich beispielhaft für weitere Initiativen in einer Welt, wo Kunst vor allem als Kunst und nicht als Ware entsteht. Geschaffen von Menschen, die außerhalb der so genannten *normalen* Gesellschaft leben, zu unserer aller Freude und für manches Sammlerglück.

- A house for the artists
- A gallery for the artists
- An open studio for guests
- A villa for events
  And now, this summer, we will be opening the Gugging Museum
- 3,500 square meters for art

3,500 square meters for the ambitious goals of supporting the artists, museums, collectors, journalists, students, art dealers, etc.

3,500 square meters for a collection of Art Brut on par with the highest standards where the best works by the Gugging artists and by renowned international representatives of this genre of art can be viewed. Made possible by foundations, purchases, loans, and gifts. Excellently situated in terms of geography and the landscape, *Art/Brut Center Gugging* is on the cultural axis between Vienna, Krems, and St. Pölten in the immediate vicinity of the 1,000-year-old Babenberg town of Klosterneuburg with its wonderful abbey and ecclesiastic art treasures.

There will be a library, study and reading rooms, a visitor lounge, and a small café restaurant. It is an attractive place for art lovers that will gain even more significance with the planned founding of an European University of Excellence on the grounds of the Gugging Museum. This range of offerings will put the *Art/Brut Center Gugging* in a central position in the genre of Art Brut around the world. Already a piece of living history today, it is hoped that it will serve as an example for additional initiatives in a world where art is above all produced as art rather than as a commodity. This art is created by people who live outside of *normal* society, much to our delight, and much to the benefit of many a collector.

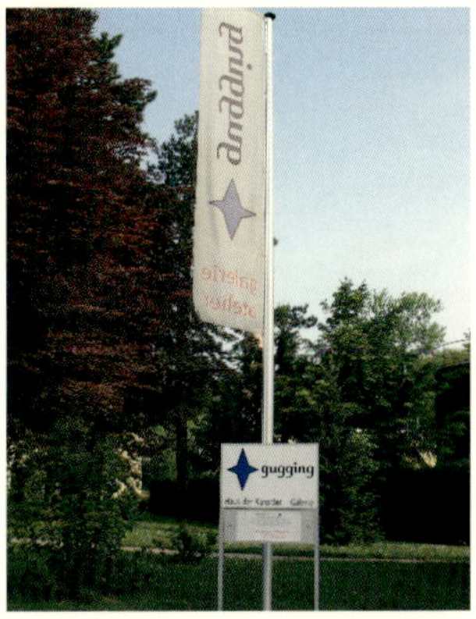

2005

wegweiser an der hauptstrasse /
signs at the main road

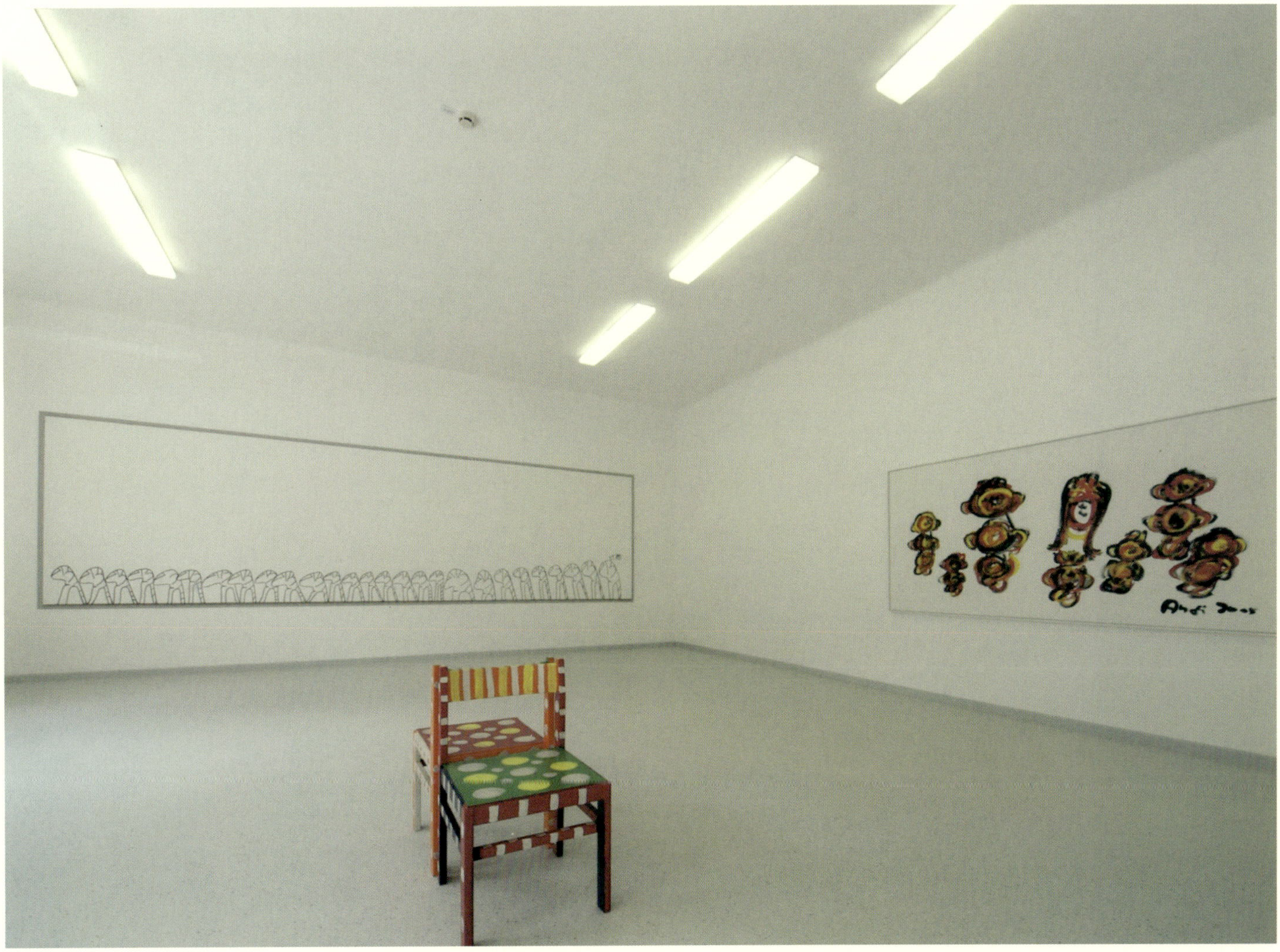

die neue galerie /
the new gallery

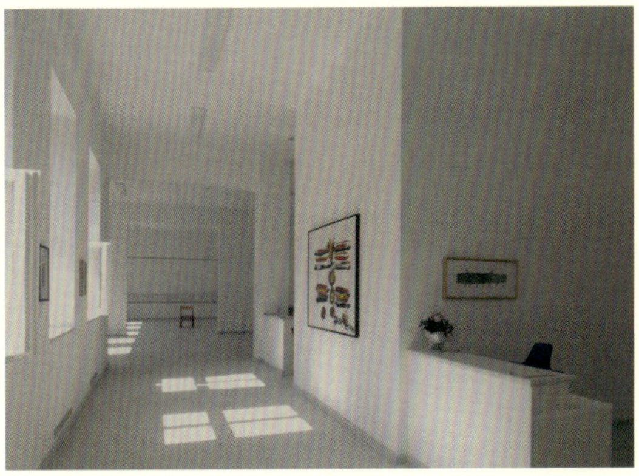

die neue galerie /
the new gallery

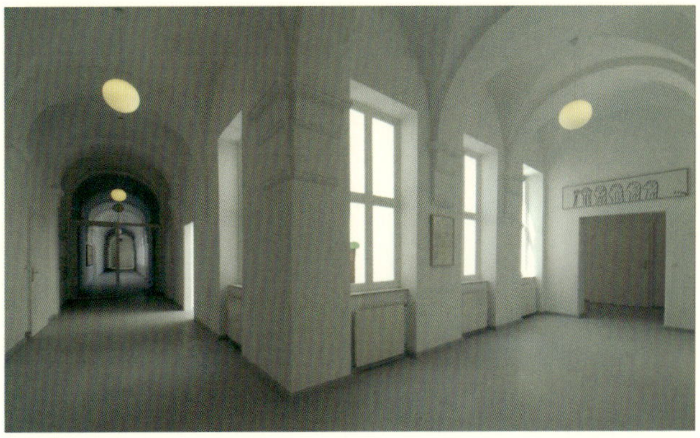

gang der galerie /
floor of the gallery

Nina Katschnig

die künstler aus gugging/ vorurteil und realität

Dieser Beitrag beschäftigt sich mit Vorurteilen, welche die Künstler aus Gugging betreffen, und mit der Realität, in der sie sind – so kann man sich dann besser ein Bild davon machen. Wirkliches Erleben passiert allerdings immer nur vor Ort. Die Werke der Künstler aus Gugging, sogar die Künstler selbst, sind Projektionsflächen für Phantasien und Wünsche – kaum jemand kommt ohne eine vorgefasste Meinung, ohne ein Vorurteil ins *Haus der Künstler* oder in die Galerie der Künstler aus Gugging.

Vorurteile, entstanden durch die eigene, ganz persönliche Geschichte und/oder durch die Gesellschaft, sind weder positiv noch negativ zu werten. Sie sind einfach da und das was sie sind: Vor–Urteile: Gedanken, Meinungen oder Bilder im Kopf, die *man* zu bestimmten Themen, Orten oder Personen hat, ohne sich genauer damit beschäftigt zu haben oder ohne etwas davon gesehen zu haben.

Die Gesellschaft hat eine große Sehnsucht nach Exoten – und als solche gelten Künstler. Seit dem Buch *Genio e follia* von Cesare Lombroso existiert verstärkt die romantische Vorstellung, dass Genie und Wahn ganz eng beieinander liegen, und da Künstler für viele etwas Geniales haben, wäre es dann auch zum Wahnsinn nicht mehr weit. Künstler zu sein ist für die heutige Gesellschaft noch immer etwas Besonderes – es ist etwas anderes, als einem *gewöhnlichen* Beruf nachzugehen. Es gibt prozentuell verhältnismäßig wenige Künstler, also haben sie an sich schon einen Sonderstatus – wie ist das jetzt aber mit den *Künstlern aus Gugging*?

Künstler, die schon seit Jahrzehnten in der Psychiatrie sind, da ihre Erkrankungen einen chronischen Verlauf genommen haben und die schließlich 1981 ein Zuhause im jetzigen Haus der Künstler gefunden haben und das wegen ihres Talentes - ihres Talentes,

the gugging artists/ prejudice and reality

This essay takes a look at the prejudices people have about the Gugging Artists and at the reality in which they exist. The hope is that it will produce better understanding. But actual experience can only take place on location. The works by the Gugging Artists, and even the artists themselves, are projection surfaces for fantasies and desires. Hardly anyone comes to the *House of Artists* or the Gallery of Gugging Artists without preconceptions or prejudices.

These prejudices are produced by each person's unique personal history and/or by society and should neither be viewed as positive nor negative. They simply exist, and they are precisely that: pre-judices – thoughts opinions, or images that we have about certain topics, places, or persons without having examined them in detail or without having realized it.

Society has an insatiable yearning for the exotic – and artists are considered exotic. Ever since Cesare Lombroso's book *Genio e follia* was published, the romantic notion that artistic genius and insanity are closely related has been popular. Since many people think that artists have something ingenious about them, insanity is never far off. To be an artist is still something special for today's society. It's something different than pursuing a conventional profession. As a percentage of the population, there are relatively few artists. So they already have a special status. But what about the *Gugging Artists?*

These artists were under psychiatric care for decades because their illnesses had become chronic. In 1981, finally, they found a home in what is now the House of Artists – all because of their talent. Their talent is to have their own vocabulary of form and the ability to express it.

künstlerisch eine eigene Formensprache gefunden zu haben.

Ein Wegweiser mit einem blauen Stern führt die Besucher durch das gesamte Areal des jetzigen Donauklinikums, vormals *Landesnervenklinik Gugging*, zum Haus der Künstler. Am Waldrand gelegen, mit den Motiven der Künstler versehen, rundherum an den Bäumen befestigte, bemalte Vogelhäuser, Schriften auf der Straße und Symbole auf den Bäumen und Steinen. So präsentiert sich das Haus der Künstler seinen Besuchern, aber was erwarten sich die Besucher eigentlich?

Es kann durchaus der Vergleich mit dem Besuch eines Indianerreservats in den USA herangezogen werden. Erstaunen und teilweise auch Enttäuschung über die Indianer mit Ray-Ban-Brillen, Jeans und Hemden, die in Autos unterwegs sind und hie und da wird auf einen historischen Brotbackofen und eine typische Küche hingewiesen. Nach all den Kinofilmen über Indianer und nach eingehender Karl-May-Lektüre stellt man sich ganz was anderes darunter vor. So ähnlich dürfte es unseren Besuchern gehen. Es rennen keine halbnackten, laut schreienden und wild gestikulierenden *Narren* herum. Es ist alles ziemlich *normal* – was auch immer das ist – und wirkt dadurch fast ein bisschen langweilig.

Das Haus der Künstler wurde von einem bekannten österreichischen Literaten, Gerhard Roth, als das *Haus der schlafenden Vernunft* bezeichnet. Besucher, die das wussten, kamen in Erwartung, etwas sehr Kindliches, Reines, ja fast Paradiesisches vorzufinden. Etwas, das sie selbst schon verloren haben. Wieder andere wollen durch einen Besuch ihre eigene Normalität bestätigt sehen.

Haben die Besucher einmal die Berührungsängste verloren, so können sie die zu diesem Zeitpunkt anwesenden Künstler kennen lernen. Das verläuft dann ganz unspektakulär und die oft erwartete oder befürchtete Freakshow bleibt aus.

Die *Galerie der Künstler aus Gugging* befindet sich im *Art/Brut Center Gugging*, einem 3500 m2 großem Gebäude, das örtlich 200 m vor dem Haus der Künstler liegt, und die meisten Besucher kommen dort hin. Diese Galerie arbeitet seit 1994 für die Künstler. Es ist eine Produzentengalerie und wurde deshalb gegründet, damit diese Künstler auf dem Kunstmarkt dieselben Chancen haben wie andere Künstler auch. Das heißt, ihre Werke sollen in Galerien und Museen ausgestellt und auch verkauft werden. Ziel war und ist es, dass die Künstler noch zu Lebzeiten etwas von ihrem Erfolg haben sollen. Dem Künstler selbst nützt es nichts, wenn seine Werke nach dem Tod hochpreisig verkauft werden. Das heißt, durch die Ausstellungstätigkeit kommen die Künstler in der Welt herum – von Basel bis New York – und präsentieren bei Vernissagen ihre Werke. Das tun sie, wie alle anderen Künstler auch, sehr gerne. Durch den Verkauf der Werke verdienen sie so wie andere Künstler auch.

Wollen die Künstler das auch – ist ihnen das recht, dass ihre Werke ausgestellt werden – wollen sie sich überhaupt davon trennen? Wollen sie Geld damit verdienen oder ist ihnen das egal? Was machen sie denn mit dem verdienten Geld?

Das sind nur einige der Fragen, die immer wieder gestellt werden – Fragen, die nicht oft genug beantwortet werden können: Ein Großteil der Künstler aus Gugging wollen nicht nur Rezipienten ihrer Arbeit, um durch deren Anerkennung ihren Selbstwert aufzumöbeln, nein, sie wollen auch, dass ihre Arbeiten gekauft werden. Die Arbeit, die sie als Künstler leisten, wird dadurch entlohnt. Sie verdienen Geld und können sich dadurch – so wie jeder andere auch – Verschiedenes

A signpost with a blue star leads visitors through the grounds of the Donauklinikum, formerly known as the *Landesnervenklinik Gugging* (Gugging Psychiatric Clinic), to the House of Artists. Situated at the edge of a forest, decorated with motifs by the artists, surrounded by painted birdhouses hanging on the trees, hand-painted lettering along the road, and symbols on the trees and stones. This is how the House of Artists presents itself to visitors. But what do the visitors actually expect?

You might compare it with a visit to an Indian reservation in the USA – the amazement and in part disappointment about seeing the Indians wearing Ray-Ban glasses, jeans, and shirts driving around in cars while a historic bread oven or a typical kitchen is pointed out here and there. After all the movies about Indians and the novels about the Wild West, you thought it would be a lot different. Our visitors might have a similar experience. There are no half-naked, screaming, wildly gesticulating *lunatics* running around here. Everything is pretty much *normal* – whatever that is – and it might even appear a little boring.

The House of Artists was referred to by a well-known Austrian writer, Gerhard Roth, as the *house of sleeping reason*. Visitors who knew that came in the expectation of finding something very childlike, pure, paradisiacal almost. Something they themselves had lost. Others, in turn, visit in a desire to confirm their own normalcy.

Once the visitors have gotten over their reservations, they can meet the artists who happen to be present. It's completely unspectacular and the often anticipated or feared freak show is absent.

The Gallery of the Artists of Gugging is in the *Art/Brut Center Gugging*, a 3,500-square-meter building that is 200 meters in front of the House of Artists. Most visitors come to the gallery, which has been operating for the artists since 1994. It is a production gallery and was founded to give these artists the same opportunities in the art market that other artists have. In other words, their works are meant to be exhibited in galleries and museums and are meant to be sold, too. The objective was and remains to give the artists a chance to benefit from their success during their lifetime. It doesn't help the artist if his works are sold at a high price after his death. As a result of the exhibition activities, the artists travel around the world – from Basel to New York – and present their works at openings. And just like any other artist, they enjoy it. Just like other artists, they earn an income from the sale of their work.

Do the artists in fact want that? Is it all right with them that their works are exhibited? Do they even want to part with them? Do they want to earn money or do they not care? What do they do with the money they earn?

These are just some of the questions people ask again and again. And they can't be answered often enough. The majority of the Gugging Artists not only want their art to be well received so that the recognition can bolster their self-esteem, they also want their work to be purchased. This is how the work they do as artists is rewarded. Just like any other work is rewarded. Not only that, they get something out of it. They earn money and – just like anyone else – they can afford to buy various things, like a vacation, a TV, an easy chair, a new jacket, or something completely banal like a pack of cigarettes. Their art is not first and foremost produced to be able to sell something – but if it happens that way, it helps improve their quality of life and self-esteem.

leisten wie z. B. einen Urlaub, einen Fernseher, Lehnstuhl, eine neue Jacke oder ganz banal: Zigaretten. Ihre Kunst entsteht nicht in erster Linie, um etwas verkaufen zu können – wenn es dann aber so ist, trägt das zur Steigerung der Lebensqualität und des Selbstwertes bei.

Die Künstler verwenden das von ihnen verdiente Geld nicht nur, um sich ihre persönlichen Bedürfnisse zu befriedigen, teilweise bezahlen sie auch für ihren Aufenthalt im Haus der Künstler in Gugging. Sie gehören nicht zu den Sozialschmarotzern, die auf Kosten der Gesellschaft leben. Im Gegenteil, beim einen oder anderen haben auch noch die Erben was davon gehabt.

Zurück zur Frage: Wollen die Künstler sich von ihren Werken trennen? So – wie für die meisten Künstler– ist auch für die Künstler aus Gugging der Entstehungsprozess wichtig. Ist die Arbeit dann abgeschlossen, so ist es meist leicht, sich davon zu trennen. Einer der Gugginger Künstler, welcher nicht immer Arbeiten in die Galerie zum Verkauf gibt, ist JOHANN GARBER – er gestaltet sein Zimmer damit. In seinem Zimmer hat er über 240 Arbeiten, die er gerne Besuchern des Hauses zeigt. Hier bekommt der Besucher wirklich Geschichten zu den Bildern zu hören.

Anders ist es mit dem Vorurteil, dass sich die Werke der Künstler aus Gugging und vieler anderer Art Brut Künstler hauptsäch-lich wegen der Storys verkaufen lassen. Storys sind in der Kunstwelt generell wichtig – warum ist das so? Können die Menschen nicht einfach ein Bild, eine Skulptur, eine Photographie oder eine Videoarbeit auf sich wirken lassen, ohne um die Lebensgeschichte des Künstlers zu wissen? Ist die Arbeit dann leichter verständlich – können wir nicht *sehen*?

Der Mensch, der hinter einer Arbeit steht, ist nie unwichtig. Dabei ist es egal, ob es sich um einen Koch, einen Tischler, einen Banker oder um einen Künstler handelt. Bei den Künstlern will man aber meist mehr als den Entstehungsprozess eines Werkes wissen – die Biographie von Kindesbeinen an ist es, was oft mehr Interesse weckt als das Werk an sich.

Krankengeschichten werden von allen Mitarbeitern im Haus der Künstler und im *Art/Brut Center Gugging* als die Privatangelegenheit der Künstler betrachtet, und somit bekommen Besucher darüber keine Auskunft. Das *Storytelling* beschränkt sich auf die Arbeitsweise des Künstlers und auf ein paar biographische Daten, aber das war es dann auch.

Es geht uns in der Galerie der Künstler aus Gugging und vielen anderen Galerien, die mit Art Brut handeln, um die Kunst und nicht um die Erkrankung des Künstlers. Die ist in diesem Zusammenhang sekundär. Die Werke werden der Kunstwelt entsprechend in Passepartouts und Rahmen präsentiert – und nicht, wie es manche Besucher bei einer *Art Brut Show* erwarten, an die Wand genagelt oder mit selbst gebasteltem Rahmen gezeigt.

Eine weitere, sehr verbreitete Meinung ist die, dass die Werke der Künstler aus Gugging billig zu erwerben sein müssten, da die Gesellschaft immerhin für ihren Aufenthalt in der Psychiatrie aufkommt. Wie oben nachzulesen ist, stimmt das so nicht. Zeitlich ist folgende Geschichte nachzuweisen:

Vor über 30 Jahren verschenkte Leo Navratil, der Begründer des Hauses, viele Zeichnungen seiner – wie er sie nannte – *Künstlerpatienten*, um deren Arbeit bekannt zu machen. Das war gut so, und nach der ersten Verkaufsausstellung 1970 bekamen die Werke einen Wert. Seit über 30 Jahren entwickelt sich nun der Marktwert der Werke

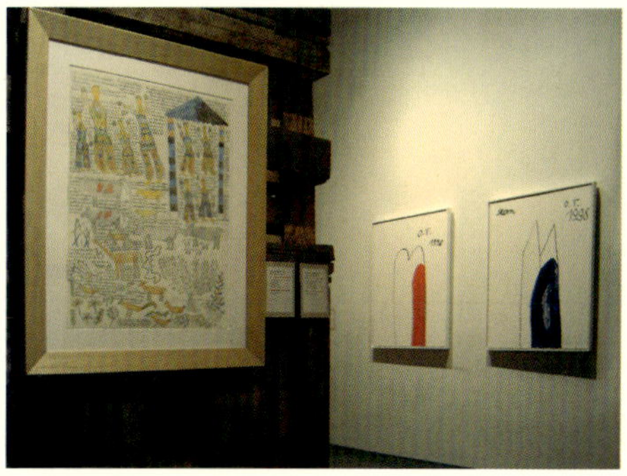

2005
Kiasma Museum, Helsinki

The artists not only use the money they earn to satisfy their personal needs – in part, they also pay for their stay at the House of Artists in Gugging. They are not social parasites who live on the costs of society. To the contrary, one or two of them have even been able to leave money to their heirs.

As for the question whether the artists want to part with their works, just as for most artists, the process of creation is important to the Gugging Artists. Once the work is complete, it's usually easy to part with it. One of the Gugging artists who does not always permit the gallery to sell his works is JOHANN GARBER. He decorates his room with them. He has more than 240 paintings and drawings in his room, and is happy to show them to visitors who come here. These visitors really get to hear some stories.

Then there is the misconception that works by the Gugging Artists and many other Art Brut artists primarily sell because of the stories. Stories are important in the art world in general. Why is that so? Can't people simply allow a painting, a sculpture, a photograph, or a video to affect them without knowing the life history of the artist? Does it make the work easier to understand? Can't we *see*?

The person behind a work product is never unimportant. It doesn't matter whether that person is a cook, a carpenter, a banker, or an artist. With artists, though, we usually want to know about more than just the production process. The artist's biography from early childhood often sparks more interest than the work itself.

All of the staff at the House of Artists and the *Art/Brut Center Gugging* consider medical histories to be the private concern of the artists, so the visitors will not get any of this kind of information. The storytelling is limited to the methodology of the artist and some general biographical data, but that's it.

At the Gallery of the Artists of Gugging, and at many other galleries that deal in Art Brut, we are interested in the art and not in the artist's illness. It is secondary in this context. The works are appropriately matted and framed – not, like some visitors of an Art Brut show expect, nailed to the wall or displayed in a handmade frame.

Another very common misconception is that works by Gugging Artists should be cheap because after all society pays for their stay at the psychiatric clinic. As mentioned earlier, this is not the case. The following genesis might help to illustrate:

More than 30 years ago, Leo Navratil, the founder of what later became the House of Artists, gave away many drawings by his *artist patients*, as he referred to them, in order to make their work known. It was a good choice – after the first exhibition with sales in 1970, the works gained in value. For more than 30 years now, the market value of the works by the Gugging Artists has been increasing. Like all other artists, they started at very low prices. The works by the Gugging Artists have been exhibited worldwide in renowned museums like the Philadelphia Art Museum, the Setagaya Art Museum in Tokyo, the Museum moderner Kunst in Vienna and Amos Anderson Museum in Helsinki, and they have also been purchased for these museums' collections.

A number of collectors and customers who have been collecting art from Gugging for some time complain about the rise in prices, since just a while ago it all cost virtually nothing. But they forget that the works in their own collections have gained in value as well.

der Gugginger Künstler und sie begannen alle, so wie andere Künstler auch, mit sehr niedrigen Preisen. Die Arbeiten der Künstler aus Gugging wurden weltweit in renommierten Museen wie etwa dem Los Angeles County Museum of Art, dem Setagaya Art Museum in Tokyo, dem Museum moderner Kunst in Wien und dem Amos Anderson Museum in Helsinki ausgestellt und auch für deren Sammlungen von Museen angekauft. Etliche Sammler und Kunden, die schon über längere Zeit Kunst aus Gugging kaufen, beschweren sich über diese Preisentwicklung – bis vor kurzem hat das ja alles noch nichts gekostet. Sie vergessen dabei aber, dass die Werke der eigenen Sammlung auch an Wert gewonnen haben.

Die Gesellschaft muss für den Aufenthalt in der Psychiatrie aufkommen – Steuergelder fließen da ein – warum also viel bezahlen? Ein Umstand, der diese Sichtweise bestimmt auch noch verstärkt, ist die jetzige Lage des Hauses der Künstler und des Art/Brut Centers Gugging. Die Psychiatrie wird allerdings in den nächsten zwei Jahren abgesiedelt und dann befindet sich dort bald eine University of Excellence. Dann steht das Haus der Künstler und das Art/Brut Center Gugging für sich alleine, und eine wichtige Hemmschwelle – nämlich erst durch das Areal der Psychiatrie gehen oder fahren zu müssen, bevor man zum Ziel kommt – fällt weg. Aber nicht nur die Hemmschwelle fällt weg – langsam, aber sicher wird auch das Psychiatrieimage des Hauses der Künstler und somit das der Künstler aus Gugging immer mehr in den Hintergrund treten und der künstlerische Aspekt in den Vordergrund kommen.

Anerkennung und Wertschätzung – für den Künstler und sein Werk – äußern sich darin, wie viel der Kunde bereit ist, für ein Kunstwerk zu bezahlen. Demnach soll die Arbeit, welche die Künstler tun, auch angemessen und gut entlohnt werden. Der viel zitierte Satz: *Was nichts kostet, ist nichts wert,* kommt auch hier zum Tragen, und der Wert, der über die Jahrzehnte geschaffen wurde, sollte sich auch bonitär festmachen.

Schließlich wäre da noch die weit verbreitete Meinung, dass man mit dem Kauf eines Werkes das *Projekt Gugging* sozial unterstützt. Das stimmt so nicht.

Die Galerie der Künstler aus Gugging orientiert sich, wie andere Galerien auch, am Kunstmarkt, und dementsprechend befremdend ist es auch, wenn man merkt, dass es einigen Kunden nicht darum geht, ein Kunstwerk zu kaufen, sondern das Projekt – den Künstler – zu unterstützen. Dieser Kauf hat dann ganz eine andere Bedeutung – es geht nicht um das Werk an sich, sondern darum, etwas Gutes zu tun –, fast ein Mäzenatentum, das da spürbar wird, Es sollte gleich sein, ob man sich ein Werk von Arnulf Rainer, Egon Schiele, JOHANN GARBER oder JOHANN HAUSER kauft. Werden etwa Arbeiten von Michel Nedjar gekauft, um diesen zu unterstützen?

Durch die langjährige Ausstellungstätigkeit und Präsenz der Künstler auf dem Markt haben ihre Werke einen Preislevel erreicht, wo es schon schwieriger wird mit der so genannten *sozialen Unterstützung.* Eine Sammlerin der ersten Stunde hat einmal gesagt: *Gugging kann man sich jetzt nicht mehr so leicht kaufen – jetzt kostet das ja schon wirkliches Geld.* Die Dame hat Recht – und auch nicht. Die Werke der *neuen Künstler* sind auch jetzt noch günstig zu erwerben, und es gibt auch preiswerte, hervorragende Graphik. Das heißt, dass es immer mehr beginnt, um das Kunstwerk an sich zu gehen – ein paar hundert Euro gibt keiner mehr leicht für ein schnelles soziales Engagement aus.

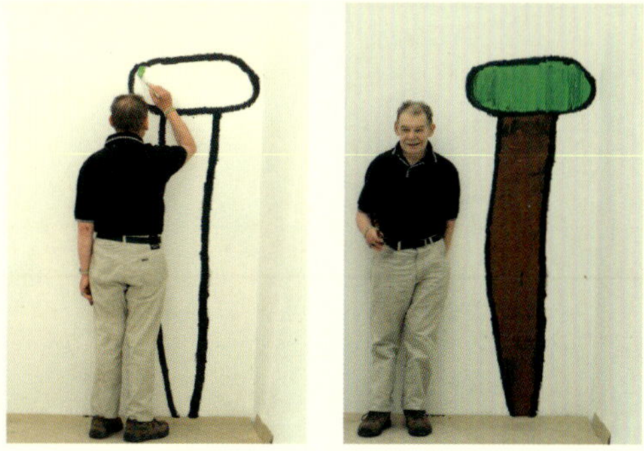

2005
Johann Korec

Society has to pay for the patients' stay in the psychiatric clinic – with tax money – so why should the art cost so much? Another factor that certainly strengthens this perception is the current position of the House of Artists and the Art/Brut Center Gugging. But the psychiatric clinic will relocate in the next two years and will soon be replaced with a University of Excellence. The House of Artists and the Art/Brut Center Gugging will then be stand-alone facilities, and an important source of inhibitions – having to pass through the grounds of the psychiatric clinic before arriving at the destination – will be eliminated. But it's not just inhibitions that will be overcome. Slowly, but surely, the psychiatric image of the House of Artists and hence the Gugging Artists will become increasingly secondary, while the emphasis on the artistic aspect will gain a more dominant position.

Recognition and appreciation for the artist and his work are expressed in how much a customer is prepared to pay for a work of art. According to this principle, the work they produce should be appropriately and well rewarded. The common platitude that *if it doesn't cost anything, it isn't worth anything* is relevant here, too. The value created in the course of the decades should be reflected in the remuneration.

Finally, there is the widespread opinion that purchasing a work supports the *Gugging project* socially. This is not the case.

Like other galleries, the Gallery of Gugging Artists orients itself to the art market, and so it is puzzling to note that some customers are not so much interested in purchasing a work of art as in supporting the project – the artist. Such a purchase has an entirely different meaning. It's not about the work itself, but about doing something good, almost a patronage in a sense. It shouldn't matter whether you're buying a work by Arnulf Rainer, Egon Schiele, JOHANN GARBER, or JOHANN HAUSER. Do people buy art by Michel Nedjar in order to support him?

Through the many years of exhibition activities and the presence of the artists on the market, their works have achieved a price level where the *social support* approach becomes a little more difficult. A person who has been collecting from the very beginning once said, *It's not so easy to buy Gugging art anymore – now it costs real money.* She's right, but she's also wrong. The works of the *new artists* can still be purchased at a reasonable price. Outstanding graphic art also is excellent value for money. In other words, it's more about the artwork itself these days – it's not so easy for anyone to lay out several hundred euros for a quick social cause.

It's now also possible to become actively involved in the new Art/Brut Center Gugging, which alongside the newly opened Gallery of the Gugging Artists and Atelier Gugging, the Die Villa event facility, and the Gugging Museum will also house the Foundation of Gugging Artists. It will be the largest center for Art Brut in the world with 3,500 square meters of space, and sponsors are more than welcome.

In the Art/Brut Center, just 200 meters from the source – the House of Artists – the artists now have larger studios, large, bright exhibition spaces, and a place where their own works can continuously be presented in a museum setting. The artists visit the new studios and the gallery often and with pleasure. They are open to the changes because they recognize the advantages and are able to accept them. We hope our visitors will feel the same way and will not get stuck on the prejudice that: *The real works were those created in the House of Artists, the canvases produced in the coal cellar.*

Engagieren kann man sich jetzt im neuen Art/Brut Center Gugging, das neben der schon eröffneten Galerie der Künstler aus Gugging, dem Atelier Gugging, der Veranstaltungshalle Die Villa nun auch das Museum Gugging für die Privatstiftung – Künstler aus Gugging beherbergen wird. Es ist mit 3500 Quadratmeter das größte Zentrum für Art Brut weltweit und Förderer dafür sind herzlich willkommen.

Mit diesem Art/Brut Center, 200 m von der Quelle, dem Haus der Künstler, entfernt, haben die Künstler nun größere Ateliers, große, helle Ausstellungsräume und einen Ort, an dem ständig ihre eigenen Werke museal präsentiert werden. Die Künstler besuchen die neuen Ateliers und die Galerie oft und gerne. Sie stehen den Veränderungen offen gegenüber, da sie durchaus die Vorteile darin erkennen und für sich annehmen können. Wir hoffen jetzt, dass es unseren Besuchern auch so geht und es nicht bei dem Vorurteil: *Die im Haus der Künstler, im Kohlenkeller entstandenen Leinwände – die waren noch richtig brut!* bleibt.

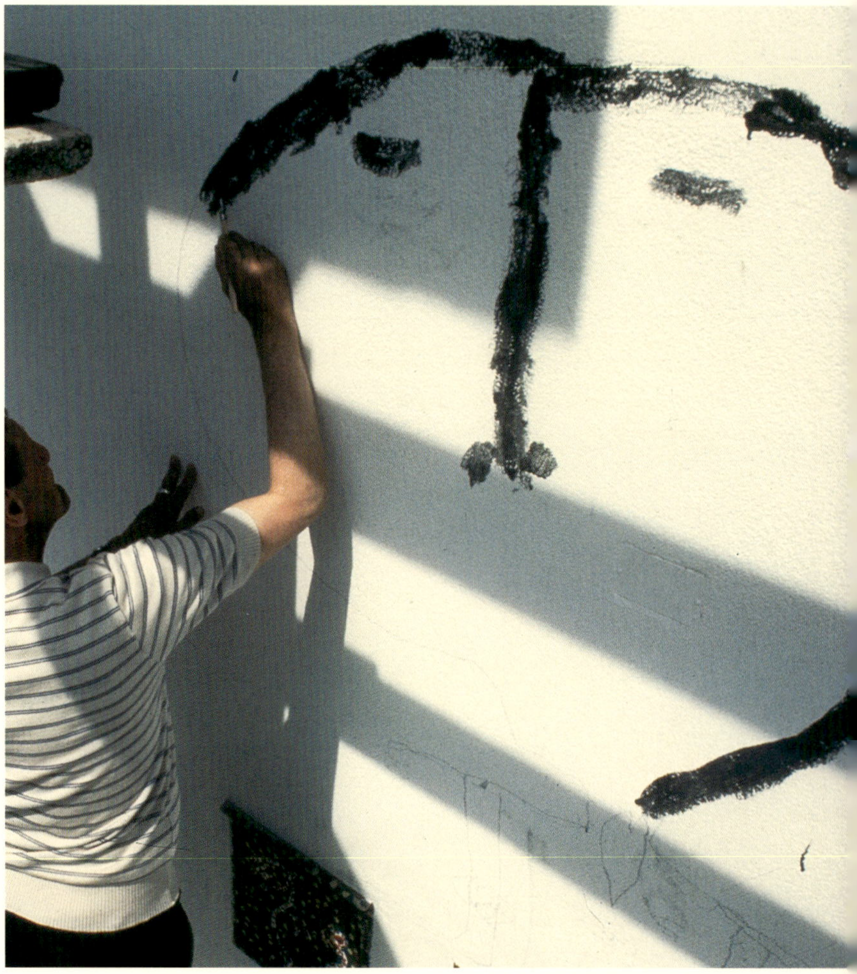

1984
schöpke

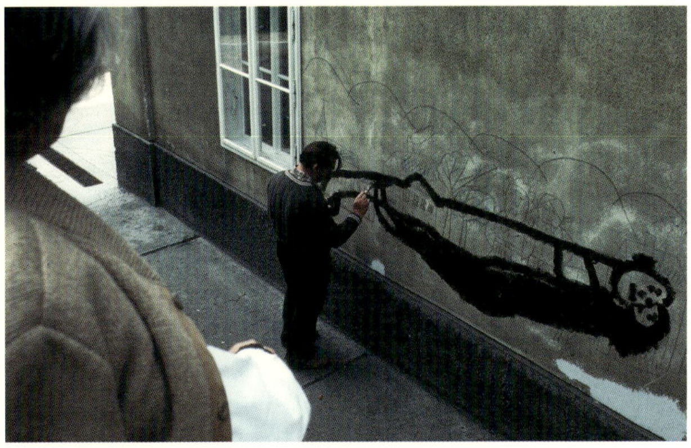

1983
korec

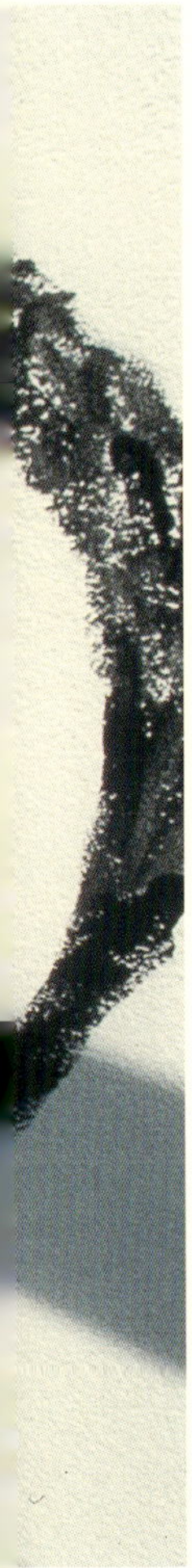

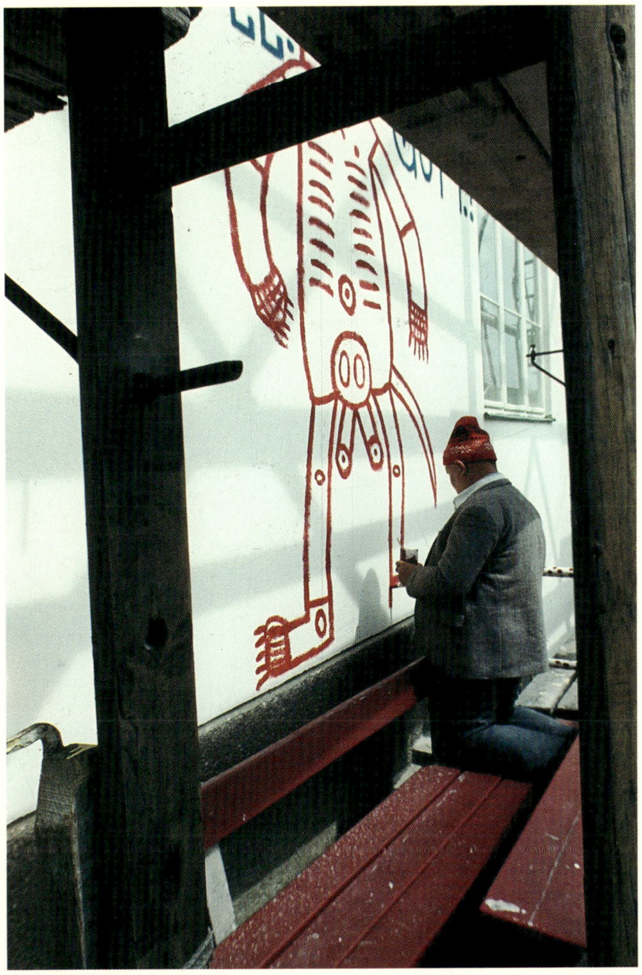

1984
walla

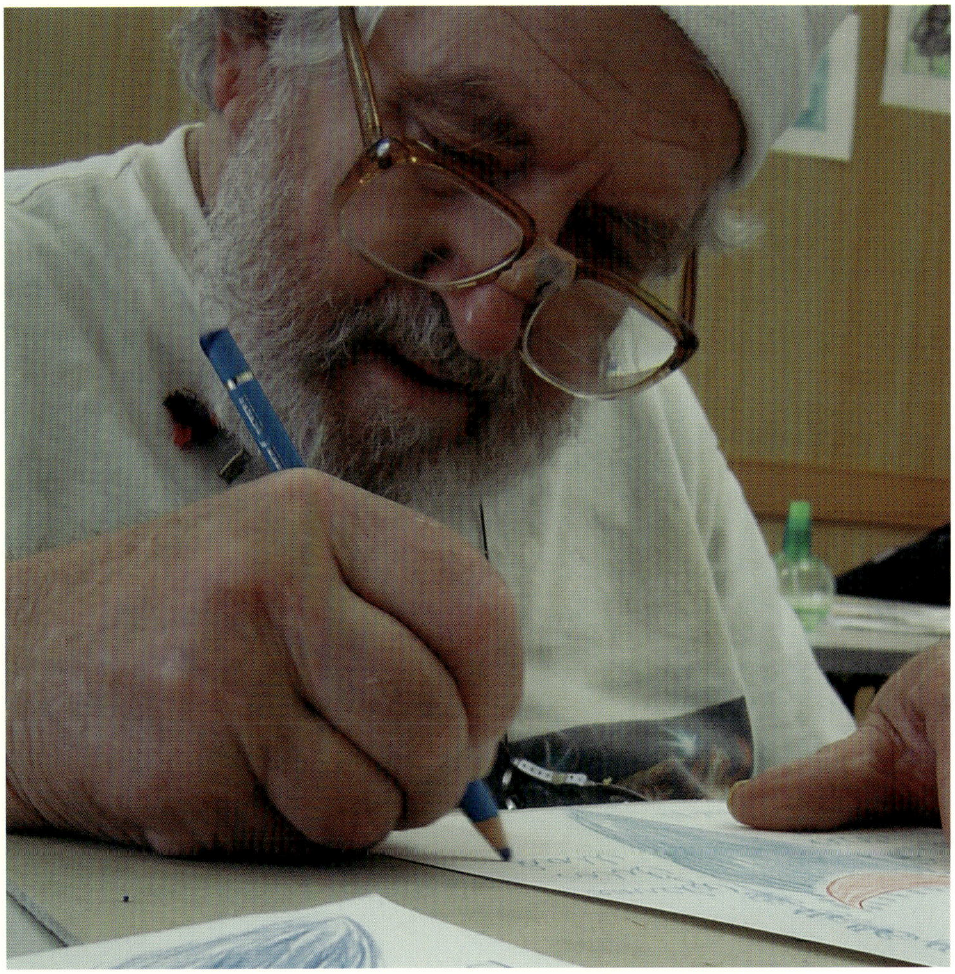

2006
schmelzer

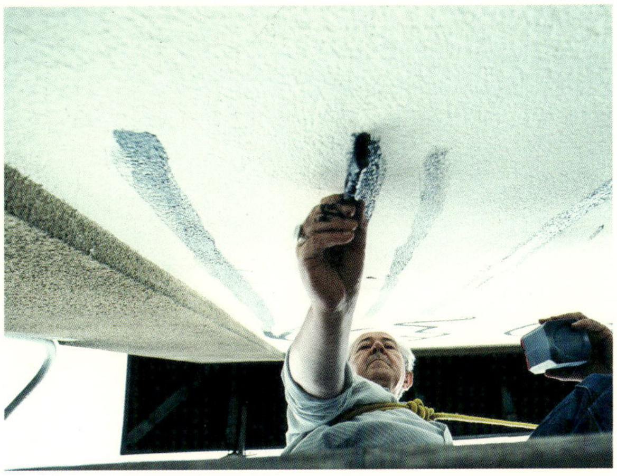

1984
tschirtner

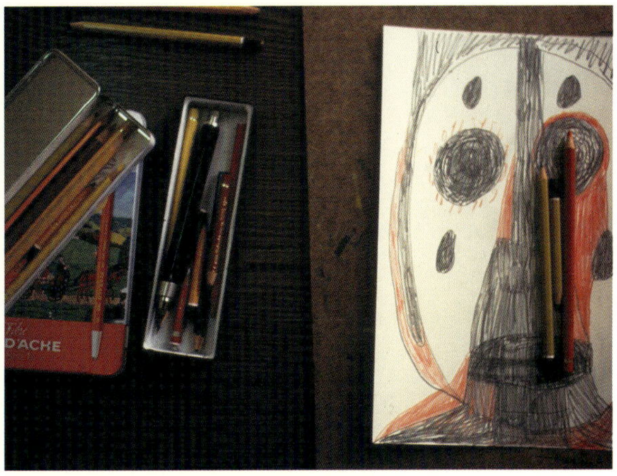

1983
horacek's arbeitsplatz / workdesk

Florian Reese

art brut und atelier

Ein Antagonismus, geradezu absurd, blanke Ironie? Prinzip und Erfahrung sprechen dafür.

Die vergangenen vierzig Jahre waren in diesem weitnuancierten Feld zwischen Kunst und Psychiatrie nur mittelmäßig erfolgreich, sofern es um klar nachvollziehbare Positionierungen ging. In dem Maße, wie das globale Interesse an Outsider Art stieg, verselbständigten sich auch ihre Konturen, was mancherorts die Qualitätsansprüche deutlich sinken ließ. Das führt zu punktuellen Eindrücken einer para-künstlerischen Bewegung, deren Fokus zunächst auf die Biographie sowie die soziale und ethnische Herkunft der Autoren gerichtet ist.

Die Kunsttherapie - als Konglomerat unterschiedlicher, nur schwer vereinbarer Schulen - ringt weiterhin zäh um allgemeine Anerkennung, und viele der zahlreichen künstlerischen Ateliers in Psychiatrien und Tagesstätten setzen sich wenig kritisch mit den eigenen Zielsetzungen sowie Arbeitsweisen auseinander und hantieren mit dem Kunst-Begriff auf beeindruckend leichtsinnige Art und Weise.

Zwar klammern einige der Ateliers wohlweislich den historischen Art-Brut-Begriff aus ihrem Selbstverständnis aus, jedoch erkennen viele im Merkmal der Eigenständigkeit und Authentizität den zentralen Aufhänger für künstlerische Qualität. Dabei handelt es sich um ein Merkmal, das eben die Art Brut bzw. Outsider Art profiliert, verteidigt und emanzipiert hat, das sie zunächst von anderen Kunstrichtungen per Definition unterscheidet. Die Authentizität dieser Kunst, so der Kanon, resultiert aus einer profunden sozialen, geistigen und kulturellen Bindungslosigkeit des Einzelgängers.

Kann also ein offenes künstlerisches Atelier oder eine künstlerische Gemeinschaft,

art brut in the studio

An antagonism? An absurdity? Outright irony perhaps? The underlying principle and experience suggest so.

As far as clearly definable positioning is concerned, the past forty years were only moderately successful in this richly nuanced field between art and psychiatry. As the global interest in Outsider Art rose, its contours took on a life of their own, and in some instances allowed quality standards to drop considerably. This leads to selective impressions of a para-artistic movement that focuses first and foremost on the biography and social and ethnic background of its authors.

Art therapy, as a conglomerate of various schools that are hard to reconcile, is still tenaciously struggling for general recognition, and many of the numerous art studios in psychiatric clinics and day treatment programs approach their objectives and methodologies with little critical examination and tamper with the definition of art in a remarkably careless manner.

While some of the studios prudently exclude the historic understanding of Art Brut from their self-conception, many recognize the characteristic of autonomy and authenticity as the central indicator of artistic quality. It is precisely this characteristic that distinguished, defended, and emancipated Art Brut or Outsider Art, that by definition set it apart from other genres of art. The authenticity of this art, according to the canon, results from a profound social, intellectual, and cultural detachment of the isolated individual.

Is it possible, then, for an open art studio or an artistic community, a colony, to serve as an appropriate environment for an Art Brut artist? Can it offer such a person anything at all, or will the painter eventually lose his touch, like the graffiti artist faced with a wall prepared by the city council,

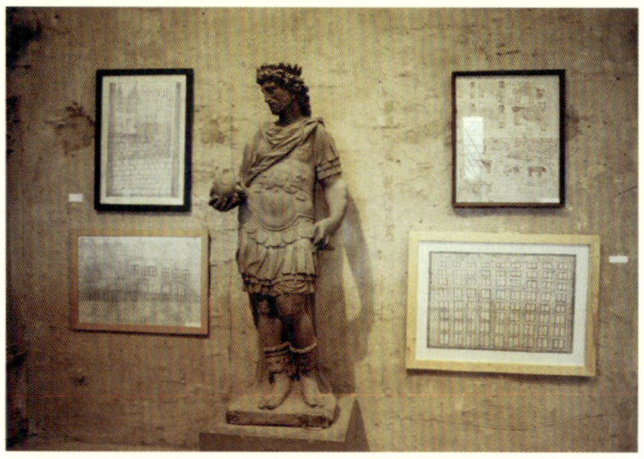

1983
Schloss Heidelberg / Heidelberg Castle

eine Kolonie das adäquate Umfeld für einen Art-Brut-Künstler sein? Kann es ihm gar etwas bieten, oder sackt der Maler hier, gleichsam wie der Sprayer dort (angesichts einer vom Stadtrat präparierten Fassade), mittelfristig ein, weil ihm mit der kultivierten Fassung entscheidende Grundlagen seines Schaffens abhanden gekommen sind?

Die Absicht der meisten Ateliers ist es, individuelle Ressourcen und Potentiale aufzuspüren und künstlerisch zu fördern. Die Strukturen ähneln sich weltweit: Menschen mit geistigen Behinderungen oder psychiatrischen Problemen besuchen die Ateliers mehr oder weniger regelmäßig und eigeninitiativ. Einige kommen im Rahmen einer geregelten Arbeitsstruktur, auch weil sie in sachlicheren Werkstätten nicht so recht *funktionieren*, andere nutzen offenere Atelierformen stetig oder sporadisch.

Hinter der Idee, geschützte Umgebungen zu schaffen, die unter Kreativität Unorthodoxeres verstehen als gehäkelte Blumenampeln, steckt die Absicht, Eigenwilliges und Irritierendes entstehen zu lassen, letztendlich Originäres soweit zu unterstützen, dass Formen der Identifikation mit Inhalten und Techniken eigenen Schaffens erzielt werden. Trotzdem kollidiert diese Idee oftmals mit den Ambitionen und Projektionen der Leiter. Dies beginnt beim starren Folgen idealisierter Wertekataloge und endet bei empfindlichen Manipulationen von künstlerischen Prozessen sowie der Ignoranz eigentlicher Begabungen. In gewisser Weise kann also nur bedingt von *geschützt* die Rede sein. Dabei werden die Fähigkeiten und Qualitäten der Einzelnen von vielen Ateliers ebenso missverstanden wie das so oft bemühte Beuys-Zitat, jeder Mensch sei ein Künstler (das wahrlich nicht mit dieser Feststellung endet).

Als persönliche und politische Mentoren tragen die Leiter der Ateliers eine hohe Verantwortung. Fehlende Kongruenz zwischen Anspruch und nach außen vermitteltem Ergebnis wirkt nicht nur unbefriedigend auf das einzelne Projekt und seine Protagonisten, sondern auf das ganze Genre, auf jene Bemühungen, die die Veröffentlichung und Etablierung beachtlicher kultureller Leistungen jenseits des rein karitativen Gedankens zum Ziel haben. Spricht man also von Kunst, begibt man sich, willentlich oder nicht, auf sehr dünnes Eis. Man möchte meinen, dass jene Instanzen, die letztendlich die Bewertung und Präsenz auf dem Kunstmarkt regulieren, ohne weiteres in der Lage sind, stets zwischen gut und *nur originell* unterscheiden zu können. Tatsächlich provozieren aber die vielen ungelenken Versuche, auf den hochdotierten Kunstebenen mitzumischen, Abwehr und Verdruss.

Es liegt in der Natur der Kunst, ziemlich selten zu sein, was aber keineswegs bedeutet, dass es jenseits der Boheme öde wird. Ganz im Gegenteil. In Europa und den USA gab und gibt es eine ganze Reihe transparenter und hervorragend organisierter Projekte, die von enormer Überzeugungskraft und Wirkung sind. Diese Projekte arbeiten ebenso spielerisch wie intelligent in kultureller Absicht und mit künstlerischen, narrativen Mitteln. Sie sind oft freier, unverkrampfter und virtuoser in der Wahl dieser Mittel als so manche Kunst-Domäne, sei es in den Bereichen Theater und Improvisation, Musik und bildende bzw. angewandte Medien. Sie nutzen diese Medien um der Kultur willen und um gleichsam Retardierungen der Gesellschaft über die Kultur zu therapieren. Die Frage ob Kunst oder *Brut* stellt sich hier auf eine sehr angenehme und erfolgreiche Weise zunächst gar nicht, die eingeschlagenen Richtungen sind stringent.

Stellt sich die Frage aber doch, sollte, in Anbetracht der Schwierigkeit, außergewöhnliche künstlerische Qualität zu bestimmen

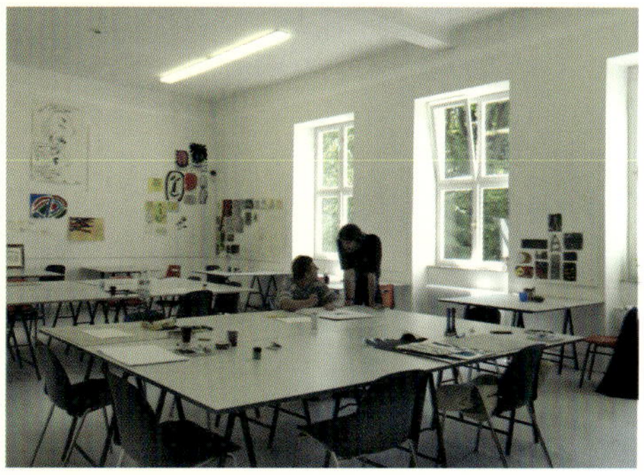

2006
Atelier Gugging

because the cultivated approach has eliminated important principles of his artistic process?

The intention of most studios is to identify resources and potentials and promote creativity. The structures are similar around the world: people with mental disabilities or psychiatric problems visit the studios on a more or less regular basis and on their own initiative. Some come in the context of a structured work environment because they can't quite *function* in more ordinary workshops. Others use open studio forms, either regularly or sporadically.

The idea to create protected environments that view creativity as something less orthodox than macramé plant hangers is inspired by the motivation to encourage the production of autonomous and uncomfortable art, and ultimately to support original work and foster forms of identification with the contents and techniques of independent art. Nonetheless, this idea often collides with the ambitions and projections of program directors. It starts with the rigid pursuit of idealized values and ends with problematic manipulations of artistic processes and an ignorance of actual talents. In some sense, then, we can speak of *protected* to a limited extent only. The capabilities and qualities of the individual are just as much misunderstood by many studios as the oft-quoted statement by Beuys that everyone is an artist (a fact that truly does not end with this pronouncement).

As personal and political mentors, studio directors have important responsibilities. A lack of congruence between needs and the results communicated to the outside world is not only dissatisfactory for individual projects and their protagonists, but reflects poorly on the entire genre, on the efforts geared at the publication and establishment of cultural achievements beyond purely charitable intentions. Once you speak of art, you tread on very thin ice – deliberately or not. You might think that the instances that ultimately regulate the evaluation and presence on the art market are readily in a position to distinguish between good and *just original.* But in fact the many awkward attempts to mingle with lofty levels of art only provoke defenses and rebuke.

It is in the nature of art to be uncommon, but this does not in any way mean that it becomes bleak outside of Bohemia. To the contrary, in Europe and in the USA there have been a number of transparent and excellently organized projects that are enormously convincing and effective. These projects are both playful and intelligent in their cultural intention and their use of artistic, narrative means. They are often freer, less inhibited, and more skillful in the selection of these means than certain other domains of art and act on various fields as theater and improvisation, music and fine or applied arts. They use these media for the sake of art and to therapeutically treat society's retardation in the realm of culture, as it were. The question whether something is art or *brut* happily and conveniently does not arise here, the directions taken are stringent.

But if the question does arise, in consideration of the difficulty of determining unusual artistic qualities and the hopelessness of verbalizing them, every contextual or practical approach, every step taken, should be taken with care. What is the minimum amount of time that the individual painter, graphic artist, or poet requires, what extent and form of support does he or she need to evolve, and when do outside influences become manipulative? Questions like these are in fact common to any art education facility.

But they are greatly intensified when the objective is to establish a suitable artistic foundation for Art Brut. Art Brut is as

und der Aussichtslosigkeit, sie zu verbalisieren, jeder inhaltliche und praktische Ansatz, jeder Schritt ein behutsamer sein. Wie viel Zeit braucht der einzelne Maler, Zeichner, Dichter wenigstens, welches Maß und welche Form der Förderung benötigt er, um sich zu entwickeln, und ab wann die Einflüsse werden unlauter. Fragen, wie man sie eigentlich aus jeder künstlerisch-edukativen Einrichtung kennt.

Diese Fragen verschärfen sich aber um ein Vielfaches, wenn ein geeigneter künstlicher Unterbau für Art Brut geschaffen werden soll. Art Brut ist so dogmatisch wie fragil. Nicht jeder Art-Brut-Künstler ist ein sturer Solitär, den jeder Versuch kunstpädagogischen Einflusses ungerührt lässt. Hilfeleistungen drohen in vielen Fällen, die Kunst zu kultivieren und damit zu brechen. Authentizität ist im besonderen Maße Voraussetzung für das Entstehen von Art Brut. Bloße Authentizität allerdings ist kein Qualitätsmerkmal und vermag Kreativität genauso wenig in Kunst zu verwandeln wie technische Finesse oder arbeitsintensive, aufwändige Produktionen.

Gugging begünstigte der Zufall gleich zweifach: Da war zum einen der glückliche Umstand außergewöhnlich hoher Dichte künstlerischer Talente unter den Patienten des gewaltig überfüllten Pavillon 2. Zum anderen handelt/e es sich ausschließlich um Menschen von ausgesprochen geringer künstlerischer Suggestibilität, um Autoren von prägnanter stilistischer Autonomie.

Niemand hatte hier je die Absicht, deren wilden Ausdruck zu zähmen, weder gestern (aus dem primären Interesse an der Pathographie) noch heute (aus dem primären Interesse an der Kunst selbst). Gugging fungierte so schon immer als ein Reservat in sich gekehrter Häuptlinge, deren Souveränität außer Frage steht.

dogmatic as it is fragile. Not every Art Brut artist is a staunch recluse unphased by any attempt at pedagogical intervention. In many instances, assistance threatens to cultivate art and hence break it. Authenticity is especially crucial in the creation of Art Brut. But authenticity alone is not a sign of quality, and it is just as incapable of transforming creativity to art as technical finesse or labor-intensive, elaborate productions.

Gugging has been favored by fortune in two ways. First of all, there was an unusually high density of artistic talent among the patients of the greatly overcrowded Pavilion 2. The other thing was the happy circumstance that nearly all of these people were characterized by exceptionally low artistic suggestibility, a laconic stylistic autonomy.

No one ever had the intention here to tame wild expression, neither in the past (out of a primary interest of pathography) nor in the present (out of a primary interest in the art itself). Gugging has always functioned as a reserve for introverted masters whose sovereignty is beyond all question.

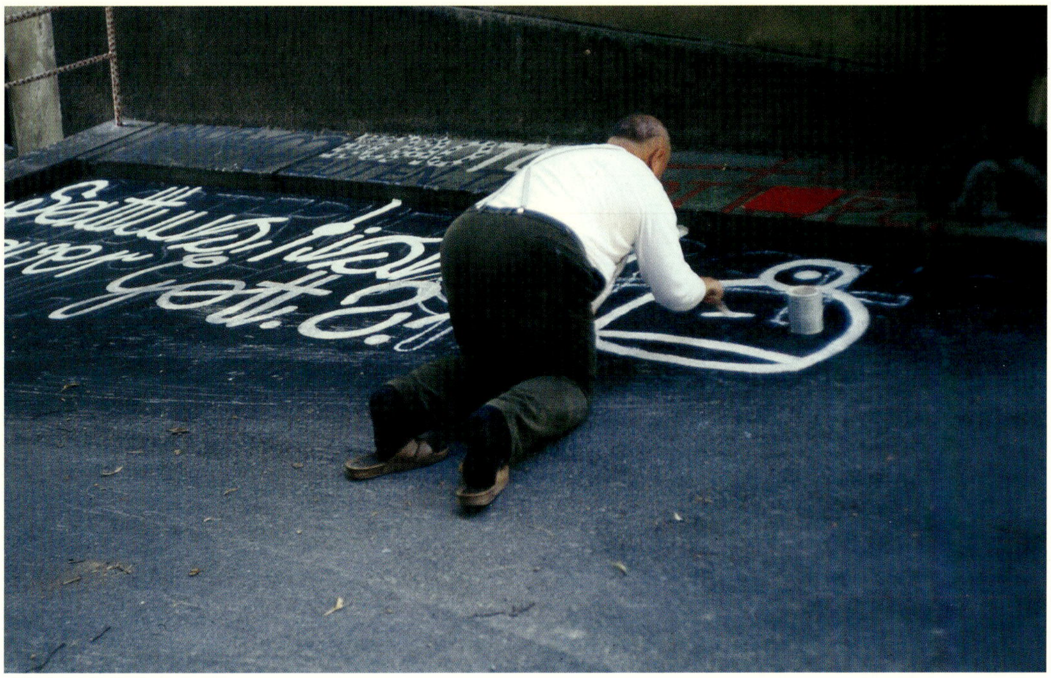

1995
walla

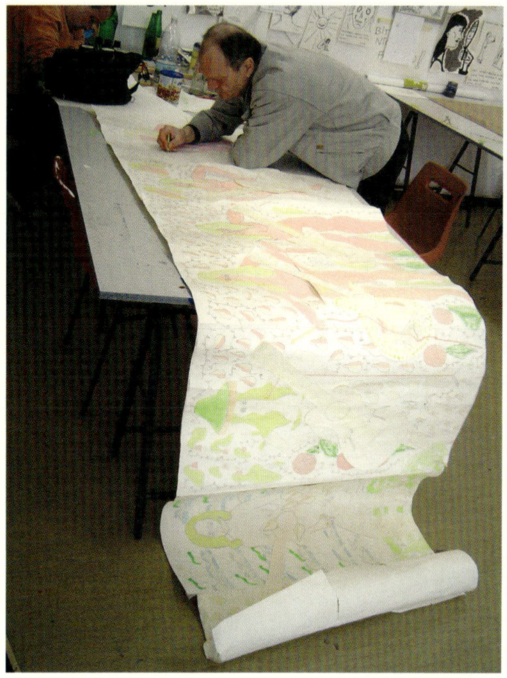

2006
vondal im atelier / in the studio

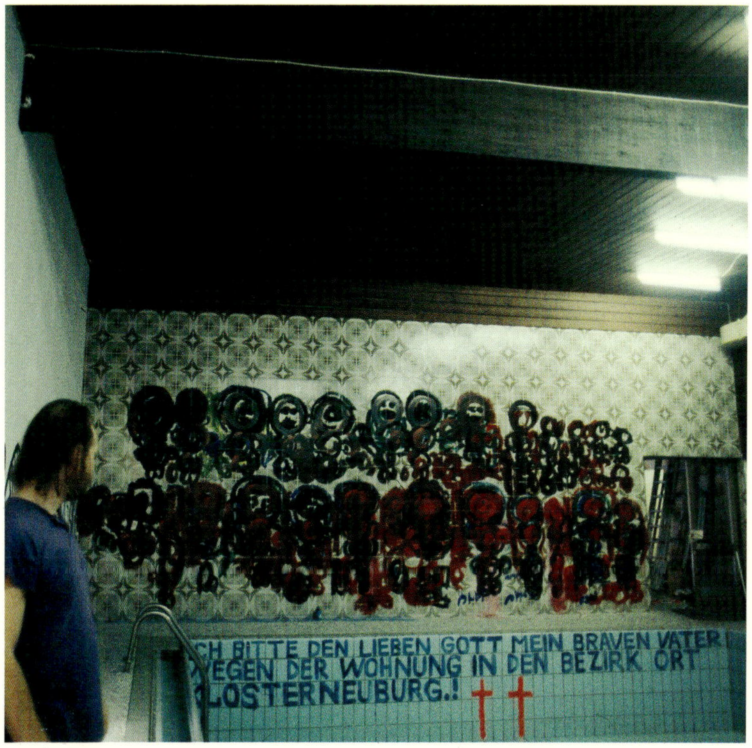

1994
steirischer herbst

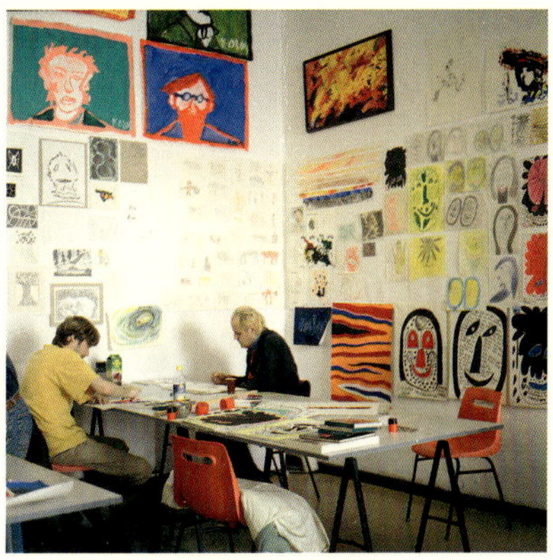

2004
atelier gugging

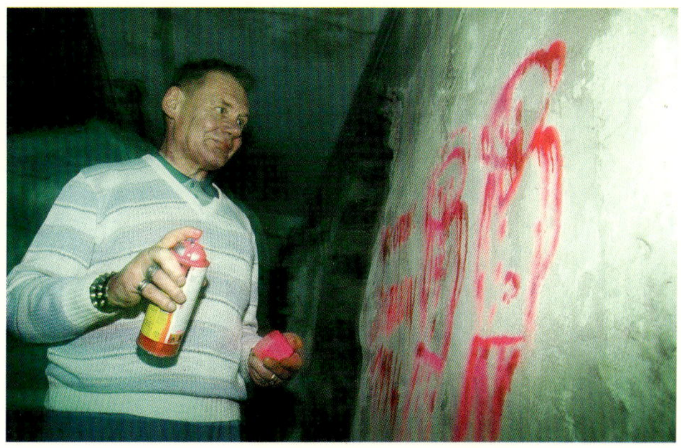

1994
korec / steirischer herbst

Roger Cardinal

ein besuch in gugging

das rätsel der spontanen kreativität

Der Ursprung des Phänomens Gugging ist und bleibt ein Rätsel. Woher kam dieser künstlerische Reichtum? Wie konnten sich so viele differenzierte Stile an gleicher Stelle und um ungefähr dieselbe Zeit entwickeln? Was für Bedingungen waren es, die das Phänomen ermöglicht haben? Wir besitzen einige Hinweise, die uns erlauben,wenigstens diese letzte Frage zu beantworten.

Zuerst müssen wir das Axiom in Betracht ziehen, laut dem – anderen Behauptungen zum Trotz – es nicht die Psychose an sich ist, die das künstlerische Talent erzeugt. Schon in den zwanziger Jahren hatte Hans Prinzhorn festgestellt, dass die spontane graphische Kompetenz bei psychisch Kranken ebenso selten ist wie bei Durchschnittsmenschen. Trotzdem scheint es wahrscheinlich, dass gewisse materielle Bedingungen den Drang zur Expression anregen.

Im Herbst 1970 wurden Werke aus Gugging in einer Avantgarde-Galerie im Zentrum von Wien ausgestellt, was die Aufmerksamkeit und Unterstützung einer nicht geringen Anzahl von österreichischen Künstlern und Intellektuellen auf sich zog.[1]

Ich betrachte dies als die entscheidende Richtungsänderung, nämlich dass man eine Zeichnung nicht mehr als unwillkürliches psychisches Symptom, sondern als zielbewusste Kreation betrachtet. Es ist dies, mit anderen Worten, der Schritt von der Passivität des Patienten zur Aktivität des Schöpfers; das heißt, aus einem Zustand der extremen psychischen Verwirrung wird ein Zustand der positiven Selbstbestimmung und Selbstbefestigung. Was diese neue Einstellung zu bestätigen scheint, ist der unvermeidliche nächste

1) Im Jahre 1973 erschien ein wichtiges Dokument in der Form eines taschenbuchgroßen Albums, in dem 51 Zeichnungen von 37 Gugginger Patienten reproduziert worden sind. Die Auswahl wurde auf Navratils Ersuchen vom jungen Wiener Künstler Peter Pongratz getroffen. In seinem Vorwort macht Navratil kein Geheimnis daraus, dass es sich um Bilder handelt, die aus der Psychopathologie kommen; er weigert sich aber, deren diagnostischen Wert zu diskutieren, indem er die Auswahl als eine Stichprobe darbietet: "Die folgenden Zeichnungen haben ungeübte Kranke ohne künstlerische Intention geschaffen." Siehe Leo Navratil & Peter Pongratz, *Der Mensch – Psychopathologische Zeichnungen / Man as Depicted in Psychopathological Art*, Klosterneuburg: Niederösterreichisches Landeskrankenhaus für Psychiatrie und Neurologie Klosterneuburg, ohne Datum [1973]. Eine kluge Diskussion des Übergangs vom diagnostischen zum ästhetischen Standpunkt gibt Professor Axel Hinrich Murken in seinem Artikel *Vom diagnostischen Hilfsmittel zum autonomen Kunstwerk* im Katalog *Künstler aus Gugging. Zur Art Brut der Gegenwart*, Oldenburg: Bibliotheks- und Informationssystem der Universität Oldenburg, 1989, S. 11-50.

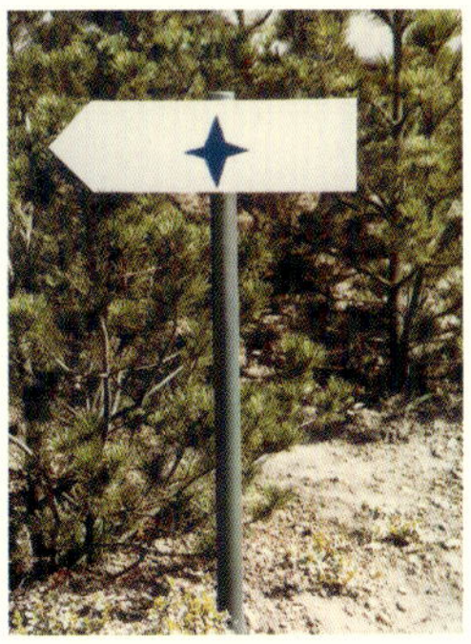

2004
wegweiser /
sign

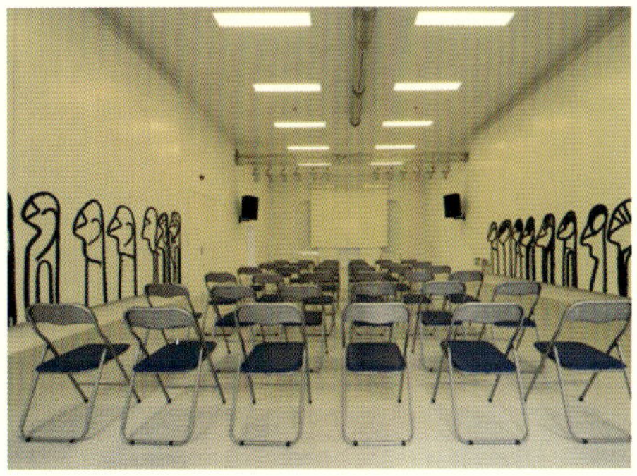

© h. schmölzer 2006
innenraum der villa /
interior of villa

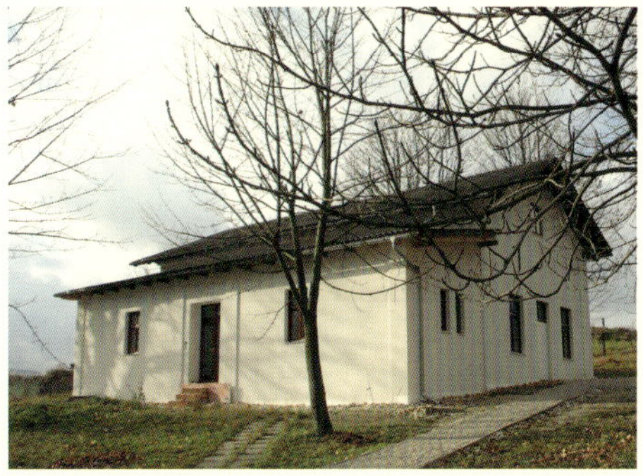

2006
villa

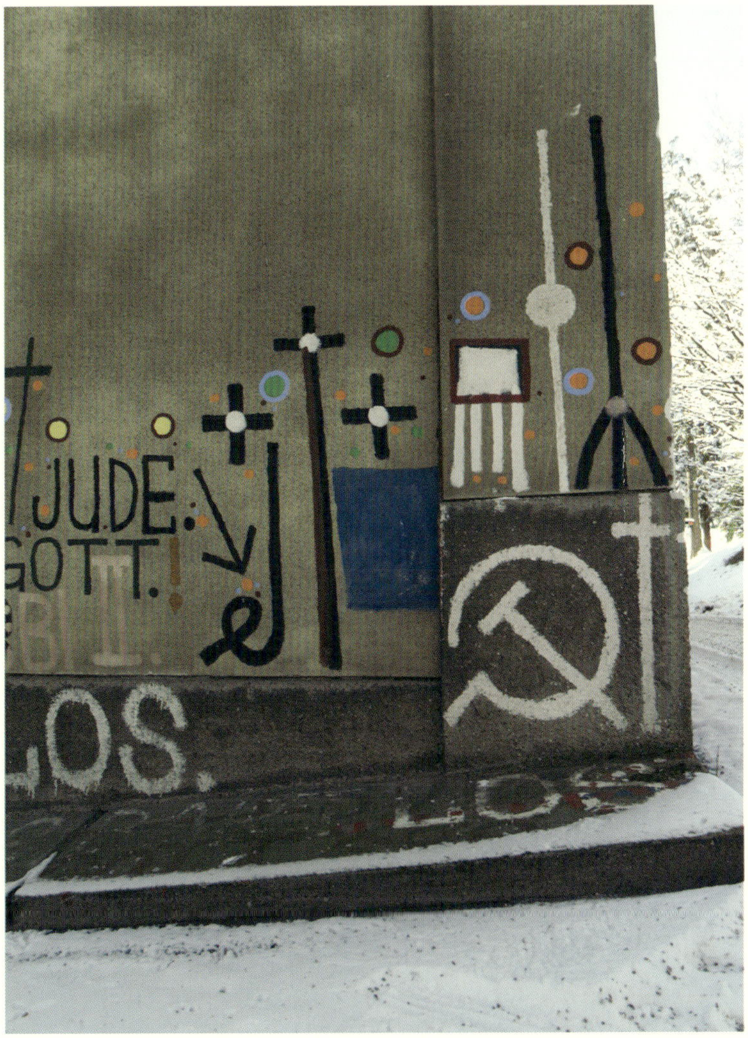

1998
mauer des hauses der künstler /
wall of house of artists

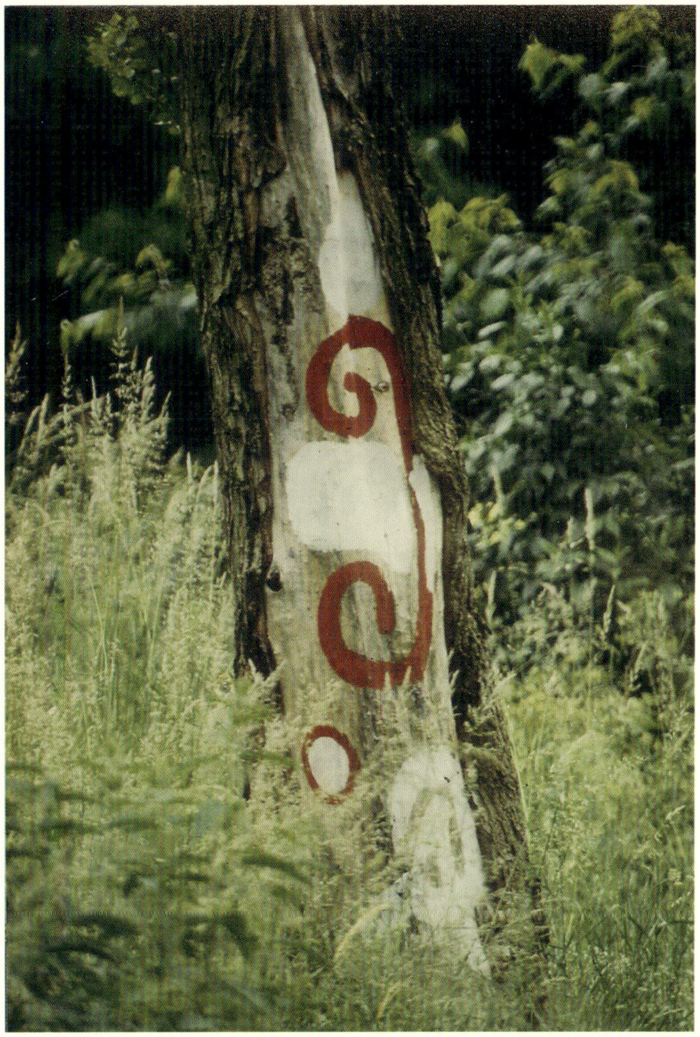

1988
symbole august wallas / symbols
of august walla

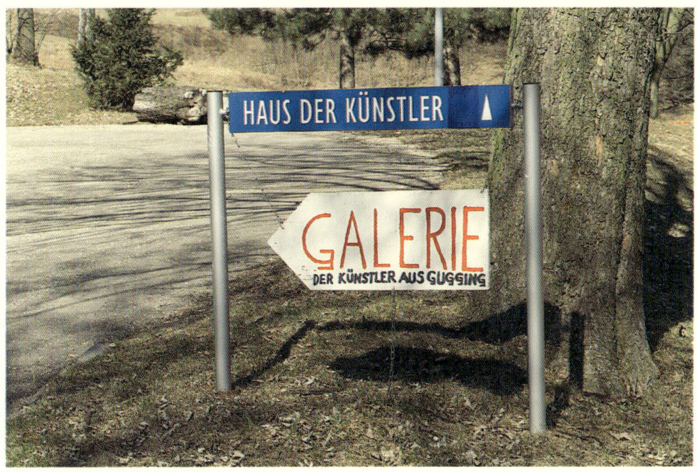

2005
wegweiser / sign

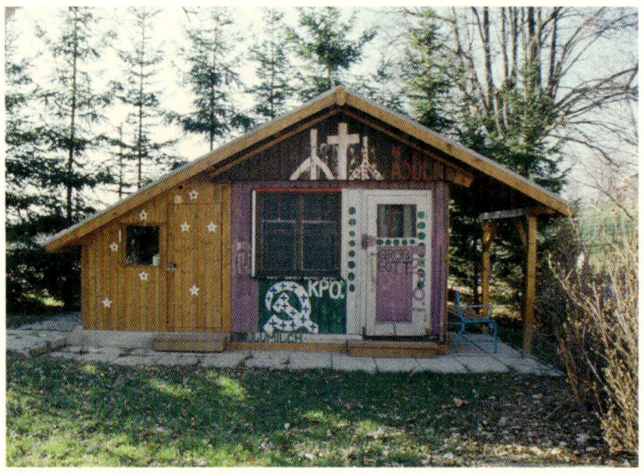

2005
walla-hütte /
walla´s hut

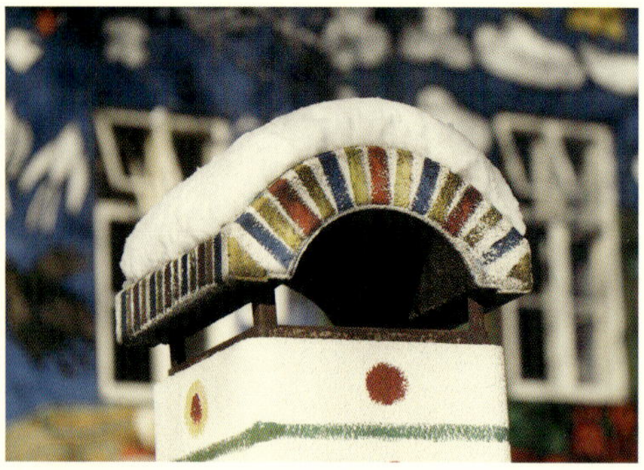

© s. roth 2004
garbers spuren /
garber´s traps

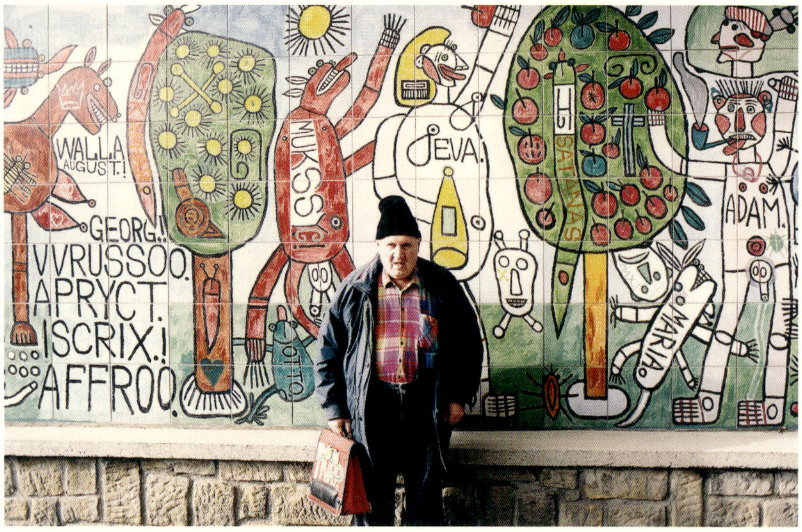

© m.vukovits 2000
walla vor keramikmalerei /
in front of his ceramic painting

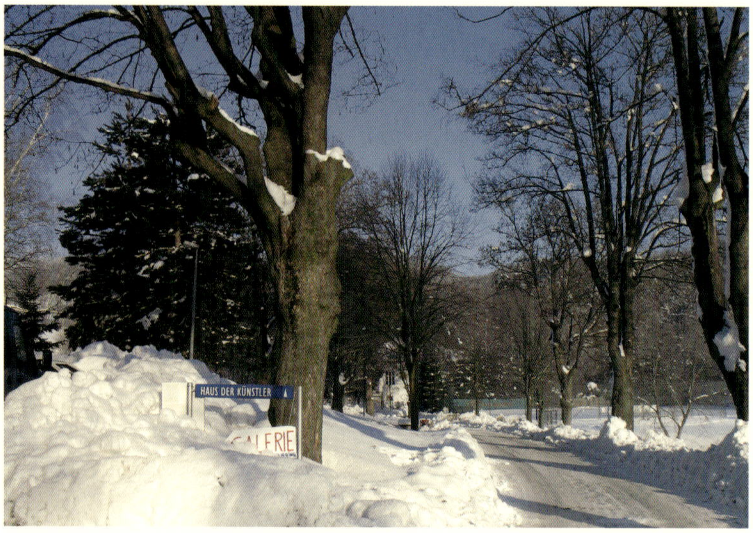

2006
winter in gugging

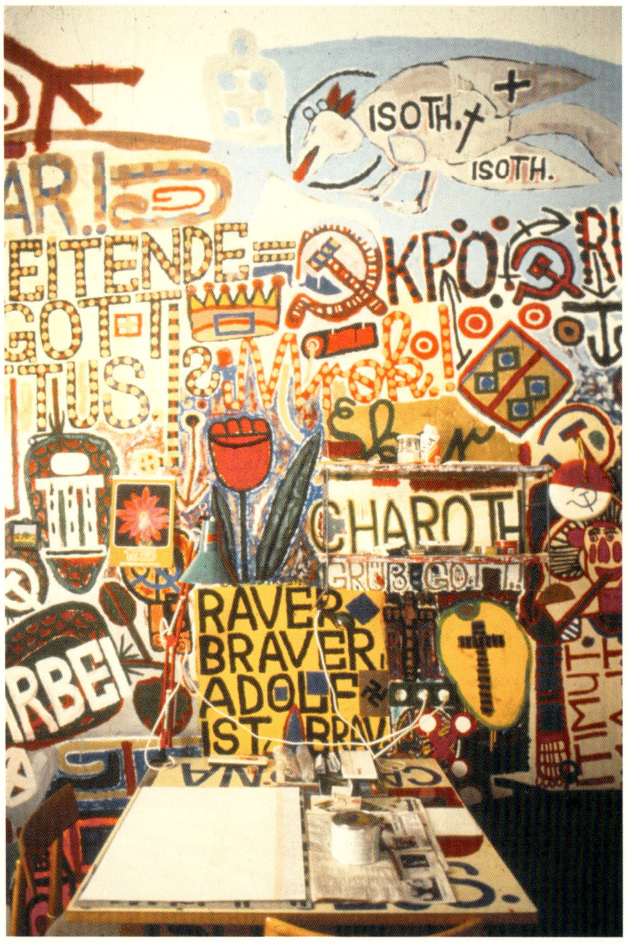

1986
walla-raum /
walla room

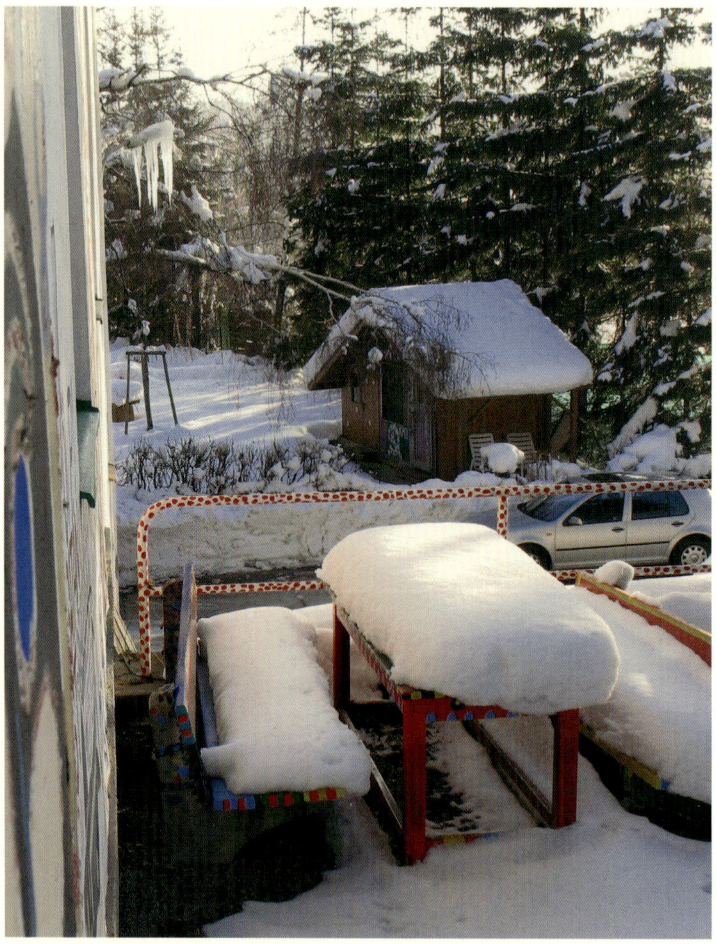

2006
vor dem haus der künstler / in front
of house of artist

Roger Cardinal

visiting gugging

the mystery of spontaneous creativity

There remains a mystery about the sources of the artistry we associate with Gugging. Whence came such talent? How did so many distinctive styles arise in the same place and at approximately the same time? What were the facilitating conditions behind the Gugging phenomenon? We have some elements of an answer, at least to the latter question.

First, we need to recall the axiom that, despite any claim to the contrary, it is not madness itself that guarantees artistic talent. As long ago as the 1920s, Hans Prinzhorn had calculated that the incidence of spontaneous graphic competence is just as rare among schizophrenics as it is in the average population. However, it seems likely that certain material conditions are conducive to the release of expressive powers. At the same time, not all such impulses lead on to concerted artmaking of quality, so that the question of inspiration is still not fully answered.

By the autumn of 1970, works from Gugging were being shown in an avant-garde gallery in the centre of Vienna, stimulating the interest and support of a considerable number of Austrian artists and intellectuals.[1]

I see this as a decisive shift, for to treat a drawing not as an involuntary psychiatric symptom but as a purposeful construction is implicitly to displace the emphasis from the passive condition of patienthood to that of active creator. This implies a progression from a state of severe mental disarray to one of positive self-definition and self-consolidation. What seems to ratify this new perspective is the inevitable next step in the material process, namely the transition from

1) A telling document appeared in 1973, in the form of a pocket-sized album with reproductions of 51 drawings by 37 Gugging inmates. The selection had been made, at Navratil's request, by the young Viennese artist Peter Pongratz, and Navratil's introduction – while making no bones about the psychopathological origin of the images – expressly declines to discuss their diagnostic potential, simply offering the selection as a sampling of the achievements of "untutored patients with no artistic aim in mind". See Navratil, Leo & Peter Pongratz, *Der Mensch – Psychopathologische Zeichnungen / Man as depicted in psychopathological art*, Klosterneuburg: Niederösterreichisches Landeskrankenhaus für Psychiatrie und Neurologie Klosterneuburg, undated [1973]. A shrewd assessment of the shift from diagnostic aid to independent artwork is given by Professor Axel Hinrich Murken in his article *Vom diagnostischen Hilfsmittel zum autonomen Kunstwerk* in the catalogue *Künstler aus Gugging. Zur Art Brut der Gegenwart*, Oldenburg: Bibliotheks- und Informationssystem der Universität Oldenburg, 1989, pp.11-50.

Schritt im materiellen Prozess, also der Übergang vom Bildmachen zum Bildzeigen. Jedes Individuum, das imstande ist, Bilder zu machen, die andere Leute gerne sehen und bewerten, kann kaum umhin, dank dieser Aufmerksamkeit, zu gedeihen und die eigene Situation neu zu überdenken. Heute ist die Unterschrift des Künstlers, die selbstbewusst die Angehörigkeit seines Werkes zu Gugging bestätigt, ein Attest für den Stolz des Autors auf sein eigenes künstlerisches Können sowie für sein gesellschaftliches Statusbewusstsein. Denn wir dürfen nicht vergessen, dass die Selbstschätzung durch die Tatsache steigt, dass jedes Werk, das bei der Galerie der Künstler verkauft wird, Geld für seinen Autor einbringt.[2]

begegnungen mit künstlern

Während meines Besuchs in Gugging im Februar 2006 habe ich versucht, mich mit mehreren Künstlern zu unterhalten. Natürlich hatte ich als Ausländer Schwierigkeiten mit ihrer Mundart. KARL VONDAL flüstert und murmelt in schwer verstehbaren Phrasen, jedoch fand ich es nicht zu schwer, ihn halbwegs zu verstehen. Zudem konnte ich mühelos die Texte lesen, die seine größeren Zeichnungen begleiten. Ich war erstaunt, wie sorgfältig er die große Zeichnung behandelte, an der er gerade arbeitete und die er aufrollte, um sie den ganzen Tag wie einen wertvollen Talisman mit sich herumzutragen. Gerne hat er seine Arbeit für mich auf dem Tisch im gemeinsamen Saal ausgerollt: Sie bestand aus mehreren zusammengeklebten Blättern und zeigte eine nackte Frau, die eine Gitarre in der Hand schwang; dazu kam noch ein Text, worin von Sex, Kaffee und Zigaretten die Rede war. Später lud er mich in sein Zimmer ein, um mir ein ähnliches, eingerahmtes Bild über seinem Bett zu zeigen sowie eine Gitarre aus Zündhölzern mit Saiten aus lockerer Wolle. (Es ist dies ein Stück aus einer früheren Karriere-Phase.)

HEINRICH REISENBAUER spricht nur selten und ist immer unterwegs: Er schlendert unaufhörlich auf und ab. Ich merke bald, dass er mich im Auge behält mit seinem schnellen nervösen Blick. FRANZ KERNBEIS ist in einem Stuhl mit einer Zigarette versunken: Viele dieser Künstler sind starke Raucher. JOHANN KOREC schleicht den Gang herunter, um einen freien Sitzplatz zu suchen, wo er sich ausruhen und eine Kippe anzünden kann; seine Zeichnungen stehen an der Wand hinter ihm, aber er ignoriert sie. Um die Asche von seiner eleganten Zigaretten-Spitze zu entfernen, verbeugt sich GÜNTHER SCHÜTZENHÖFER und hält eine feierliche Rede, deren Sinn ich leider nicht ausmachen kann. Dann lädt er mich auf sein Zimmer ein, um rituellerweise jede Zeichnung an der Wand zu identifizieren: ein Löffel, ein Baum usw. Er hat eine große Sammlung von Compact-Discs sowie eine Menge kleiner Spielzeuge.

JOHANN GARBER ist ein aufgeweckter und aktiver Mann mittleren Alters. Nach dem Hinschied AUGUST WALLAS scheint er die Rolle des *Hausmalers* übernommen zu haben. Seine Pinselstriche sind überall auf den elektrischen Schaltern zu sehen, und die Diensträume sind mit seinen bunten Farben aufgeheitert. Mit Begeisterung macht er mich auf seine Arbeit am Ofen im Untergeschoss aufmerksam. Er hat das Glück, ein eigenes Zimmer zu haben, wo er die Wände bis in alle Ecken mit seinen schelmischen Zeichnungen bedeckt. Nebenher bastelt er bunte Vogelhäuserl, die er zu Dutzenden draußen an die Bäume nagelt. Er eilt geschäftig hin und her, damit alle wissen, dass er im Begriff ist, eine Einkaufs-Expedition zu unternehmen.

2) Die Galerie der Künstler wurde im Jahre 1994 formell eingerichtet mit dem Auftrag, die Erzeugnisse der Gugginger Künstler auszustellen, zu publizieren und zu verkaufen. Die Künstler verdienen 70% durch den Verkauf. Mit dem Faktor des finanziellen Gewinns hat sich Achim Jägers in einer soziologischen Studie über Gugging und seine Beziehungen zur Außenwelt auseinander gesetzt. Jägers war als Praktikant sechs Monate im Hause tätig. Er bespricht die einmalige Entwicklung und Zusammensetzung des Gugginger Unternehmens und zeigt, dass er damit einverstanden ist, obwohl er bezweifelt, dass andere Institutionen in derselben Weise funktionieren könnten: *Gugging ist und bleibt ein Sonderfall.* Siehe Jägers, Achim, *Von Gugging Aus...Das Haus der Künstler und die Folgen. Eine kritische Betrachtung von innen und / nach außen*, Innsbruck: Verlag Integrative Psychiatrie, 1998.

artmaking to art-display – the showing of one's work to others. Any individual capable of making images that other people are willing to admire and value is likely to thrive on their praise and to see their own situation in fresh terms. Nowadays, the assertive signature which proclaims the authorship of a given work at Gugging is testimony to the creator's pride in both his artistic prowess and his social standing: for we must not overlook the impact on self-esteem which derives from the rule whereby any work which is sold through the Artists' Gallery earns money for its maker.[2]

encounters with artists

During my visit to Gugging in February 2006, I made an attempt to communicate with several of the artists, despite the difficulties I have in grasping their dialect. KARL VONDAL whispers and mumbles in incomprehensible phrases, yet I grasped the drift of what he was saying and could indeed quite easily read the texts which accompany his larger drawings. I marvelled at his attachment to the large drawing he was currently working on and which he rolled up and carried from place to place during the day, like some very precious talisman. He was keen to unroll it for me on a table in the common room. It consisted of several sheets glued together, with a drawing of a naked woman brandishing a guitar and a long accompanying text referring to sex, coffee and cigarettes. Later, he beckoned me into his room to show me a similar image framed above his bed, as well as a guitar made from matchsticks with slack strings made of wool (a piece from an earlier phase of his career).

HEINRICH REISENBAUER hardly ever speaks, and is rarely still, being an obsessional stroller, up and down, up and down. I notice that he keeps track of me in quick nervous glances. FRANZ KERNBEIS is slumped on a chair with a cigarette: many of the artists are heavy smokers. JOHANN KOREC sidles down the corridor and finds a free seat at which to lounge and light up; his drawings are on the wall behind him, but he ignores them. Bending over to tap the ash from his elegant cigarette-holder, GÜNTHER SCHÜTZENHÖFER makes a ceremonious speech (whose meaning I unfortunately cannot follow) before guiding me to his room and ritually naming the objects depicted in each of his drawings on the wall: a spoon, a tree, and so forth. He has amassed a large collection of compact discs, and another of small toys.

JOHANN GARBER is an alert and active fellow in his late fifties. He seems to have taken over from Walla as the resident decorator, annotating such things as light-switches and painting whole areas of the service rooms in bright colours. He is eager to point out his handiwork on the boiler in the basement. He is fortunate in having a bedroom all to himself, and has festooned it with hundreds of his impish drawings. Another of his sidelines is the production of dozens of colourful nesting-boxes which he nails up on the trees outside. He bustles about importantly, letting everyone know that he is about to leave on a shopping expedition.

OSWALD TSCHIRTNER, now in his eighties, behaves like a prince in exile, complaining about his discomforts and spending much of the day in his private room. I was introduced to him as he sat in his armchair with a much-thumbed copy of the Bible at his elbow; and I shook his ice-cold hand. Meek and subservient as befits the passive persona with which he has been associated – he never makes a drawing unless asked – he throws a tantrum when one of the staff tries

2) The Artists' Gallery was formally instituted in 1994 in order to exhibit, publicize and market the work of the Gugging artists, who currently benefit from 70% of any sale. The issue of financial gain is discussed in a sociological study of Gugging and its external relations written by Achim Jägers, who spent six months as an intern at the House. Jägers considers the unique development and constitution of the Gugging enterprise and expresses his approval thereof, albeit he remains sceptical as to whether other institutions could function in quite the same way: *Gugging is, and will remain, a special case.* See Jägers, Achim, *Von Gugging Aus...Das Haus der Künstler und die Folgen. Eine kritische Betrachtung von innen und / nach außen*, Innsbruck: Verlag Integrative Psychiatrie, 1998.

OSWALD TSCHIRTNER ist jetzt über achtzig Jahre alt. Wie ein Prinz im Exil klagt er über seine Beschwerden und sitzt fast den ganzen Tag in seinem Zimmer. Ich wurde ihm vorgestellt, als er in seinem Fauteuil saß, ein abgegriffenes Exemplar der Bibel an seiner Seite. Ich schüttelte seine eiskalte Hand. Er scheint bescheiden und unterwürfig, wie es seiner passiven Persönlichkeit, die sich in seiner Arbeit andeutet, geziemt – er fängt nie eine Zeichnung an, wenn man ihn nicht dazu auffordert. Dennoch ist er sehr aufgebracht, wenn eine Angestellte ihn einlädt, sich ein bisschen zu bewegen: *Furchtbar!*, ruft er überlaut und vollkommen entrüstet. Seine minimalen Skizzen sind überall im Hause aufgehängt, und eine außerordentlich große Malerei nimmt den Ehrenplatz in der Galerie in dem neuen Gebäude ein. Es ist, als ob TSCHIRTNER für den Ruf des Hauses genug getan hat und jetzt sein Recht behaupten will, ein bisschen Frieden zu haben. Ich glaube nicht, dass er sich viel daraus macht, dass er im Herbst 2005 eine Einzelausstellung in einer Galerie in Tokio hatte.

JOSEF SCHMELZER ist ebenfalls ein alter Herr, der erst vor zwei Jahren ins Haus kam. Er zieht es vor, den Tag in einem bequemen Lehnstuhl am Ende des Korridors zu verbringen, von wo aus er alles, was so läuft, zur Kenntnis nehmen kann. Er hat einen klaren Blick und ist sehr höflich; sein Gespräch ist voll von Andeutungen über seine Füße, die ihm weh tun. Noch einer, der mich gern begrüßt, ist ARNOLD SCHMIDT. Er bemüht sich beständig, meinen Blick zu fangen, meine Hand zu schütteln oder sich nach meiner Gesundheit zu erkundigen. Früher hatten seine kleineren Bilder mich nicht sehr beeindruckt; bei diesem Besuch bin ich jedoch auf seine größeren Werke gestoßen und diese haben mir sehr imponiert. Ich mache ihn auf sein sehr gelungenes Gemälde aufmerksam, das ein Flugzeug darstellt und das in der Küche über dem Schüttstein aufgehängt ist. Er ist offensichtlich erfreut und gerührt. Ich erinnere mich an meine Begegnungen mit Outsider-Künstlern an verschiedenen Orten der Welt: Es ist oft der Fall, dass sie sehr empfindlich sind, wenn man ihre Werke beurteilt, so dass man es vermeiden muss, etwas Kritisches zu sagen. Dasselbe gilt natürlich auch für professionelle Künstler oder Möchtegern-Maler. Sicher ist es eine Voraussetzung des authentischen Ausdrucks, dass der Künstler verletzlich ist.

Das Gegenteil gilt für JOHANN FISCHER. Er kultiviert ein gelassenes und weises Aussehen. Für mich ist er *der Profi*, ist immer korrekt gekleidet, mit einem neu gebügelten Hemd und einer schicken Baseball-Kappe: Er würde sicher nie auf die Idee kommen, diese verkehrt zu tragen. Ich plaudere mit ihm in dem gemeinsamen Saal und deute auf eins seiner Bilder, in dem ich viele Vögel bemerkt habe. Wenn ich ihn bitte, seine schriftliche Bemerkungen zu kommentieren – *die diebische Elster, ein Vogel, im ruhenden Zustand, ein Eier legender Hahn* –, antwortet er lediglich mit einem amüsierten und ironischen Kichern; sein zwinkerndes Auge scheint zu sagen: *Das ist Ihre Sache, ich hab das Meine getan.* Ich fühle mich sehr von seinem doppelten Diskurs, in dem Zeichnen und Schreiben zusammenfließen, angetan; mit Sorgfalt lese ich seine feierlichen Schriften, die spontan und sehr geistreich wirken.

LEONHARD FINK kommt täglich ins Atelier im Nachbarhaus, wo er den Morgen in scherzendem Gespräch mit Florian Reese verbringt und zugleich an seinen Zeichnungen arbeitet. Diese sind intensive Bleistift-Zeichnungen und stellen Tiere und phantastische Paläste dar. Wir plaudern ein bisschen über sein Werk, das mich beeindruckt, da es eine seltsame Mischung von Komischem und Erhabenem darstellt. Nebenan sitzt ein anderer Tagesgast, eine junge Frau namens LAILA BACHTIAR. Sie arbeitet an einem

to get him to take a little exercise. His minimalist sketches are hung all about the house, while an unusually large mural takes pride of place on the end wall of the new Gallery in the nearby Centre. It is as though TSCHIRTNER has done more than enough for the reputation of the House, and now asserts his right to a little peace and quiet. I somewhat doubt that he is interested in the fact that, last autumn, he had a solo show in a gallery in Tokyo.

Another old-timer is JOSEF SCHMELZER, who lives in the house since two years. Nowadays he prefers to spend his time in a comfortable armchair at the end of the corridor, where he can survey everything that is going on. He is bright-eyed and courteous; his conversation is punctuated with references to his aching feet. Another welcoming figure, ever eager to catch my glance or shake my hand, and to make a polite enquiry as to my health, is ARNOLD SCHMIDT. I had not previously found his smaller pictures very interesting, but on this visit I discover his impressive large-scale works. When I draw attention to his excellent painting of an airplane that hangs above the sink in the kitchen, he is clearly touched and pleased. This reminds me of my meetings with Outsiders in other parts of the world: it is often the case that they are ultra-sensitive to any appraisal of their work, so that one tries to avoid saying anything at all critical. However, much the same thing applies to one's encounters with professional or would-be professional artists. Perhaps it is a condition of all authentic expression that it makes the artist feel vulnerable.

JOHANN FISCHER, by contrast, cultivates a serene and sagacious look. I think of him as *the professional*, for he is always well turned out, with a clean shirt and a neat baseball cap. I speak to him in the common room, near one of his pictures, in which I notice lots of birds. When I press him to comment on his captions – *the thieving magpie, a bird in a state of rest, a cockerel that lays eggs* – he responds with an amused and ironic chuckle, twinkling his eye at me as if to say:
It is up to you to work it out. I have done my bit. I am much taken by his twin system of drawing interspersed with writing, and devote myself to the careful reading of his elaborate scripts, which reflect a high order of native wit.

LEONHARD FINK attends the nearby studio on a daily basis, and spends his mornings chaffing constantly with Florian Reese, the monitor, while working at his densely charged pencil-drawings of towers and fantasy palaces. We converse a little about his work, which I find quite haunting, a mixture of the comical and the sublime. Nearby is another day visitor, a young woman called LAILA BACHTIAR. She huddles over her latest piece, studiously filling in a loose grid-pattern with regular strokes of a thick soft pencil. She seems intent on gradually converting the entire sheet of paper into all-over darkness. This opacity seems comforting rather than frightening.Witnessing her concentration, I feel moved, remembering Paul Klee's dictum that when he was working at a picture, he was really working on his own self. LAILA is nervous and very reserved, though I can see she is pleased that I take the trouble to sit with her. I am aware that I would need far more time to gain her full confidence.

Werk, indem sie einen lockeren Raster mit regelmässigen Strichen ausfüllt. Sie benutzt einen dicken, weichen Bleistift und scheint darauf zu zielen, das Blatt in etwas endgültig Dunkles zu verwandeln. Wie ich ihre Konzentration beobachte, fühle ich mich sehr bewegt; ich erinnere mich an das Wort Paul Klees, der einmal sagte, dass – wenn er mit einem Bild beschäftigt sei – er in Wirklichkeit an sich selbst arbeite. LAILA ist nervös und sehr reserviert, doch sehe ich, dass es ihr Freude macht, als ich mir die Mühe nehme, bei ihr zu sitzen; aber ich weiß, dass es einige Zeit dauern würde, um ihr volles Vertrauen zu gewinnen.

die kunst aus gugging

Es ist eine heikle Frage, ob die Kategorien der Psychopathologie für die heutige Künstlergruppe noch zutreffen. Es kann wohl behauptet werden, dass Konzepte wie Schizophrenie, Depression, Autismus usw. immer noch notwendig sind, wenn man das Verhalten und die Bedürfnisse des Individuums zu beurteilen hat, sei es auch in einem so geschützten Milieu wie hier. Gemäß der neuen Gesinnung in Gugging ist es nicht mehr denkbar, mit einer medizinischen Diagnose eine Person zu definieren und abzugrenzen.

Es bleibt die Frage, wie man die außerordentlichen Produkte dieser Institution eigentlich nennen soll. Sicher scheint mir nur, dass es nicht genügt, von 'Kunst' allein und ohne nähere Definition zu sprechen. Das Phänomen Gugging ist mit einem ganz bestimmten Kontext und Geschehen verbunden: Wenn man seine Geschichte näher studiert, findet man, dass die Ansprüche immer deutlicher hervortreten. Heutzutage darf niemand mehr glauben, dass das, was hier passiert, die Frucht eines glücklichen Zufalls sei, einfach ein spontanes Wunder. Das will nicht heißen, die Gugginger Künstler seien programmiert und ihr Schaffen im Voraus geplant, denn es gibt, mindestens im Prinzip, keinen Versuch, die Thematik, die Malweise oder den Stil ihrer Kreationen zu bestimmen. Obwohl es sich keineswegs um eine Kunstschule oder eine Kunstbewegung handelt, kann man nicht leugnen, dass es hier um eine Stätte des Erfindens, um einen Ort für künstlerische Produktion geht – also um ein ganz spezifisches Unternehmen, um ein Projekt. Das Haus der Gugginger Künstler befindet sich an einem recht abgelegenen Ort. Es liegt etwas ganz Poetisches in seiner Nähe zum Wienerwald: Besonders an einem Wintertag im Februar, mit dem Glanz des Sonnenscheins auf einem nahen, von purem Schnee bedeckten Anhang, schien mir das Haus vom Alltag und von den wechselnden Strömungen der heutigen Gesellschaft wunderbar distanziert zu sein. Dürfte es so sein, dass Gugging seine raison d'être darin findet, dass es von allem weit entfernt liegt? Ist es gerade seine Marginalität, die seine Fruchtbarkeit und seinen Erfolg garantiert? Jean Dubuffet hätte das sicher so gesehen.

Es mag sein, dass Gugging immer noch einmalig ist, und doch ist die Idee seiner Marginalität nun sicher überholt: Heute muss sein Status als Outsider-Ort neu vermessen werden. Vielleicht ist die Grenze zwischen Wildnis und Kultur der Ort, von dem man die Welt am besten beobachten kann. Ich glaube nicht mehr, dass man heute noch den Outsider-Künstler als einen, der seine Lebenschance verpaßt hat, sehen kann. Eher betrachte ich ihn als einen, der erstaunlicherweise als erster am Endziel anlangt, wie ein Rennpferd, dem keiner eine Chance gegeben hat und das gegen alle Erwartung mit 500 gegen 1 gewinnt. Meiner Meinung nach hat Gugging dieses Rennen gewonnen. Es hat die Außenwelt überrascht und ihre Aufmerksamkeit auf sich gezogen: Zwar ist nicht sicher,

the art of gugging

It is a difficult question whether the categories of psychopathology are still applicable to today's team of artists. Some will contend that concepts such as schizophrenia, manic-depression, autism and so forth are still necessary if one is fully to appreciate an individual's behaviour and private needs, even within a protected environment such as this. Yet the new ethos of Gugging insists that no medical diagnosis should be allowed to define and delimit the person.

It remains to decide what name to give to the exceptional products of this establishment. Undoubtedly it is not satisfactory to speak of 'art' without further qualification. The Gugging phenomenon belongs to a specific context and set of circumstances which, when one looks closely, appear more and more sophisticated as time goes by. Today, no-one would take what is happening here to be a lucky accident, a spontaneous miracle. This is not to imply that the arts of Gugging are programmed or rehearsed, for there is, in principle at least, no attempt to regulate the thematics, the formats or the styles of creation. And yet, if not a school or a movement, this is undeniably a locus of invention, a site of art production, an enterprise, even a project. I spoke earlier of the House and its placement at the very edge of things. I find a poetic resonance in its proximity to the Wienerwald, and on a wintry day in February, with the sunshine gleaming on a nearby slope of virgin snow, it seemed wonderfully detached from everyday life and the vicissitudes of contemporary society. Could it be that Gugging's raison d'être resides in its lying far from everything else? Does it thrive on its marginality, as Jean Dubuffet might have said?

Unique it may still be, yet Gugging's marginality is a thing of the past, and its *Outsider* status needs to be reassessed. Perhaps the edge of the wilderness is the best place from which to see the wider cultural picture. Rather than argue that the Outsider is one who has missed his chance in life, I would rather see him as the one who, like the racehorse which nobody thinks capable of winning, somehow manages to reach the finishing-post first: against all expectation, the 500-to-1 gamble pays off. I think Gugging has managed just such a feat. Having startled the world outside and caught its attention, it is now obliged to assume a role on a wider stage. Whether or not everyone entirely understands its inner constitution, Gugging cannot avoid functioning as a model or an inspiration for other projects, given the fast-growing number of institutions supporting artmakers with special needs.[3]

During my Gugging visit, I went to the renowned Essl Foundation in nearby Klosterneuburg, which had mounted an ambitious survey of Austrian art of the nineteenth and twentieth centuries. It included avant-garde works by such stars as Arnulf Rainer, Alfred Hrdlicka, Fritz Wotruba and Wolfgang Hollegha. Amid these, I stumbled upon an alcove with large paintings by three Gugging artists: HAUSER, WALLA and KAMLANDER. Inserted into this elite company without special pleading, the works were entirely at ease: they seemed assertive, self-possessed, fearless.

Professor Navratil finally retired as director of the Gugging enterprise in 1986.[4] Since that time, his successor, Dr Johann Feilacher, has rigorously followed the logic and momentum outlined above, striving to de-emphasize psychiatric concerns in favour of aesthetic priorities. His declared goal is to launch the Gugging group into the art-world proper, arguing that any supposed

3) Prominent among such centres worldwide are Creative Growth, USA; La Tinaia, Italy; Arts Project, Australia; Musée de l'Art différencié, Belgium; Kunsthaus Kannen, Germany; Atelier Heerenplaats, Netherlands; Gaia, Denmark; Trastad Samlinger, Norway; Galerie Tak, Poland; Project Ability, Scotland; and Barrington Farm, England. Whether dealing with art made by the mentally ill or those with learning difficulties, nearly all these institutions are grappling with the choice between the circumscribed field of art-as-therapy and a challenging exposure to the art-world at large.

4) Navratil has gone on to publish extensively on issues related to art and mental disorder, in particular developing ideas about what he sees as the fundamental creative functions and their corresponding stylistic traits. Among several publications on this theme may be cited his *Die Überlegenheit des Bären. Theorie der Kreativität*, Munich: Arcis Verlag, 1995.

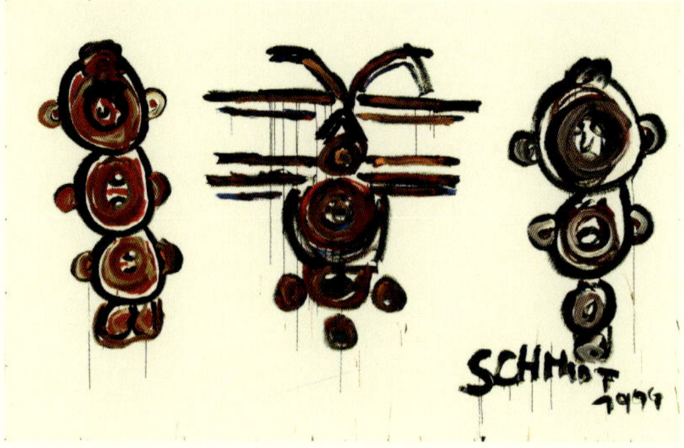

1999
Schmidt: Flugzeug / Airplane

dass alle seine Bewunderer seine innere Bewandtnis richtig erfassen. Dessen ungeachtet kann Gugging als Modellfall oder als Inspiration für andere Projekte wirken, umso mehr, als es eine schnell wachsende Anzahl von Institutionen gibt, deren Ziel es ebenfalls ist, kunstschaffende Menschen mit speziellen sozialen Bedürfnissen zu unterstützen.[3]

Während meines Besuchs in Gugging ging ich zum berühmten Kunsthaus Essl im nahen Klosterneuburg, welches einen kühnen Überblick von der Kunst Österreichs im neunzehnten und im zwanzigsten Jahrhundert darbot. Darin fand man avantgardistische Werke von Arnulf Rainer, Alfred Hrdlicka, Fritz Wotruba und Wolfgang Hollegha. Inmitten dieser Sammlung stieß ich auf große Gemälde von drei Gugging-Künstlern: HAUSER, WALLA und KAMLANDER. In dieser elitären Gesellschaft, eingeführt ganz ohne Plädoyer, behaupteten sich diese Werke absolut problemlos: Sie schienen sogar maßgebend, selbstbewußt, furchtlos.

Nach seinem langen Dienst als Leiter des Zentrums für Kunst-Psychotherapie ist Professor Navratil 1986 in den Ruhestand getreten.[4] Seitdem hat sein Nachfolger, Dr. Johann Feilacher, rigoros die Logik und den Schwung beibehalten, die ich hier skizziert habe, d.h. er bemüht sich, der ästhetischen Perspektive gegenüber der psychiatrischen den Vorrang zu geben. Seine Absicht ist es, Gugging in die größere Kunstwelt einzugliedern, indem er den Standpunkt vertritt, dass ein angebliches psychologisches Defizit mit dem Status dieser kreativen Gruppe gar nichts zu tun hat. Der rote Faden im ganzen Gugginger Unternehmen, sagt er, liege in dem Versuch, seine Beziehung zur allgemeinen Kunst zu normalisieren. Kunst sei eine elementare menschliche Aktivität, die das Recht auf ihre eigene Existenz hat, ohne Rücksicht auf eine etwaige Trennung zwischen Profis und Amateuren oder zwischen *Insiders* und *Outsiders.* Ich glaube, dass es sein Endziel ist, die alten Etiketten – *psychopathologische Kunst, diagnostische Zeichnung, zustandsgebundene Kunst, Art Brut, Outsider Ar*t usw. – endgültig loszuwerden. Er will eine zuverlässige Stabilität aufbauen: Gugging soll Garantie sein für ästhetische Qualität als ein Ort, der seine Definition und seine Rechtfertigung lediglich in der künstlerischen Beziehung findet.

Mir scheint, dass es noch einige Zeit dauern wird, bis das allgemeine Publikum die Kunst von Gugging in diesem höheren Sinn akzeptiert. Es dürfte nicht so leicht sein, die Leute davon zu überzeugen, dass Gugging nichts anderes als eine Künstlerkolonie ist. Und auf lange Sicht steht fest, dass die subtile und komplexe Evolution von Gugging auf keinen Fall als bloße historische Fußnote betrachtet werden kann.

3) Unter den vielen Anstalten in der Welt dürfen wir die folgenden wichtigen Beispiele nennen: Creative Growth, USA; La Tinaia, Italien; Arts Project Australia, Australien; Musée de l'Art différencié, Belgien; Kunsthaus Kannen, Deutschland; Atelier Heerenplaats, Niederlande; Gaia, Dänemark; Trastad Samlinger, Norwegen; Galerie Tak, Polen; Project Ability, Schottland, und Barrington Farm, England. Ob sie psychisch kranke oder geistig behinderte Menschen behandeln, stehen fast alle diese Anstalten vor der Wahl, entweder im begrenzten Gebiet der Kunst-als-Therapie zu bleiben oder in ein Verhältnis zur allgemeinen Kunstwelt einzutreten.

4) Des Weiteren hat Navratil vielfach über das Verhältnis zwischen Kunst und psychischen Störungen geschrieben. Insbesondere entwickelt er Hypothesen über die *kreativen Grundfunktionen* und die daran anknüpfenden stilistischen Merkmale. Unter seinen vielen Schriften zu diesem Thema zitieren wir sein Buch *Die Überlegenheit des Bären.* Theorie der Kreativität, München: Arcis Verlag, 1995.

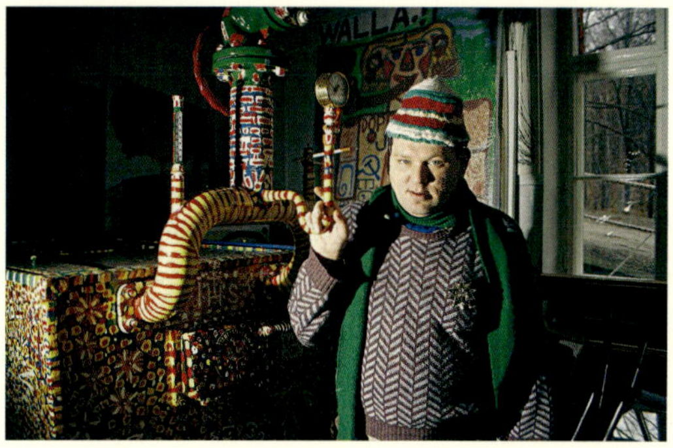

2006
Garber mit bemalten Ofen / Garber with painted stove

psychological deficit is of no relevance to their status as creators. The essence of Gugging, he insists, lies in the effort to normalize their relation to artmaking, seen as a central human activity that should exist independently of any segregation of professionals from amateurs, or of *insiders* from *outsiders*. I believe that his ultimate objective is to get rid of all the old labels – *psychopathological art, diagnostic drawing, statebound art, Art brut, Outsider Art* and the rest – and to stabilize Gugging as a centre of artistic excellence, a site defined and validated purely in terms of art.

My impression is that there is still some distance to travel before popular audiences can absorb the art of Gugging in this spirit. It may prove difficult to persuade them that Gugging is in fact an artists' colony pure and simple. And in the long term, the question remains whether the subtle complexities of Gugging's evolution can ever be relegated to a historical footnote.

Jane Kallir

gugging im zusammenhang mit art brut, amerika und der welt

Die Anerkennung von Art Brut und Außenseiterkunst als eigene künstlerische Genres erfolgte aufgrund einer Besessenheit mit der *Andersartigkeit*, die zum ersten Mal um die Wende zum 20. Jahrhundert ernstere Beachtung fand. Zwar hatte es in früheren Epochen schon eine Vielzahl von nicht-akademischen Kunstarten wie Volkskunsthandwerk, Amateurmalerei und Kunst von geisteskranken Menschen gegeben, doch die Gralshüter der Hochkultur schenkten solch minderwertigen Schöpfungen erst gar keine Aufmerksamkeit. Der *edle Wilde* existierte als philosophischer Begriff, war der Kunst jedoch fremd. Schließlich stellte die Kunst die unangefochtene Domäne des europäischen Erbadels und des wohlhabenden amerikanischen Bildungsbürgertums dar. Während des neunzehnten Jahrhunderts verschoben sich die Grenzen zwischen den Klassen infolge von Industrialisierung und Vermischung von Volksgruppen durch Migration und Imperialismus. Dies führte zu noch nie vorher gesehenen Konfrontationen zwischen herrschenden und untergeordneten Völkern. Die Tatsache, dass man gleichzeitig gezwungen und unfähig war, mit den „anderen“ zurande zu kommen, wurde das Leitmotiv des 20. Jahrhunderts und trug zu seinen vielen Völkermorden bei. Der Zusammenbruch von einst stabilen aristokratischen Imperien war Anlass für den Ersten Weltkrieg. Dieser wiederum löste Hitlers Vergeltungsdrang, sein Streben nach der Oberherrschaft über Europa und in der Folge den Zweiten Weltkrieg aus. Beide Weltkriege waren Anlass einer Welle ernsten Interesses von Seiten der kulturellen Elite für die autodidaktische Kunst, die Kunst der *anderen*.

Im 20. Jahrhundert hoben die an autodidaktischer Kunst Interessierten immer wieder verschiedenartige Aspekte der *anderen* hervor. Der erste *Außenseiter*, der nach *innen* gebracht wurde, war der berühmte malende Zöllner Henri Rousseau. Ihn erkannten

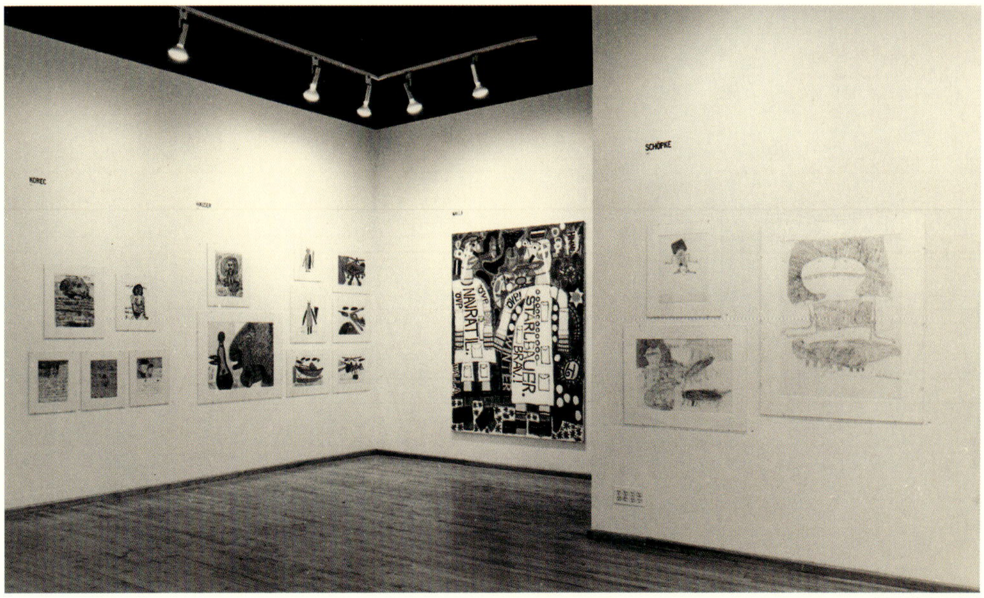

New York, 1986

european outsiders / rosa esman gallery

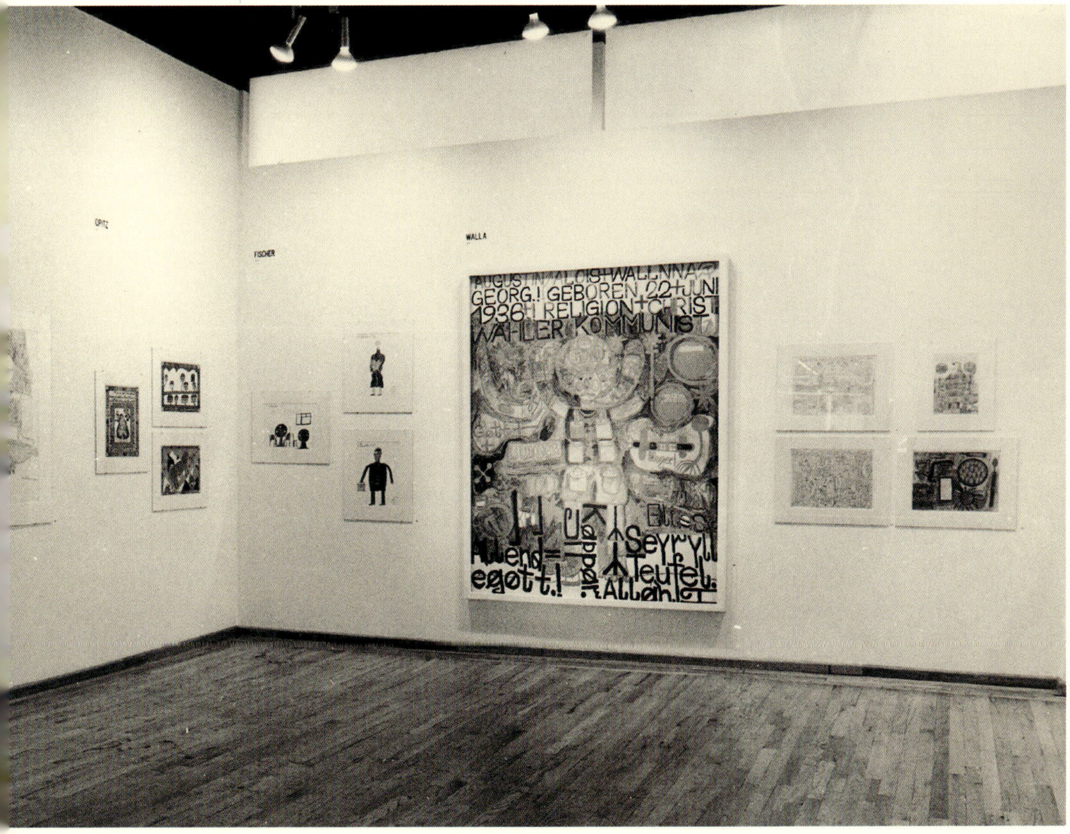

New York, 1986

european outsiders / rosa esman gallery

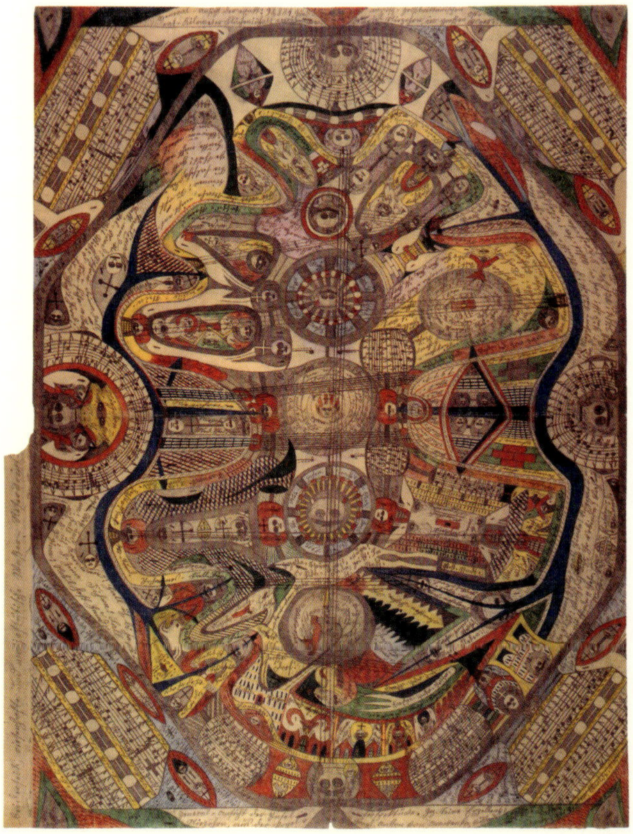

1911

wölfli

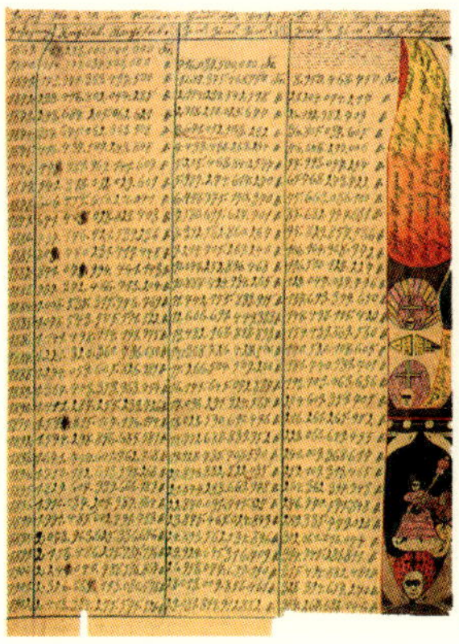

1914

wölfli

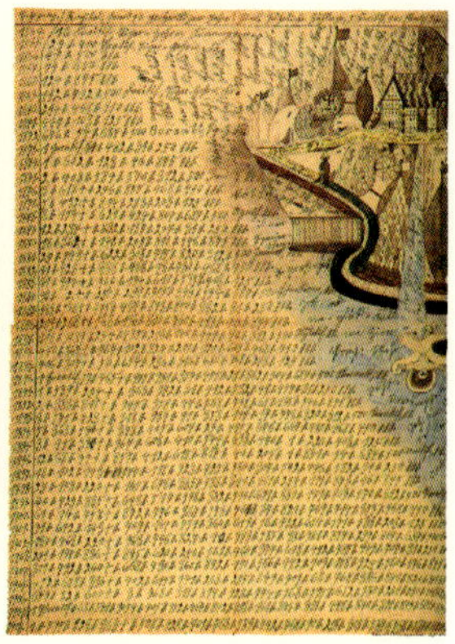

1912

wölfli

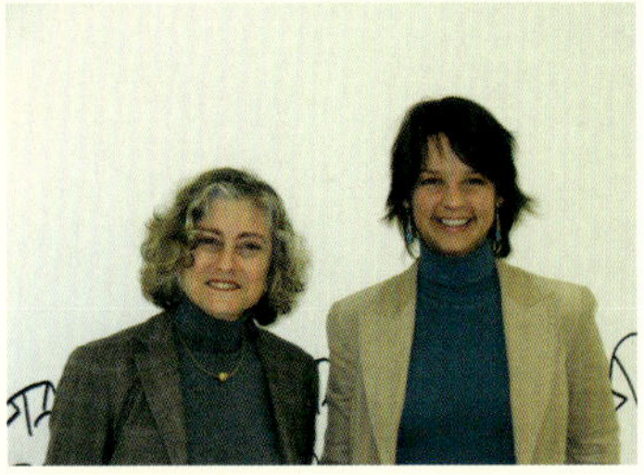

2005
kallir, katschnig

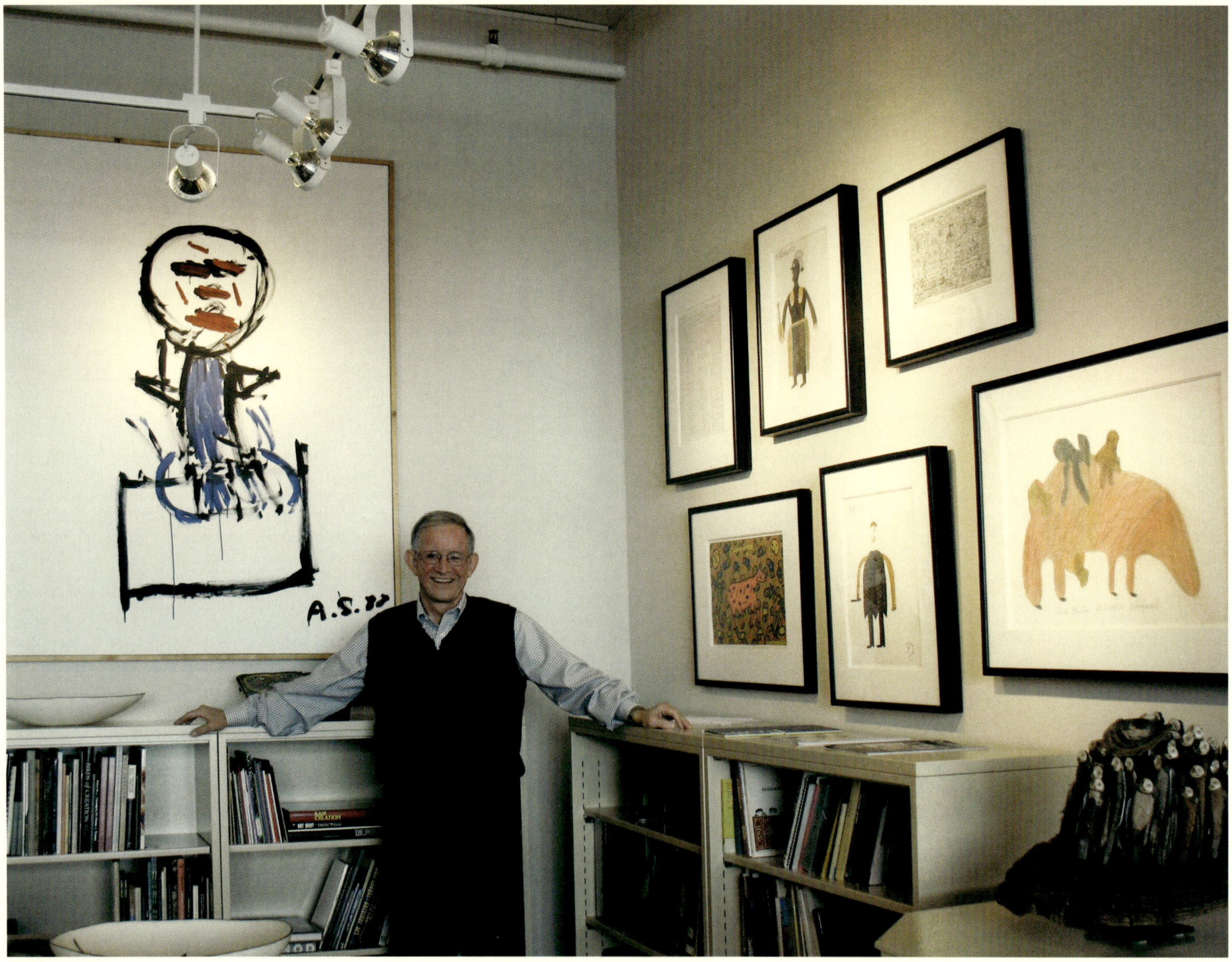

Milwaukee, 2005
petullo

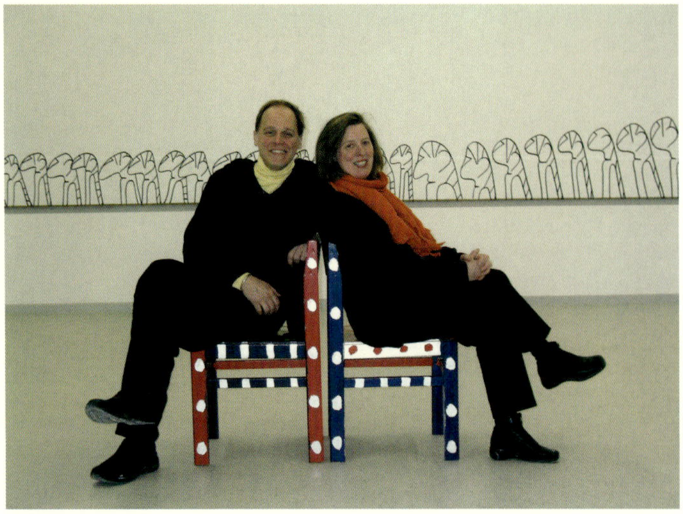

2005
vick, stone

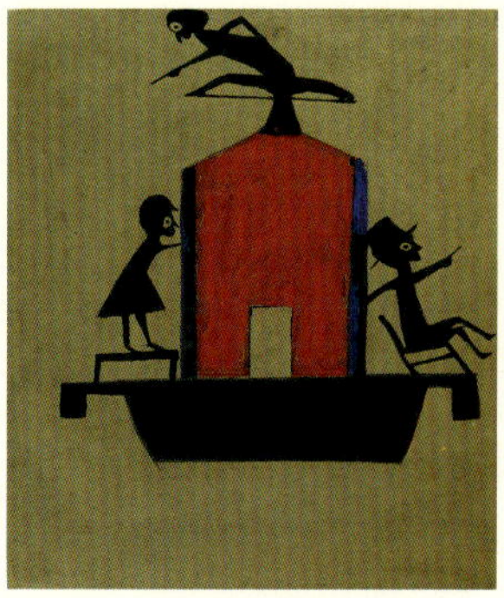

© Ricco Maresca Gallery, New York
Bill Traylor, Ohne Titel / untitled
ca. 1939-42, 32,5 x 17,5 cm
Tempera, Bleistift / tempera, pencil

Jane Kallir

gugging in the context of art brut, america and the world

The recognition of Art Brut and *outsider* art as distinct genres of expression derived from an obsession with *otherness* that first came into focus around the turn of the last century. Although a broad array of non-academic art—folk craft, amateur painting and art by the mentally ill—existed inearlier eras, the arbiters of high culture paid such lowly creations no mind. The *noble savage* existed as a concept in philosophy but not in art, which was the unchallenged purview of the hereditary aristocracy and, in democratic America, of the educated moneyed classes. During thenineteenth century, however, the readjustment of class boundaries occasioned by industrialization and the mingling of disparate populations through migration and imperialism sparked heretofore unknown confrontations between dominant and subservient peoples. The simultaneous need and inability to deal with the *other* became a leitmotif of twentieth-century history, contributing to its many genocides. The crumbling of once stable aristocratic empires touched off World War I, which in turn triggered Hitler's retaliatory quest for European domination and World War II. And for each world war, there was a concomitant surge of interest in selftaught art, the art of the *other,* on the part of the cultural elite. The waves of interest in self-taught art that recurred throughout the twentieth century tended to emphasize differing aspects of the *other*. The first *outsider* to be brought *inside* was the famous painting toll collector Henri Rousseau. Embraced by Picasso in France and Kandinsky in Germany, Rousseau was the original *naïf,* a paragon of childlike innocence. It was Kandinsky, a prolific theorist, who promulgated the notion that artists without formal training are better able to capture the *inner resonance* of their subjects than those whose spontaneity has been dulled by rote schooling. After World War I, this ideal of artistic purity would find broader commercial acceptance through the intervention of the art historian and dealer

Picasso in Frankreich und Kandinsky in Deutschland an. Rousseau war der erste *Naive*, ein Paradebeispiel kindlicher Unschuld. Kandinsky machte sich sehr viele Gedanken zur künstlerischen Theorie und verbreitete die Ansicht, dass Künstler ohne formale Ausbildung besser die *innere Resonanz* ihrer Sujets erfassen konnten als all jene, deren Spontaneität durch akademische Routine abgestumpft war. Nach dem Ersten Weltkrieg fand dieses Ideal von künstlerischer Reinheit aufgrund der Bemühungen des Kunsthistorikers und – händlers Wilhelm Uhde größeren kommerziellen Anklang. Er vereinte eine ganze Gruppe von nicht-akademischen Künstlern um sich, die er *Maler des Heiligen Herzens* nannte. In den zwanziger Jahren verbreiteten die Psychiater Hans Prinzhorn und Walter Morgenthalter eine weitere, dunklere Sicht der *Außenseiterkunst*. Diese beiden Ärzte von der Heidelberger Psychiatrischen Klink bzw. der Berner Waldauklinik suchten Zugang zu kreativen Tiefen, indem sie die künstlerische Produktion ihrer geisteskranken Patienten analysierten. Viele Surrealisten waren mit Prinzhorns und Morgenthalers Forschungen vertraut und machten sich die Nutzung unbewusster Impulse zum vorrangigen Ziel.

Nach dem zweiten Weltkrieg brachte der Surrealismus den wichtigsten Verfechter der *Außenseiter*, den Künstler Jean Dubuffet, hervor. Er verwendete den Begriff Art Brut, rohe Kunst, um eine Schaffensweise zu beschreiben, die von der tradierten Kultur nicht verdorben war. Die Art Brut stellte eine unmittelbare Reaktion auf den Wahnsinn zweier weltweit geführten Kriege dar. Aus Verzweiflung über die menschliche Zivilisation suchte Dubuffet bei Randgruppen nach Hoffnung und Inspiration. Diese fand er in der Arbeit von geisteskranken und vollkommen unangepassten Menschen sowie von spirituellen Medien. Dubuffet verband die beiden vor den Kriegen gängigen Begriffe von autodidaktischer Kunst zu einem und schrieb der Arbeit von Menschen, die aus der Gesellschaft ausgegrenzt waren, eine primitive Unschuld und Reinheit zu. Art Brut führte in der Folge zum Begriff *Outsider Art* (*Außenseiterkunst*), der Titel des ersten auf Englisch erschienenen Buches über das Thema, das der britische Kunsthistoriker Roger Cardinal verfasste. Allerdings ging sowohl bei der Übersetzung des Begriffs *art brut* als auch bei der Verpflanzung des Genres von Europa in die Vereinigten Staaten etwas verloren.

Die allgemeine Anerkennung von nicht-akademischer Kunst wurde in Amerika von Europäern propagiert und setzte sich erst ziemlich spät durch. In der Folge wurde das Genre im Land auch auf recht einzigartige Weise interpretiert. Wie in Europa verwendeten frühe moderne Künstler in Amerika *naive* Kunst, um ihren eigenen unorthodoxen formalen Experimenten Gültigkeit zu verschaffen. Als Amerika in den Zeiten der großen Depression in den dreißiger Jahren seine ersten eigenen autodidaktischen Maler *entdeckte*, wurde dieses Genre zu einem Sammelbecken für verschiedene Vorstellungen von nationaler Identität. Wie die gleichzeitig arbeitenden Regionalisten symbolisierten die autodidaktischen Künstler die Stärke des Kernlandes im Vergleich zur korrupten Großstadt. Sie standen stellvertretend für uramerikanische Konzepte wie Erfindungskraft, Freiheit und Individualismus. In Amerika, wo Klassenunterschiede öfter verleugnet werden als in Europa, stärkten die autodidaktischen Künstler den Mythos von Egalitarismus. So wie die Kunstelite während der Depression die Künstler aus der Arbeiterklasse lobte, so wurden die afroamerikanischen Kunstschaffenden in den achtziger und neunziger Jahren des zwanzigsten Jahrhunderts gefördert. Damals versuchte Amerika mit seinem fest im Bewusstsein verankerten Rassismus zurande zu kommen. Während sich in Europa eine riesige Kluft zwischen den Vertretern der *naiven*

Wilhelm Uhde, who cobbled together a whole group of untrained *Painters of the Sacred Heart.* However, in the 1920s another, darker view of the *outsider* emerged, courtesy of the psychiatrists Hans Prinzhorn and Walter Morgenthaler. Working, respectively, at the Heidelberg Psychiatric Clinic and the Waldau Clinic in Bern, these two doctors sought access to the creative depths by studying the art of mental patients. The harnessing of unconscious impulses became a primary goal of the Surrealists, many of whom were familiar with Prinzhorn's and Morgenthaler's research. Surrealism spawned the preeminent post-World-War-II champion of *outsiders,* the artist Jean Dubuffet. Art Brut (raw art), the term he coined to describe art untainted by received culture, was a direct response to the insanity of global war. Despairing of civilization, Dubuffet looked to its margins for hope and inspiration, which he found in the work of mental patients, spiritual mediums and extreme outcasts. In effect, Dubuffet melded the two pre-war conceptions of selftaught art, ascribing primordial innocence and purity to the work of social deviants. Art Brut in turn spawned *outsider* art, the title chosen by the British art historian Roger Cardinal for the first English-language book on the subject. However, something was literally lost in translation and in the transplantation of the genre from Europe to the United States. Mainstream recognition of non-academic art was a European import that was welcomed to the U.S. rather belatedly and, in the process, given a uniquely American interpretation. As in Europe, America's early modernists used *naïve* art to ratify their own unorthodox formal experiments. But in the depths of the Depression, when America's first homegrown self-taught painters were *discovered,* the genre quickly became a repository for all sorts of notions about national identity. Like the contemporary Regionalists, self-taught artists of the 1930s represented the strength of the heartland as against the corrupt big city. They represented native ingenuity, freedom and individualism. In America, where class divisions are more commonly denied than is the case in Europe, self-taught artists bolstered the myth of egalitarianism. Just as the art-world elite lauded working-class artists during the Depression, that same elite promoted African-American creators in the 1980s and '90s, when America was struggling to overcome its legacy of entrenched racism. Whereas in Europe, a sharp rift developed between proponents of *naïve* art and avatars of Art Brut, Americans were far less inclined to engage in such theoretical hair-splitting. To them, folk art, *naïve* art and *outsider* art were all different expressions of pretty much the same thing. The term Art Brut is used rarely in the United States, and then chiefly to denote foreign phenomena. Those who have a serious professional commitment to what is amorphously referred to as *the field* also attempt to distance themselves from the term *outsider,* preferring the more neutral, if also problematical, adjective *self-taught.* Given the connection between America's interest in self-taught art and the affirmation of national identity, it is not surprising that American collectors, dealers and museums have always tended to favor domestic exemplars of the genre. This phenomenon is by no means unique to the United States; Germans, for example, are the foremost collectors of German *naives,* and the Swiss evince an affinity to *cow parades* that stretch back to nineteenth-century Appenzell. Recently, the popularity of *outsider* art and Art Brut has created a handful of international superstars, such as the Swiss Adolf Wölfli and the American Henry Darger. Nevertheless, selftaught art, with its oblique ties to parochial folk traditions and its specific locus in place and persona, has proved more resistant to internationalization than mainstream art. Since taking over Leo Navratil's position as Director of the Gugging Haus der Künstler in 1986, Johann Feilacher has tried diligently to raise

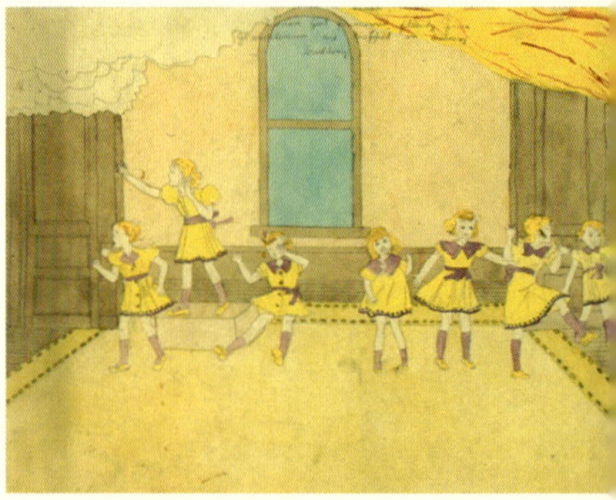

Kunst und den Verfechtern der Art Brut auftat, waren die Amerikaner viel weniger geneigt, sich mit solch theoretischer Haarspalterei zu beschäftigen. Für sie stellten Volkskunst, *naive* Kunst und *Außenseiterkunst* schlechthin verschiedene Aspekte von mehr oder minder derselben Sache dar. Der Begriff Art Brut wird in den Vereinigten Staaten selten gebraucht und wenn, dann meistens nur, um ein ausländisches Konzept zu beschreiben. All jene, die sich beruflich ernsthaft mit dieser vage zusammengefassten Kunstszene beschäftigen, versuchen sich vom Begriff *outsider art* abzugrenzen und ziehen den neutraleren, nicht weniger unproblematischen Ausdruck *self-taught* (*autodidaktische*) Kunst vor.

Da zwischen Amerikas Interesse an autodidaktischer Kunst und der Bekräftigung von nationaler Identität eine Verbindung besteht, ist es nicht weiter verwunderlich, dass amerikanische Sammler, Kunsthändler und Museen einheimische Vertreter des Genres meistens bevorzugt behandeln. Diese Haltung beschränkt sich allerdings nicht nur auf die Vereinigten Staaten. Die Deutschen sind z. B. die wichtigsten Sammler der deutschen *Naiven.* In der Schweiz sind *Kuhparaden,* die bis ins Appenzell des neunzehnten Jahrhunderts zurückgehen, äußerst beliebt. In der jüngsten Vergangenheit haben die populäre Außenseiterkunst und die Art Brut eine Handvoll von internationalen Superstars wie den Schweizer Adolf Wölfli und den Amerikaner Henry Darger hervorgebracht. Mit ihren versteckten Verbindungen zu provinzlerischen Volkstraditionen und ihrer Verankerung an einem bestimmten Ort und mit einer bestimmten Person widersetzt sich die autodidaktische Kunst der Internationalisierung jedoch stärker als die etablierte Kunst.

Seit Johann Feilacher die Direktorenposition des Gugginger Haus der Künstler von Leo Navratil im Jahr 1986 übernahm, versucht er beständig *seine* Künstler über Österreichs Grenzen hinaus bekannt zu machen. In Zusammenarbeit mit dem Sammler Sam Farber organisierte Rosa Esman in ihrer New Yorker Galerie im Jahr 1986 die erste amerikanische Ausstellung von Künstlern aus Gugging. Im Jahr 1988 wurden die Gugginger Künstler in die Ausstellung *Outsider Art from Europe* miteingeschlossen, die an den Universitäten von Connecticut und Northern Illinois in Chicago und am Massachusetts College of Art gezeigt wurde. Die Parsons School of Design in New York stellte einige Künstler aus Gugging in ihrer Ausstellung *Portraits from the Outside* im Jahr 1990 vor. Weitere Ausstellungen wie jene im Moore College of Art in Philadelphia im Jahr 1991 und in der Phyllis Kind Galerie in Chicago im Jahr 1992 konzentrierten sich ausschließlich auf Gugging. Im gleichen Jahr wurden einige Gugginger Künstler in die bahnbrechende Übersichtsschau *Parallel Visions: Mainstream Artists and Outsider Art* im Los Angeles County Museum of Art aufgenommen. Obwohl diese Ausstellungsgeschichte beeindruckend erscheinen mag, ist *Gugging* in Amerika kaum zu einem eingeführten Begriff avanciert. Nur die Ausstellung *Parallel Visions* fand in einem großen Museum statt, ordnete die *Außenseiter* den etablierten modernen Künstlern jedoch ganz offensichtlich unter.

Im Jahr 1993 war der Begriff *Außenseiterkunst* im amerikanischen Bewusstsein und am Kunstmarkt so weit verankert, dass die Gründung der Outsider Art Fair, einer Messe für Außenseiterkunst, gerechtfertigt schien. Seit damals findet sie jeden Januar in New York statt. In den folgenden Jahren brachten viele Kunsthändler Werke aus Gugging auf die Messe, unter ihnen Heike Curtze aus Wien, Susanne Zander aus Köln, Judy Saslow aus Chicago und meine Galerie St. Etienne. Wie in jedem anderen Sammelbereich verfolgen die Käufer von Werken aus Gugging unterschiedliche Ziele. Vielen fehlt

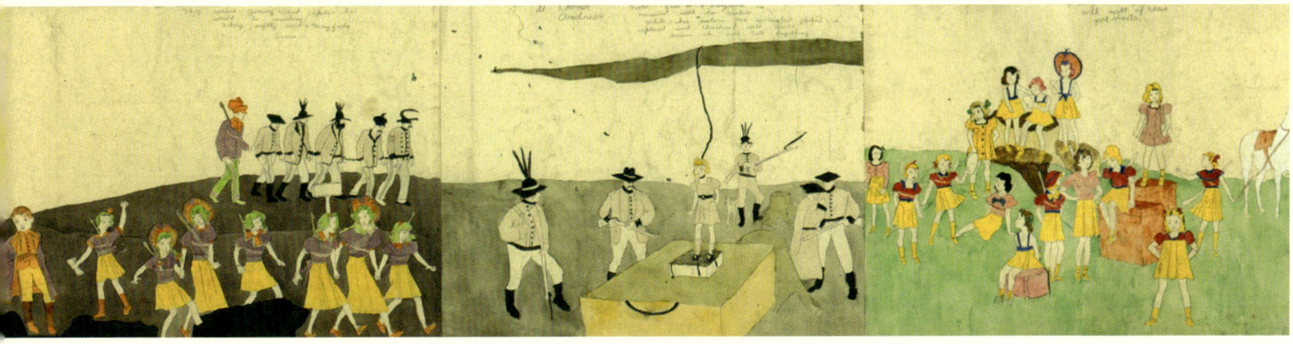

© Ricco Maresca Gallery, New York
Henry Darger, Violet geht... / Violet goes..., ca. 1950-60
47,5 x 180 cm, Wasserfarben, Bleistift / watercolor, pencil

the profile of *his* artists outside of Austria. Rosa Esman, working together with the collector Sam Farber, mounted the first American exhibition of the Gugging artists at her New York gallery in 1986. In 1988, Gugging artists were included in the exhibition *Outsider Art from Europe,* which traveled to the University of Connecticut, Northern Illinois University in Chicago and the Massachusetts College of Art. The Parsons School of Design in New York featured several Gugging artists in its 1990 show *Portraits from the Outside.* Shows focusing exclusively on Gugging followed: at Moore College of Art in Philadelphia in 1991, and at the Phyllis Kind Gallery in Chicago in 1992. That same year, some of the Gugging artists were included in the groundbreaking survey *Parallel Visions: Mainstream Artists and Outsider Art* at the Los Angeles County Museum of Art. Impressive though this exhibition history may seem, however, it hardly made *Gugging* a household name in the U.S. Of all the shows, only *Parallel Visions* took place at a major museum, and it clearly subordinated the *outsiders* to mainstream modernists. By 1993, *outsider* art had become sufficiently entrenched in the American consciousness and marketplace to justify the establishment of the Outsider Art Fair, which since then has been held every January in New York City. Over the ensuing years, many dealers have brought Gugging works to the Fair, among them Heike Curtze from Vienna, Susanne Zander from Cologne, Judy Saslow from Chicago, and my own Galerie St. Etienne. As is the case with any area of collecting, buyers of Gugging work tend to vary in their approach. Many lack a sustained commitment to the field, and simply select a single piece because it moves them. Of those who do have an-indepth focus on *outsider* art, Gugging work has featured most prominently in the collections of Americans who already have an international orientation, such as Sam Farber, Robert Greenberg, Anthony Petullo and Bob Roth. Gugging has never become a *must* for all American *outsider* collectors, in the way that artists such as James Castle, Henry Darger, Martin Ramirez or Bill Traylor seem to have. Nor are Gugging artists anywhere near as widely collected in the U.S. as the stars of the Corcoran Museum's trendsetting 1982 exhibition *Black Folk Art in America* (Sam Doyle, Sister Gertrude Morgan, Elijah Pierce, Nellie Mae Rowe, Moses Tolliver, Joseph Yoakum, etc.).

In the mid 1990s, the Galerie St. Etienne began representing the Gugging artists in New York, and we have since included them in many group exhibitions as well as in two feature presentations, *That Way Madness Lies: Expressionism and the Art of Gugging* (1997) and *'Our Beautiful and Tormented Austria': Art Brut in the Land of Freud* (2001). Although both shows were well received, some of the criticism points to the inherent difficulty many Americans have with the European concept of Art Brut. Dubuffet's idea of singling out mental patients as exemplars of creative purity makes Americans profoundly uncomfortable. *Notions of a continuum from madness to genius are a crock,* wrote Peter Schjeldahl in the Village Voice (February 11, 1997). *In . . . psychosis, we confront a closed loop, an inside of hermetic association from which we are utterly excluded. To be charmed by psychotic art is possible but trivial, like enjoying the sound of a language we do not understand.* Americans love *outsider* artists for their deviant biographies: the homeless ex-slave discovered on the streets of Montgomery, Alabama; the prisoner who embroiders miniature pictures from the threads of unraveled socks; the recluse who collects string and creates a secret trove of drawings in his filthy rented room. But the American dream requires that we domesticate these deviants, and so even as we bask in their biographies, we deny the seriousness of their problems. Psychosis, understandably,

ein anhaltendes Engagement für das Genre. Sie wählen ein Einzelwerk aus, weil es sie berührt. Gugginger Werke sind hauptsächlich in *Outsider*-Sammlungen von Amerikanern wie Sam Farber, Robert Greenberg, Anthony Petullo und Bob Roth vertreten, deren Sammlungen bereits eine internationale Orientierung haben. Gugging ist für amerikanische Sammler von *Außenseiterkunst* niemals ein absolutes Muss geworden wie es Künstler wie James Castle, Henry Darger, Martin Ramirez und Bill Traylor anscheinend sind. Ebenso werden die Gugginger Künstler in den Vereinigten Staaten nicht annähernd so viel gesammelt wie die Stars der zukunftsweisenden Ausstellung *Black Folk Art in America* (Sam Doyle, Sister Gertrude Morgan, Elijah Pierce, Nellie Mae Rowe, Moses Tolliver, Joseph Yoakum, etc.), die im Corcoran Museum im Jahr 1982 gezeigt wurde.

Mitte der neunziger Jahre begann die Galerie St. Etienne damit, die Gugginger Künstler in New York zu vertreten. Seit damals haben wir sie in viele Gruppenausstellungen und wichtigen Schauen wie *That Way Madness Lies: Expressionism and the Art of Gugging* im Jahr 1997 und *‚Our Beautiful and Tormented Austria:' Art Brut in the Land of Freud* im Jahr 2001 gezeigt. Obwohl beide Ausstellungen großen Anklang fanden, wiesen einige Kritiker darauf hin, dass viele Amerikaner mit dem europäischen Begriff von Art Brut ein grundlegendes Problem haben. Dubuffets Vorstellung, dass man geisteskranke Patienten als Beispiele von kreativer Reinheit hervorheben kann, geht Amerikanern gegen den Strich. *Die Vorstellung von einem Kontinuum vom Wahnsinn zum Genie ist Blödsinn,* schrieb Peter Schjeldahl in der Village Voice am 11. Februar 1997. *In ... der Psychose sind wir mit einem geschlossenen Kreis konfrontiert, der Innenseite einer hermetischen Assoziation, von der wir vollkommen ausgeschlossen sind. Es ist möglich, dass man von psychotischer Kunst fasziniert ist, jedoch recht trivial. Genauso gut könnte man den Klang einer Sprache lieben, die man nicht versteht.* Amerikaner mögen die *Außenseiterkünstler* wegen ihrer andersartigen Lebensgeschichte: Sie bewundern den obdachlosen Ex-Sklaven, der in den Straßen von Montgomery, Alabama entdeckt wurde, den Häftling, der Miniaturbilder aus den Fäden von aufgetrennten Socken stickt und den Einzelgänger, der Schnüre sammelt und in seinem schmutzigen Untermietszimmer einen geheimen Schatz an Zeichnungen hervorbringt. Dem amerikanischen Traum zufolge müssen diese unangepassten Menschen jedoch domestiziert werden. Selbst wenn wir uns an ihren Lebensgeschichten ergötzen, leugnen wir, wie schwer ihre Probleme sind. Dass uns die Psychose Angst macht, ist ganz klar.

Im Gegensatz dazu haben die Psychiater am Landeskrankenhaus Maria Gugging schon immer eine ehrliche, professionelle Beziehung zu Psychotikern gehabt. Wie viele Psychiater verwendete Leo Navratil ursprünglich Zeichnungen zu Diagnosezwecken. In den fünfziger Jahren bemerkte er jedoch, dass einige seiner Patienten Werke von außerordentlicher Qualität hervorbrachten. Er schickte Dubuffet diese Blätter, und dieser pries die Zeichnungen sofort als authentische Art Brut. In der Folge wählte Navratil talentierte Patienten aus und begann mit ihnen intensiver zu arbeiten. Von Anfang an unterschied sich das Gugging-Projekt von herkömmlichen Kunsttherapieprogrammen dadurch, dass die Künstler aufgrund ihres Talentes ausgewählt wurden. Johann Feilacher legt noch größeren Wert auf diesen Aspekt des Programms als sein Vorgänger. Talent, so merkt er an, ist unter geisteskranken Patienten so selten zu finden wie in der Allgemeinbevölkerung. Ohne das Haus der Künstler hätten die Talente aus Gugging niemals Zugang zur etablierten Kulturszene, denn sie sind viel zu krank, zu arm und zu ungebildet. Gugging stellt

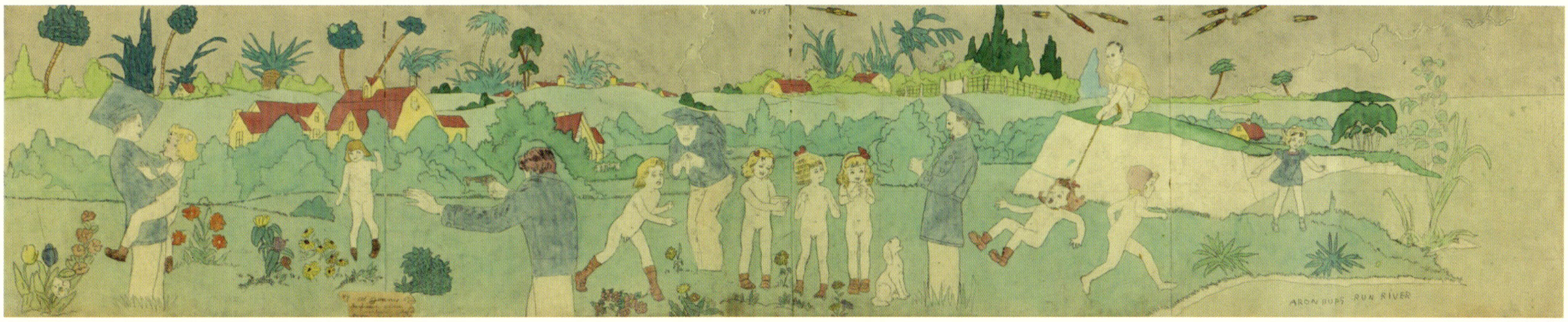

© Ricco Maresca Gallery, New York
Henry Darger, Bei Jennie Richee... / At Jennie Richee...
ca. 1950-60, 47,5 x 180 cm, Wasserfarben, Bleistift / watercolor, pencil

scares us. By comparison, the psychiatrists at the Landeskrankenhaus Maria Gugging have always had a straightforward, professional relationship to psychotics. Like many psychiatrists, Leo Navratil originally used drawings for diagnostic purposes, but in the 1950s he noticed that some of his patients were doing work of exceptional quality. He sent samples to Dubuffet, and the drawings were promptly anointed as genuine Art Brut. Hereafter, Navratil began to single out talented patients and to work more intensively with them. From the outset, the Gugging project differed from conventional art therapy programs in that the artists were specifically chosen for their talent. Johann Feilacher has placed even more emphasis on this aspect of the program than did his predecessor. Talent, he observes, is as rare among mental patients as it is among the general population. Without the *Haus der Künstler,* the Gugging artists would never have access to the mainstream art world: they are far too ill, too poor and too uneducated. Gugging, then, provides a vital conduit for these artists, giving professional meaning to their lives and encouraging them to develop their talent. Nonetheless, they have been acclaimed internationally not because of their illnesses, but because of the quality of their work. The Haus der Künstler has helped lead the way in encouraging the public to see the art of the mentally ill as art, rather than as the product of an inferior, ghettoized *other.* Although indebted to Dubuffet's pioneering work, Gugging in fact embodies a conceptual break with conventional notions of Art Brut. Art Brut and all the other approaches to self-taught art that emerged during the twentieth century suffered from similar inherent contradictions. For one thing, the ascription of intrinsic purity to self-taught artists was neither objectively verifiable nor true. It is, after all, no more possible to determine whether an artist has a *sacred heart* than it is to X-ray his or her soul. And the paradigm of purity clashed head-on with the fact of external influence. As it turns out, many self-taught artists teach themselves in exactly the same way that trained artists do: they look at things and then poach from an array of preexisting sources. Only for self-taught artists, those sources are ad hoc, rather than selected by the art-world's educational superstructure. There was also something insidious about the mainstream's idealization of the self-taught artist's ostensible purity. A self-taught artist could be disqualified, driven from the temple of Art Brut and back into the no-man's land of inept anonymity, for being too knowing or too ambitious. The whole point was that selftaught artists were accidental modernists, creating works that looked like sophisticated art without deliberately intending to. By denying the self-taught artist's intentionality, the art-world mainstream denied these artists the right to be taken seriously. Insofar as the discipline of art history has traditionally treated art works as texts, the purpose of which is to communicate an artist's conscious or unconscious intent, the doctrine of *purity* made it impossible to properly study self-taught artists and therefore impossible to admit them to the canon. The *other* was acknowledged, even petted and pampered, but at the same time safely ensconced in a position subordinate to that of the mainstream elite. Most of the attributes – purity, innocence, iconoclasm, individualism – ascribed to *outsiders* had less to do with them than with the projected needs of the mainstream. In practice, the mainstream's relationship to self-taught artists was largely formal, as though by claiming a similar pictorial language, trained artists could appropriate those self-same projected values. This formal relationship was double-edged: the mainstream singled out self-taught artists who unwittingly confirmed its own preexisting aesthetic proclivities, and trained artists also borrowed specific stylistic tropes from their uneducated colleagues. Formalism became the primary way in which modernism

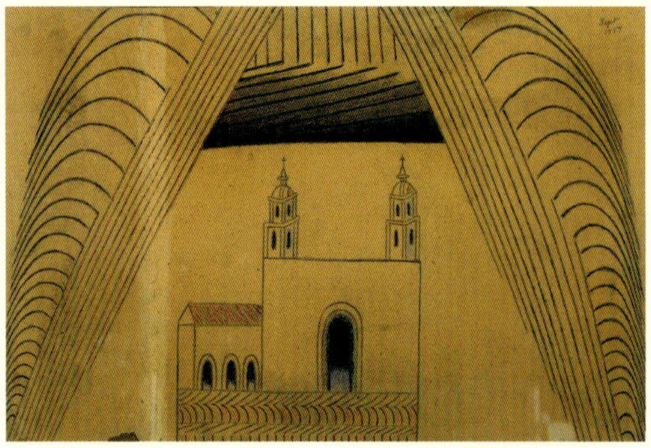

© Ricco Maresca Gallery, New York
Martin Ramirez, Ohne Titel / untitled
ca. 1950's, 45 x 77,5 cm,
Mischtechnik / mixed media

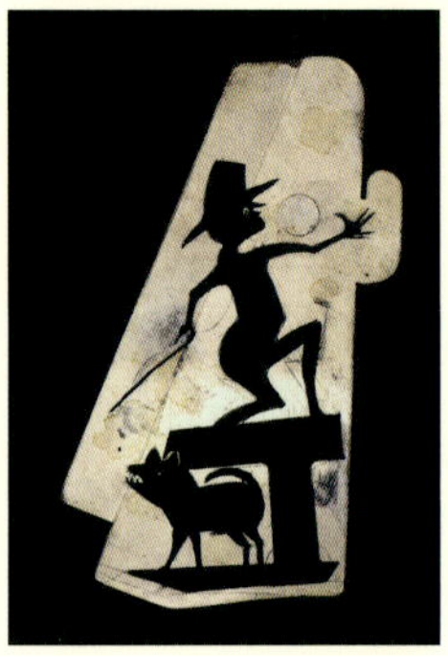

© Ricco Maresca Gallery, New York
Bill Traylor, Ohne Titel / untitled, ca.1939-42,
35 x 17,5 cm, Tempera, Bleistift /
tempera, pencil

deshalb eine lebenswichtige Verbindung für diese Künstler dar und verleiht ihrem Leben eine berufliche Bedeutung, indem es sie dabei unterstützt, ihr Talent zu entwickeln. Sie sind nicht aufgrund ihrer Krankheit, sondern aufgrund der Qualität ihrer Arbeit international anerkannt. Das Haus der Künstler hat bahnbrechende Arbeit geleistet, die Öffentlichkeit davon zu überzeugen, die Werke der geisteskranken Künstler als wirkliche Kunst zu betrachten und nicht als minderwertiges Produkt von ghettoisierten *anderen.* Obwohl Gugging in der Schuld von Dubuffet und seinen Pionierleistungen steht, vollzieht es einen begrifflichen Bruch mit den herkömmlichen Vorstellungen von Art Brut.

Art Brut und alle anderen Zugänge zur autodidaktischen Kunst des 20. Jahrhunderts waren von einander ähnlichen, inhärenten Widersprüchen gekennzeichnet. Zum einen war die Tatsache, dass man autodidaktischen Künstlern eine ihnen wesenhafte Reinheit zuschrieb, weder objektiv nachprüfbar noch wahr. Man kann schließlich ebenso wenig bestimmen, ob ein Künstler ein *heiliges Herz* hat, als dass man seine Seele röntgen kann. Und das Paradigma von der Reinheit stand in krassem Widerspruch zu der Tatsache, dass es auch Einflüsse von außen gab. Wie sich herausstellte, lernen autodidaktisch arbeitende Künstler auf genau dieselbe Weise wie Künstler, die eine Ausbildung abgeschlossen haben: Sie sehen sich in ihrer Umwelt um und wählen bestimmte Elemente aus einer Vielzahl von bereits existierenden Quellen aus. Allerdings ergeben sich diese Quellen für den Autodidakten im Moment und sind nicht von dem der Kunstwelt übergeordneten Bildungssystem vorgegeben. Die generelle Idealisierung der angeblichen Reinheit des autodidaktischen Künstlers hat auch etwas Heimtückisches an sich. Ein autodidaktischer Künstler konnte sich disqualifizieren, aus dem Tempel der Art Brut vertrieben und ins Niemandsland der unfähigen Anonymität zurückgeschickt werden, wenn er zu viel wusste oder zu viel Ehrgeiz an den Tag legte. Das Wichtigste an dem autodidaktischen Künstler war, dass er durch Zufall zur Moderne gestoßen war und Werke schuf, die wie ausgereifte Kunst aussahen, ohne dass er es je beabsichtigt hätte. Indem sie dem autodidaktischen Künstler seine Absichtlichkeit verweigerte, sprach die etablierte Kunstwelt diesen Künstlern auch eine ernsthafte Anerkennung ab. So weit die Kunstgeschichte traditionellerweise Kunstwerke als Text betrachtet hat, deren Zweck ist, die bewusste oder unbewusste Absicht des Künstlers zu vermitteln, machte es die Doktrin der *Reinheit* unmöglich, autodidaktische Künstler richtig zu analysieren. Dadurch war ihnen auch eine Aufnahme in den Kanon verwehrt. Der *andere* wurde anerkannt, sogar gehätschelt und getätschelt, aber gleichzeitig sicher in einer Position verankert, die der etablierten Elite untergeordnet war.

Die meisten Attribute, mit denen *Außenseiter* beschrieben wurden – Reinheit, Unschuld, Ikonoklasmus, Individualismus – hatten weniger mit ihnen selbst als mit den Bedürfnissen zu tun, die die etablierte Kunst auf sie projizierte. In der Praxis war die Beziehung des Establishments zu autodidaktischen Künstlern hauptsächlich formaler Natur, als ob sich akademisch gebildete Künstler dieselben projizierten Werte aneignen könnten, indem sie eine ähnliche Bildsprache verwendeten. Diese formale Beziehung ist ein zweischneidiges Schwert: Die etablierte Kunst hob autodidaktische Künstler hervor, die unwissentlich ihre eigenen, bereits existierenden ästhetischen Neigungen bestätigten. Geschulte Künstler borgten sich auch spezifische stilistische Themen von ihren ungebildeten Kollegen aus. Der Modernismus wurde hauptsächlich mit Hilfe des Formalismus erklärt und der breiten Öffentlichkeit verkauft, besonders in den Vereinigten Staaten. In den Jahren unmittelbar nach dem Zweiten

was explained and sold to the broader public, especially in the U.S. In the years immediately after World War II, the histories of diverse modernist movements in places like Russia, Italy, Germany and Austria were pruned in order to present a clean, linear developmental trajectory from prewar Paris to postwar New York. The whole idea of a single international art *center* presupposed a high degree of coordination and unity of intent. Modernism's subsidiary *isms* were seen to comprise cohesive teams of artists engaged in a joint mission to advance the global cause of art. Tastemakers such as the Museum of Modern Art's founding director Alfred Barr wielded immense influence through their ability to channel the messy products of artistic enterprise into neat formalist schemes. Today, the formalist linearity once ascribed to modernist development has been generally discredited, both as art history and as a prescriptive mandate for aspiring artists. Artists are encouraged to take their inspiration from anything and everything that moves them, reaching back in time through all of art history, and absorbing more recent visual phenomena like cartoons, comics and film as well. Contemporary artists give all cultural sources equal weight, drawing no distinction between *high* and *low* art. There are no rules or restrictions regarding the use of materials, either. *New media* such as video and computers are welcomed into an arena once dominated by painting and sculpture, as are formerly *inferior* modes of expression like photography. This diversity has created a confusing welter of objects and styles. There are no longer any gatekeepers comparable to Barr controlling access to the citadel of high art. For the most part, curators and critics now follow paths blazed in an increasingly freewheeling and decentralized marketplace. Globalization has for the first time created a true *art world,* assimilating collectors and artists from all over. Although many dealers are still based in New York, the art scene has become a moveable feast, decamping regularly to Basel, Miami, London or wherever in accordance with art-fair schedules. Globalization has forced a new confrontation with the *other,* both in terms of individual players and in terms of diverse traditions. The current approach to self-taught art is in many respects an extension of the heterogeneity born of globalization, and as such differs decisively from earlier, modernist attitudes to the genre. Mainstream contemporary art and self-taught art are joined not merely by formal similarities, but by a kinship of content. Common themes include war, violence, abuse and the exploitation of the weak by the strong. Children's-book iconography is employed both within and beyond the mainstream to explore adult issues of sexual aggression. The idea of mapping the unconscious – either through semiabstract images or though literal maps – is another unifying motif. Many artists, trained as well as self-taught, see art-making as a devotional act with redemptive potential, or attempt to harness the spiritual powers perceived in found objects. Debased, non-art materials – pipe-cleaners, feathers, beads, mailing tubes and the like – are proliferating in all quarters. Ritual, counting and formal repetition are no longer seen merely as the hallmarks of obsessive disorder, but rather can suggest a connection with the divine by revealing the patterns underlying the visible world. The conceptual links between the work of *insiders* and *outsiders* suggest that today the most substantive difference between the two may be the way they are labeled and marketed. After all, to the extent that they exist outside the nine-to-five job grind that preoccupies most people, all artists are economic *outsiders.* And all artists, if they are any good, are passionate and driven. The act of segregating *outsiders* according to their biographies is becoming increasingly shallow and pointless. The minor detail of having gone, or not gone, to art school seems similarly irrelevant when all the

Weltkrieg wurden die Geschichten von diversen modernen Bewegungen in Russland, Italien, Deutschland und Österreich so zurechtgeschneidert, dass sie einen sauberen, linearen Entwicklungsweg von Paris vor dem Krieg nach New York nach dem Krieg ergaben. Die gesamte Vorstellung eines einzigen *Zentrums* für internationale Kunst setzt einen hohen Grad an Koordination und einheitlicher Absicht voraus. Die der Moderne untergeordneten *Ismen* setzten sich anscheinend aus kohärenten Künstlerteams zusammen, die den gemeinsamen Auftrag hatten, Kunst global zu propagieren. Trendsetter wie Alfred Barr, der begründende Direktor des Museum of Modern Art, genossen einen ungeheuren Einfluss, weil sie die unordentliche künstlerische Produktion in ordentliche formalistische Schemen pressen konnten.

Heute ist die formalistische Linearität, die einst der Moderne zugeschrieben wurde, im Allgemeinen in Verruf geraten, sowohl als Kunstgeschichte wie auch als vorgeschriebener Auftrag für angehende Künstler. Künstler werden dazu aufgefordert, sich von jedem und allem, das sie berührt, inspirieren zu lassen, ganz weit in der Kunstgeschichte zurückzugehen und visuelle Elemente aus Zeichentrickfilmen, Comics und Spielfilmen in ihre künstlerische Produktion aufzunehmen. Künstler der Gegenwart geben allen kulturellen Quellen gleiches Gewicht und machen keinen Unterschied zwischen *high* und *low art*. Im Bezug auf die zu gebrauchenden Materialien gibt es eben so wenige Regeln oder Einschränkungen. *Neue Medien* wie Video und Computer, sowie ehemals *minderwertige* Ausdrucksweisen wie die Fotografie sind in einer Domäne willkommen, die einst von Malerei und Bildhauerei beherrscht wurde. Diese Vielfalt hat zu einer verwirrenden Anzahl von Objekten und Stilen geführt. Es gibt auch keine Hohepriester wie Alfred Barr mehr, die bestimmen, wer Zugang zum Tempel der hohen Kunst hat. Meistens folgen die Kuratoren und Kritiker Trends, die von einem immer freier laufenden, dezentralisierten Kunstmarkt vorgegeben werden. Die Globalisierung hat zum ersten Mal eine wirkliche *Kunstwelt* geschaffen und Sammler und Künstler aus aller Herren Länder zusammengebracht. Obwohl viele Händler noch immer in New York ansässig sind, ist die Kunstszene zu einem beweglichen Feiertag geworden, der regelmäßig in Basel, Miami, London oder wo auch immer in Übereinstimmung mit dem Terminkalender von Kunstmessen zelebriert wird. Die Globalisierung hat zu einer neuen Konfrontation mit den *anderen* geführt, sowohl was die einzelnen Spieler als auch die verschiedenen Traditionen betrifft.

Der gegenwärtige Zugang zu autodidaktischen Künstlern ist in vielerlei Hinsicht ein Resultat der aus der Globalisierung hervorgegangenen Heterogenität und unterscheidet sich als solcher wesentlich von den Haltungen, die die Moderne gegenüber dem Genre einnahm. Gegenwartskünstler mit akademischer Ausbildung und Autodidakten sind nicht nur durch artverwandte formale Ansätze, sondern auch durch ähnliche Inhalte verbunden. Gemeinsam behandeln sie Themen wie Krieg, Gewalt, Missbrauch und die Ausnutzung des Schwachen durch den Starken. Die Ikonographie von Kinderbüchern wird sowohl innerhalb wie auch außerhalb der etablierten Kunst verwendet, um erwachsene Themen wie sexuelle Aggression zu behandeln. Die Vorstellung, dass man das Unterbewusstsein kartographisch durch halbabstrakte Bilder oder durch tatsächliche Landkarten erfassen kann, ist ein weiteres verbindendes Motiv. Viele ausgebildete Künstler wie auch Autodidakten betrachten den schöpferischen Prozess als einen Akt der Hingabe, der auch erlösende Wirkung haben kann. Oder aber sie versuchen spirituelle Kräfte für sich nutzbar zu machen, die gefundenen Objekten innewohnen. Minderwertige Materialien, die nicht aus der Kunst stammen wie Pfeifenreiniger,

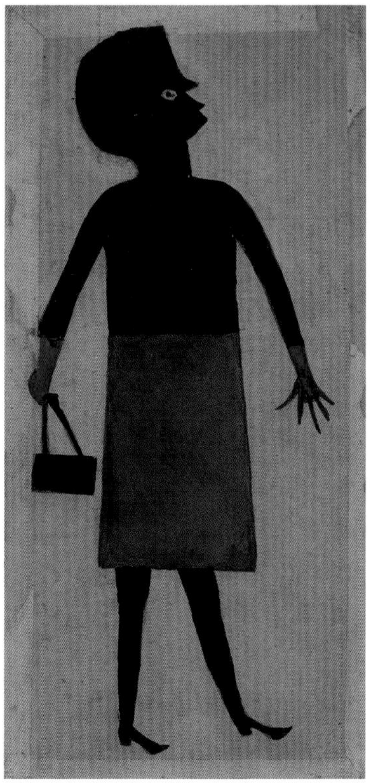

© Ricco Maresca Gallery, New York

Bill Traylor, Ohne Titel / untitled, ca.1939-42
22,5 x 49 cm, Tempera, Bleistift / tempera, pencil

world's a school. In the future, we may hope for an environment in which all art is judged on its merits, irrespective of superficial labels. Terms such as Art Brut, *outsider*, *naïve* and self-taught have little scholarly utility, in that they designate artists who have nothing in common except their deviance from a mainstream norm. There are, of course, subgroups within these catchall categories that do share meaningful attributes. Some selftaught African-American artists, for example, have kindred ties to certain local and historical traditions. However, labeling such artists as *outsiders* does nothing to help us understand their work, and is in fact inherently disrespectful of the artists' original context and influences. To truly absorb the *other* into the mainstream, we must honor the artist's intentions and judge the art by its success in fulfilling those intentions – just as we have always judged mainstream art. A lot of inferior *outsider* art will not pass this test and will as a result fall by the wayside. However, the best examples of self-taught art will not only survive, they will for the first time be fully understood and appreciated. Institutions such as the Haus der Künstler will be important in the future not because they segregate differently abled artists from the mainstream, but because they give those artists a chance to shine as equals within a mainstream context. Globalization has produced many ill effects, from economic exploitation and environmental degradation to terrorism, but it has also helped to break down the barriers separating us from the *other*. It is encouraging to think that, at least in some quarters, the divisions between disparate peoples are diminishing in the face of our common humanity.

Federn, Perlen, Versandrohre und dergleichen nehmen überall überhand. Rituelle Handlungen wie Zählen und formale Wiederholungen werden nicht mehr nur als Kennzeichen einer Zwangsneurose betrachtet, sondern können eine Verbindung zum Göttlichen darstellen, indem sie die der sichtbaren Welt zugrunde liegenden Muster ans Licht rücken.

Die begrifflichen Verbindungen zwischen der Arbeit eines *Insiders* und eines *Outsiders* lassen vermuten, dass heute der wesentlichste Unterschied zwischen ihnen die Art und Weise ist, wie sie etikettiert und verkauft werden. Schließlich sind alle Künstler insoweit wirtschaftliche *Außenseiter*, als dass sie keinem geregelten Arbeitsleben von 9 Uhr morgens bis 5 Uhr abends nachgehen. Wenn Künstler etwas taugen, dann sind sie alle passioniert und ehrgeizig. Die Vorgangsweise, *Außenseiter* nach ihren Lebensläufen abzusondern, wird immer banaler und sinnloser. In einer Zeit, wo die ganze Welt Schule ist, scheint das kleine Detail, ob man auf eine Kunstakademie gegangen ist oder nicht, irrelevant.

In der Zukunft dürfen wir auf eine Lebenswelt hoffen, in der alle Künste nach ihrem Verdienst beurteilt werden, ohne Rücksicht auf irgendwelche oberflächlichen Etiketten. Begriffe wie Art Brut, *Außenseiter*, *naive* oder *autodidaktische* Kunst haben geringen wissenschaftlichen Nutzwert, da sie Künstler bezeichnen, die nichts anderes gemeinsam haben als ihrer Abweichung von den Normen der etablierten Kunstwelt. Innerhalb dieser allumfassenden Kategorien gibt es natürlich Untergruppen, die wirklich sinnvolle Attribute gemein haben. Einige autodidaktische afroamerikanische Künstler sind z. B. mit bestimmten örtlichen und historischen Traditionen verbunden. Wenn man solche Künstler jedoch als *Außenseiter* abstempelt, trägt das nicht zum besseren Verständnis ihrer Werke bei, sondern wertet ihren ursprünglichen Kontext und ihre Einflüsse ab. Um die *anderen* wirklich in der etablierten Kunstwelt aufzunehmen, müssen wir die Absichten der Künstler respektieren und sie danach bewerten, ob sie diese Absichten erfüllt haben, so wie wir die Werke der kulturellen Kunst seit jeher beurteilt haben. Eine große Menge minderwertiger *Außenseiterkunst* wird diese Prüfung nicht bestehen und deshalb auf der Strecke bleiben. Die besten Beispiele autodidaktischer Kunst werden nicht nur überleben, sondern zum ersten Mal vollkommen verstanden und geschätzt werden. Organisationen wie das Haus der Künstler werden in der Zukunft wichtig sein, nicht weil sie Künstler mit anderen Fähigkeiten aus der etablierten Kunst absondern, sondern weil sie diesen Künstlern die Chance geben, in einem allgemeinen Kontext gleichwertig aufzutreten. Die Globalisierung hat viele Nachteile mit sich gebracht, von der wirtschaftlichen Ausbeutung und der Schädigung der Umwelt bis hin zum Terrorismus. Sie hat jedoch auch zur Abtragung der Grenzen beigetragen, die uns von den *anderen* trennen. Der Gedanke, dass die Grenzen zwischen unterschiedlichen Völkern angesichts unseres gemeinsamen Menschtums zumindest in einigen Bereichen verschwinden, macht Mut.

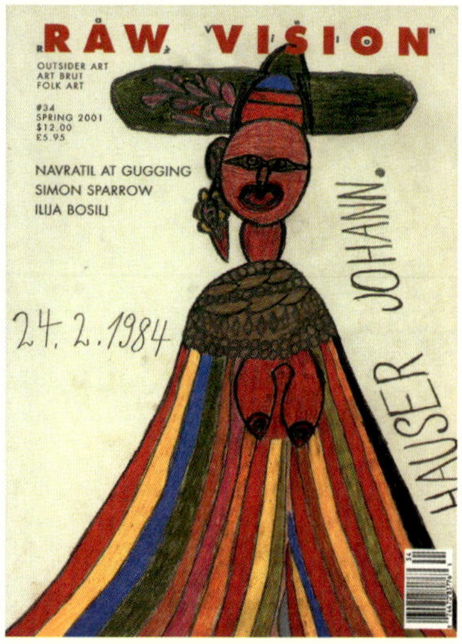

2001
raw vision #24

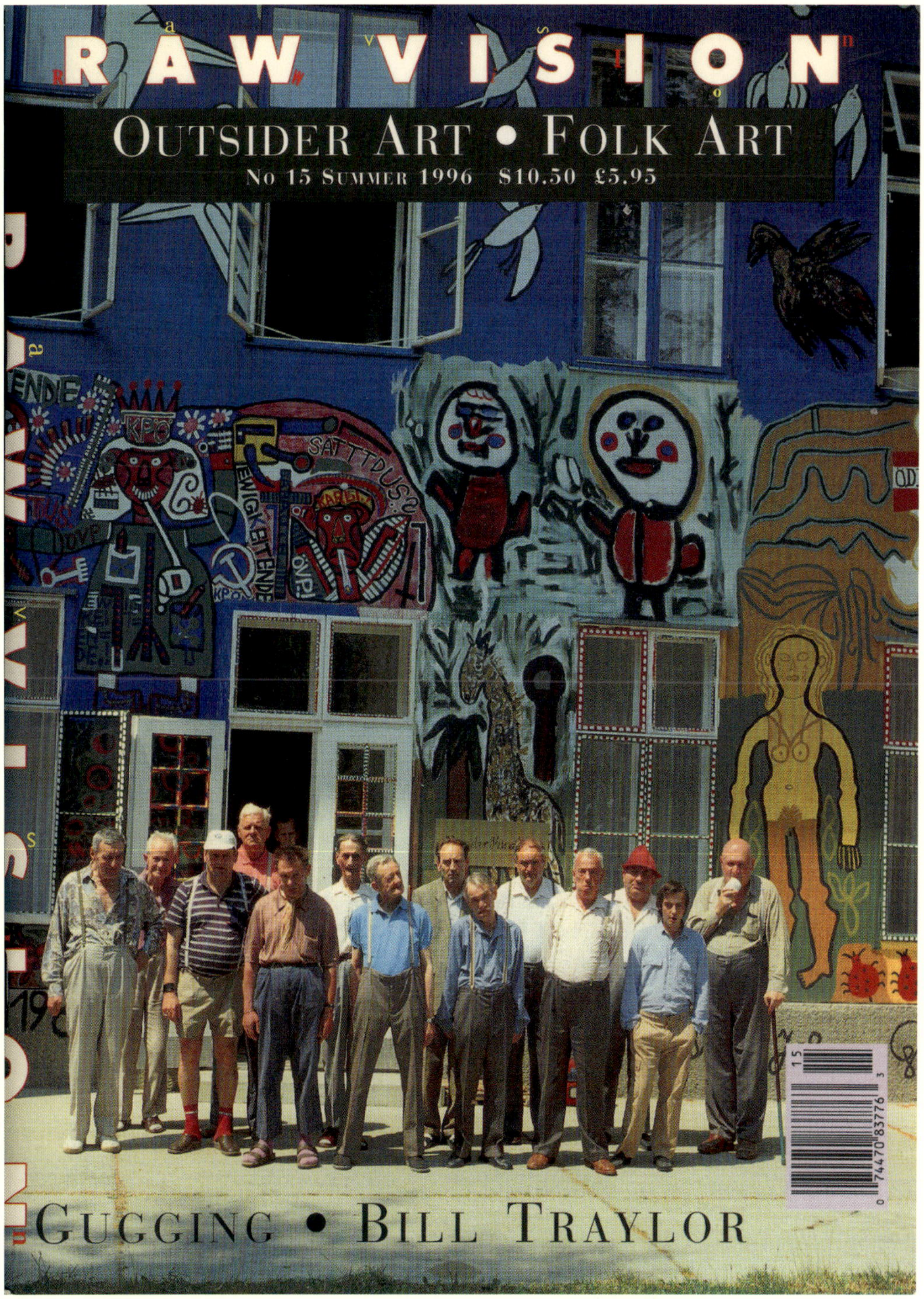

1996
raw vision #15

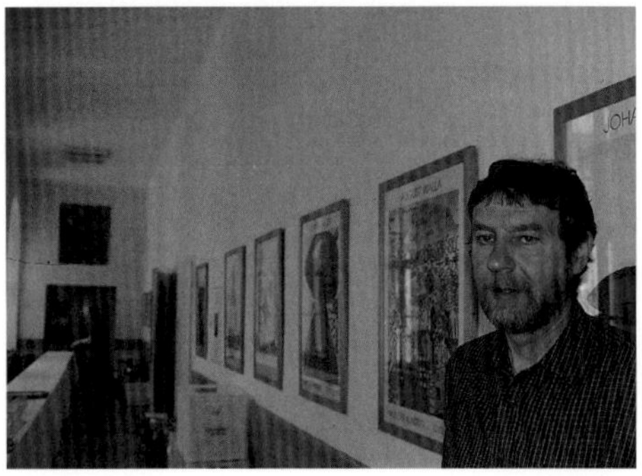

John Maizels

Die erste Ausgabe des Magazins Raw Vision erschien im Jahr 1989. Ziel war, ein internationales Publikum mit der Außenseiterkunst vertraut zu machen. Es war das erste und bleibt auch weiterhin das einzige Journal für Art Brut und Außenseiterkunst. Im Jahr 1989 war das Haus der Künstler in Gugging bereits ein Begriff. All jene, die sich für Art Brut interessierten, kannten die Werke der Gugginger gut, und die Künstler wurden in der *Collection de l'art brut* in Lausanne präsentiert.

Unter der Führung von Dr. Leo Navratil vergrößerte sich der Bekanntheitsgrad der Werke dieser besonderen, talentierten Künstler. Raw Vision gelang es jedoch, das Oeuvre der Künstler einer größeren Leserschaft auf der ganzen Welt nahe zu bringen.

Der erste Artikel, der ausschließlich Gugging gewidmet war, erschien in unserer zweiten Nummer im Jahr 1989. Autor war Dr. Johann Feilacher. Er konzentrierte sich auf die Zeichnungen von OT, OSWALD TSCHIRTNER. Dr. Feilacher beschrieb, wie Tschirtner mit seiner einzigartigen Strichführung in die Länge gezogene Formen in einem perfekt ausbalancierten Raum zu Papier bringt.

Die fünfte Ausgabe von Raw Vision aus dem Jahr 1991 stellte die Arbeit von JOHANN GARBER in den Mittelpunkt. Dies ist ein weiterer Künstler, der sich auf seine Strichführung konzentriert. Seine Kompositionen sind jedoch viel komplizierter als die von TSCHIRTNER. GARBER kreiert Szenen aus der Stadt oder Landschaften, die dicht bevölkert mit Tieren und Figuren sind.

raw vision und gugging

Zur vierzehnten Ausgabe von Raw Vision trug Dr. Navratil einen Artikel zum Gedenken an den großartigen JOHANN HAUSER bei. Darin zollte er dem Werk des vielleicht stärksten Gugginger Künstlers

raw vision and gugging

Raw Vision magazine was started in 1989 with the purpose of bringing Outsider Art to a wide international audience. It was the first and remains the only international journal of Art Brut and Outsider Art. By 1989, of course, the Gugging Haus der Künstler was already firmly established. The work of the artists was well known by followers of Art Brut and artists from Gugging were represented at the *Collection de l'art brut* in Lausanne.

Under the direction of Dr. Leo Navratil, the importance of the works by these special and talented artists had become widely known. However, Raw Vision magazine was able to introduce the works of these artists to a broader audience all around the world.

The first article purely about a Gugging artist that we published in Raw Vision was in our second edition, published in 1989. Written by Dr. Johann Feilacher, it introduced the drawings of OT, OSWALD TSCHIRTNER. His unique line delineated elongated forms that sat within a perfectly balanced space.

The fifth issue of Raw Vision, in 1991, featured the work of JOHANN GARBER, another artist who draws in line. But his compositions were much more complex than TSCHIRTNER'S and focused on themes such as cityscapes and landscapes closely packed with animals and figures.

Raw Vision No.14 published a memorial piece on the great JOHANN HAUSER by Dr. Navratil, a fitting tribute to perhaps the most powerful of the Gugging artists. HAUSER'S strong compositions and figures came to epitomize the unique work of the Haus der Künstler and his drawing of a blue star became its symbol.

gebührenden Tribut. HAUSERS kraftvolle Kompositionen und Figuren verkörpern das einzigartige Werk des Hauses der Künstler. Sein *Blauer Stern* wurde zum Symbol der Gruppe.

Die Titelgeschichte über Gugging in der nächsten Ausgabe von Raw Vision wurde abermals von Dr. Navratil geschrieben und verfolgte die Beziehung zwischen Art Brut und Psychiatrie. In der 34. Nummer von Raw Vision im Jahr 2001 veröffentlichten wir ein langes Interview mit Dr. Navratil, in dem er den Weg zur Errichtung des Hauses der Künstler und seine Theorien über *zustandsgebundenen* Ausdruck beschrieb.

Die 50. Sonderausgabe von Raw Vision enthielt einen Text von Nina Katschnig zu einem klassischen Werk von OSWALD TSCHIRTNER. Sie steuerte auch den Text für einen Artikel in der 51. Ausgabe des Journals bei. Darin befasste sie sich mit zwei neuen Mitgliedern des Hauses der Künstler, GUNTHER SCHTZENHÖFER und KARL VONDAL, und zeigte auf, wie die Arbeit in Gugging fortschritt.

Raw Vision ist sehr stolz darauf, mit Gugging über Jahre hinweg in Beziehung zu stehen. Zu diesem besonderen Anlass möchten wir allen Gugginger Künstlern gratulieren, sowohl jenen in der Vergangenheit wie auch all jenen, die in der Gegenwart in Gugging arbeiten. Wir möchten auch dem Gründer Dr. Leo Navratil und seinem Nachfolger Dr. Johann Feilacher für all die harte Arbeit danken, die sie erbracht haben, um die Bedeutung und Stellung der Gugginger Künstler in der internationalen Kunstszene fest zu verankern. Dr. Feilacher wird von einem wunderbaren Team unterstützt, aus dem ich Nina Katschnig stellvertretend hervorheben möchte. Dieses Team hat erfolgreich dazu beigetragen, dass das Werk der Gugginger Künstler international anerkannt und respektiert wird.

This was followed by the cover story on Gugging in the next issue of Raw Vision, also written by Dr. Navratil's, traced the relationship between Art Brut and psychiatry. In a lengthy interview published in Raw Vision No. 34 in 2001, Dr. Navratil described the process of establishing the Haus der Künstler and his theories of *statebound* expression.

The special 50th edition of Raw Vision contained a text by Nina Katschnig on a classic work by OSWALD TSCHIRTNER. She also contributed an article for Raw Vision No. 51 on two newcomers to the Haus de Künstler, GÜNTHER SCHÜTZENHÖFER and KARL VONDAL, showing how the work of Gugging continues to develop and evolve.

Raw Vision is very proud to have been associated with Gugging over the years and on this special occasion offers its congratulations to all the artists of the Haus der Künstler, both past and present, and also to the founder, Dr. Leo Navratil, and his successor, Dr. Johann Feilacher, who has worked so hard to establish the influence and position of the Gugging artists in the international scene. He is well supported by his team, especially by Nina Katschnig, and they have succeeded in making the Gugging artists well known and respected across the world.

werke / works

Die Titel sind wegen orthographischer Eigenwilligkeiten im Deutschen frei übersetzt.
On account of their peculiar spelling in German, all titles were translated freely.

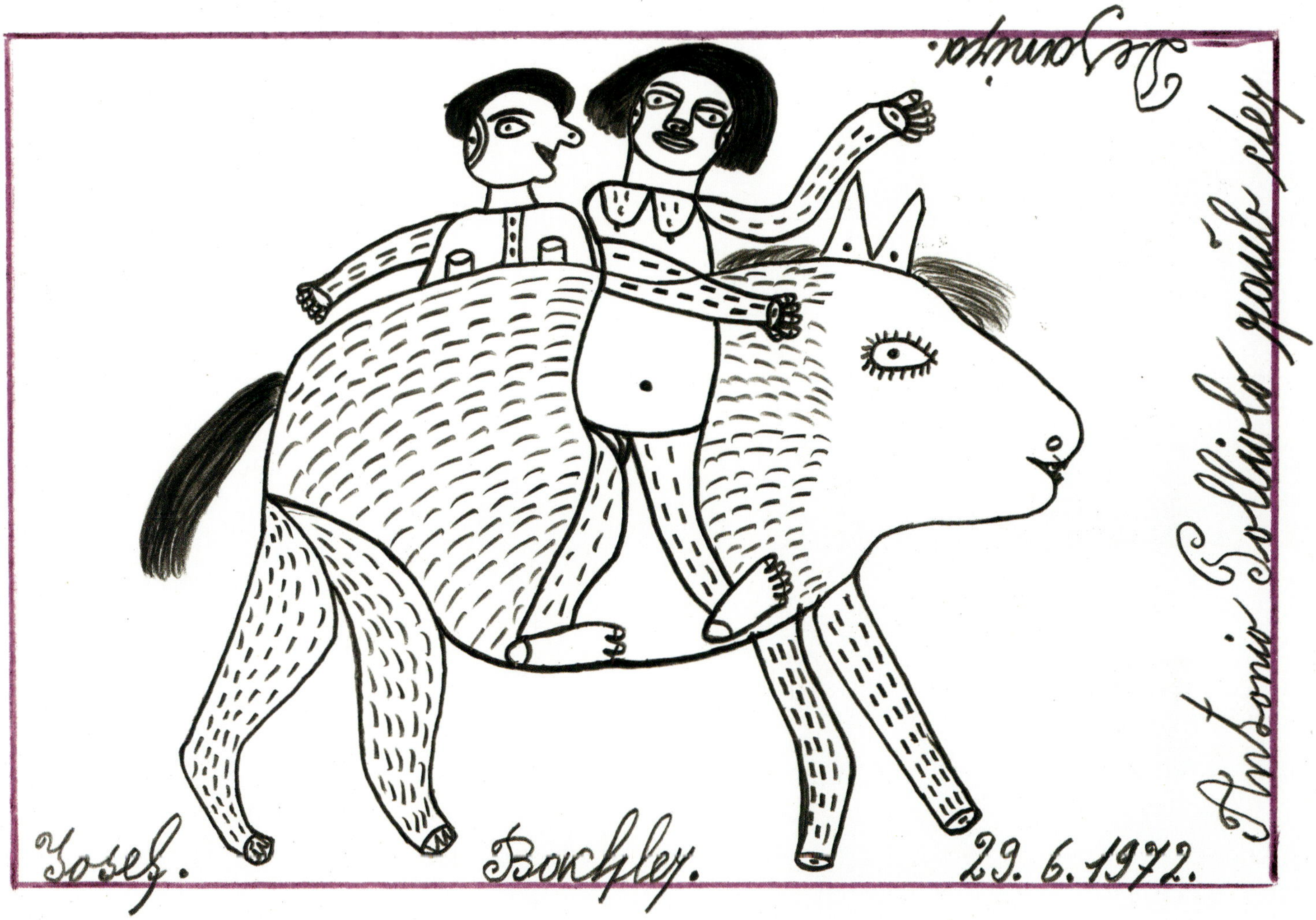

Josef Bachler
Antonio Polliolo … /
Antonio Polliolo …
1972, 21 x 29,7 cm
Bleistift, Farbstift /
pencil, color pencil
Privatsammlung

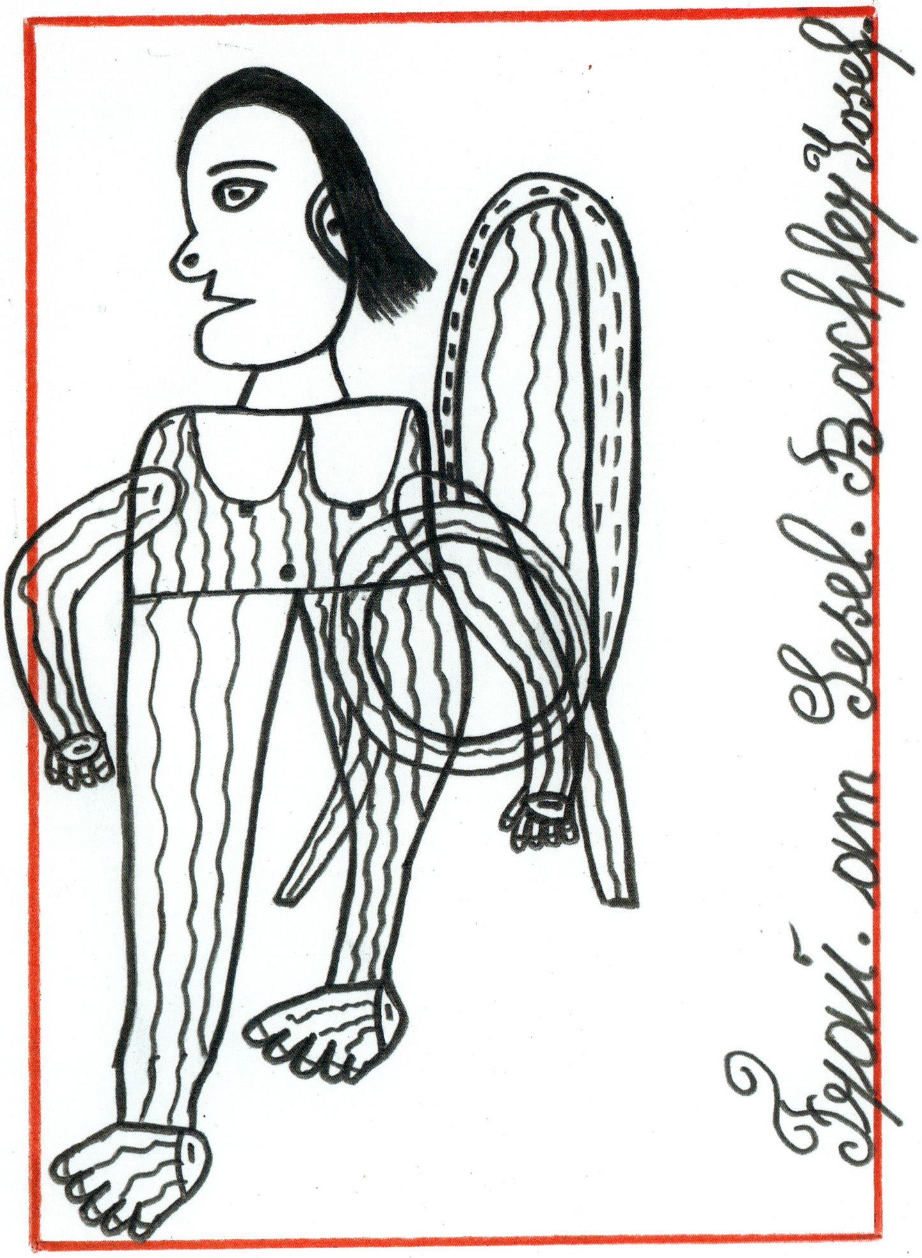
Frau. am Sesel. Bachler Josef

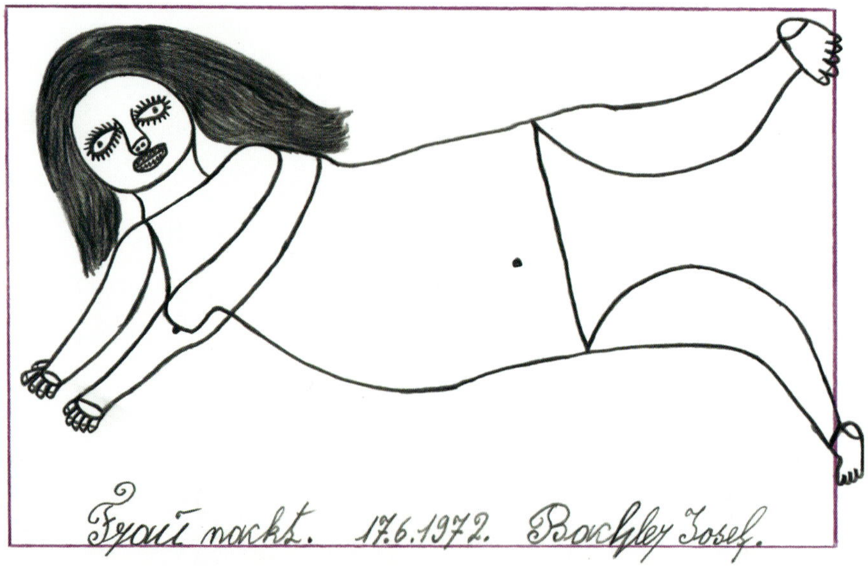
Frau nackt. 17.6.1972. Bachler Josef.

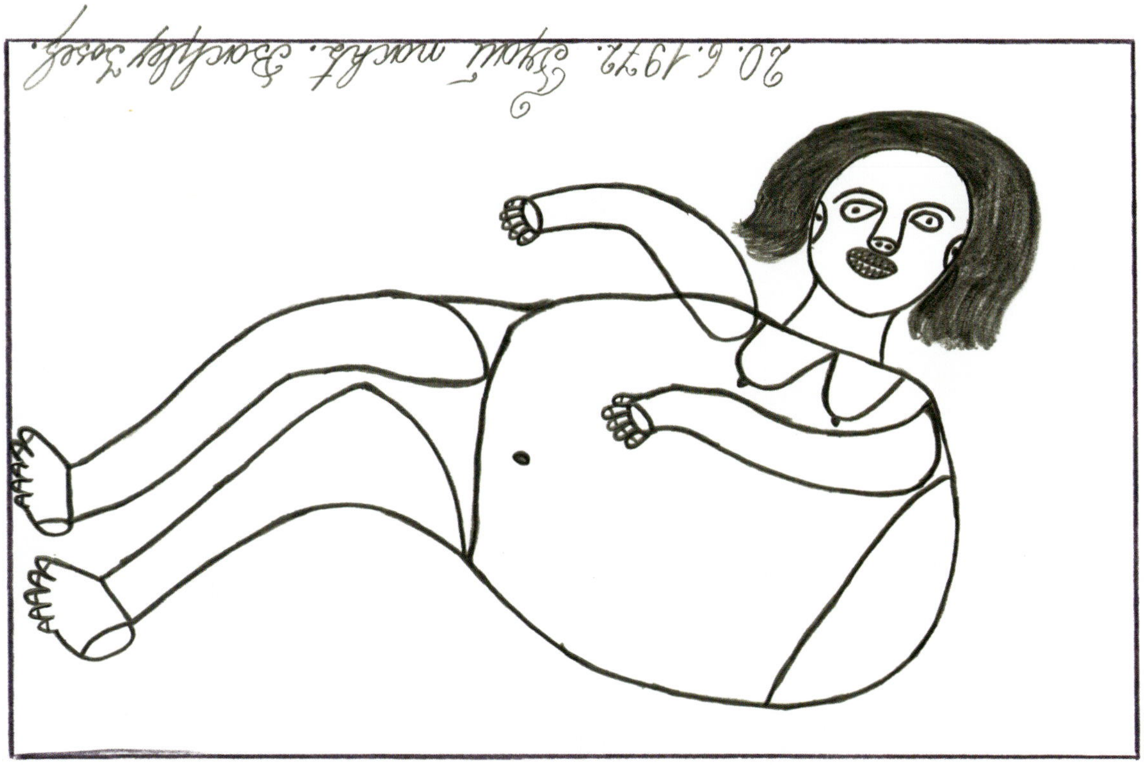

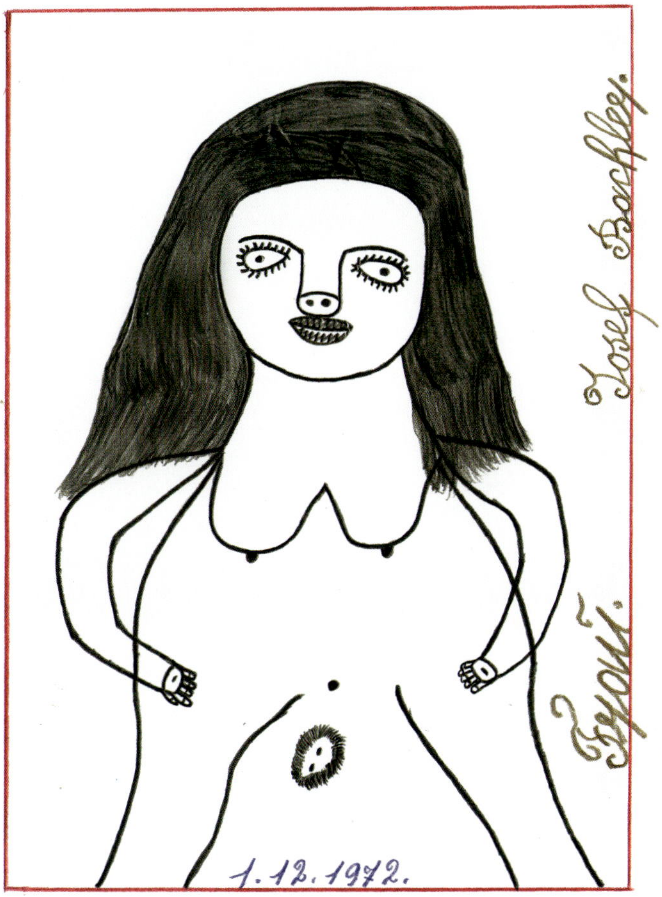

Josef Bachler
Frau am Sesel /
Woman on a Chair
Undatiert / undated
21 x 14,8 cm
Bleistift, Farbstift /
pencil, color pencil
Sammlung Arnulf Rainer

Josef Bachler
Frau nackt /
Woman naked
1972, 20,4 x 30,1 cm
Bleistift, Farbstifte /
pencil, color pencils
NÖ Landesmuseum
Sammlung Leo Navratil

Josef Bachler
Frau nackt /
Woman naked,
1972, 20,4 x 30,1 cm
Bleistift, Farbstift /
pencil, color pencil
NÖ Landesmuseum
Sammlung Leo Navratil

Josef Bachler
Frau / Woman,
1972, 29,7 x 21 cm
Bleistift, Farbstifte /
pencil, color pencils
NÖ Landesmuseum
Sammlung Leo Navratil

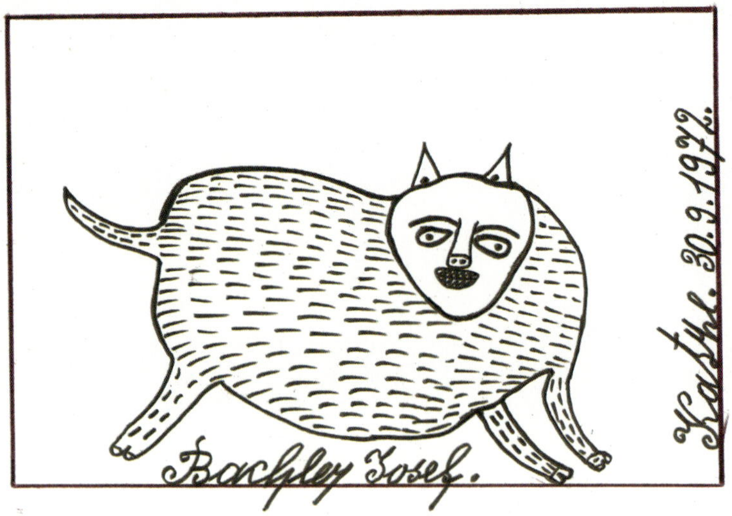
Bachler Josef.
Katze. 30.9.1972.

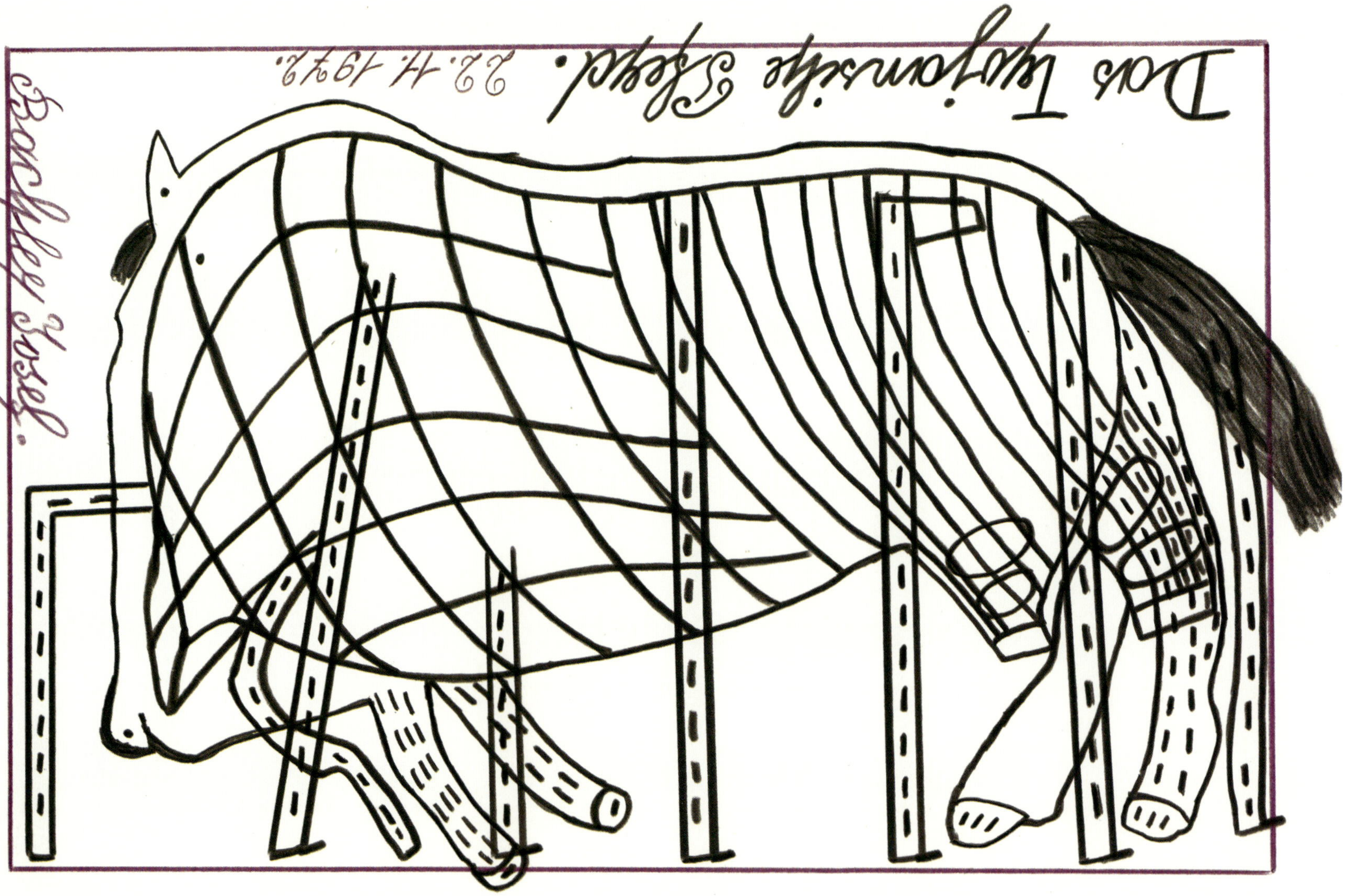
22.11.1972.
Bachler Josef.

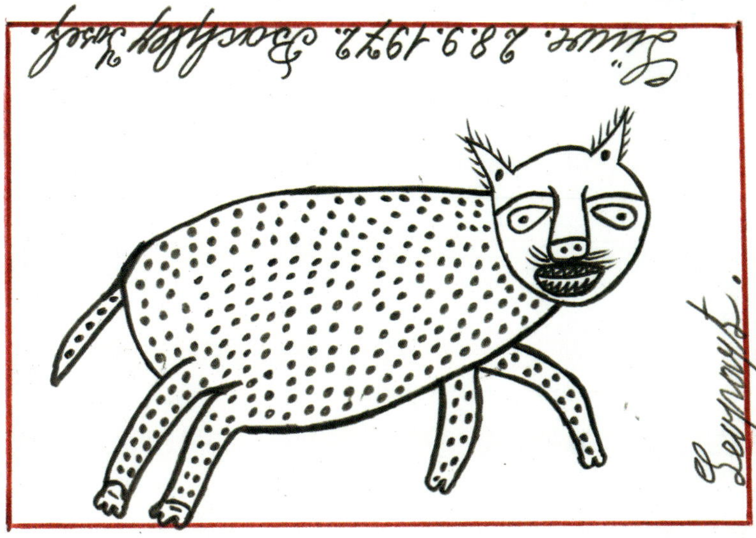

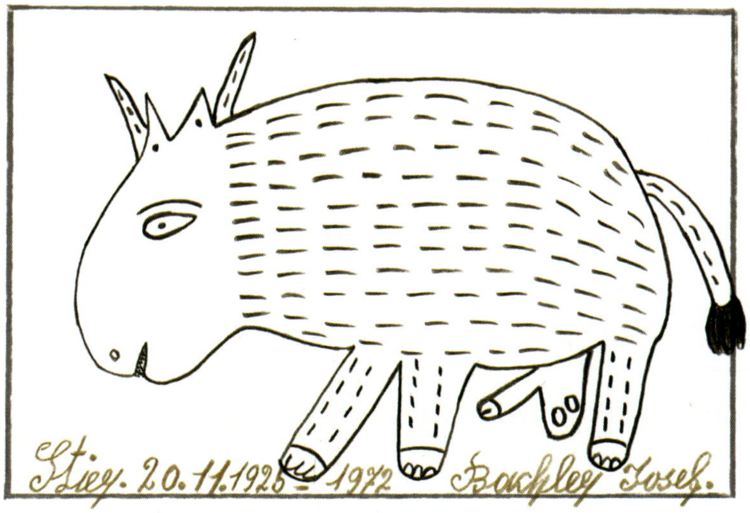

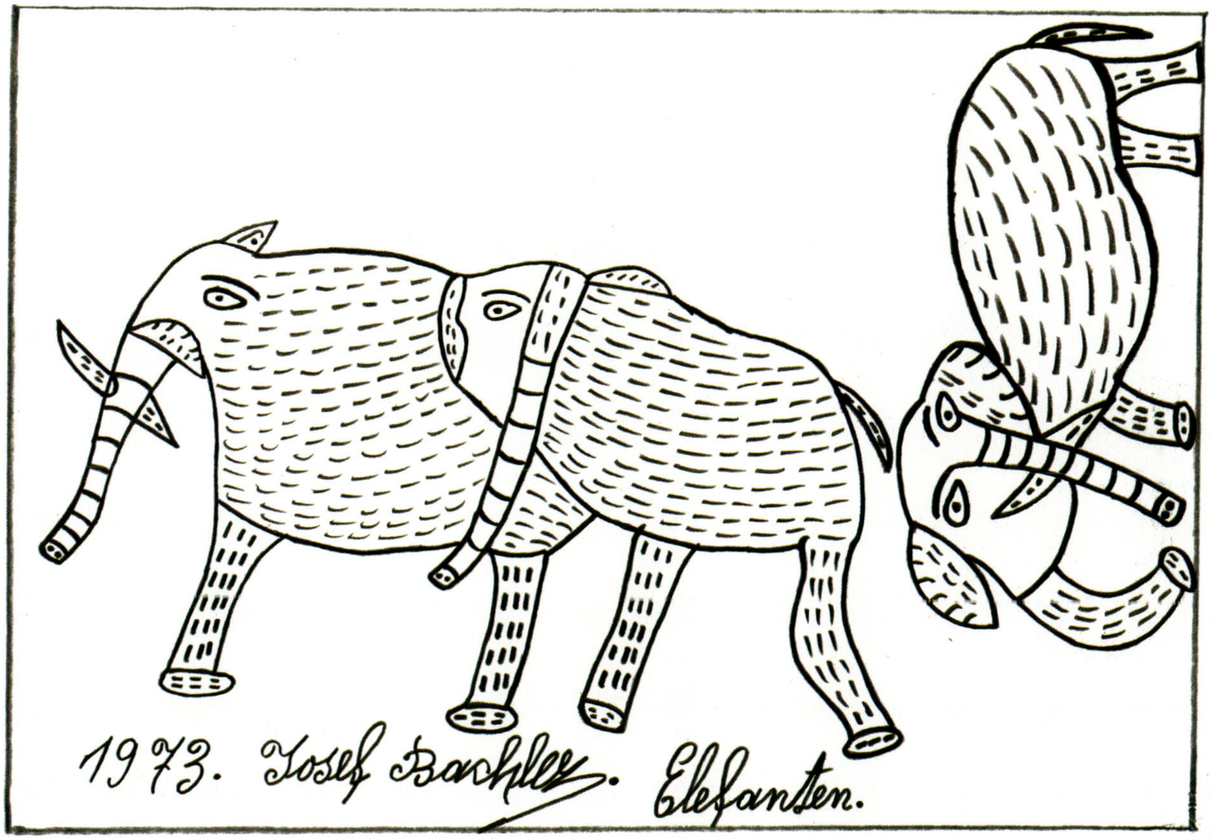

Josef Bachler
Katze / Cat
1972, 14,9 x 21 cm
Bleistift, Farbstift /
pencil, color pencil
Sammlung Arnulf Rainer

Josef Bachler
Das Trojanische Pferd /
The Trojan Horse
1972, 21 x 29,7 cm
Bleistift, Farbstift /
pencil, color pencil
NÖ Landesmuseum
Sammlung Leo Navratil

Josef Bachler
Leopart / Leopard
1972, 14,8 x 21 cm
Bleistift, Farbstift /
pencil, color pencil
Sammlung Arnulf Rainer

Josef Bachler
Stier / Bull
1972, 14,8 x 21 cm
Bleistift, Farbstifte /
pencil, color pencils
NÖ Landesmuseum
Sammlung Leo Navratil

Josef Bachler
Elefanten / Elephants
1973, 22 x 30,1 cm
Bleistift, Farbstift /
pencil, color pencil
NÖ Landesmuseum
Sammlung Leo Navratil

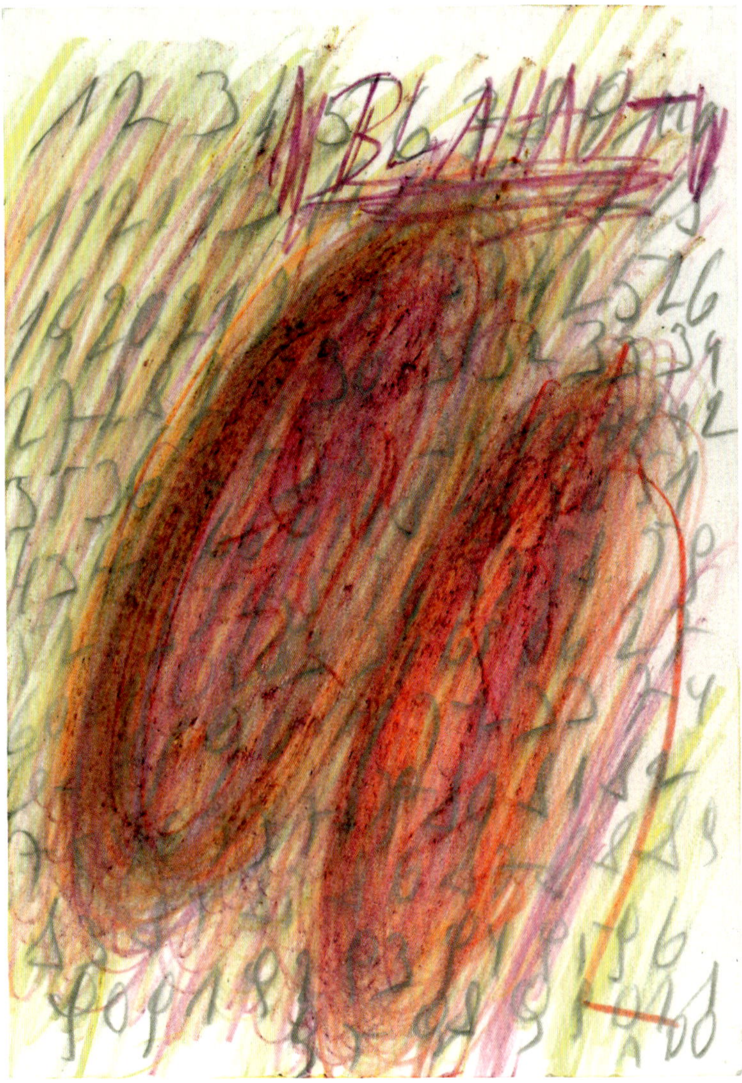

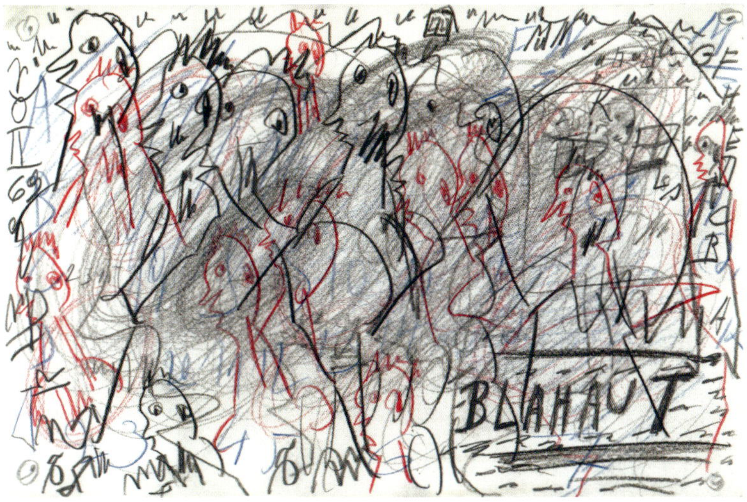

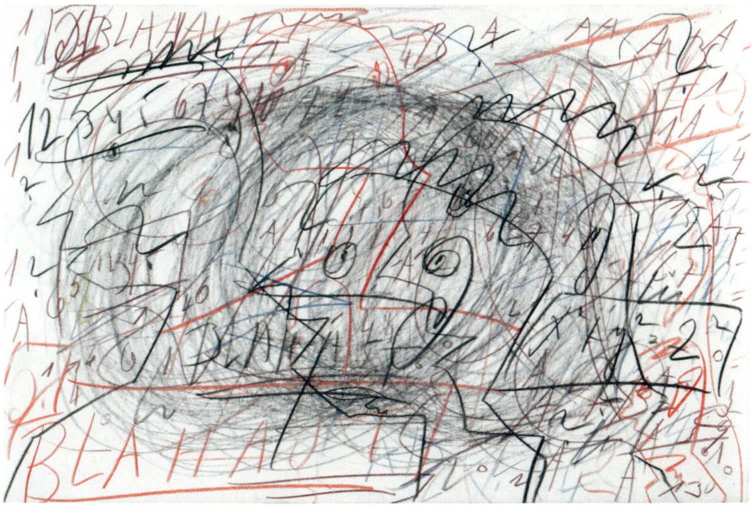

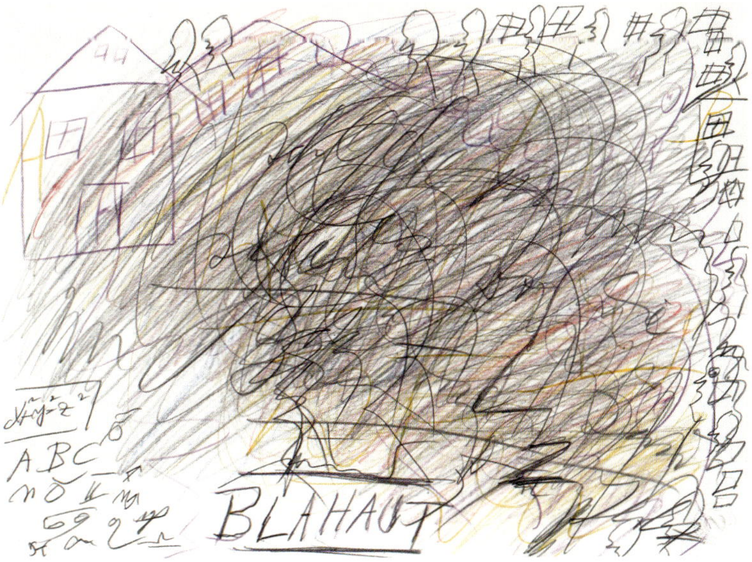

Josef Blahaut
Ohne Titel / Untitled
Undatiert / undated
14,7 x 10,4 cm
Bleistift, Farbstifte /
pencil, colour pencils
Sammlung Helmut Zambo

Josef Blahaut
Köpfe / Heads
Undatiert / undated
21 x 30 cm
Bleistift, Farbstifte /
pencil, color pencils
Sammlung Helmut Zambo

Josef Blahaut
Zwei Köpfe /
Two Heads
Undatiert / undated
20,7 x 29,6 cm
Bleistift, Farbstifte /
pencil, color pencils
Sammlung Helmut Zambo

Josef Blahaut
Ohne Titel / Untitled
1980, 30 x 40 cm
Bleistift, Farbstifte /
pencil, color pencils
Privatsammlung

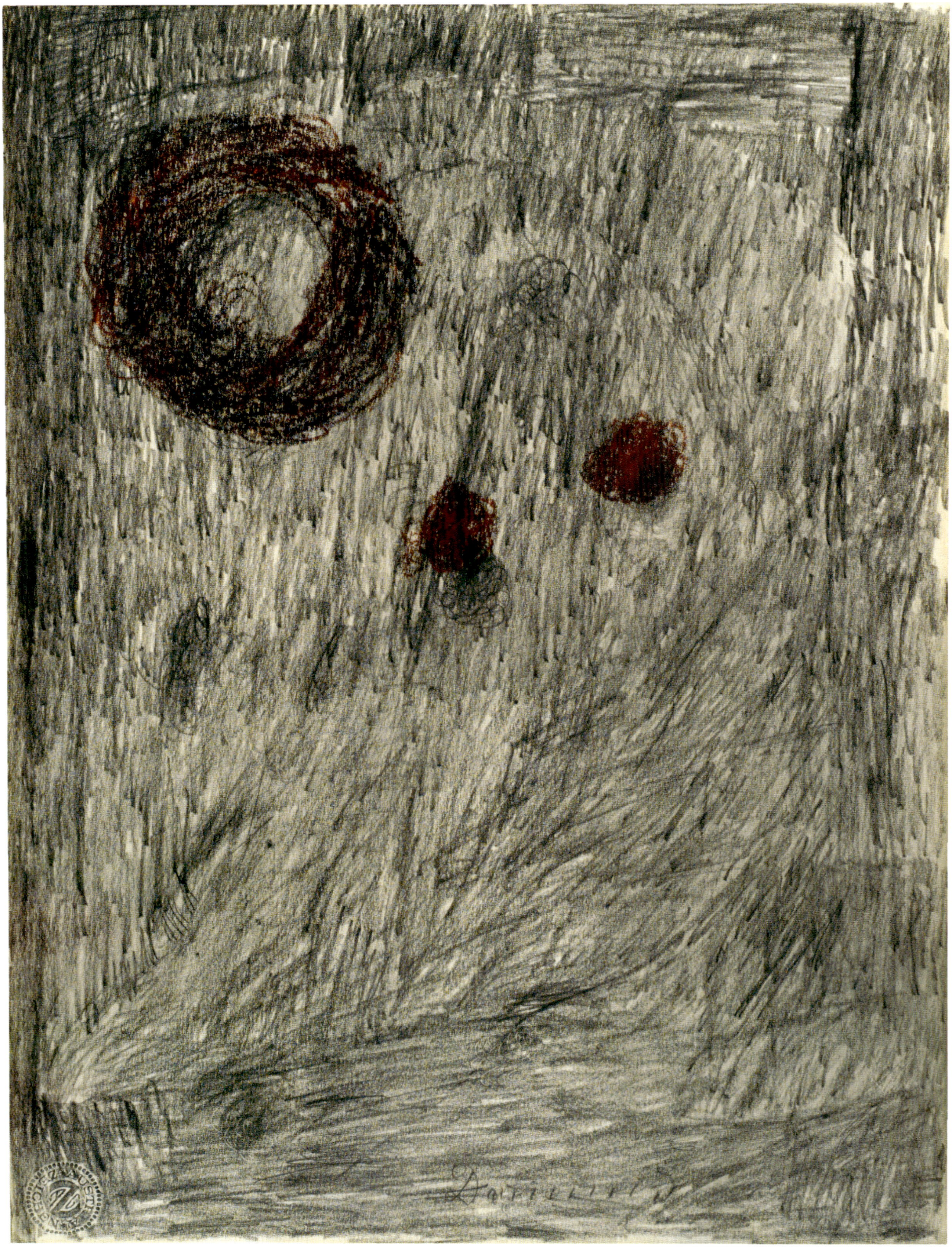

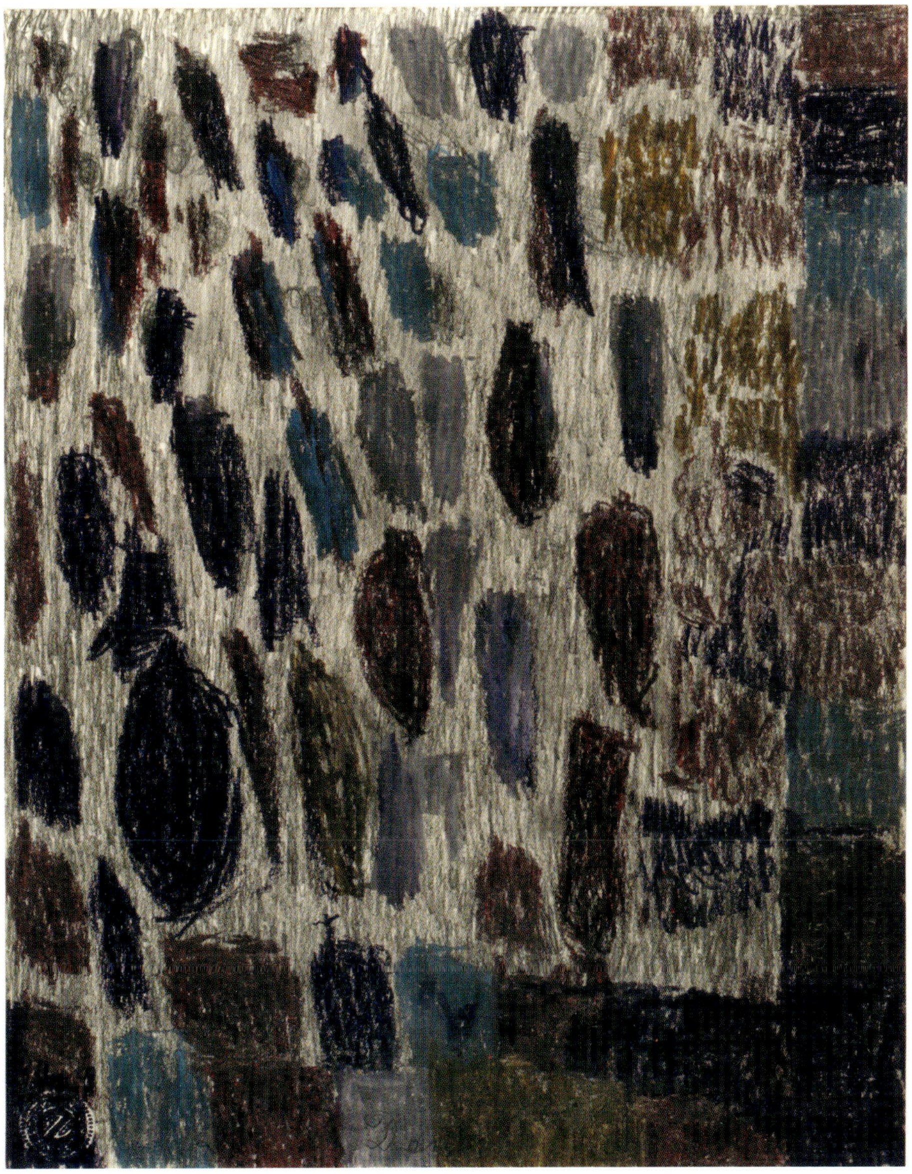

Anton Dobay
Ohne Titel / Untitled
Undatiert / undated
40 x 30 cm, Bleistift,
Wachskreide /
pencil, crayons
Privatstiftung -
Künstler aus Gugging

Anton Dobay
Stillleben mit Blumen /
Still life with Flowers
1981, 40 x 30 cm
Bleistift, Wachskreide /
pencil, crayons
Privatstiftung -
Künstler aus Gugging

Anton Dobay
Gegenstand / Object
Undatiert / undated
40 x 30 cm
Bleistift, Kohle,
Wachskreide /
pencil, charcoal,
crayons
Privatstiftung -
Künstler aus Gugging

Anton Dobay
Blumen in blauer Vase
(nach Jan Breughel) /
Flowers in Blue Vase
(after Jan Breughel)
1981, 40 x 30 cm
Bleistift, Wachskreiden /
pencil, crayons
Privatstiftung -
Künstler aus Gugging

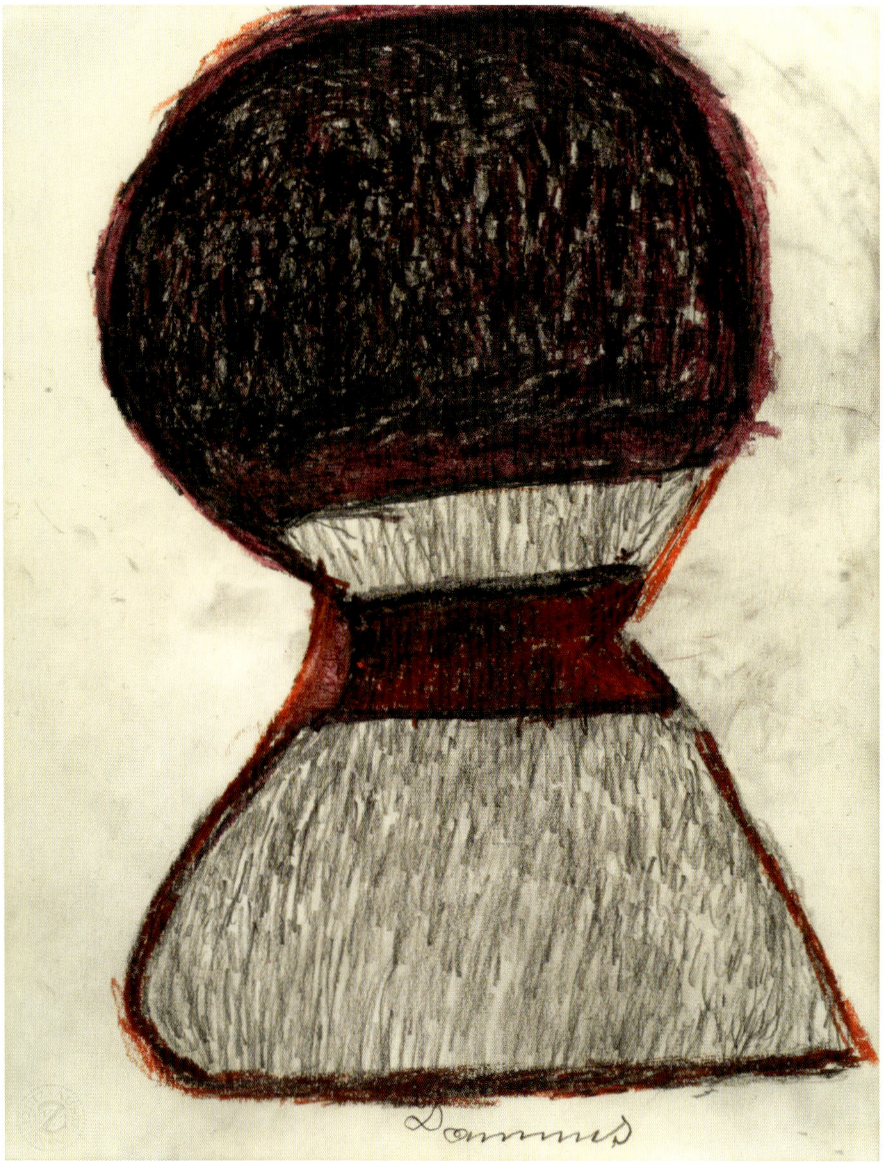

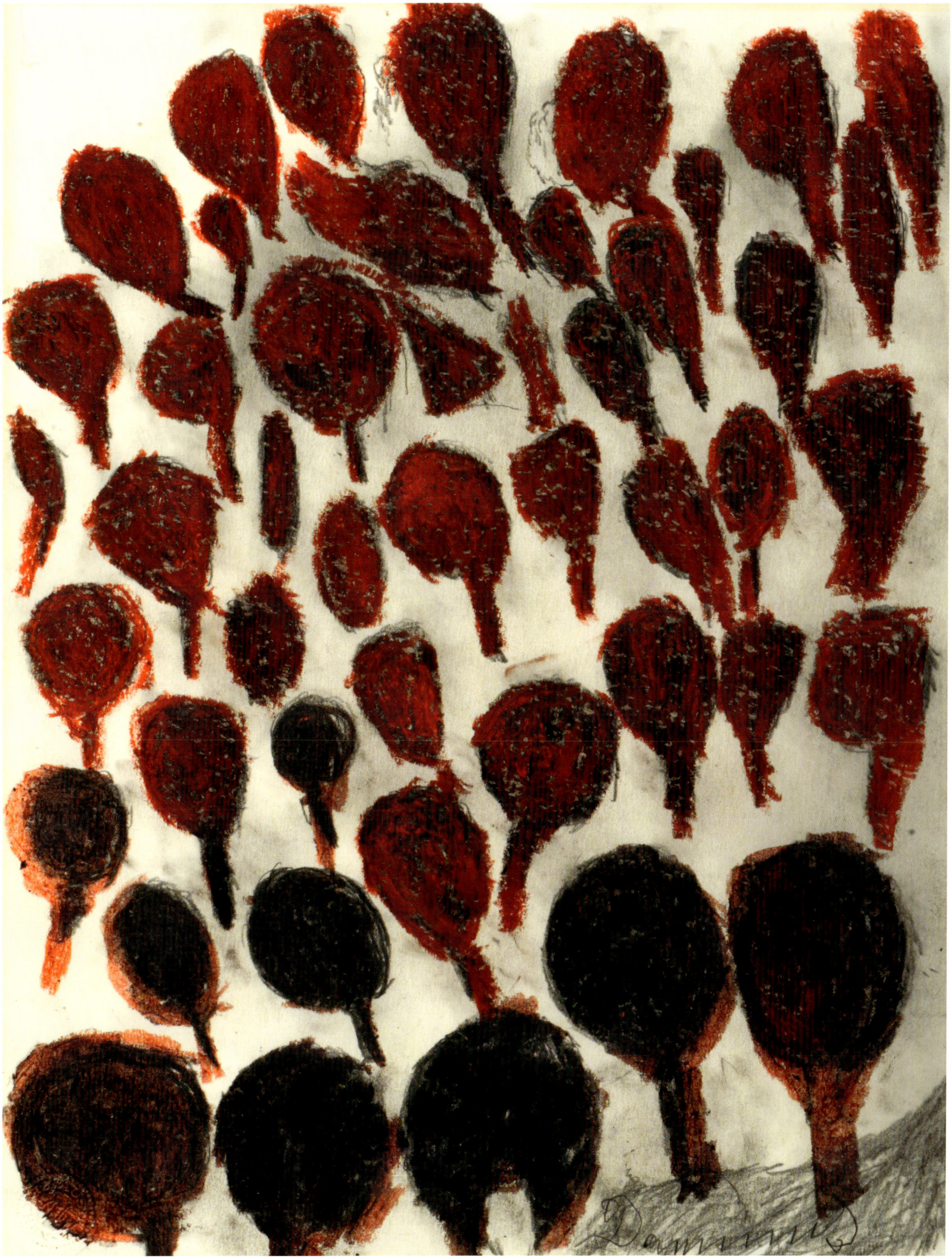

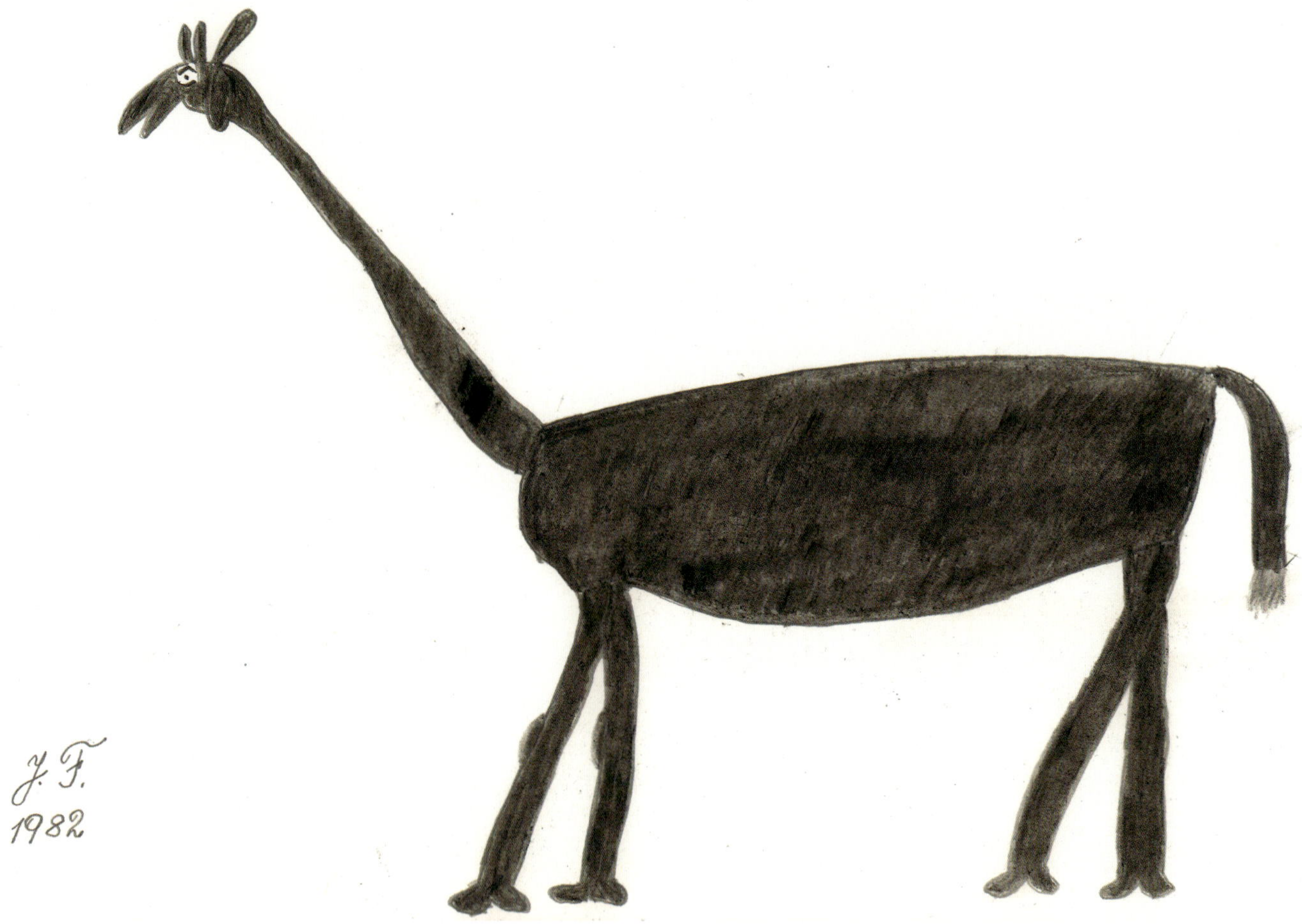
J. F.
1982

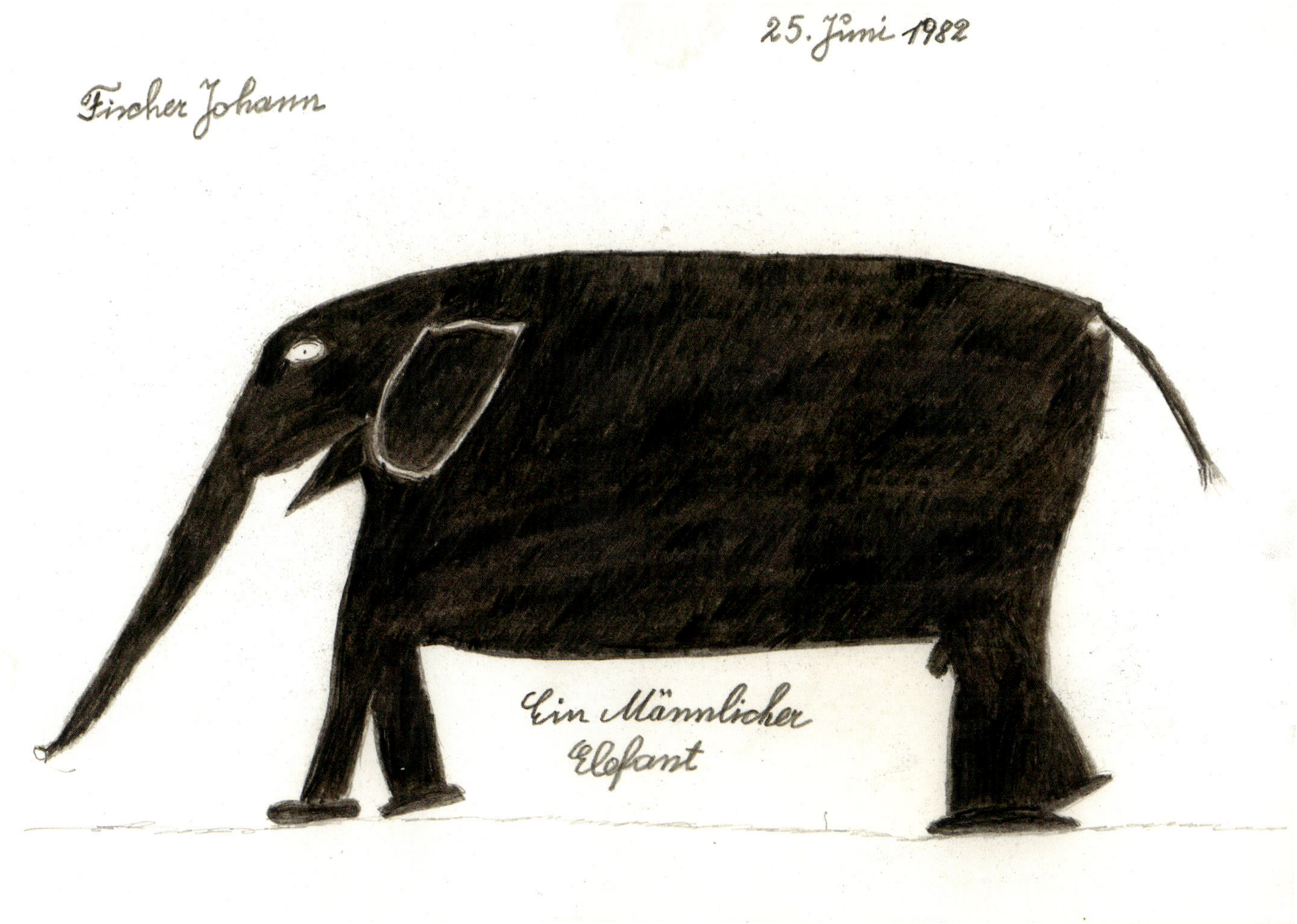

Johann Fischer
Giraffe / Giraffe
1982, 20,9 x 29,6 cm
Bleistift, Farbstift /
pencil, color pencil
Privatsammlung

Johann Fischer
Ein männlicher
Elefant /
A Male Elephant
1982, 20,9 x 29,6 cm
Bleistift, Farbstift /
pencil, color pencil
Privatsammlung

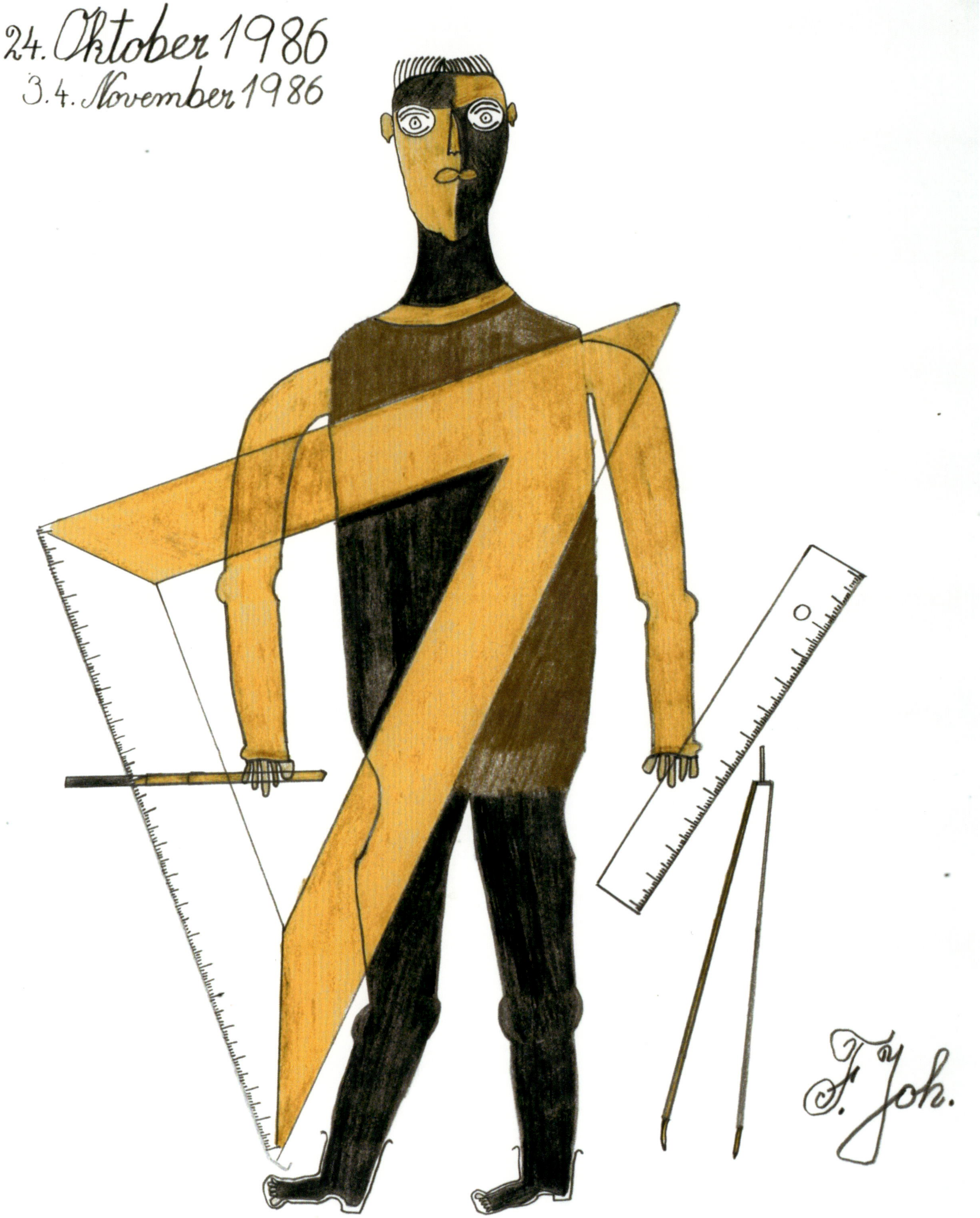
24. Oktober 1986
3.4. November 1986
J. Joh.

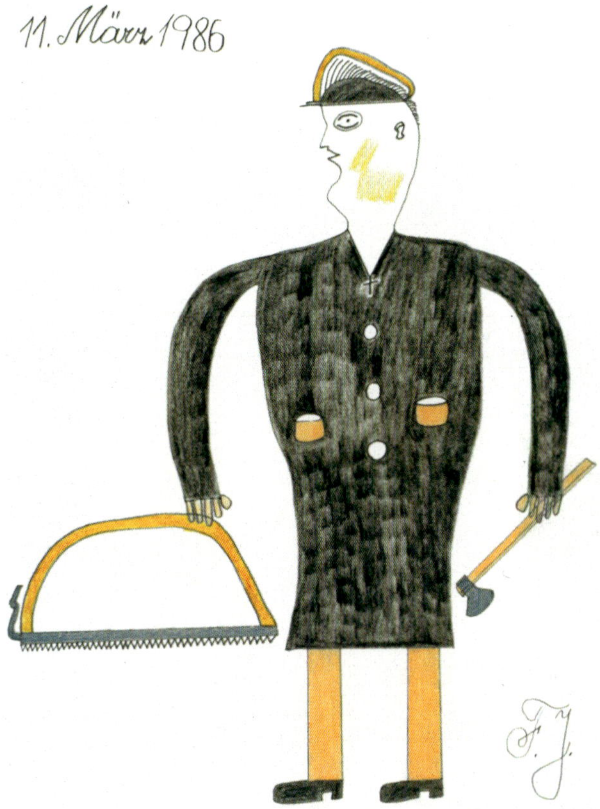

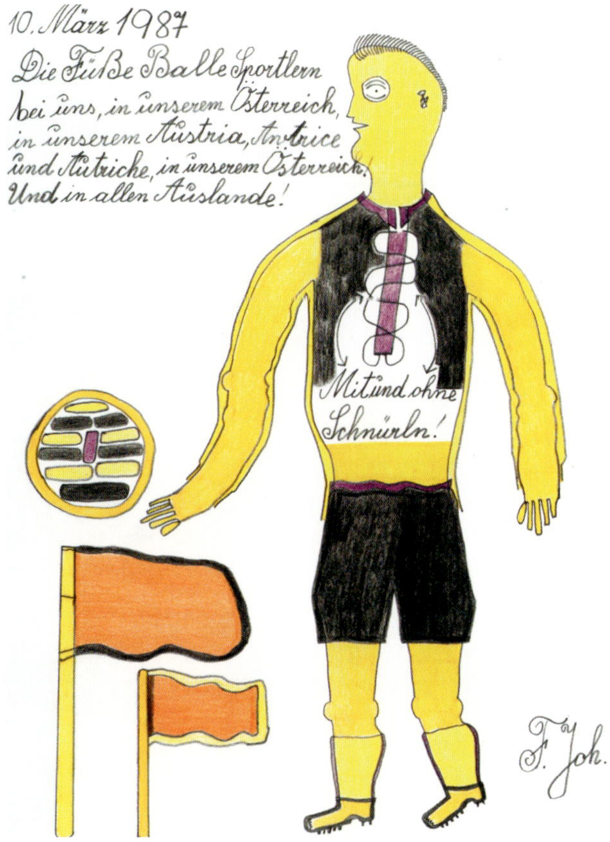

Johann Fischer
Techniker / Technician
1986, 40 x 30 cm
Bleistift, Farbstifte /
pencil, color pencils
Privatsammlung

Johann Fischer
Die jungen Männer /
The young Men
1986, 41 x 31cm
Bleistift, Farbstifte /
pencil, color pencils
Privatstiftung -
Künstler aus Gugging

Johann Fischer
Fußballer / Footballer
1987, 40 x 30 cm
Bleistift, Farbstifte /
pencil, color pencils
Privatsammlung

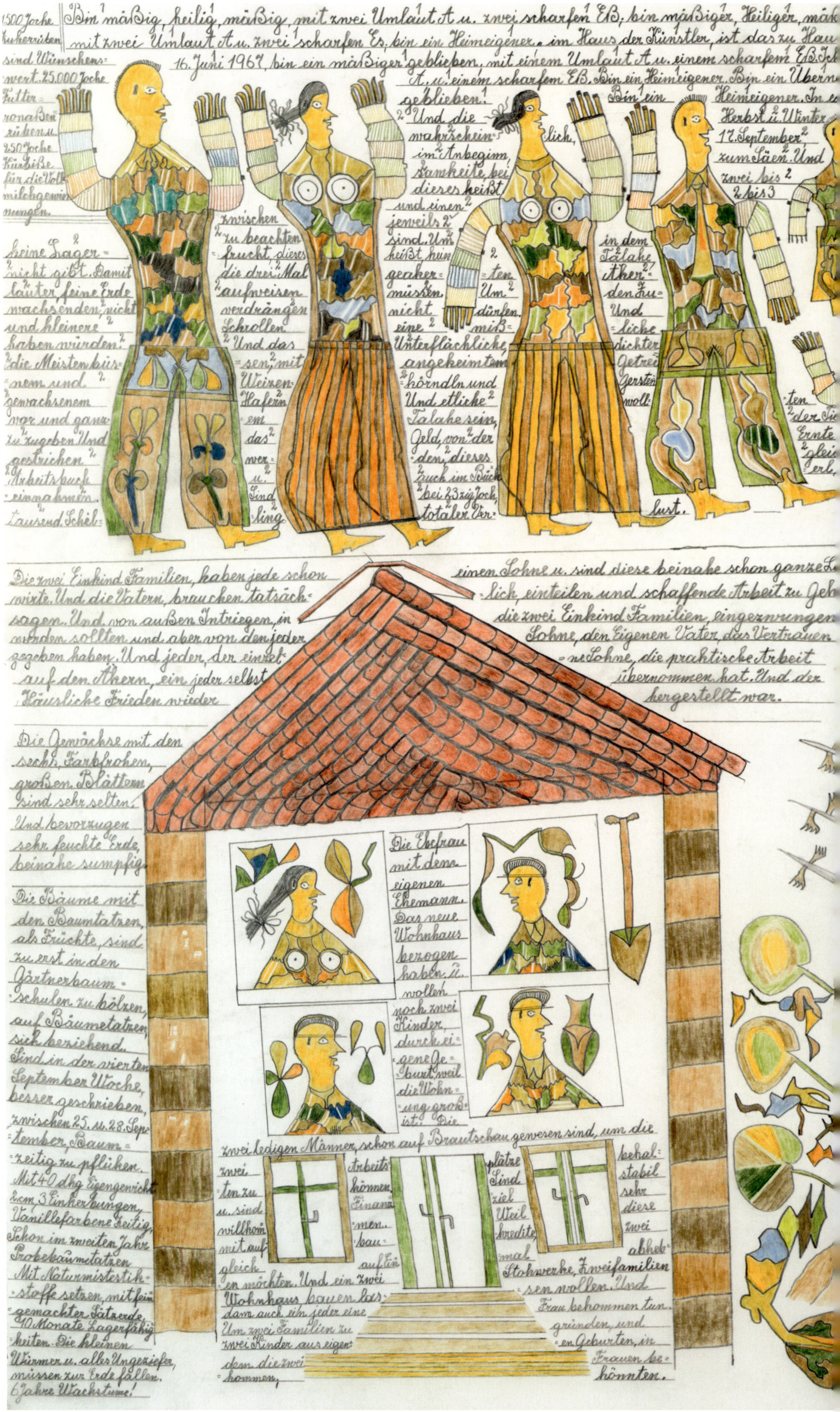

Johann Fischer
Bin mäßig, heilig … /
I am Moderate, Holy …
1999, 62,5 x 88 cm
Bleistift, Farbstifte /
pencil, color pencils

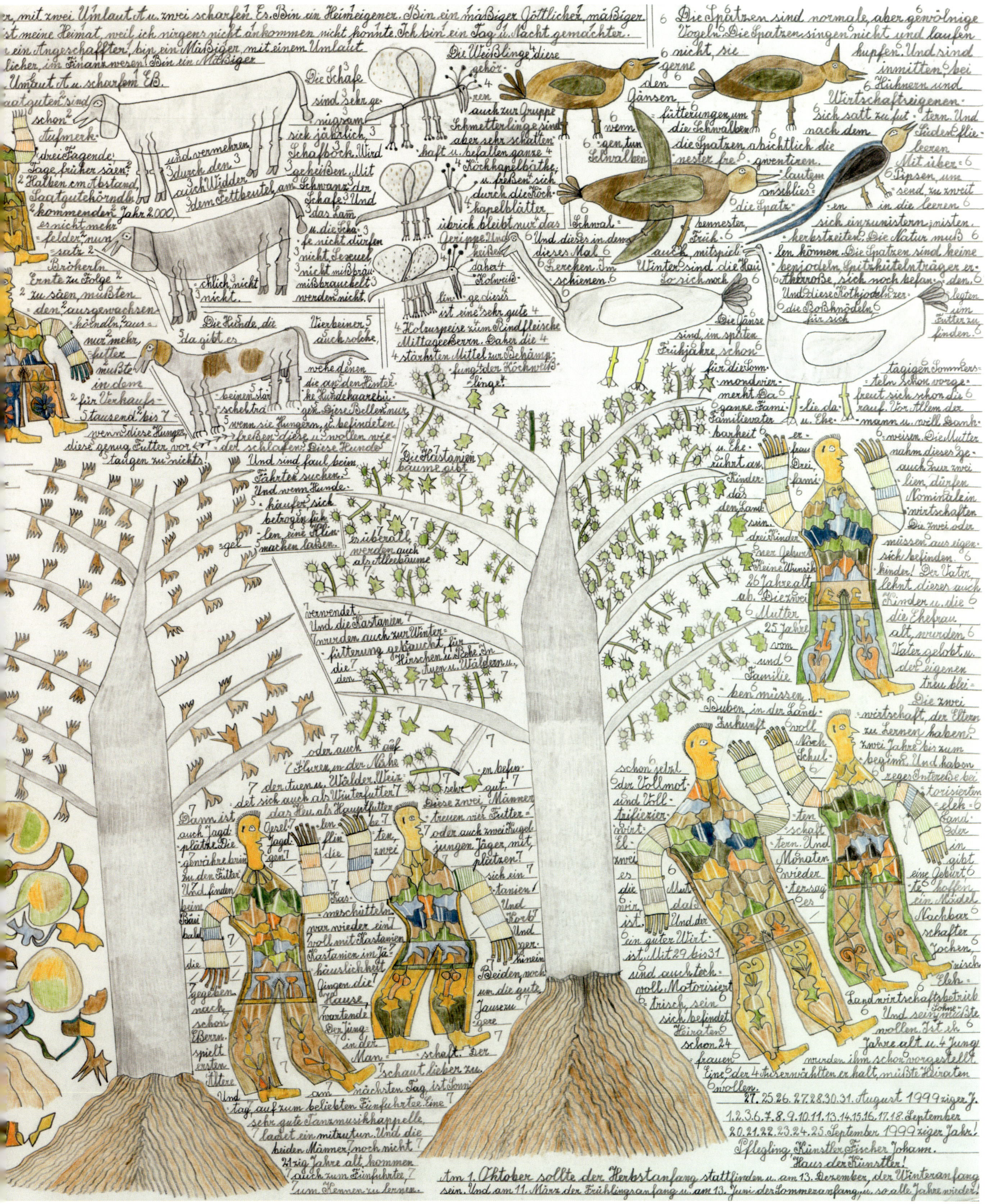
mit zwei Umlaut A u. zwei scharfen Es. Bin ein Heimeigener. Bin ein mäßiger Göttlicher, mäßiger
ist meine Heimat, weil ich nirgens nicht ankommen nicht konnte. Ich bin ein Tag u. Nacht gemachter.
Die Spatzen sind normale, aber gewöhnige Vögeln. Die Spatzen singen nicht und laufen nicht, sie hupfen. Und sind
Die Schafe sind sehr genügsam
Die Weißlinge diese gehören auch zur Gruppe Schmetterlinge sind aber sehr schatten haft u. befallen ganze Kochkapelblätter
Die Hunde, die Vierbeiner auch solche
Die Kastanien bäume gibt es überall werden auch als Alleebäume verwendet.
Und die Kastanien wurden auch zur Winter fütterung gebraucht, für Hirschen u. Rehe in den Auen u. Wäldern u.
oder auch auf Fluren, in der Nähe der Auen u. Wälder.
Dann ist auch Jagd
Landwirtschaftsbetrieb
27. 25. 26. 27. 28. 30. 31. August 1999ziger J.
1. 2. 3. 6. 7. 8. 9. 10. 11. 13. 14. 15. 16. 17. 18. September
20. 21. 22. 23. 24. 25. September 1999ziger Jahr!
Pflegling Künstler Fischer Johann.
Haus der Künstler!
Am 1. Oktober sollte der Herbstanfang stattfinden u. am 13. Dezember der Winteranfang
sein. Und am 11. März der Frühlingsanfang u. am 13. Juni der Sommeranfang, u. so alle Jahre wieder!

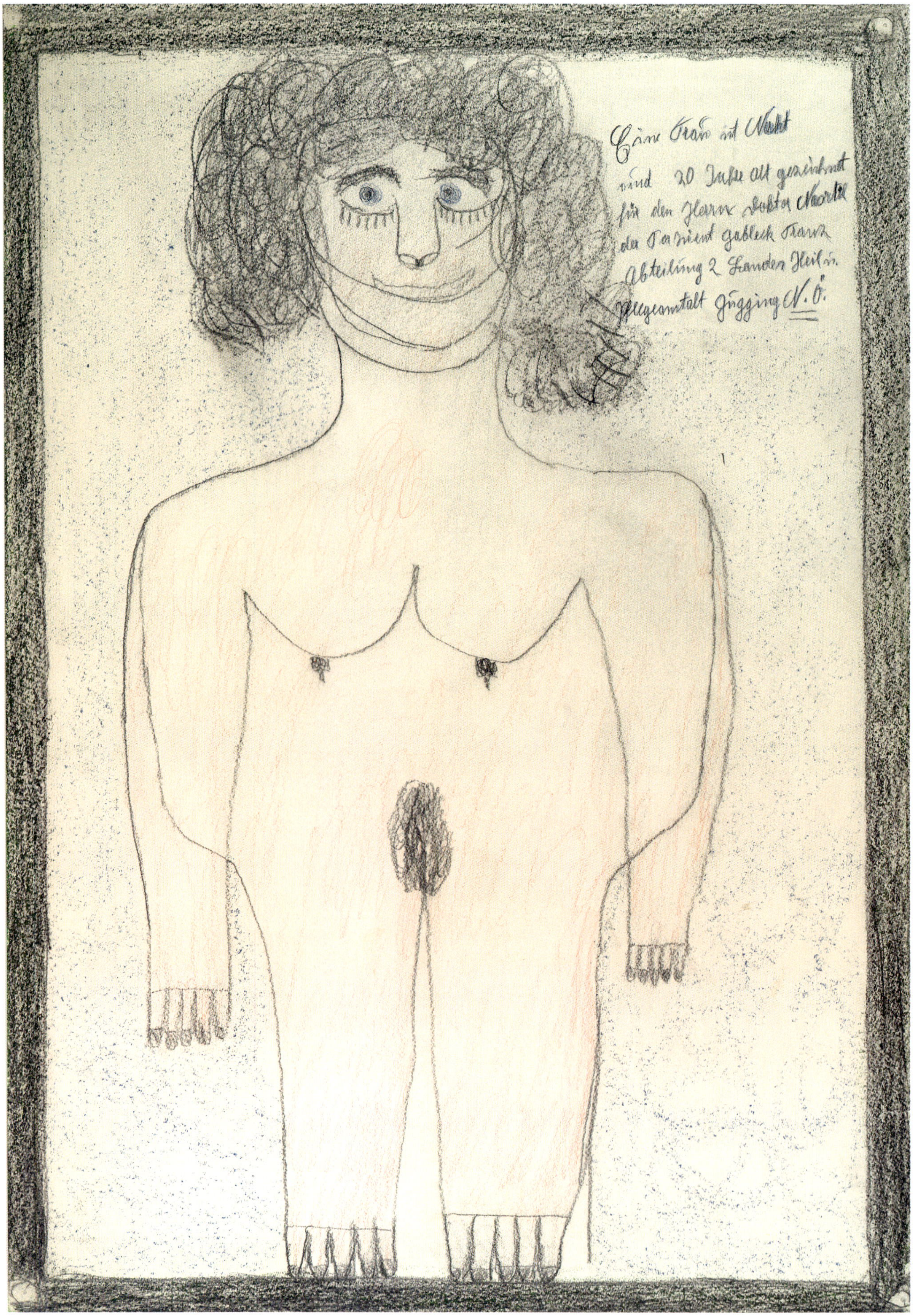
Äine Frau ist Nakt
und 20 Jahre alt gezeichnet
für den Herrn Doktor Navratil
der Patzient Gableck Franz
Abteilung 2 Landes Heil u.
Pflegeanstalt Gugging N.Ö.

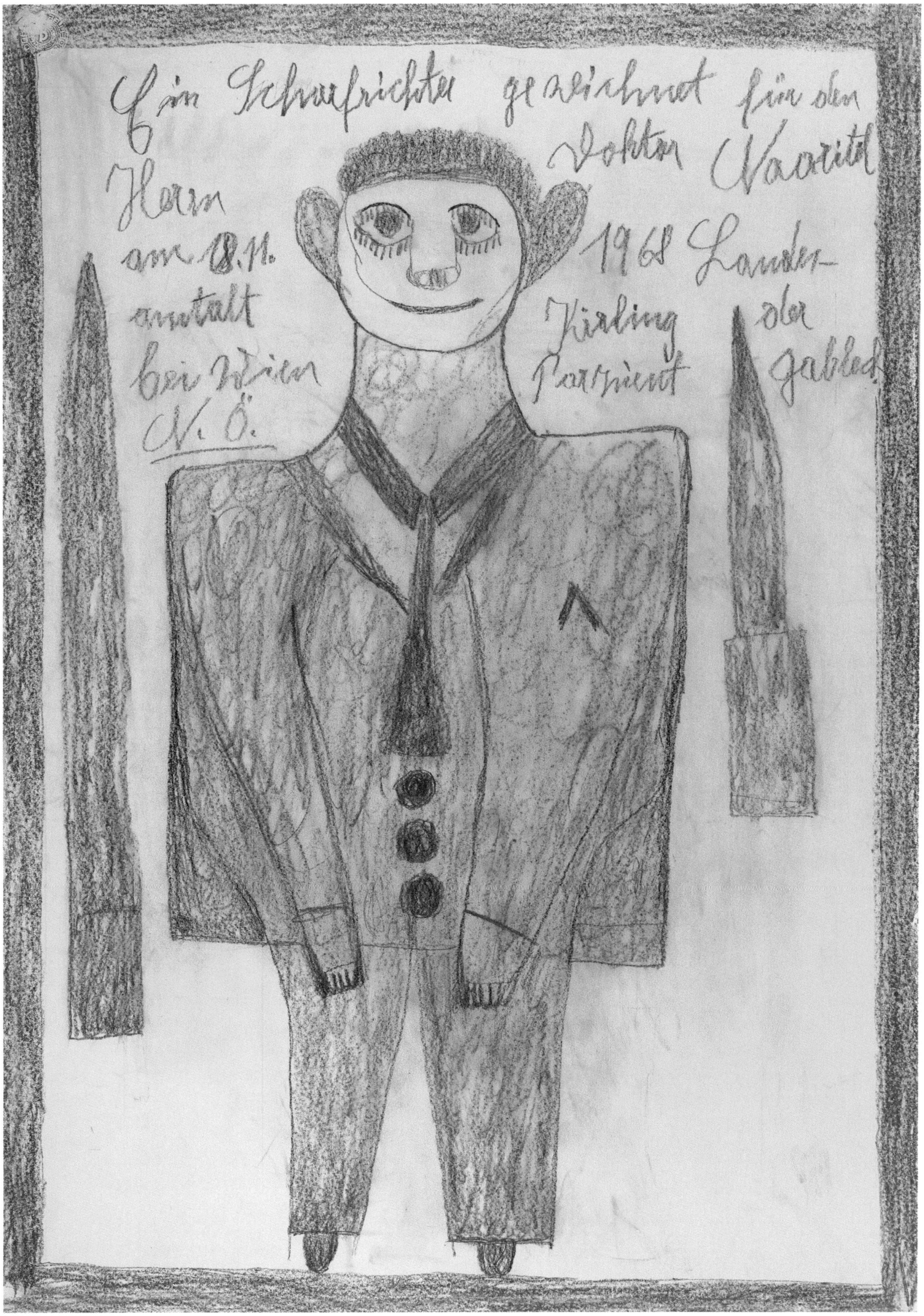
Ein Scharfrichter gezeichnet für den
Doktor Navratil
Herrn
am 8.11.
1968 Landes-
anstalt
Kierling
der
bei Wien
N. Ö.

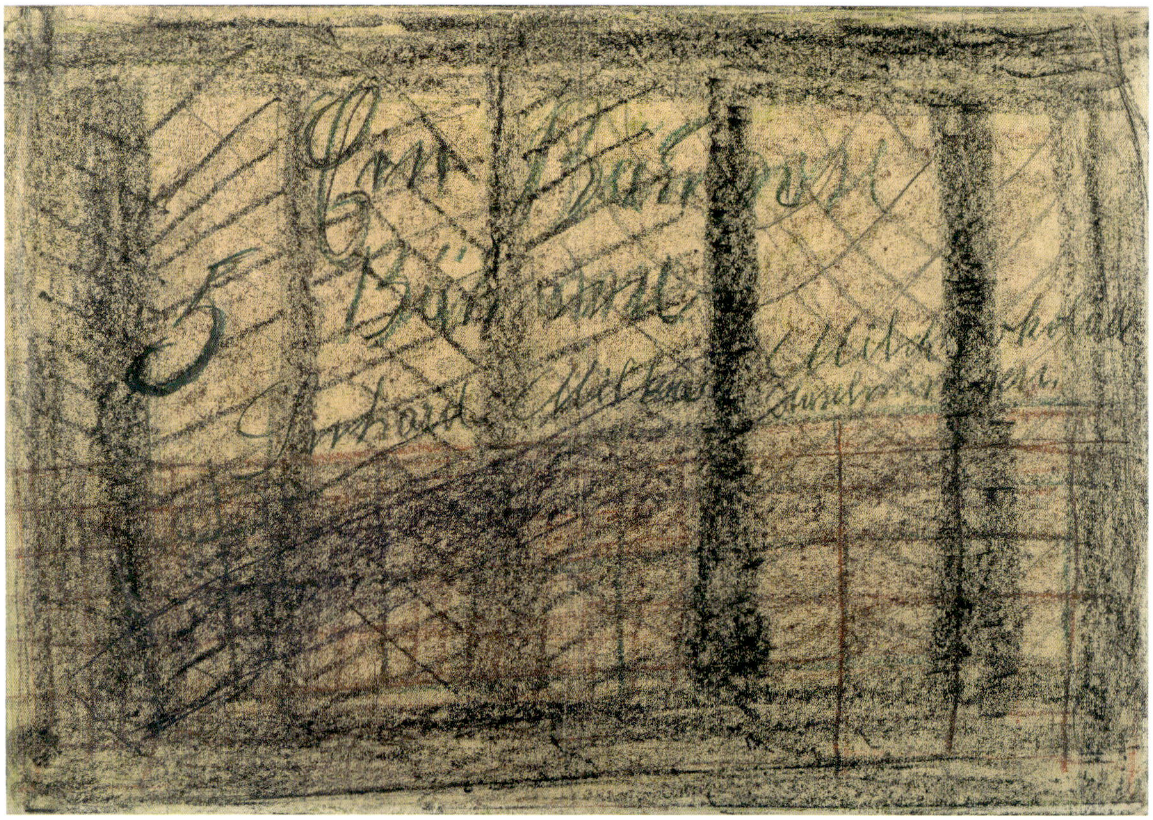

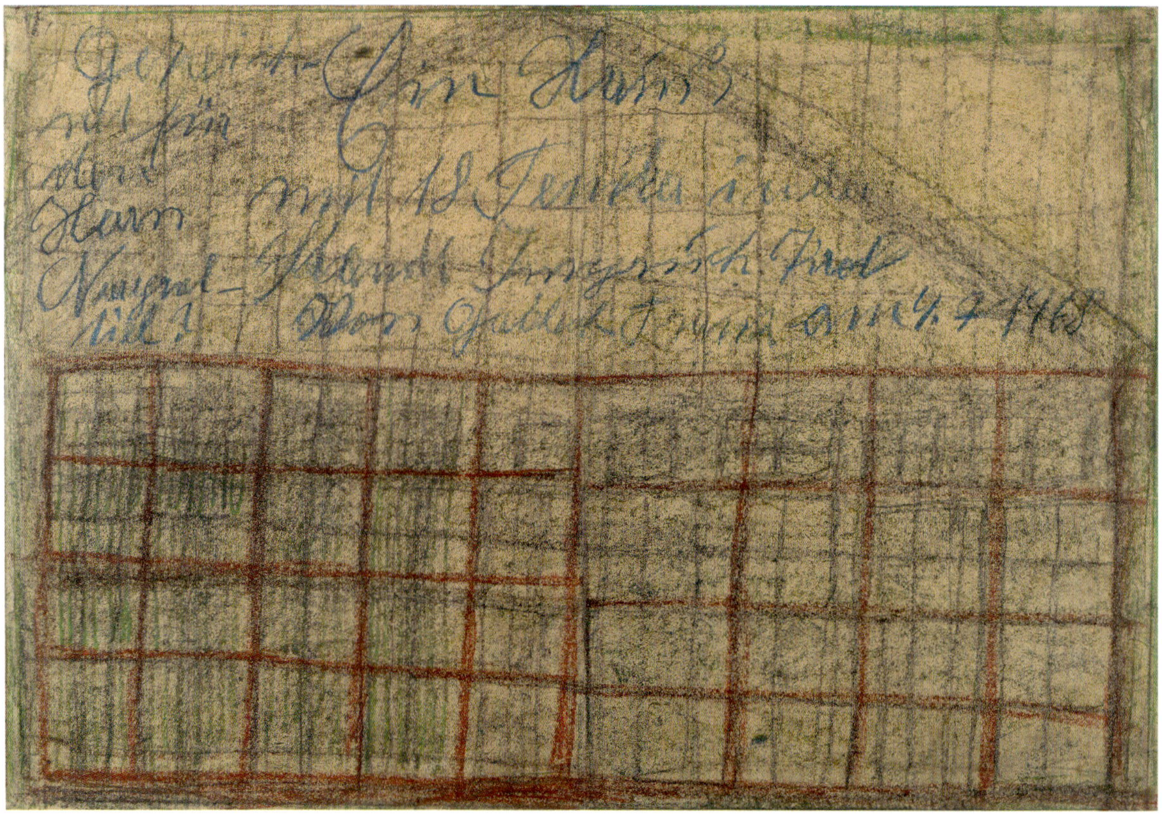

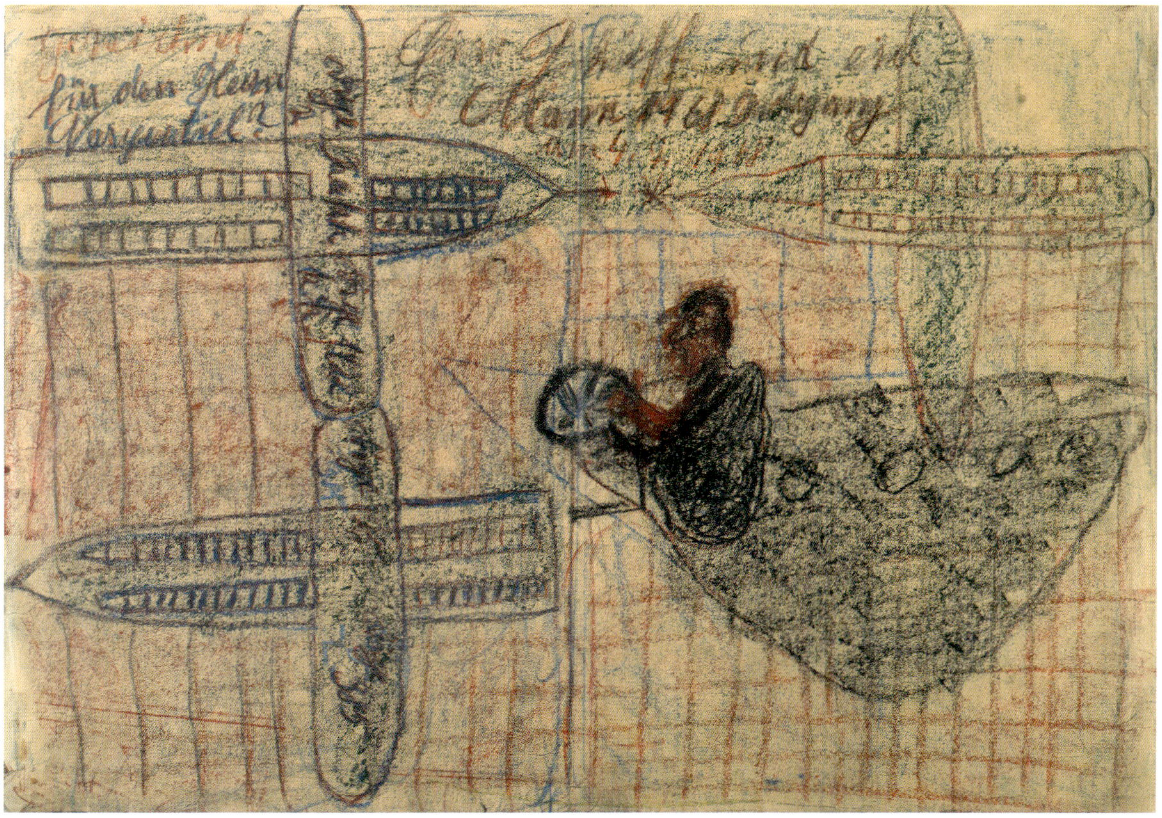

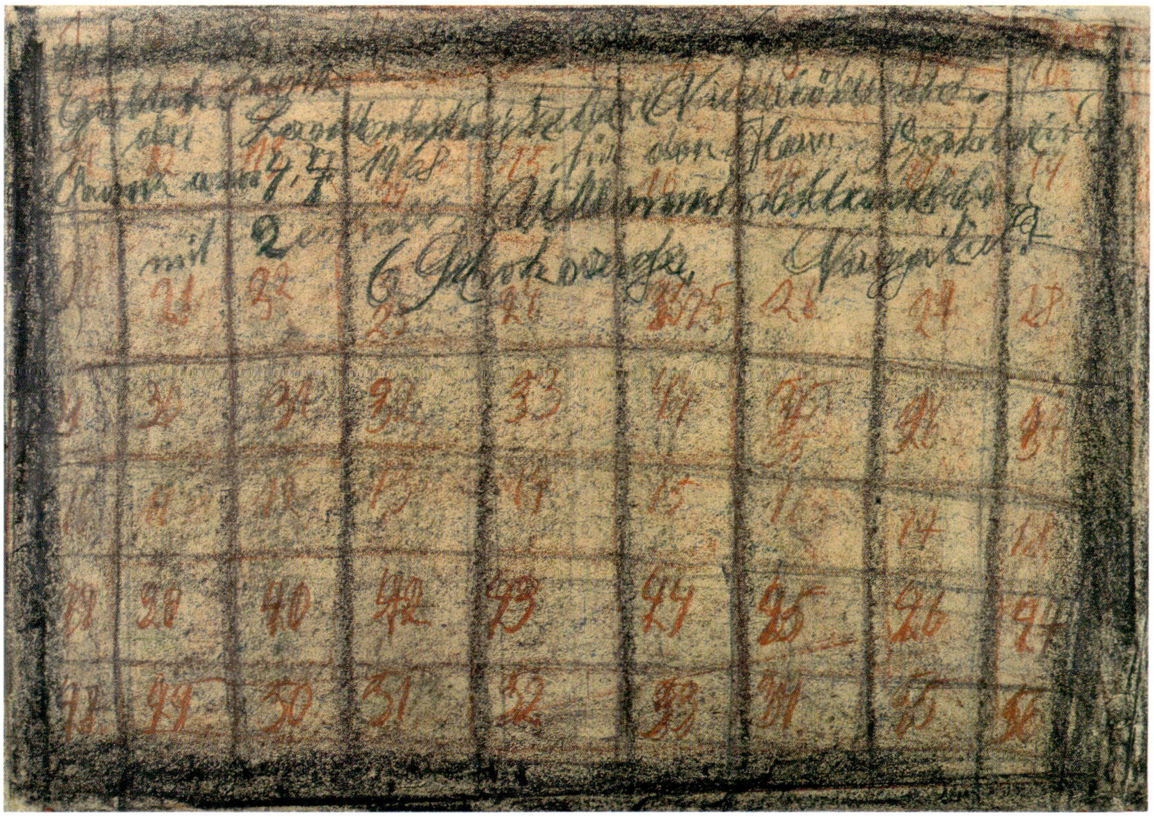

Franz Gableck
Eine Frau ist Nakt ... /
A Woman is naked ...
Undatiert, undated
88 x 60 cm
Bleistift, Farbstifte,
Wachskreide /
pencil, color pencil,
crayons
Privatsammlung

Franz Gableck
Ein Scharfrichter ... /
An Executioner
1968, 90 x 62,5 cm
Bleistift, Farbstifte /
pencil, color pencils
Privatsammlung

Franz Gableck
5 Bäume / 5 Trees
1968, 45 x 62,8 cm
Farbstifte /
color pencils
Privatstiftung -
Künstler aus Gugging

Franz Gableck
Ein Hauß / a House
1968, 44,8 x 63 cm
Farbstifte /
color pencils
Privatstiftung -
Künstler aus Gugging

Franz Gableck
Ein Schiff / A Ship
1968, 44,8 x 63 cm
Farbstifte /
color pencils
Privatstiftung -
Künstler aus Gugging

Franz Gableck
Raster / Grid
1968, 44,7 x 63,2 cm
Farbstifte /
color pencils
Privatstiftung -
Künstler aus Gugging

Franz Gableck
Ein Autostadion ... /
Motor-racing Circuit ...
1968, 86 x 61 cm
Bleistift, Farbstifte,
Wachskreiden /
pencil, color pencils,
crayons
Privatsammlung

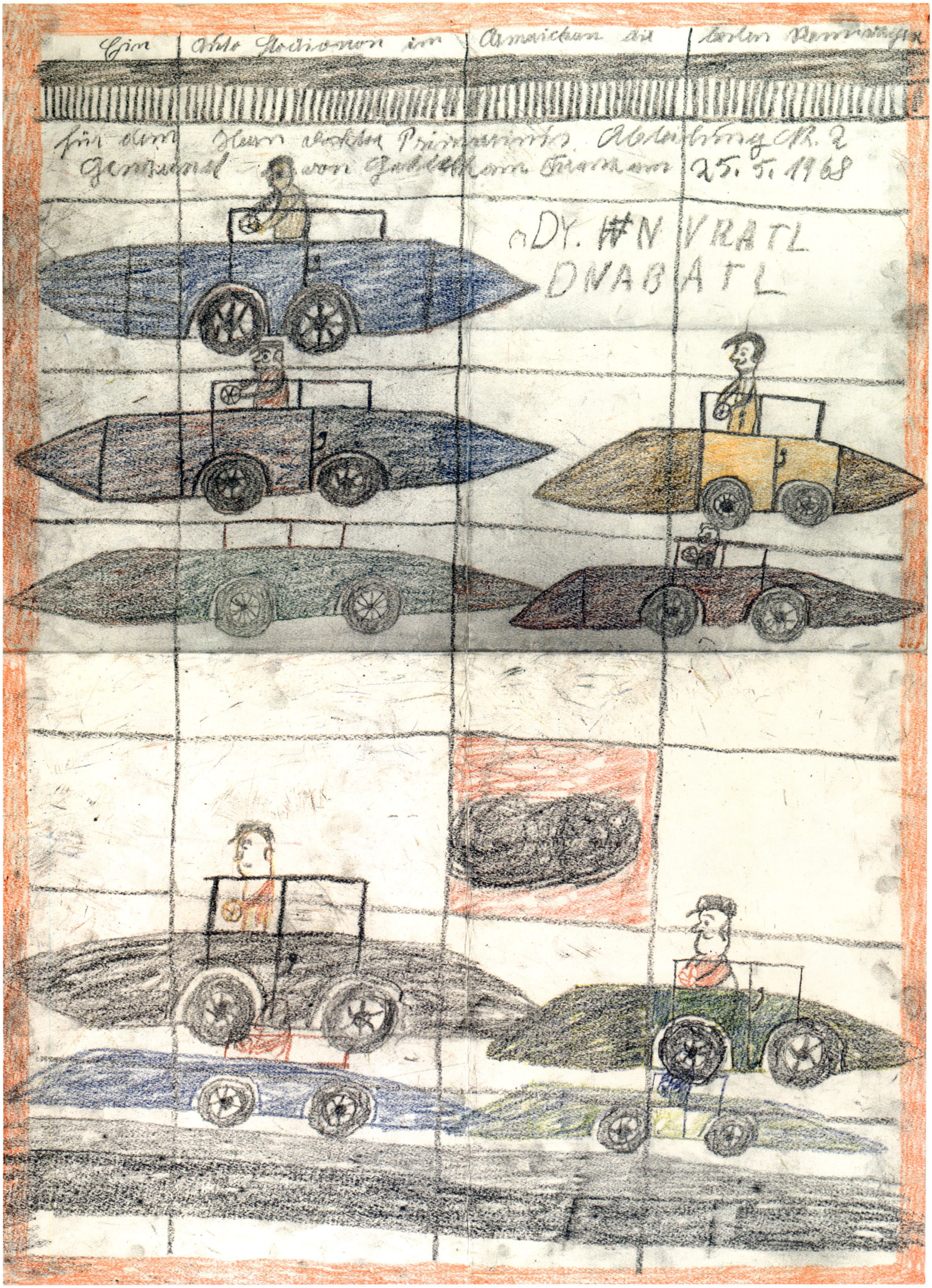
25. 5. 1968
DY. #N VRATL
DNABATL

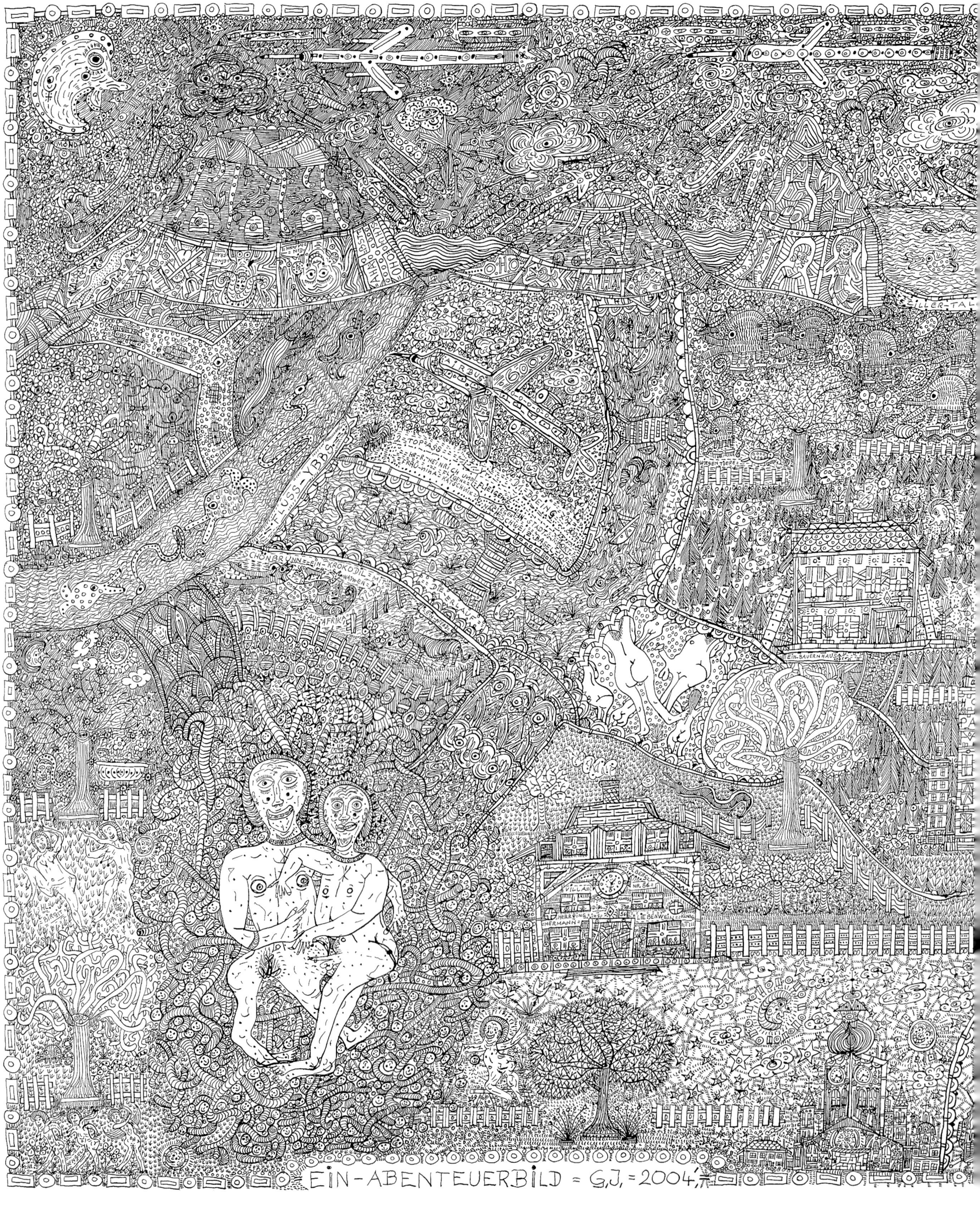
MOND
FLUSS-YBBS
AIRBUS
EIN-BAUERNHAUS
AUS-AFRIKA
EIN-ABENTEUERBILD = G.J, =2004,-

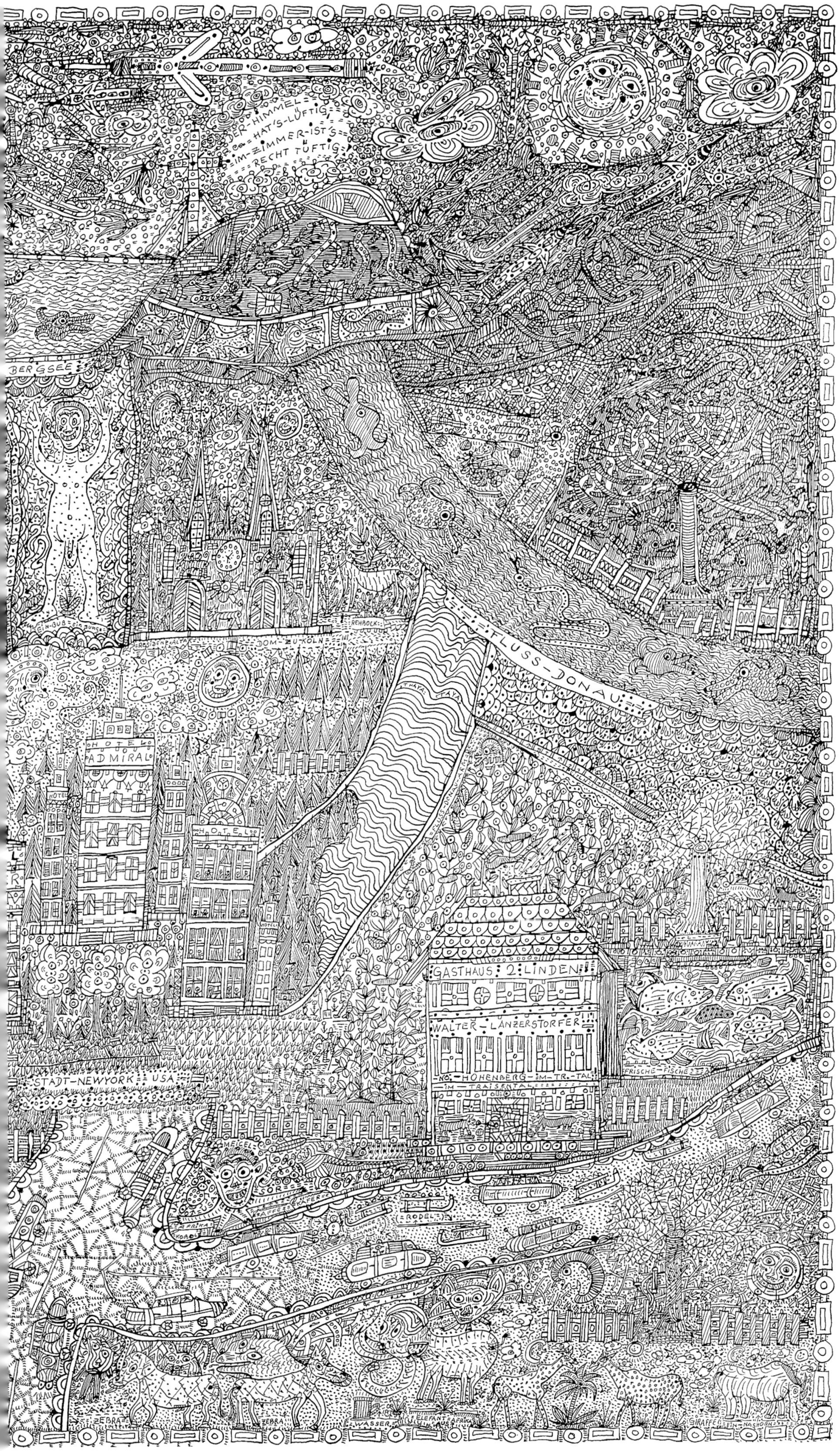

Johann Garber
Ein Abenteuerbild / Adventure Picture
2006, 72,9 x 101,7 cm
Tusche / Indian ink

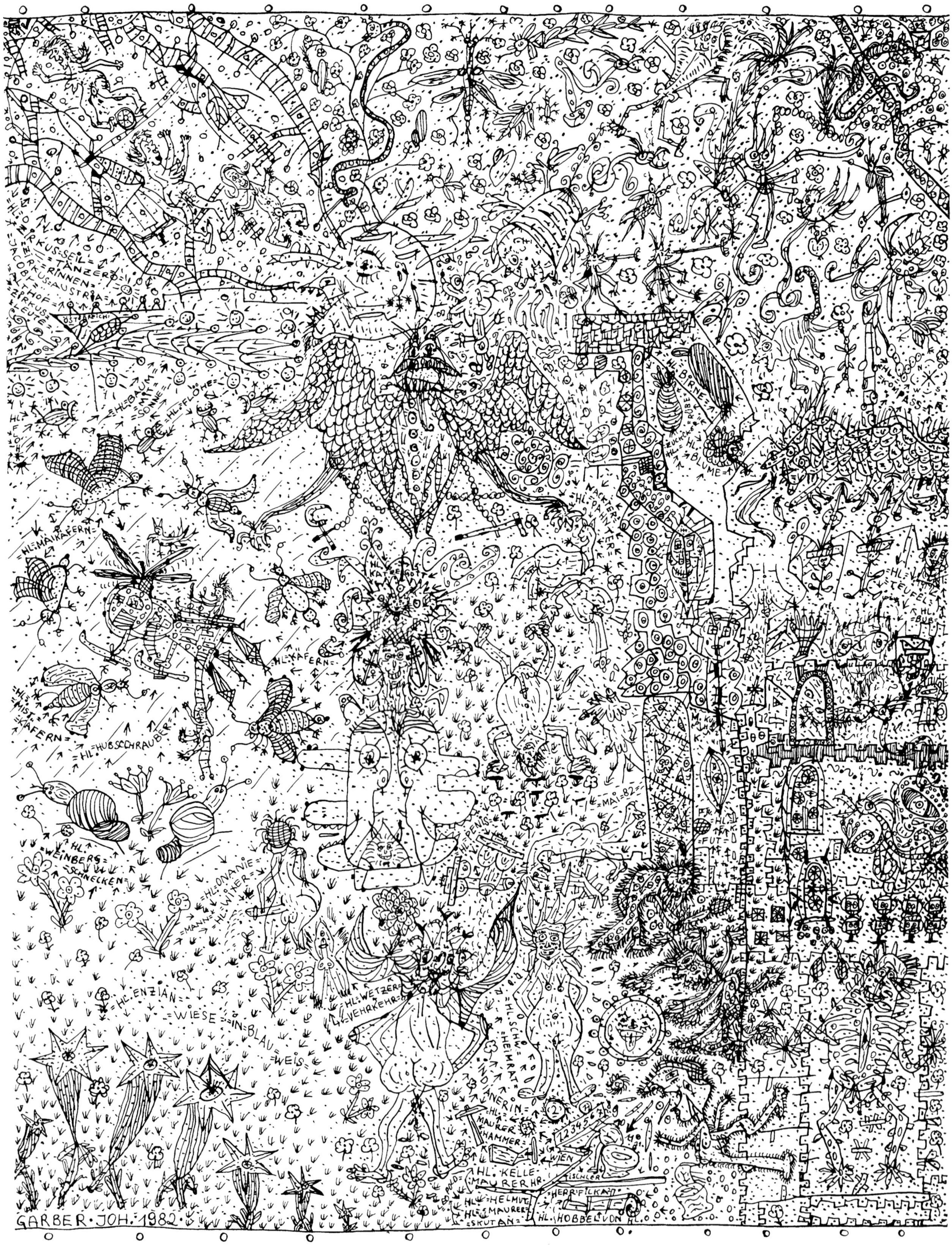
ZIRKUS-SEIL-TÄNZER
ZIRKUS AUSTRIA
HL: BAUM
SONNE
HL: FLÖHE
HL: MAIKÄFERN
HL: KÄFERN
HL: HUBSCHRAUBER
HL: MIST-KÄFERN
HL: WEINBERG-SCHNECKEN
HL: ONANIE
HL: WIXER
MANN
HL: ENZIAN
WIESE IN BLAU WEIS
HL: WETZER VERKEHR
HL: PENIS
MAI 82
HL: FUT
HL: BIRNE
HL: BLUME
KOMPASS
HL: TEUFEL
HL: BUB
HL: MAURER HAMMER
HL: KELLE MAURER HR.
WIEN
TISCHLER
HERR FILKA
HL: HELMUT
HL: MAURER SKUTAN
HL: HOBBEL VON HL.
GARBER·JOH. 1982

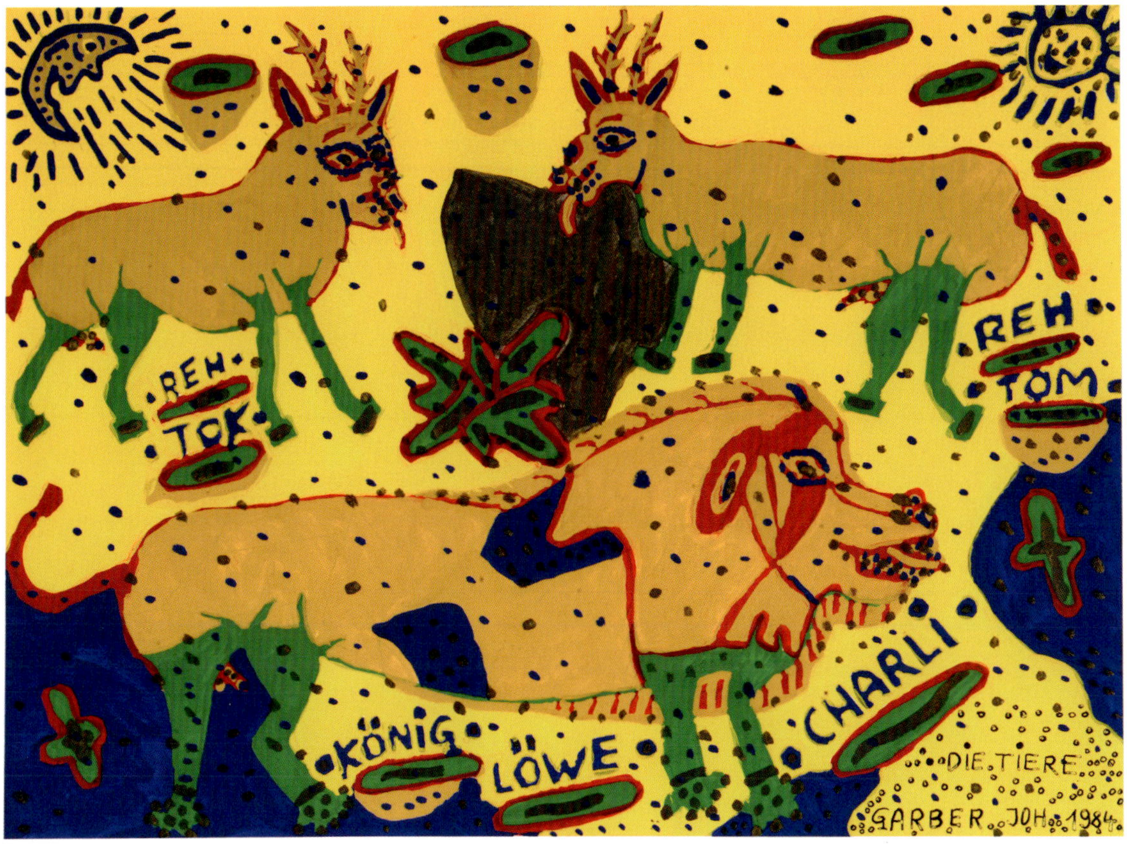

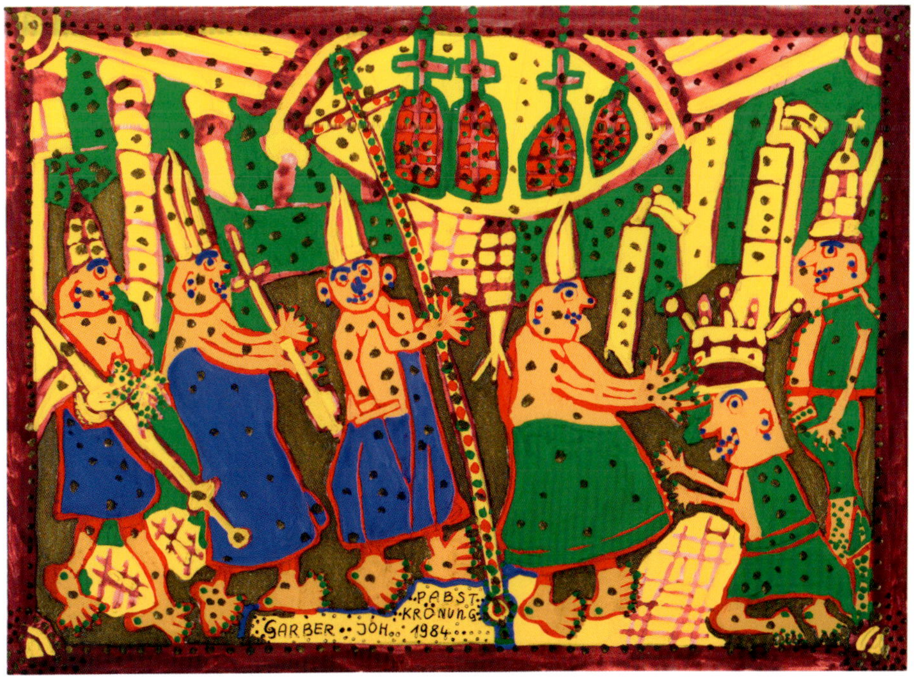

Johann Garber
Die Heiligen /
The Saints
1982, 30 x 40 cm
Tusche / Indian ink
Privatsammlung

Johann Garber
Die Tiere / The Animals
1984, 30 x 40 cm
Tusche, Deckfarben /
Indian ink, tempera
Privatsammlung

Johann Garber
Pabstkrönung /
Papal Coronation
1984, 30 x 40 cm
Tusche, Deckfarben /
Indian ink, tempera
Privatsammlung

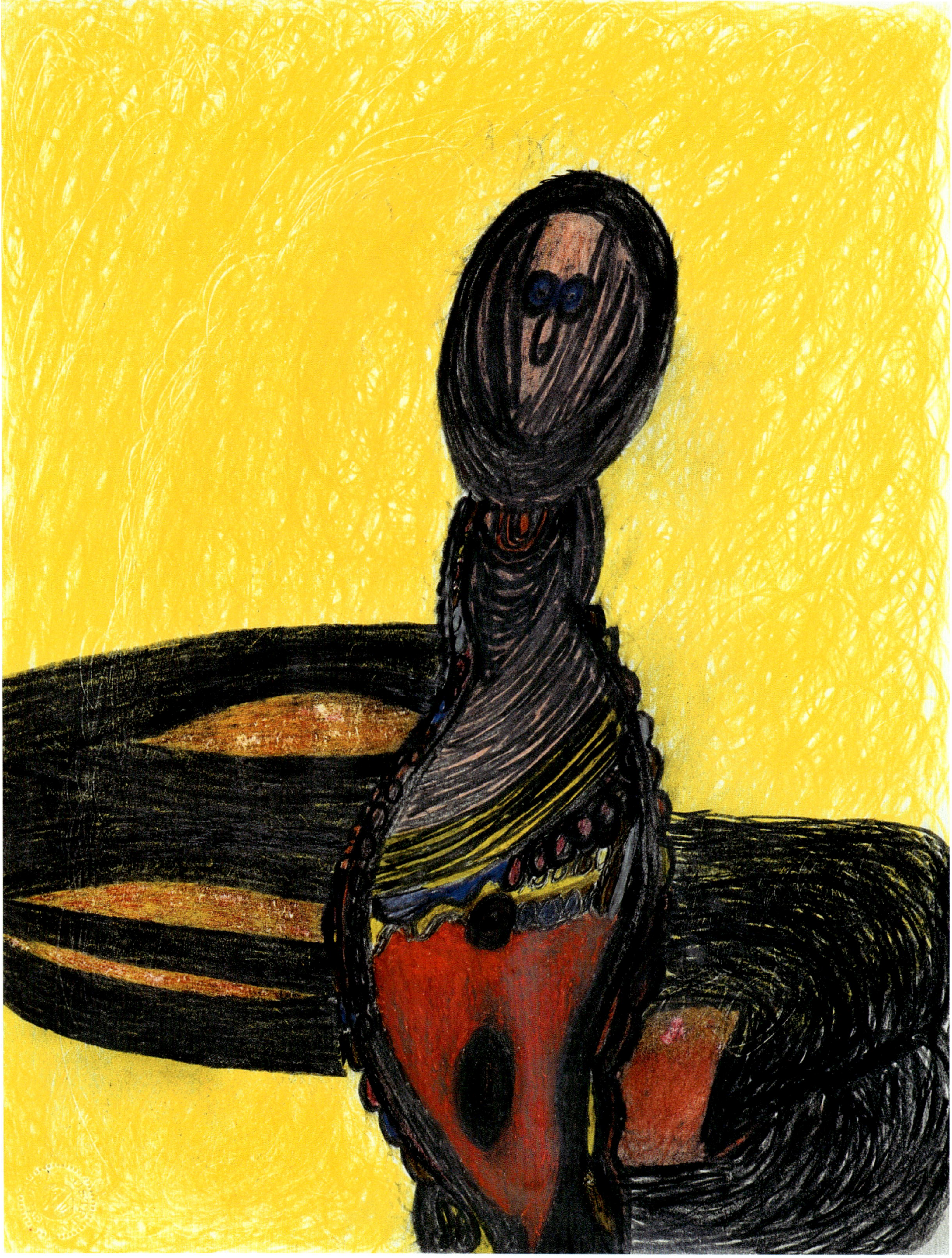

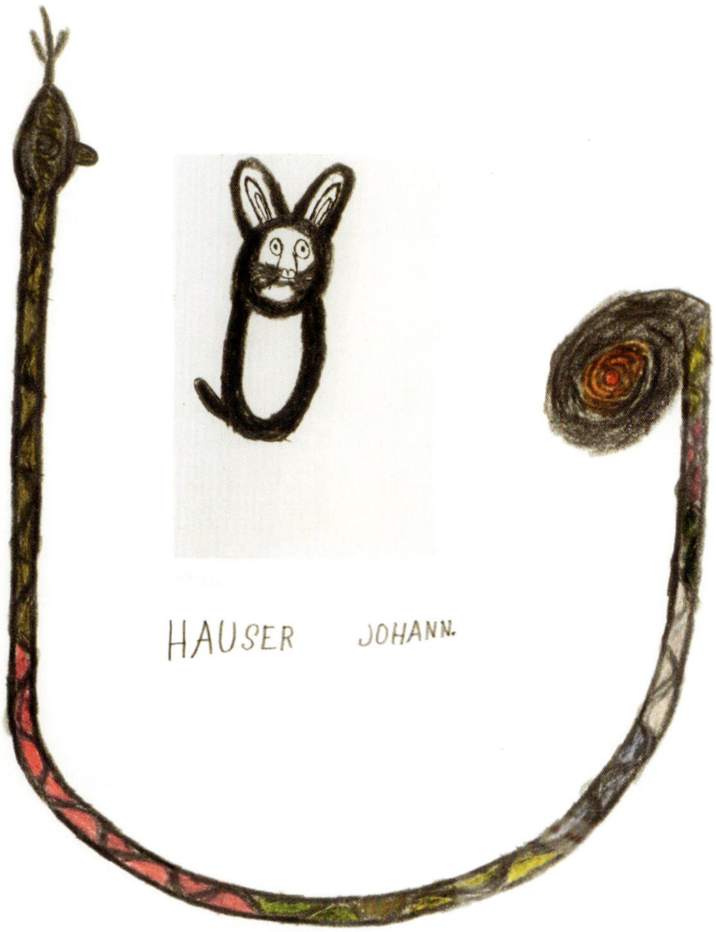

Johann Hauser
Frau auf gelbem Grund / Woman on Yellow Background
1986, 40 x 30 cm
Bleistift, Farbstifte / pencil, color pencils
Privatsammlung

Johann Hauser
Schlange auf Radierung *Hase* / Snake on Etching *Bunny*
1970, 40 x 30 cm
Bleistift, Farbstifte auf Ätzradierung / pencil, color pencils on etching
Sammlung Helmut Zambo

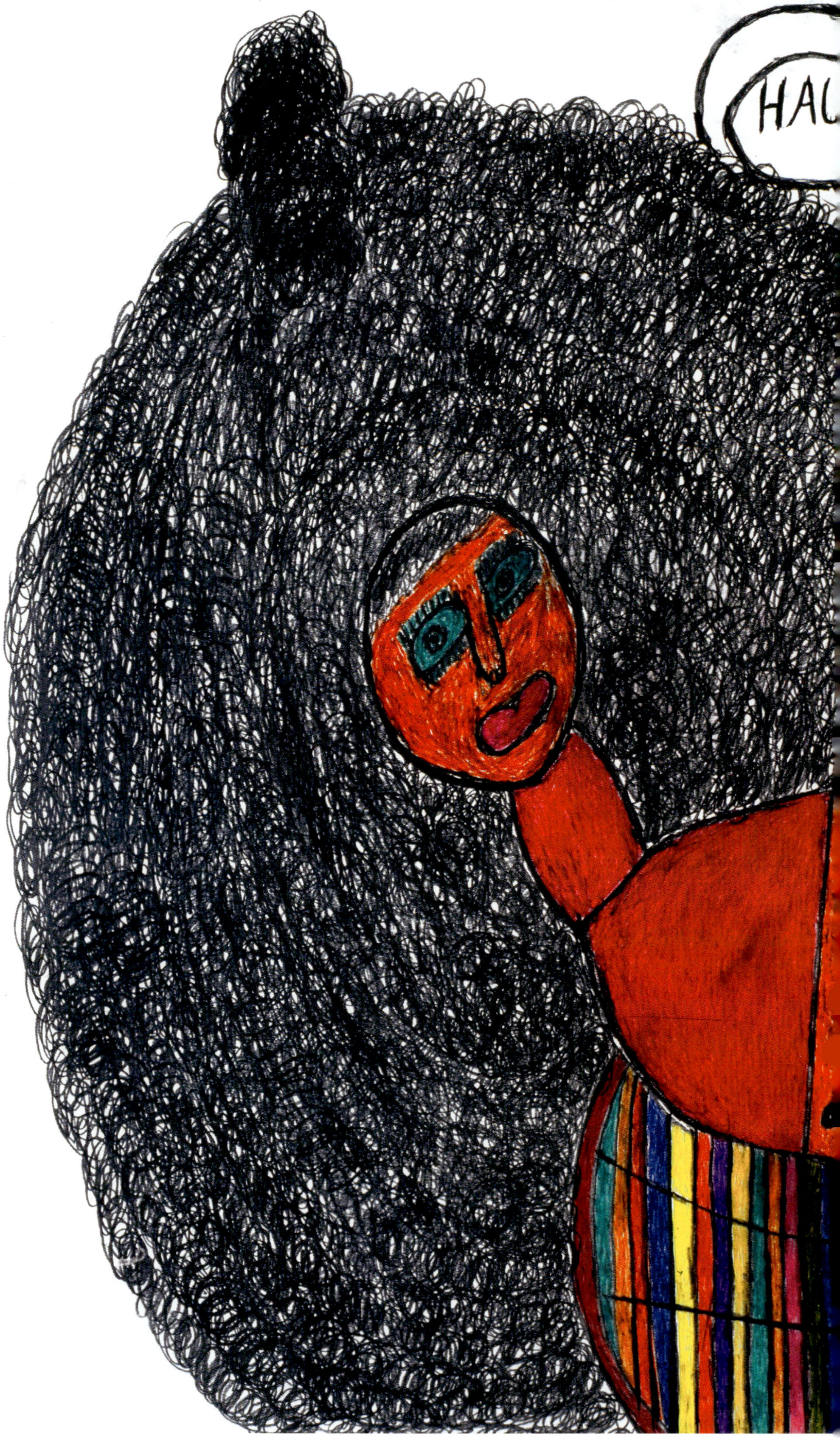

Johann Hauser
Liegende Frau /
Lying Woman
1994, 62,4 x 86 cm
Bleistift, Farbstifte /
pencil, color pencils
Sammlung Helmut Zambo

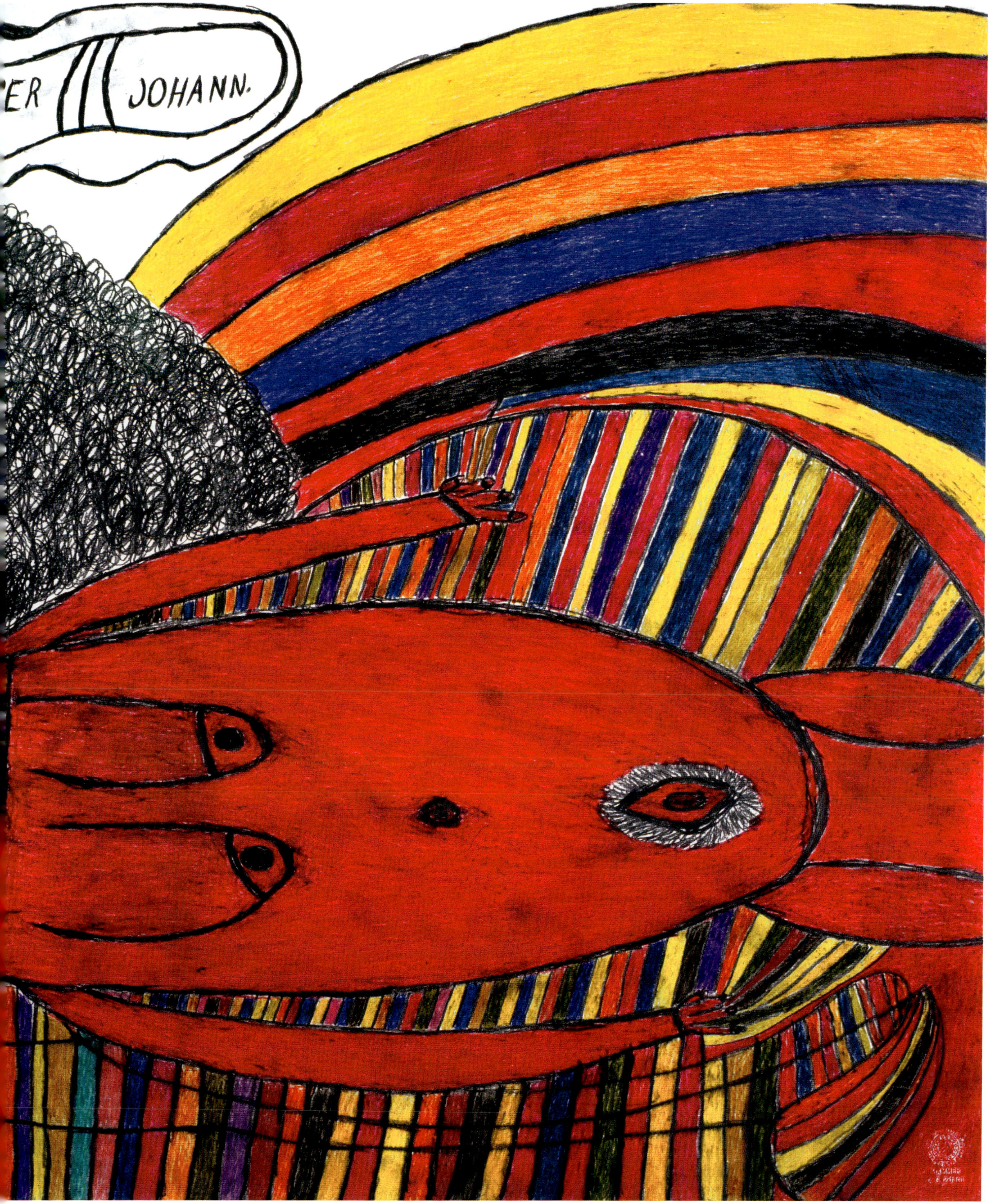
ER JOHANN.

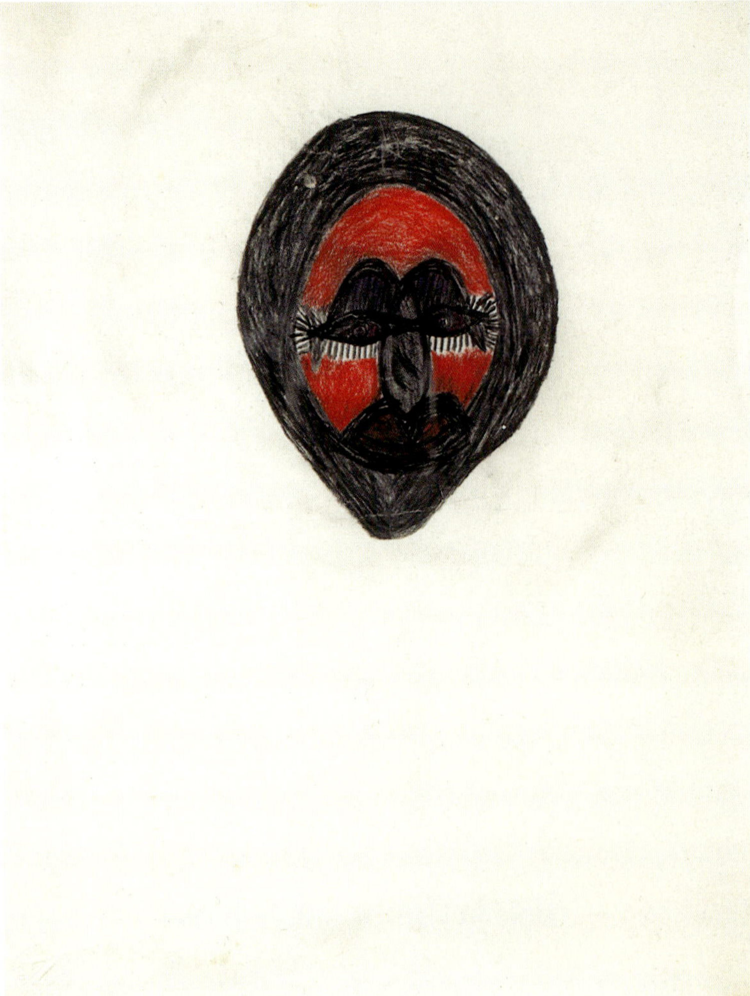

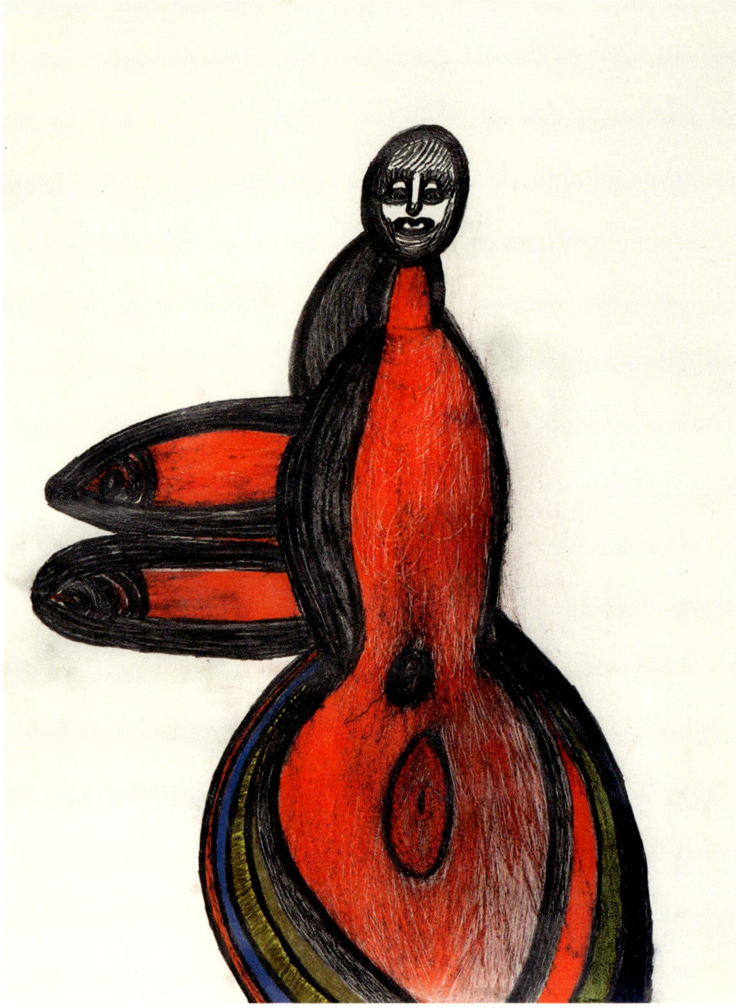

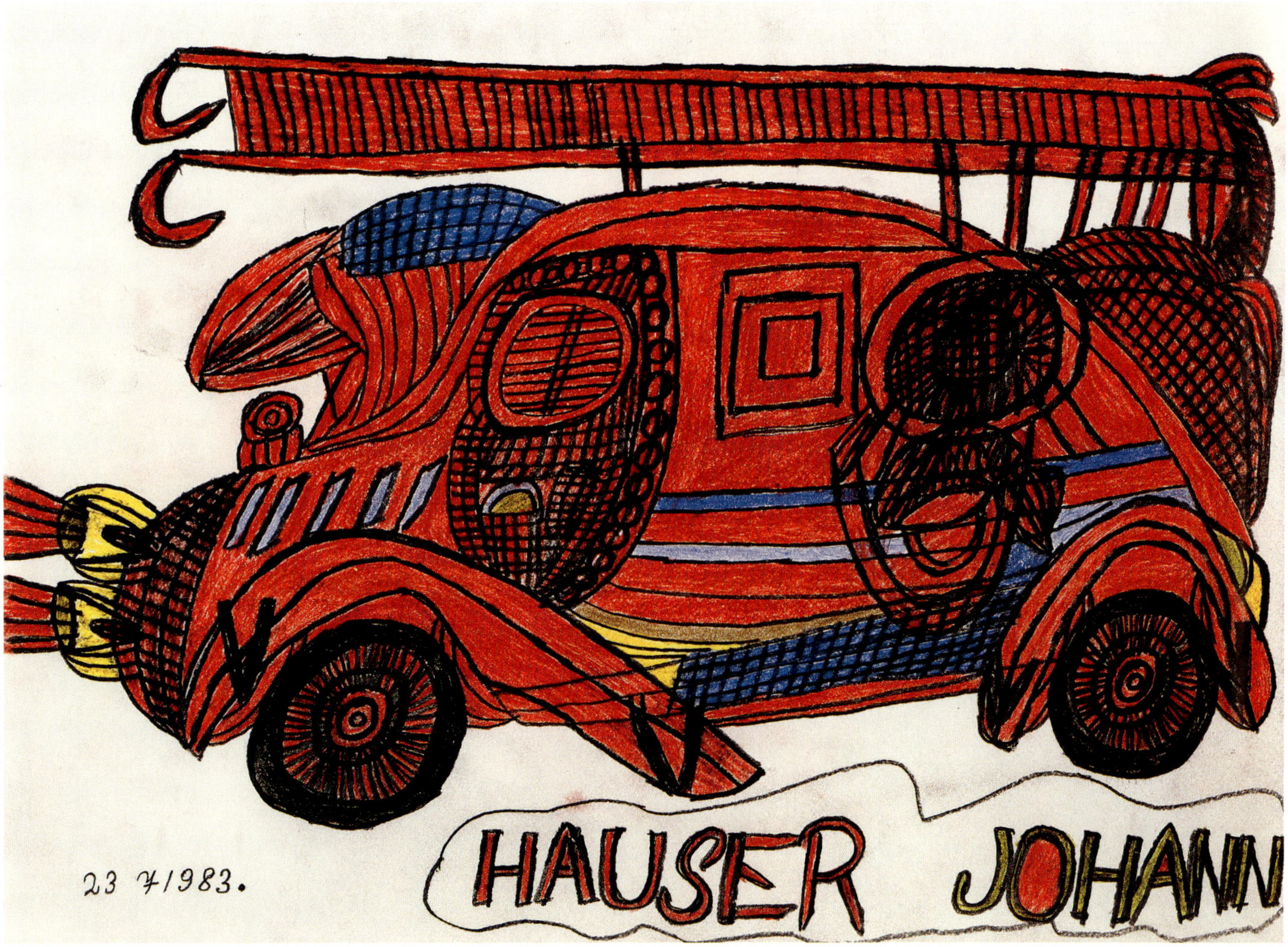

Johann Hauser
Kopf / Head
1969, 40 x 30 cm
Bleistift, Farbstifte /
pencil, color pencils
Sammlung Helmut Zambo

Johann Hauser
Roter Frauenakt /
Red Woman Nude
1985, 62 x 44 cm
Bleistift, Farbstifte /
pencil, color pencils
Privatsammlung

Johann Hauser
Feuerwehrauto /
Fire Engine
1983, 30 x 40 cm
Bleistift, Farbstifte /
pencil, color pencils
Sammlung Helmut Zambo

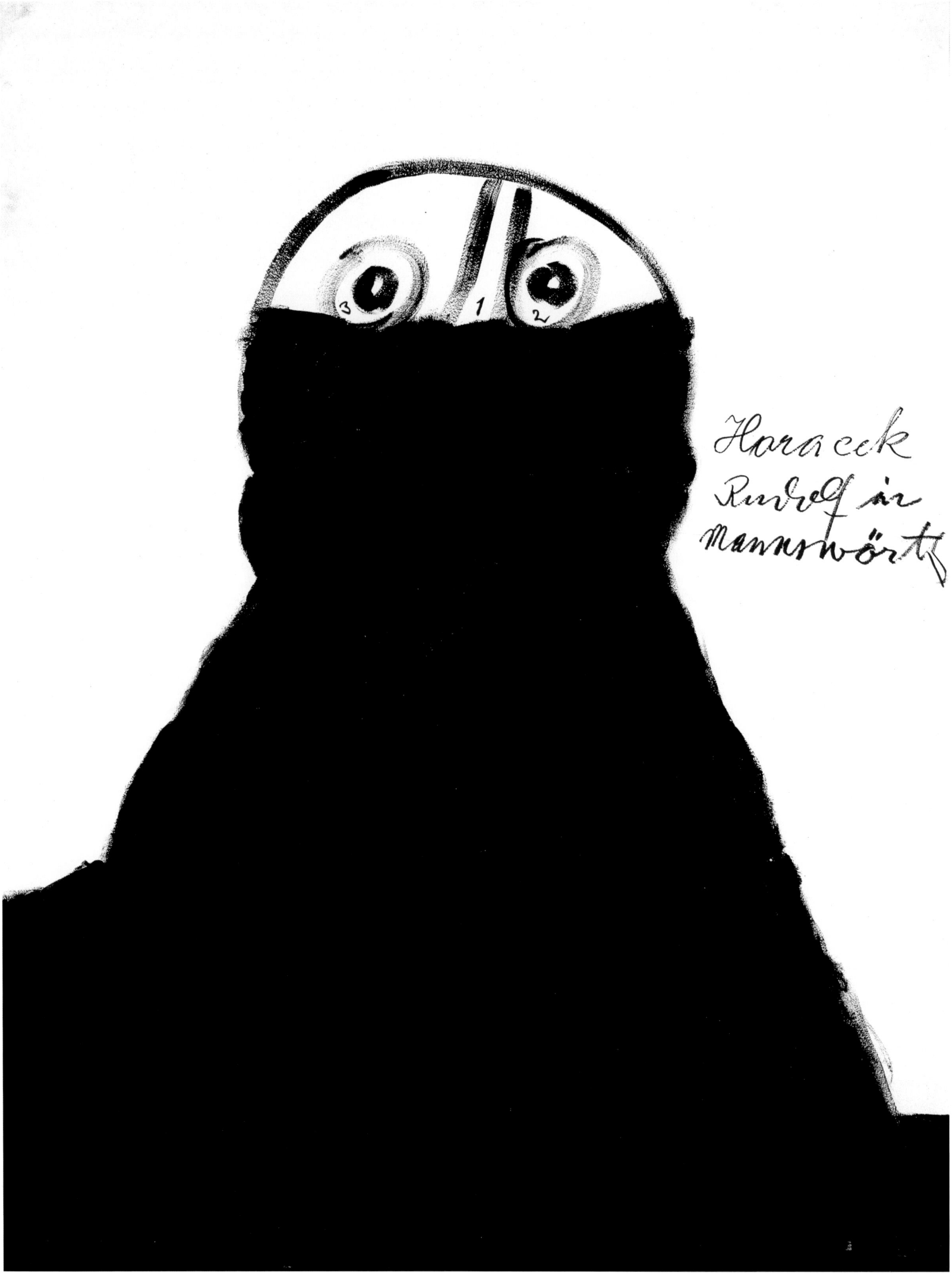
Haraeck
Rudolf in
Mannswörth
3
1
2

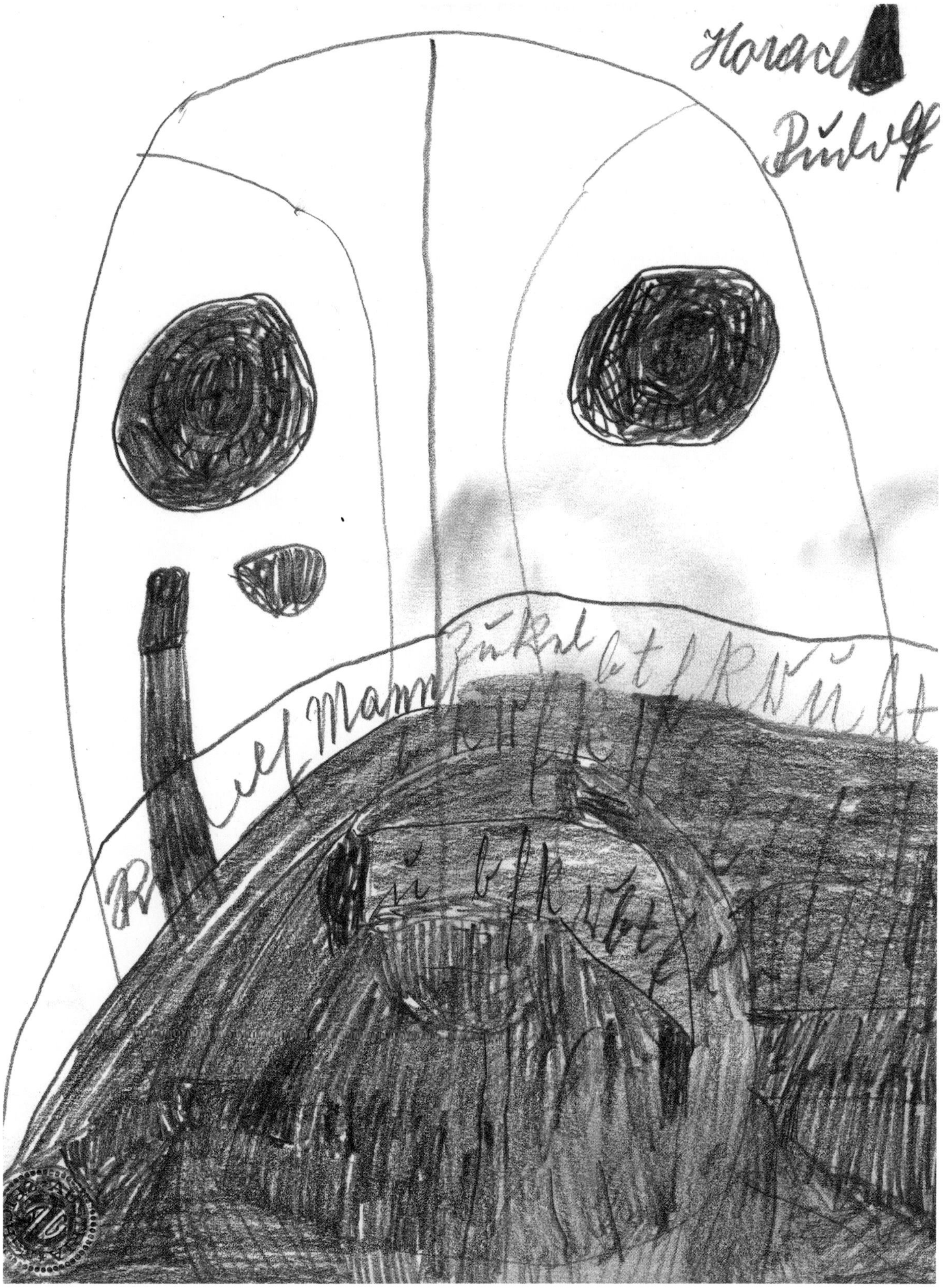

Rudolf Horacek
Horacek Rudolf in Mannswörth /
Horacek Rudolf in Mannswörth
1984, 186,8 x 140,5 cm
Acryl auf Holz /
Acryl on wood
Privatsammlung

Rudolf Horacek
Kopf / Head
Undatiert / undated
30 x 21,9 cm
Bleistift / pencil
Privatsammlung

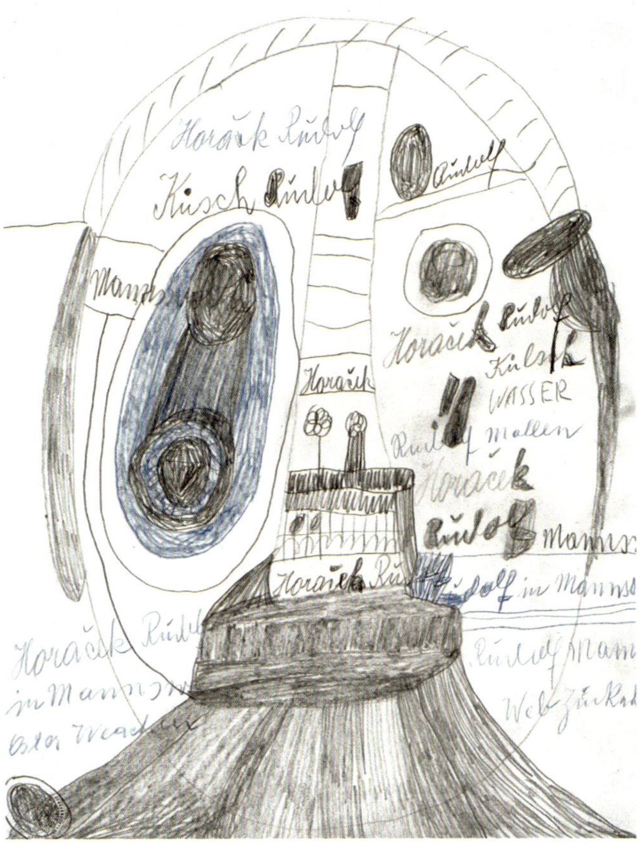
WASSER

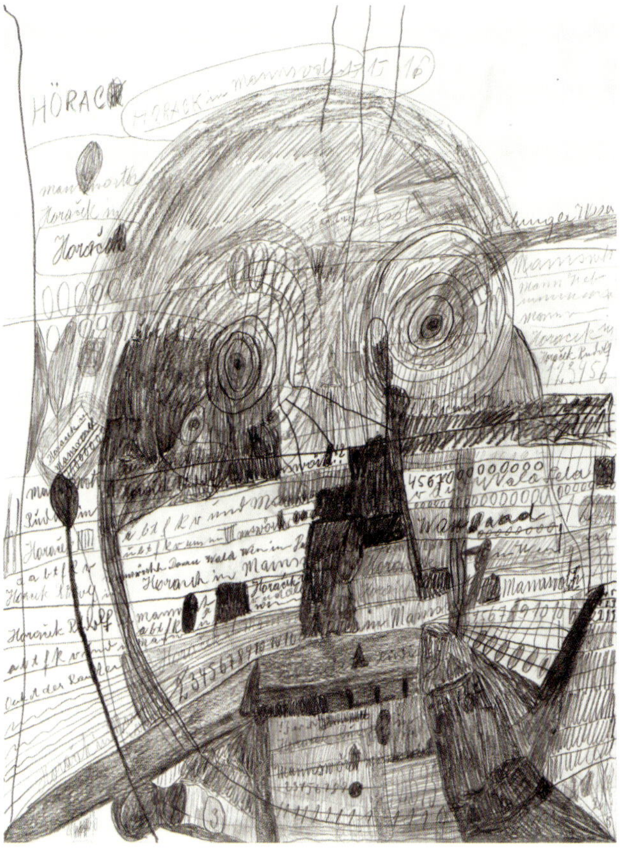
HÖRAC

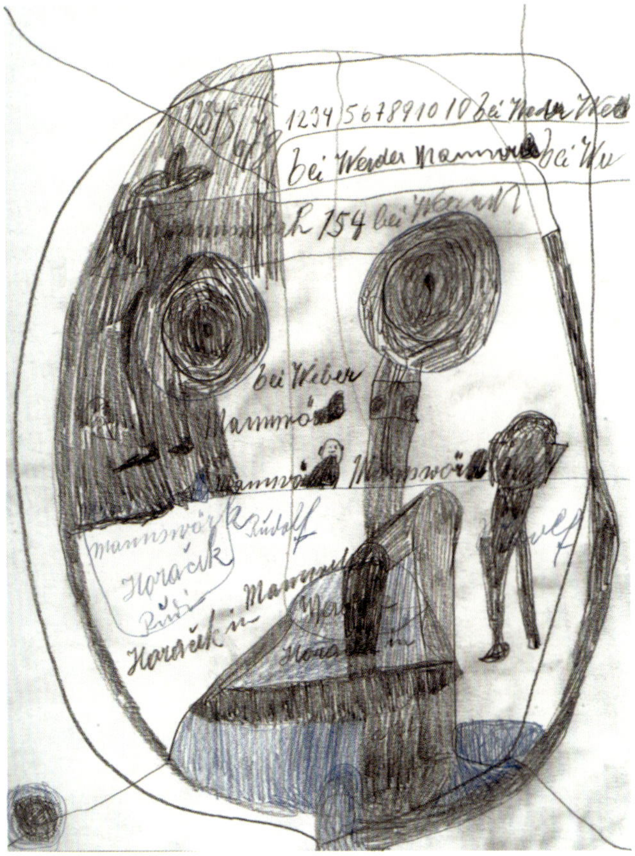
1 2 3 4 5 6 7 8 9 10
bei Weber

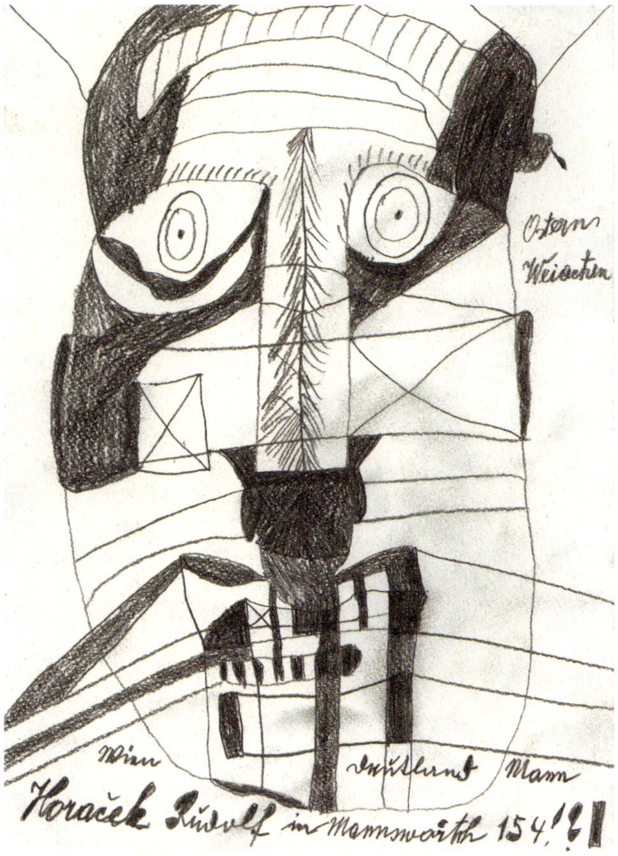
Ostern
Weiachten
Horaček Rudolf in Mannswörth 154!

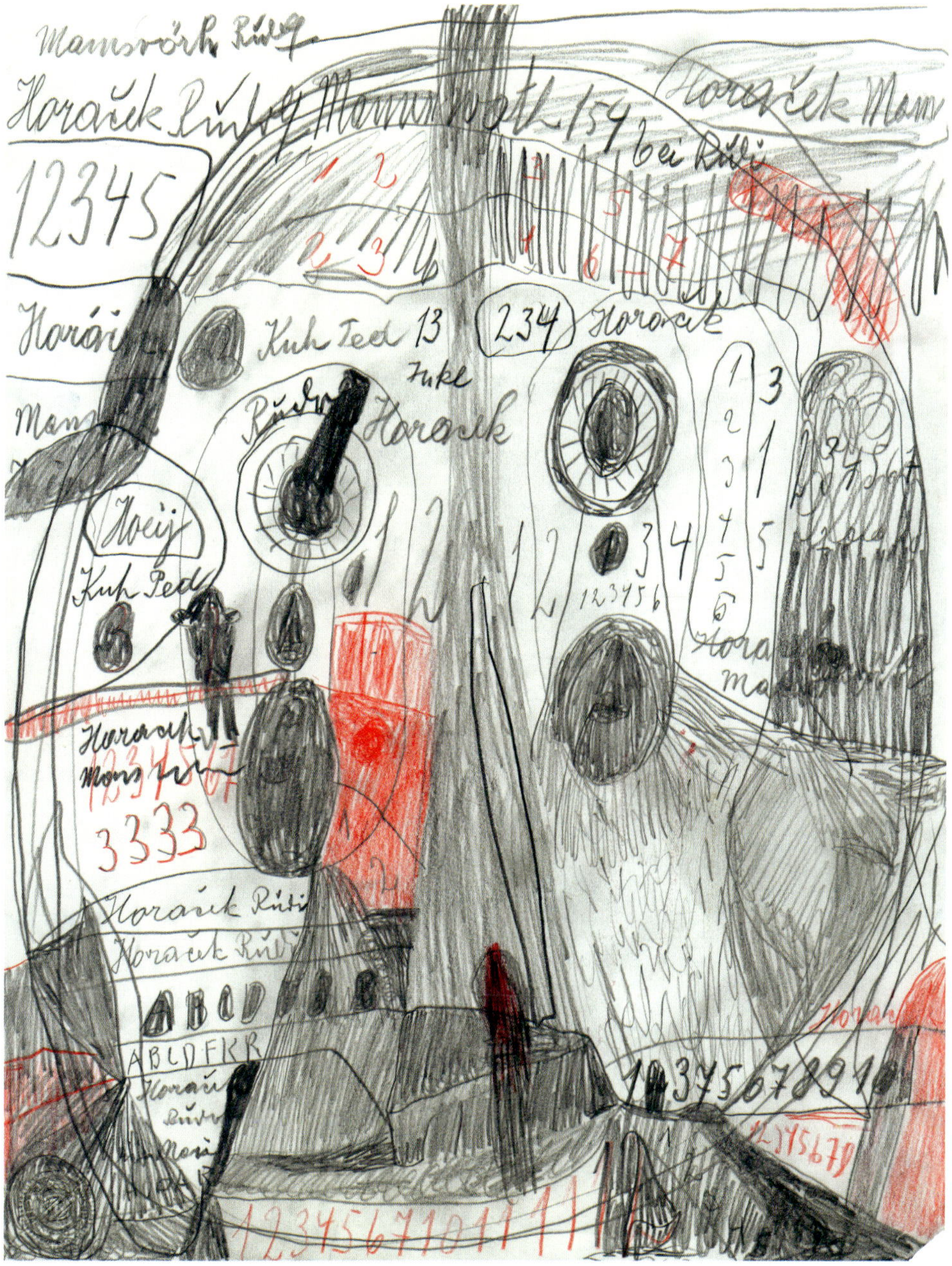

Rudolf Horacek
Kopf / Head
Undatiert / undated
40 x 30 cm
Bleistift, Farbstifte / pencil, color pencils
Privatsammlung

Rudolf Horacek
Kopf / Head
Undatiert / undated
69,3 x 49,7 cm
Bleistift / pencil
Privatsammlung

Rudolf Horacek
Kopf / Head
Undatiert / undated
40 x 30 cm
Bleistift, Farbstifte / pencil, color pencils
Privatsammlung

Rudolf Horacek
Ostern Weiachten / Eastern Chrismas
1979, 29,9 x 21 cm
Bleistift / pencil
Privatsammlung

Rudolf Horacek
Kopf / Head
Undatiert / undated
40 x 30 cm
Bleistift, Farbstift / pencil, color pencil
NÖ Landesmuseum
Sammlung Leo Navratil

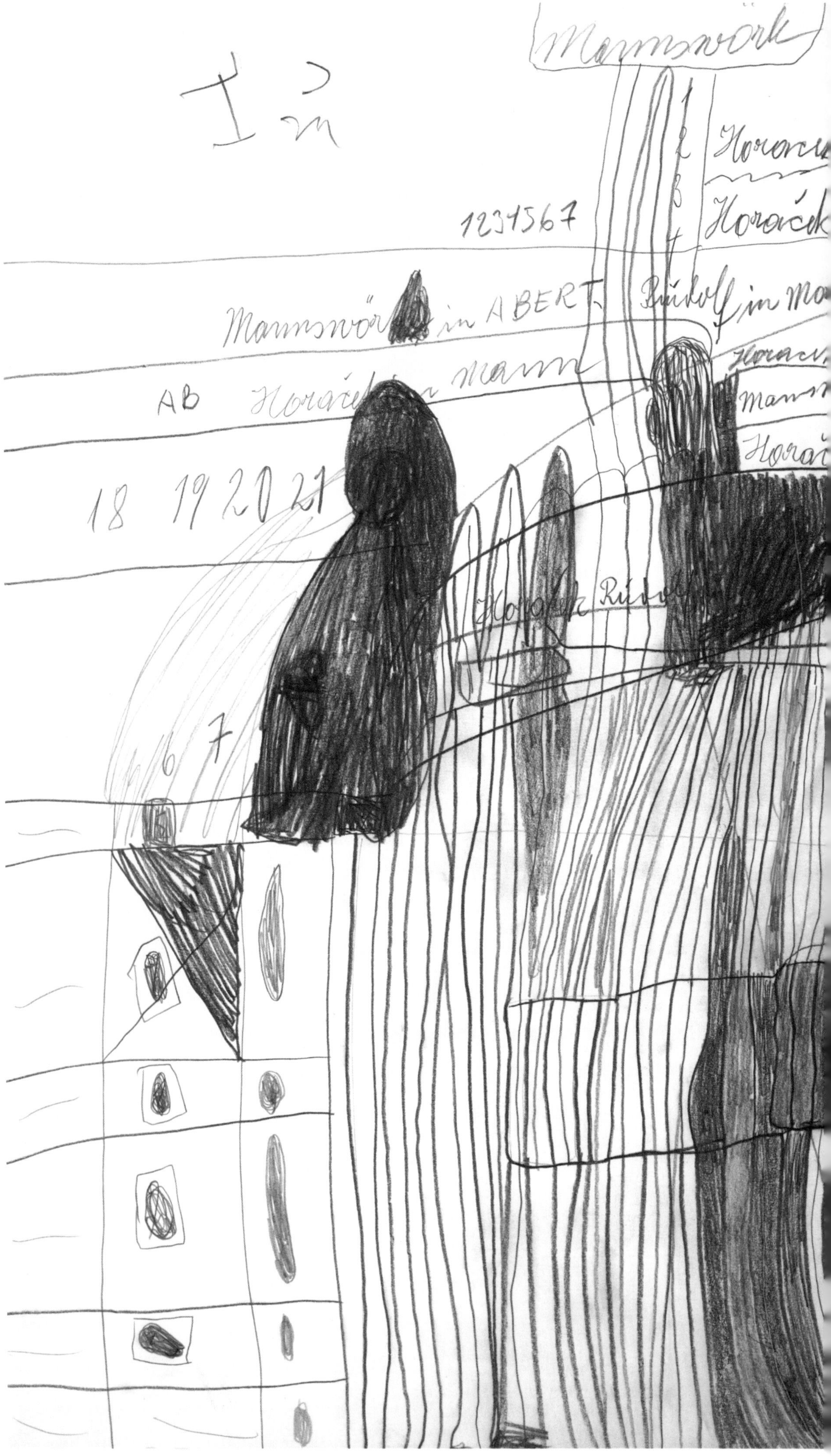

Rudolf Horacek
Ohne Titel / Untitled
Undatiert / undated
62,5 x 87,9 cm
Bleistift, Farbstifte /
pencil, color pencils
Privatsammlung

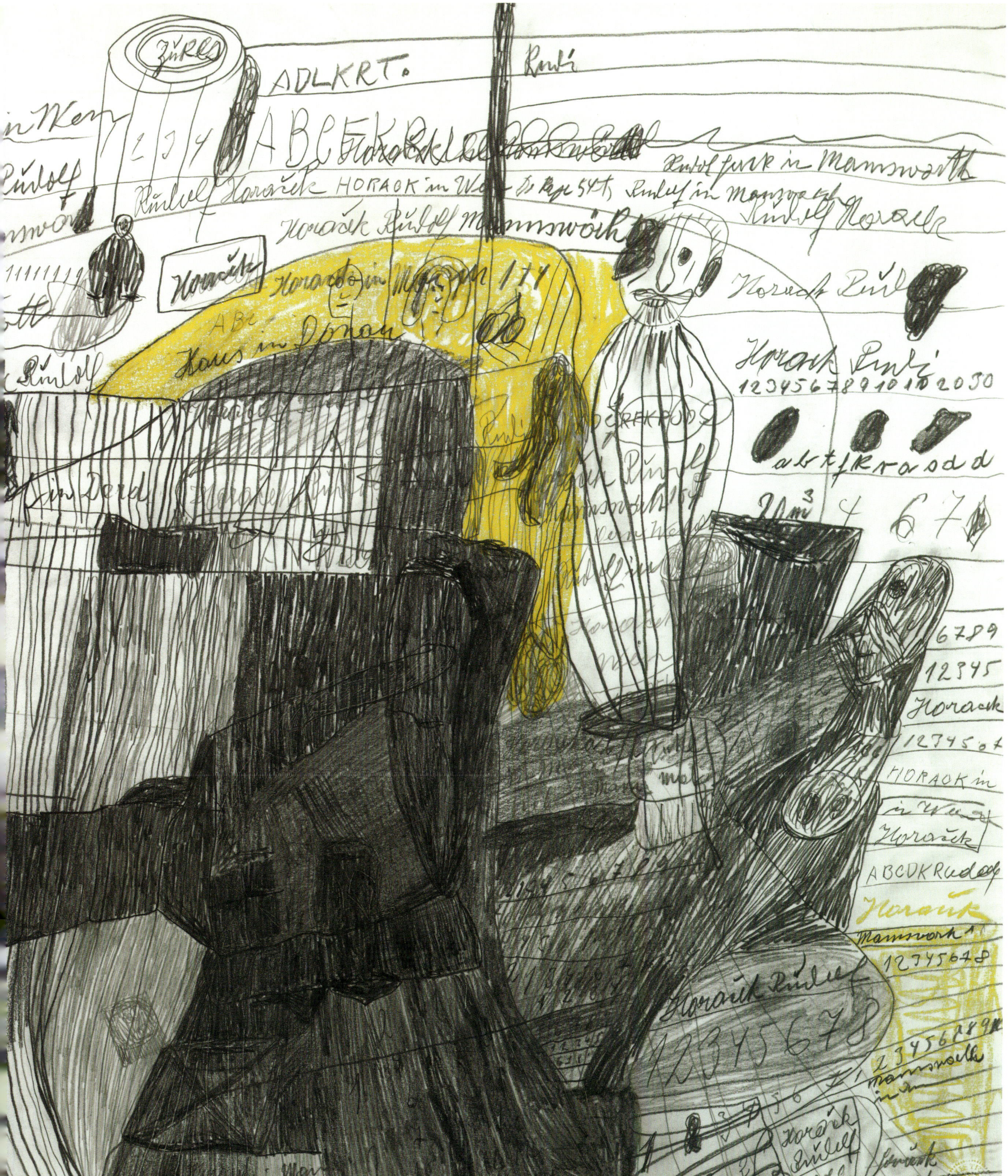
ADLKRT.
Rudolf Horaček HORAOK in
Horack Rudi
12345678910
abrfkrasdd
Haus in Donau
in Dorf
6789
12345
Horack
HORAOK in
Horaček
ABCDKRudolf
12345678
Horaček Rudolf
12345678

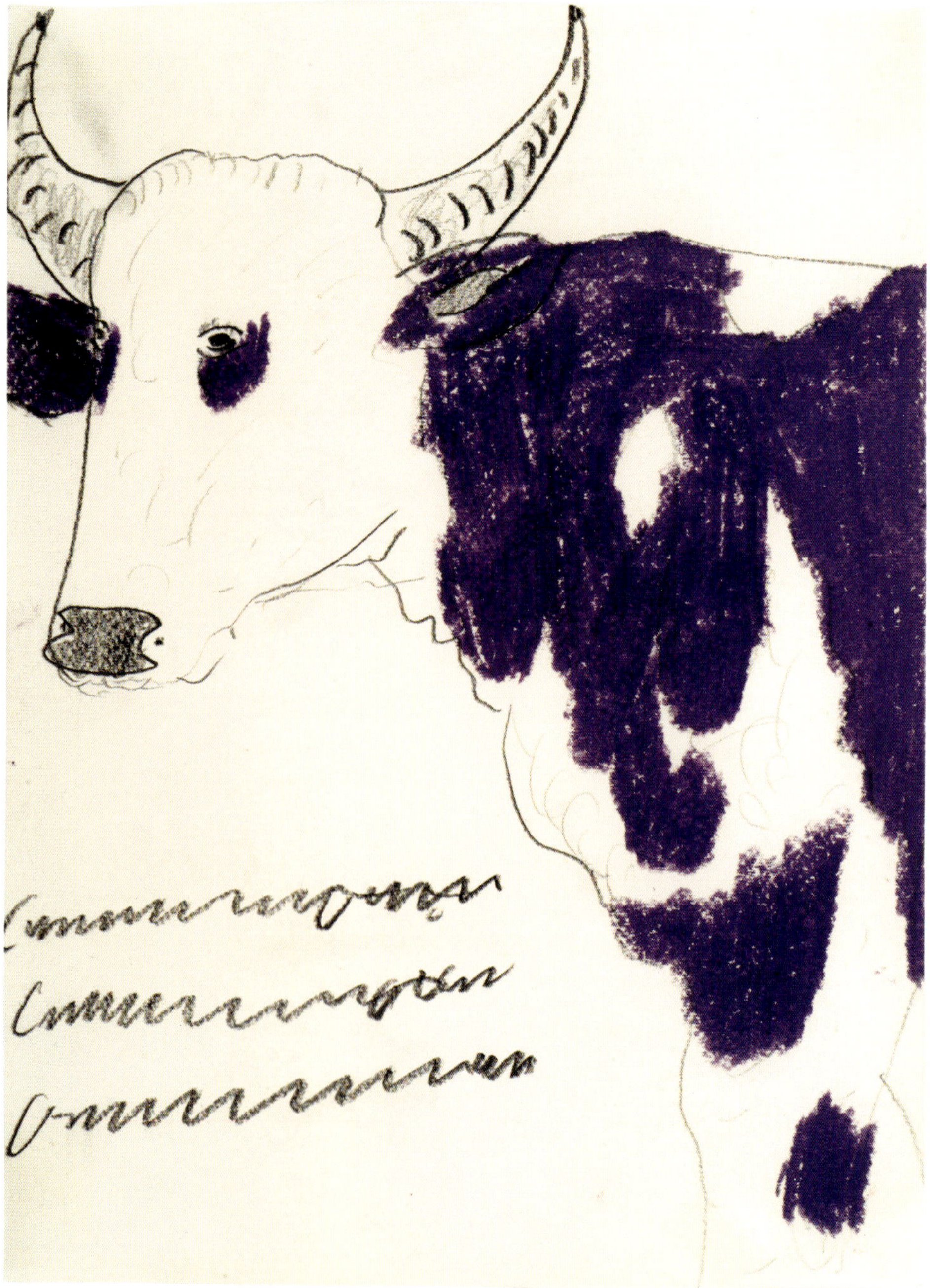

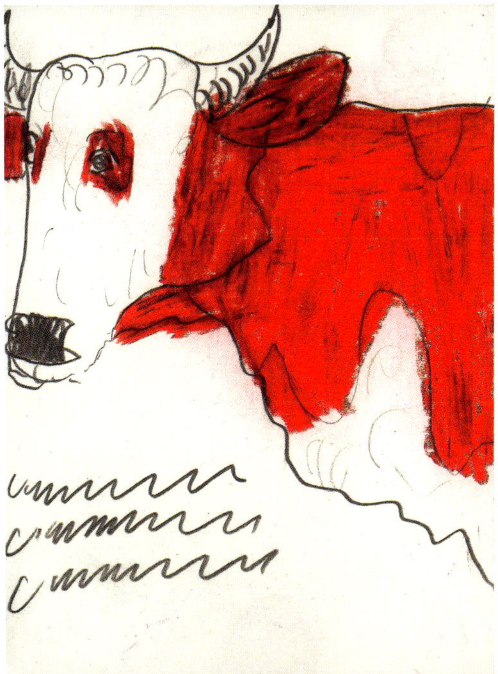

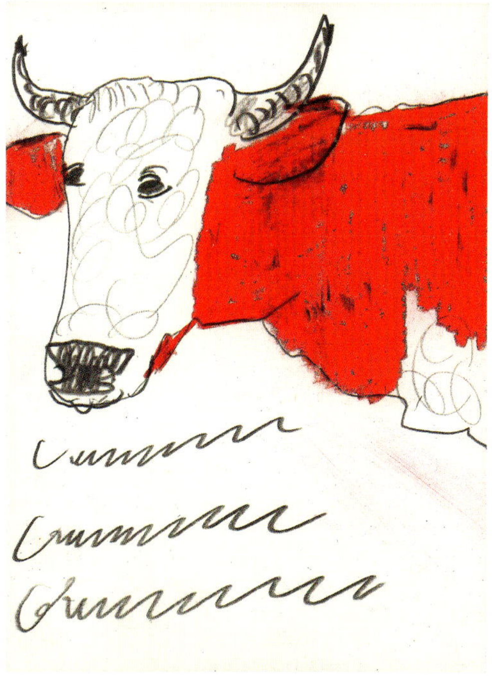

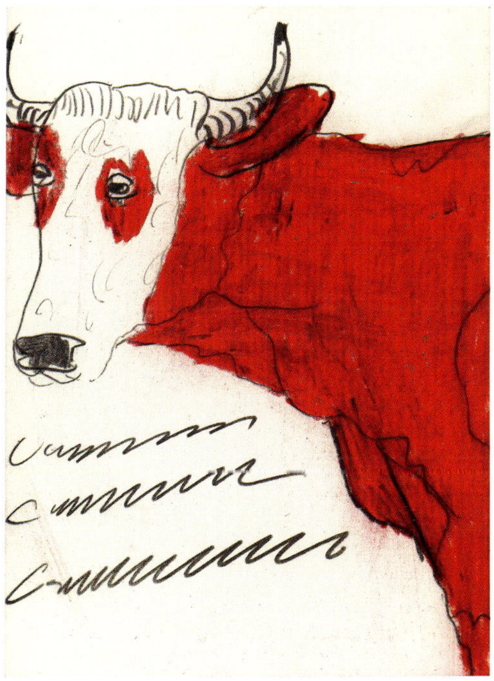

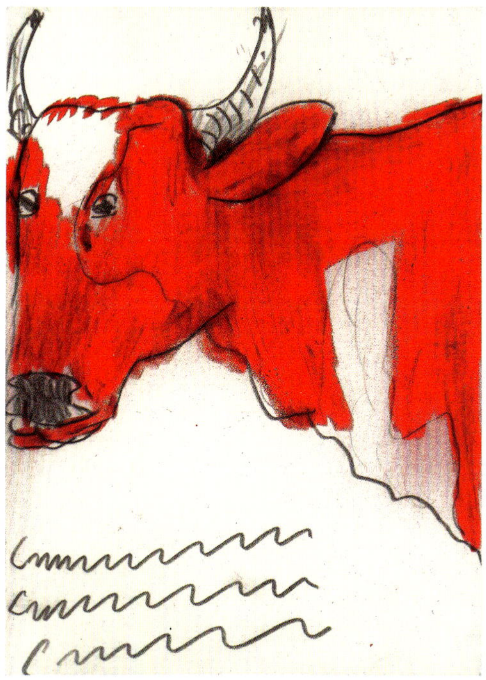

Franz Kamlander
Kuh / Cow
Undatiert / undated
30,2 x 21,5 cm
Bleistift, Wachskreide /
pencil, crayon
Sammlung Helmut Zambo

Franz Kamlander
Kuh / Cow
Undatiert / undated
14,8 x 10,5 cm
Bleistift, Farbstift /
pencil, crayon
Privatsammlung

Franz Kamlander
Kuh / Cow
Undatiert / undated
14,8 x10,5 cm
Bleistift, Farbstift /
pencil, color pencil
Privatsammlung

Franz Kamlander
Kuh / Cow
Undatiert / undated
14,8 x 10,5 cm
Bleistift, Farbstift /
pencil, color pencil
Privatsammlung

Franz Kamlander
Kuh / Cow
Undatiert / undated
14,8 x 10,5 cm
Bleistift, Farbstift /
pencil, color pencil
Privatsammlung

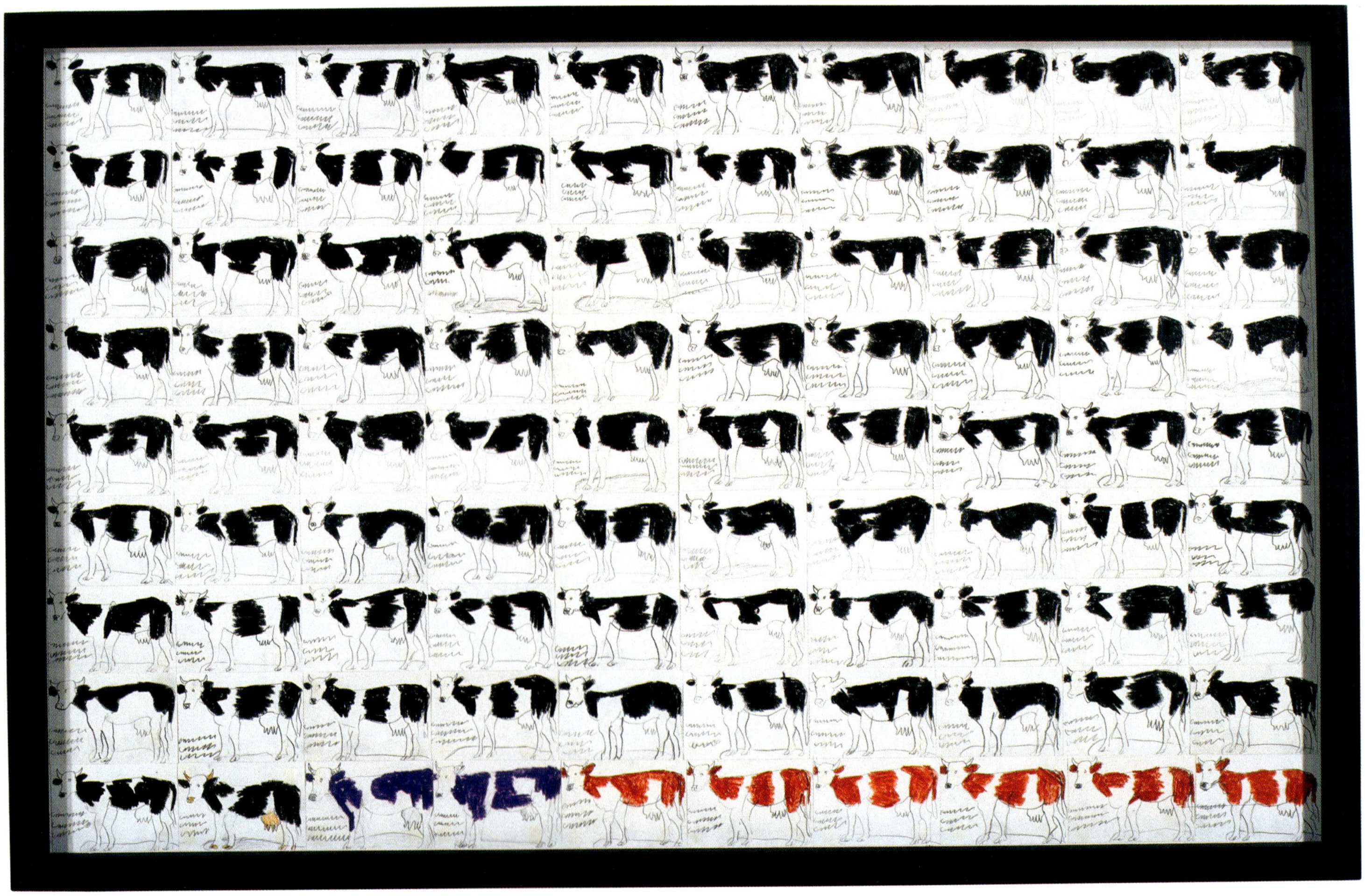

Franz Kalmander
90 Kühe / 90 Cows
1983, 10,5 x 14,5 cm
Bleistift, Wachskreide /
pencil, crayon
Sammlung Helmut Zambo

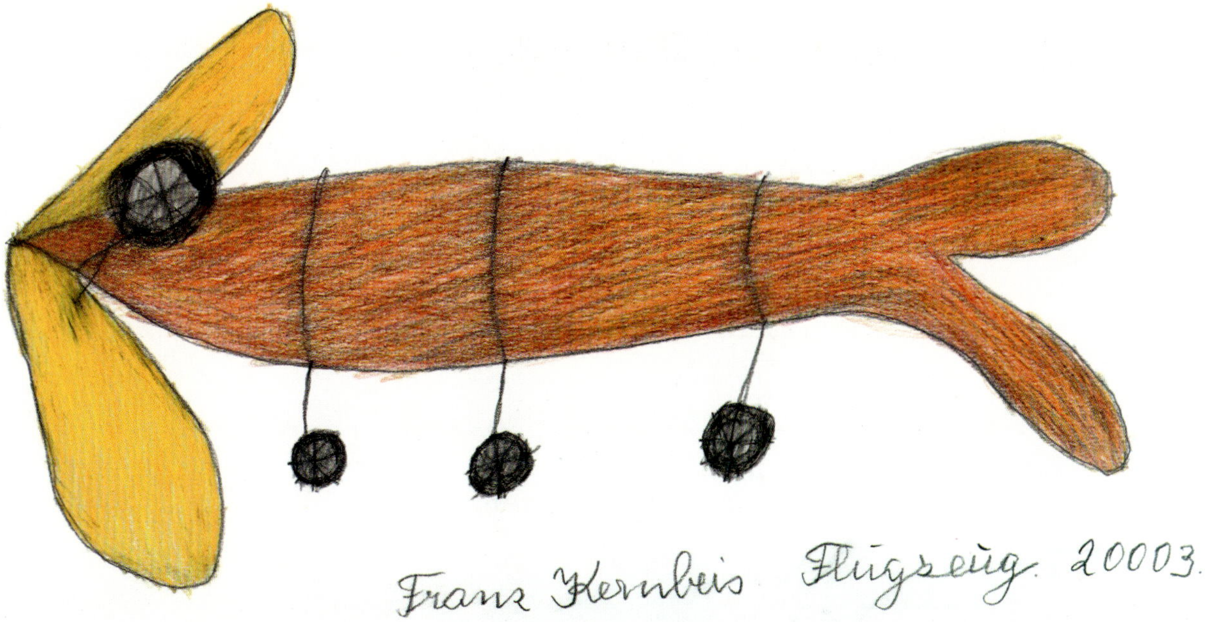

Franz Kernbeis
Flugzeug / Airplane
2003, 22,8 x 45,8 cm
Bleistift, Farbstifte /
pencil, color pencils

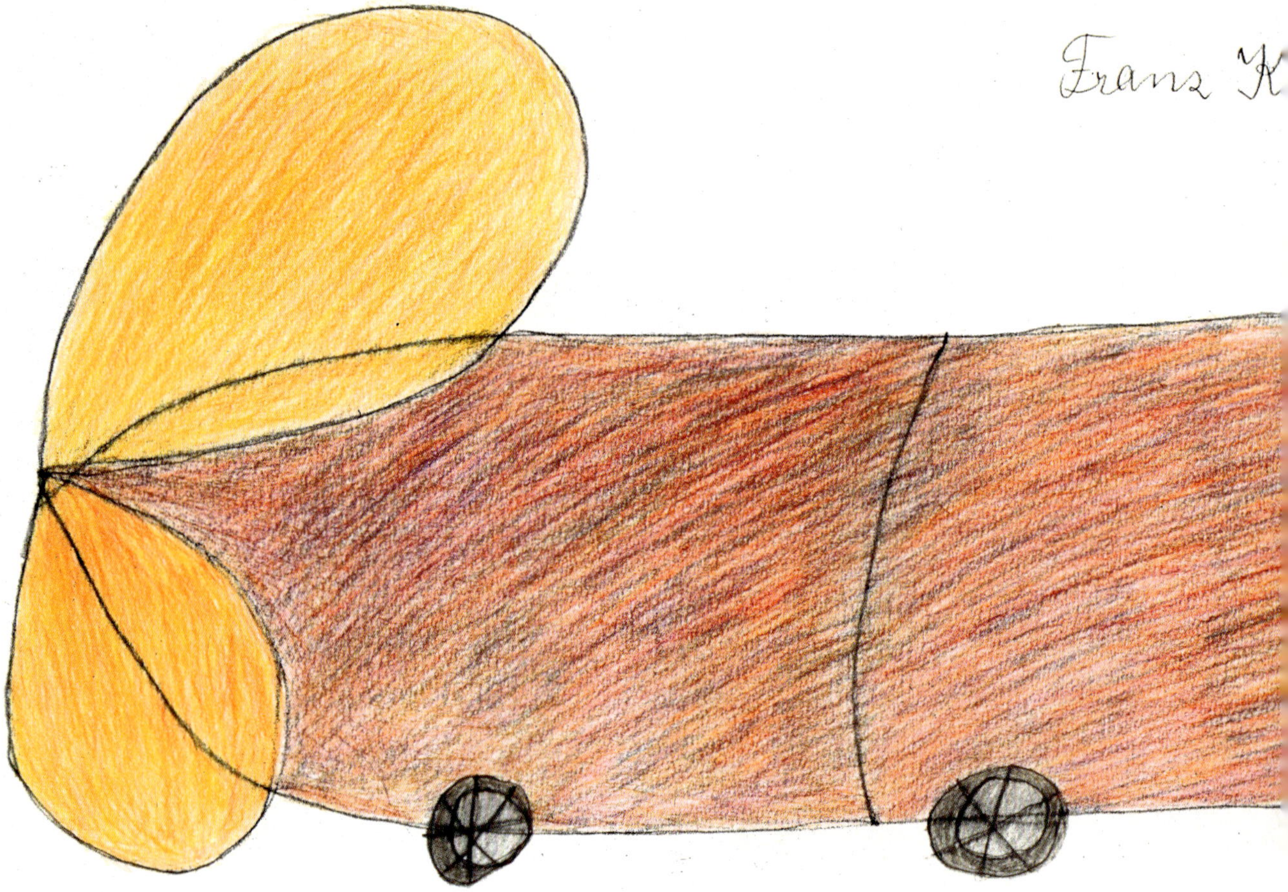
Franz K

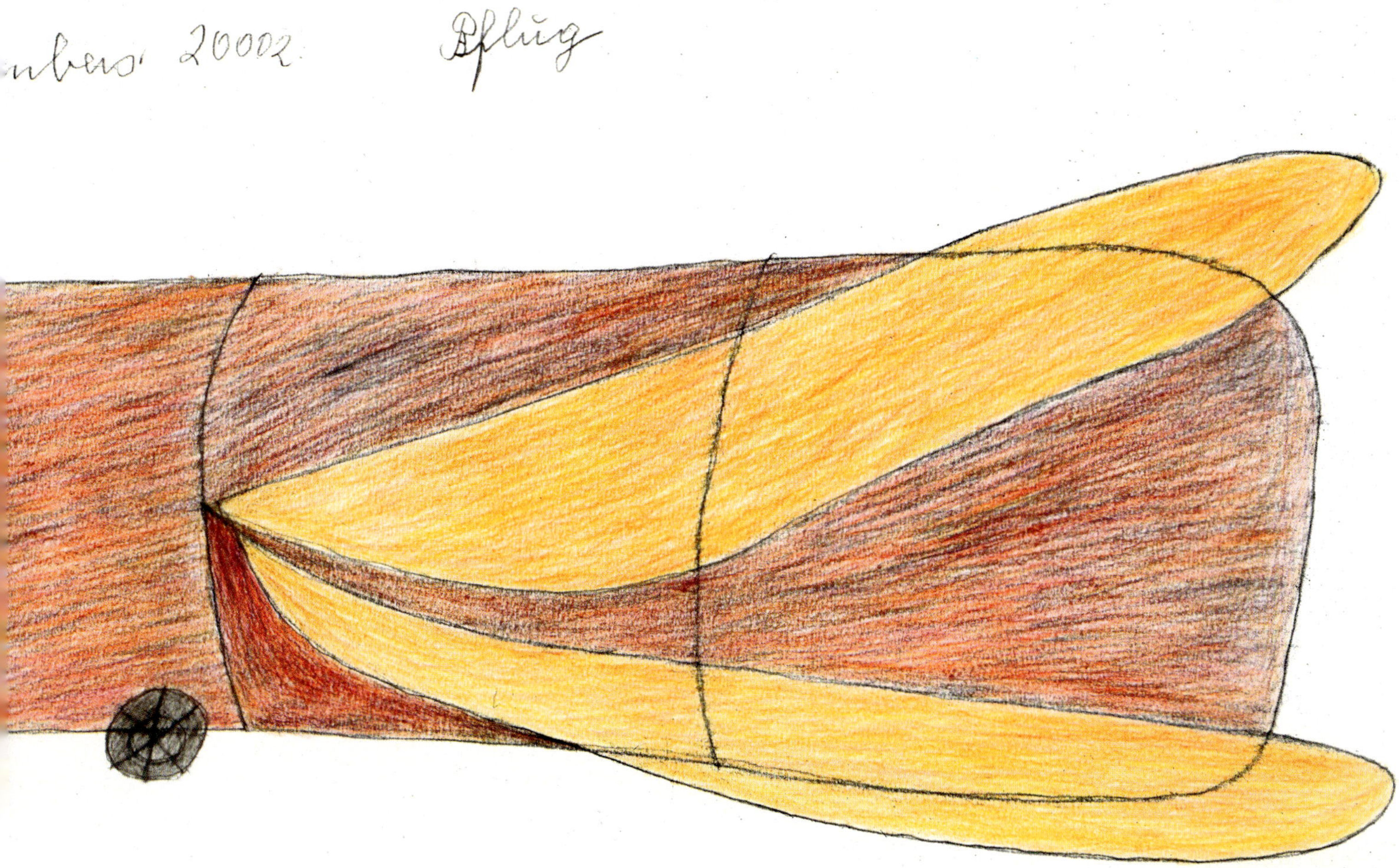

Franz Kernbeis
Pflug / Plow,
2002, 33 x 101,9 cm
Bleistift, Farbstifte,
Aqua-Monolith /
pencil, color pencils,
Aqua-Monolith
Sammlung Hannah Rieger

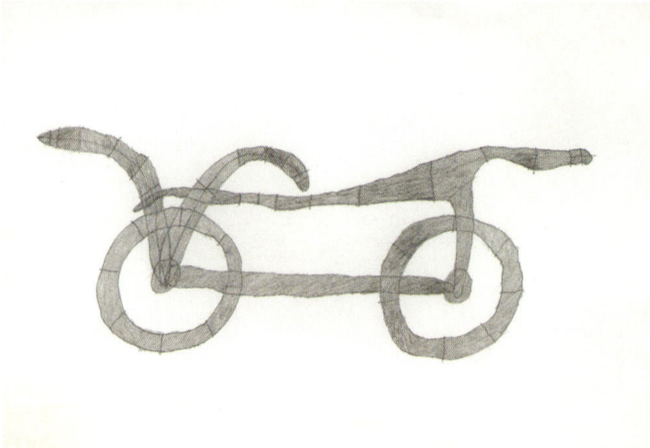

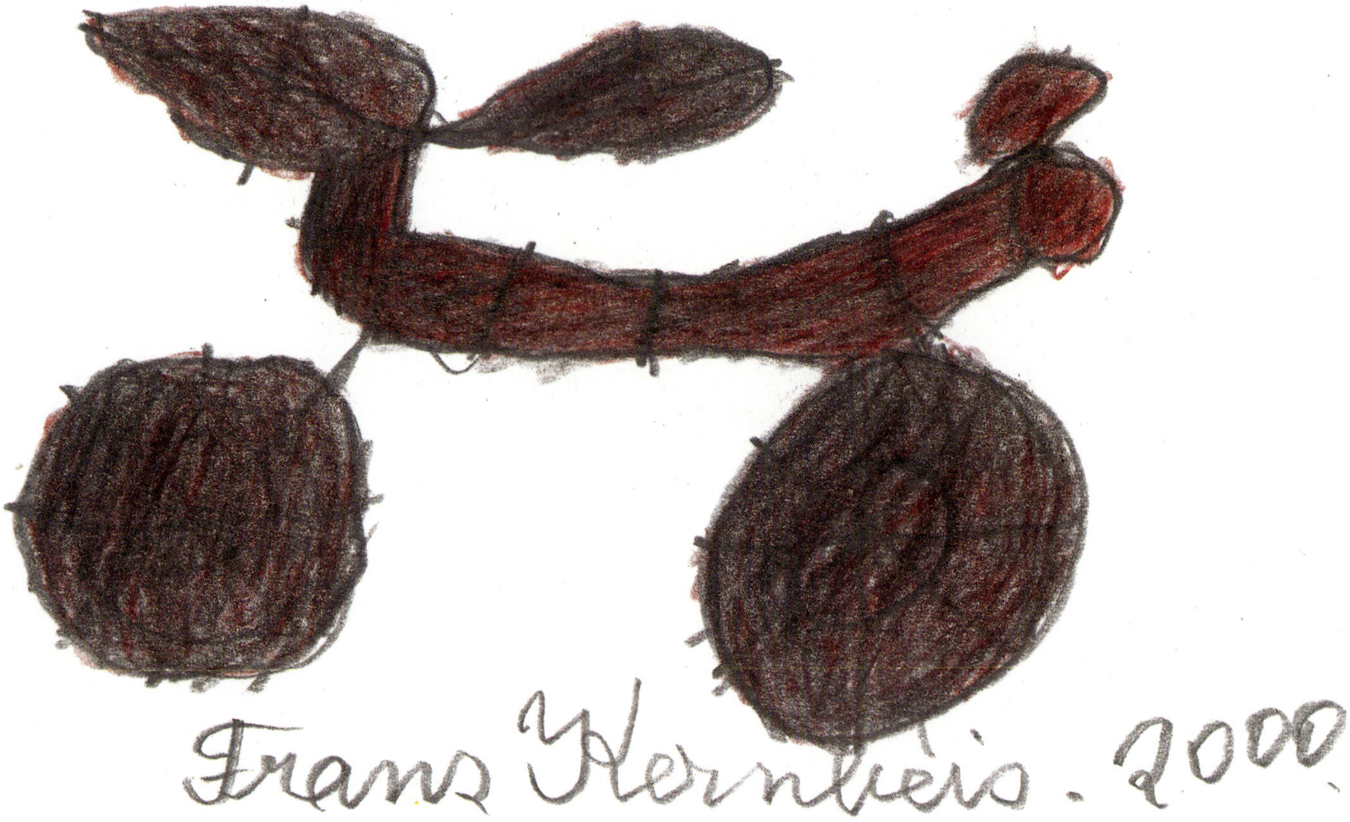
Franz Kernbeis . 2000

Franz Kernbeis
Fahrrad / Bicycle
1979, 20,9 x 30 cm
Bleistift / pencil
Privatsammlung

Franz Kernbeis
Fahrrad / Bicycle
2000, 10,4 x 14,7 cm
Bleistift, Farbstifte / pencil, color pencils
Privatstiftung - Künstler aus Gugging

Franz Kernbeis
Kuh / Cow
2000, 14,7 x 20,9 cm
Bleistift, Farbstifte / pencil, color pencils
Privatstiftung - Künstler aus Gugging

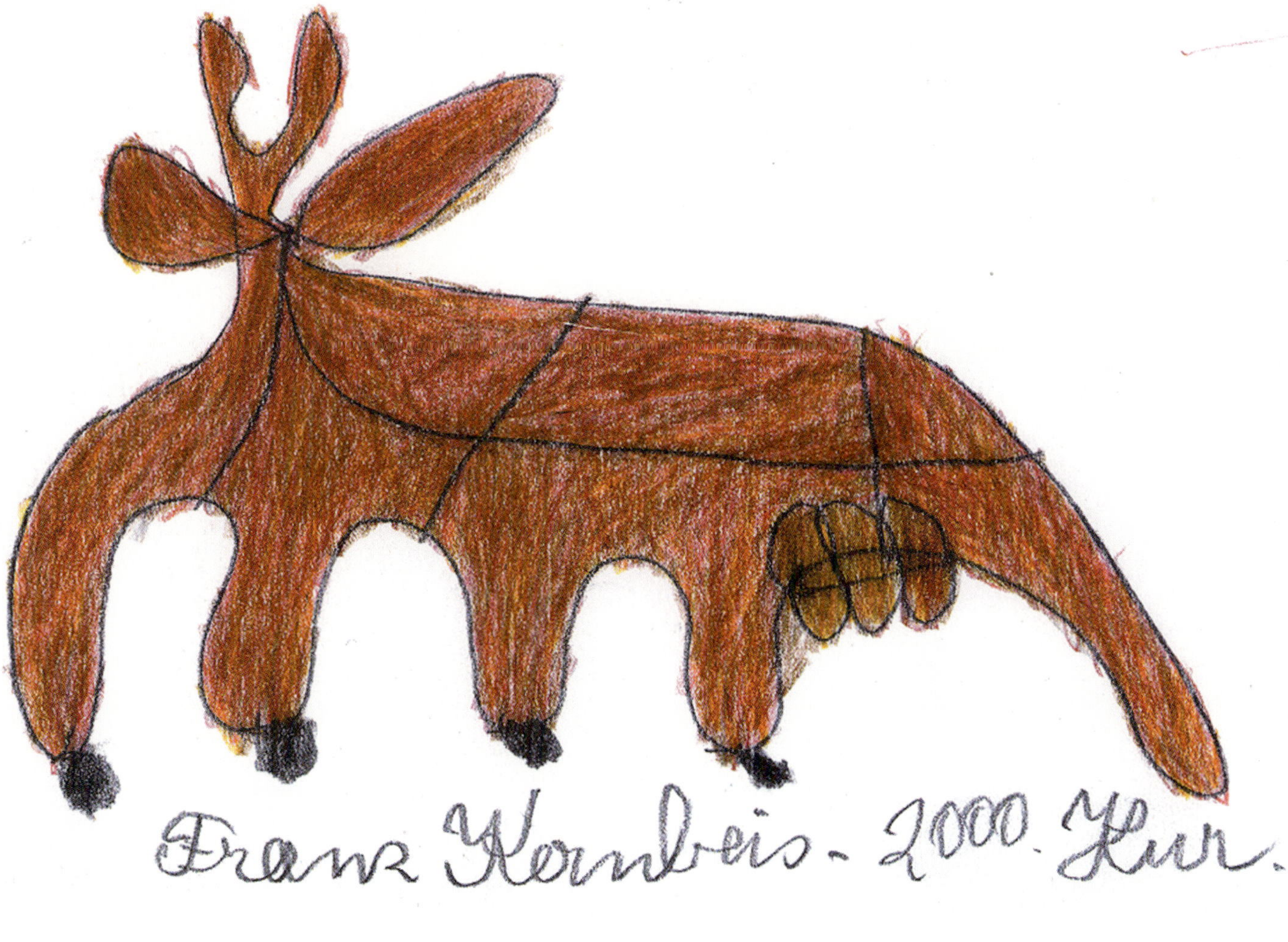

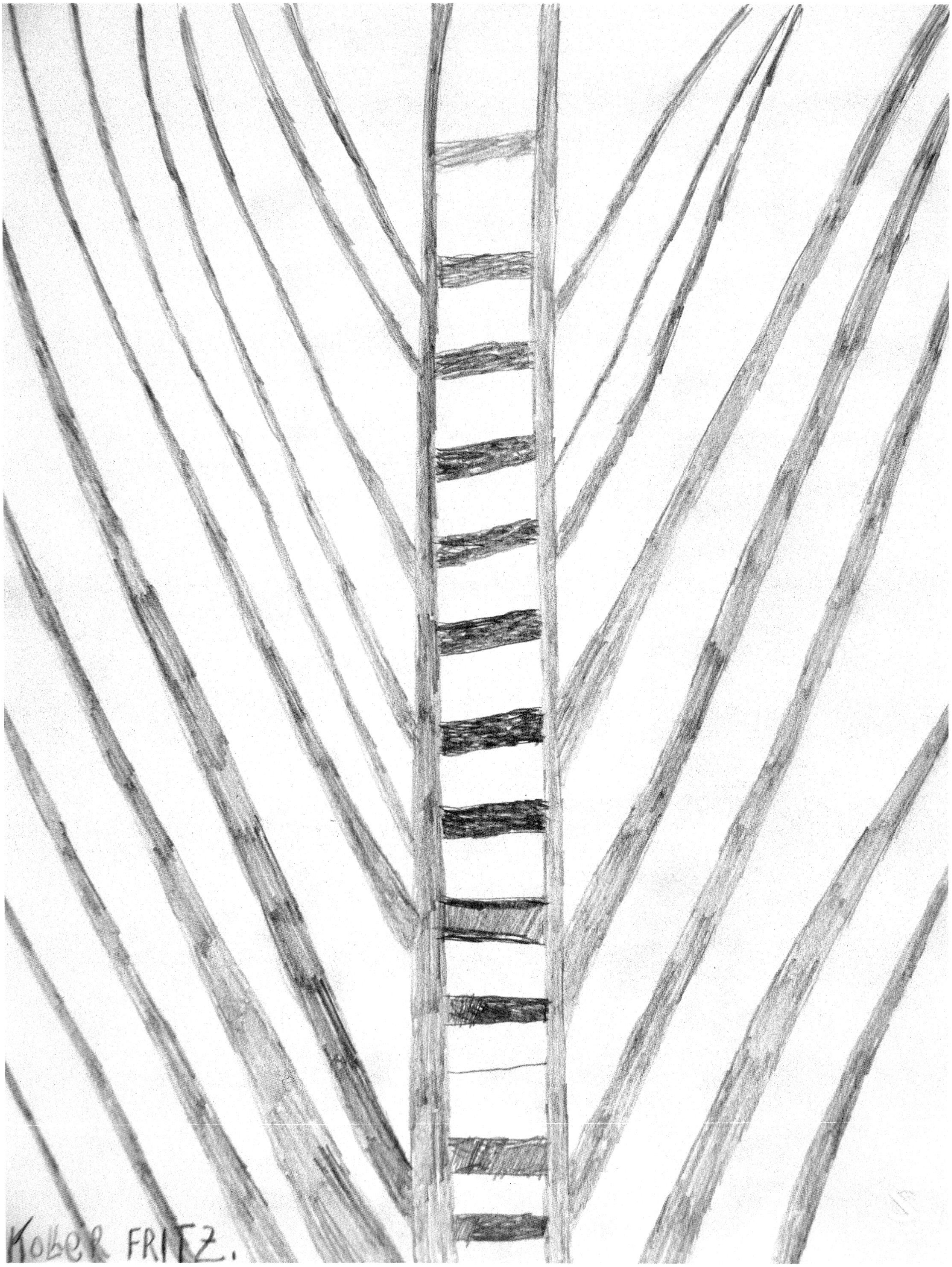
Kober FRITZ.

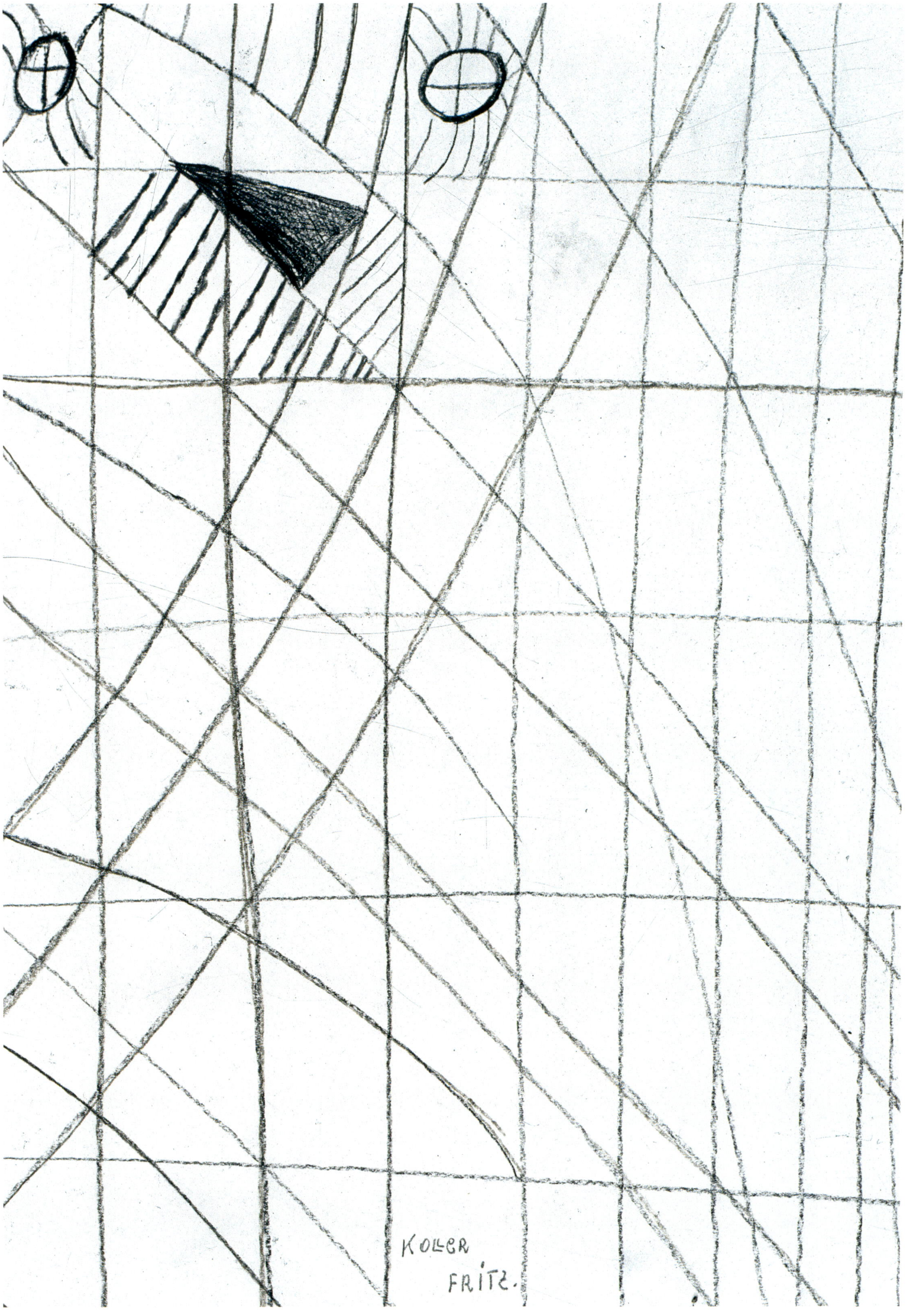
KOLLER
FRITZ.

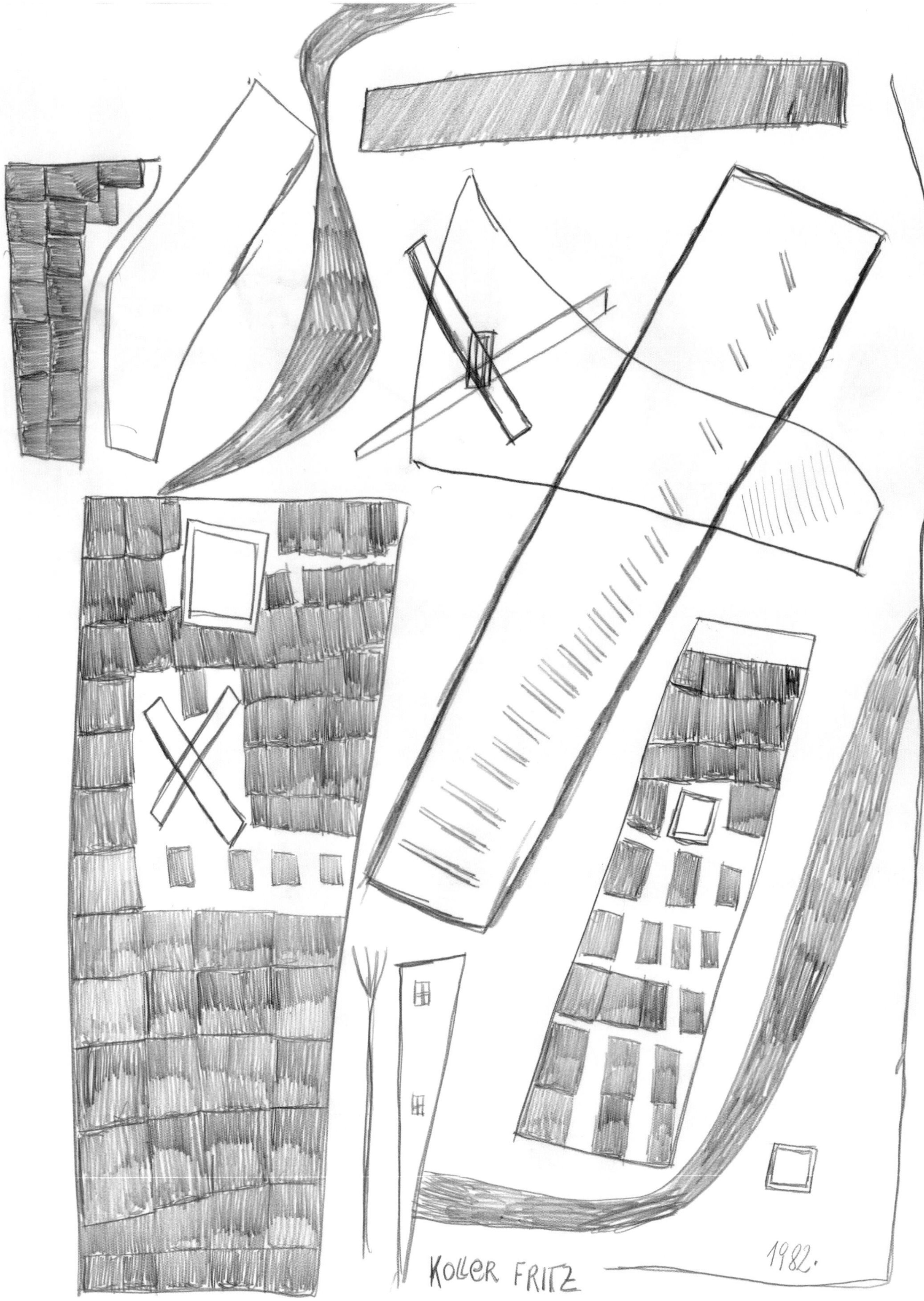
KOLLER FRITZ
1982.

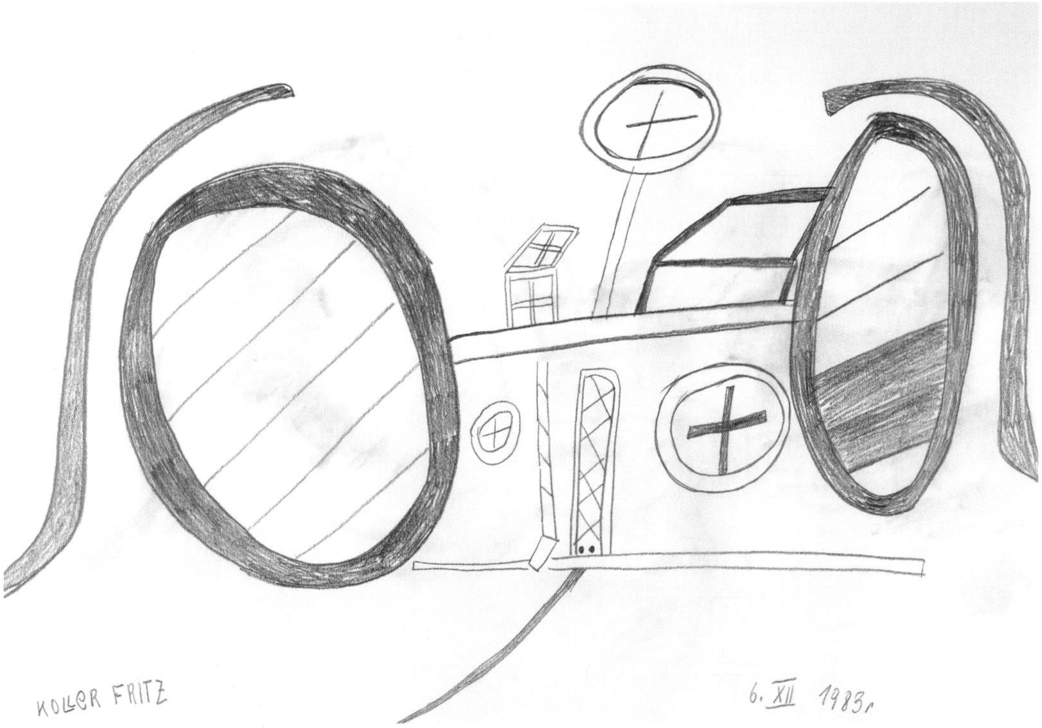

Fritz Koller
Maibaum / Maypole
1980, 40 x 30 cm
Bleistift / pencil
Sammlung Josef Schroll

Fritz Koller
Ohne Titel / Untitled
1991, 44 x 31,2 cm
Bleistift / pencil
Sammlung Josef Schroll

Fritz Koller
Mühle / Mill
1982, 64,9 x 50 cm
Bleistift / pencil
Privatsammlung

Fritz Koller
Auto / Car
1983, 49,8 x 69,8 cm
Bleistift /pencil
Privatsammlung

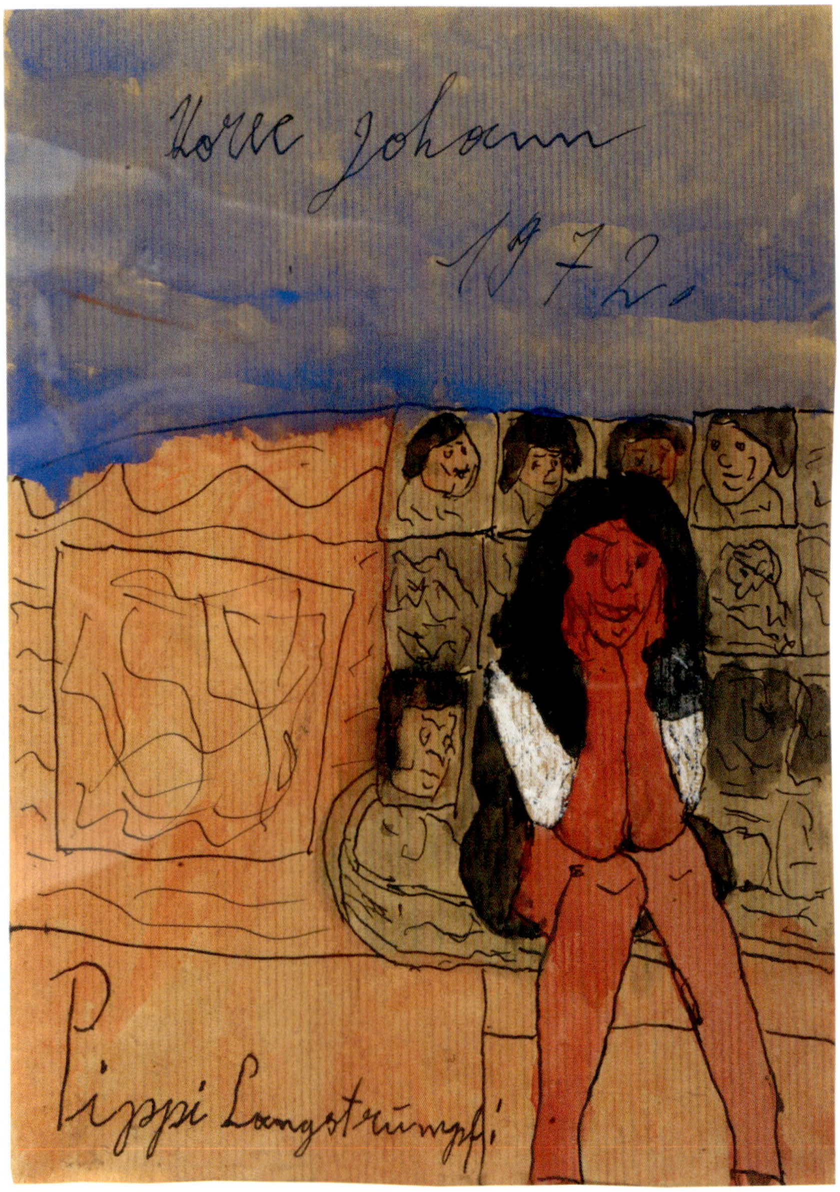
Korec Johann
1972.
Pippi Langstrumpf!

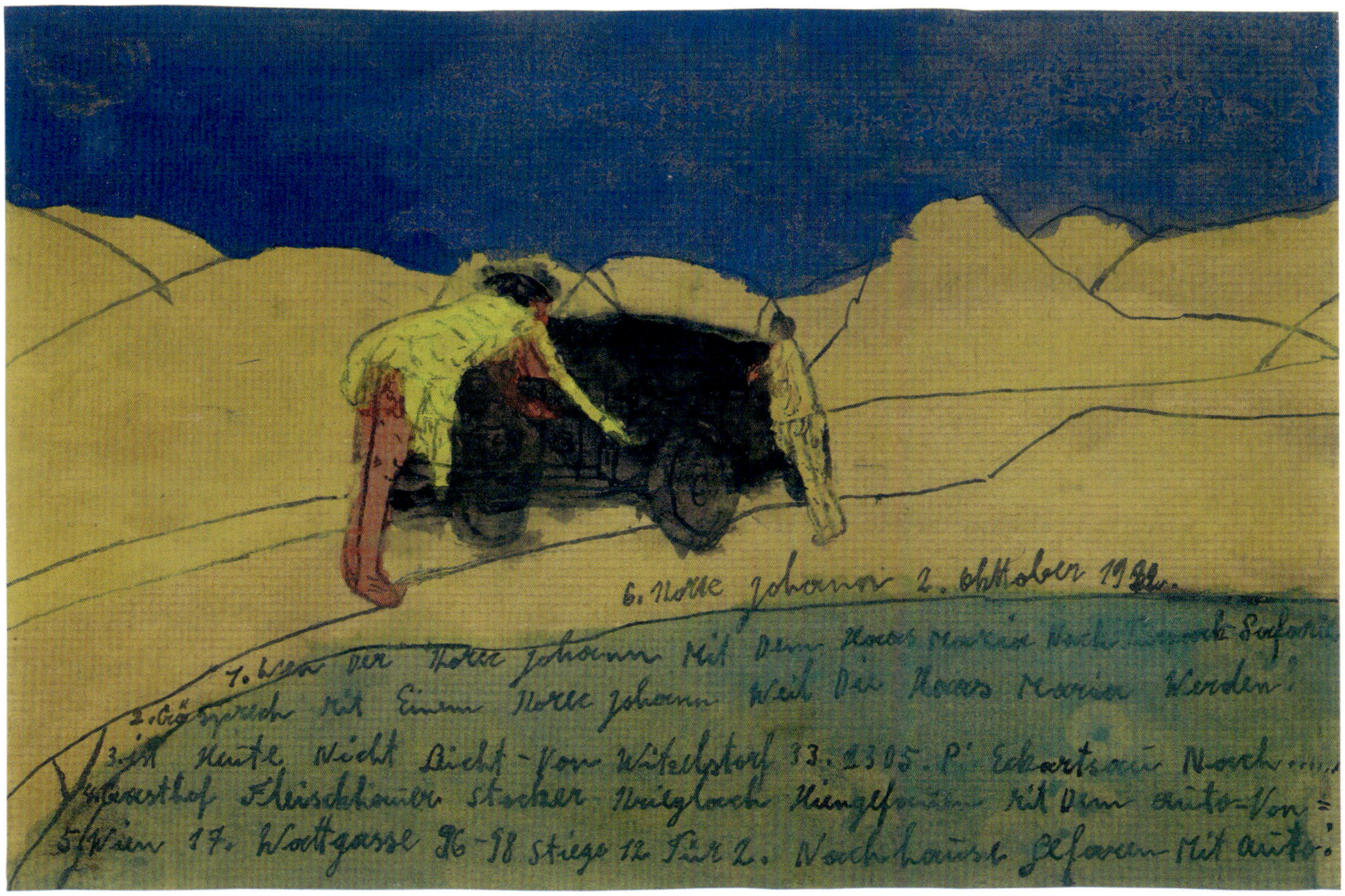

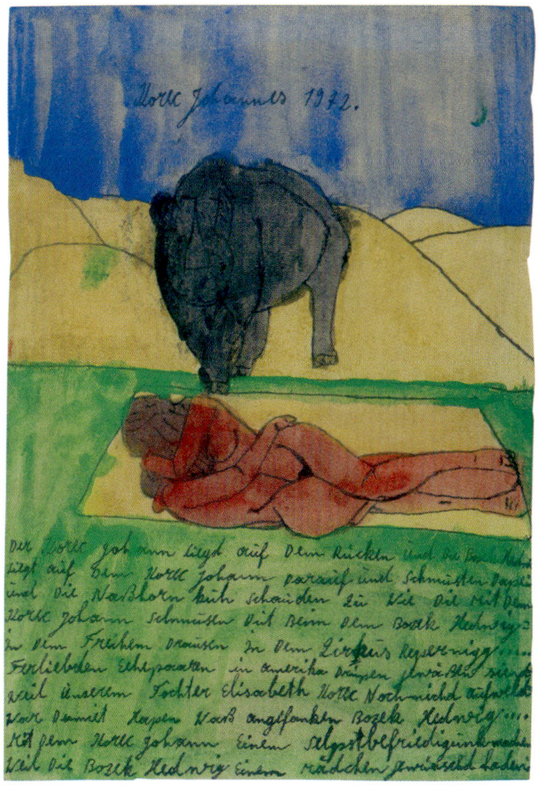

Johann Korec
Pippi Langstrumpf / Pippi Langstocking
1972, 29,6 x 20,6 cm
Tusche, Aquarellfarbe / Indian ink, aquarell
Sammlung Helmut Zambo

Johann Korec
Szene im Safaripark / Scene in Safari-Park
1972, 20,7 x 29,8 cm
Tusche, Aquarellfarbe / Indian ink, aquarell
Sammlung Helmut Zambo

Johann Korec
Nashorn / Rhinoceros
1972, 30,6 x 20,8 cm
Tusche, Aquarellfarbe / Indian ink, aquarell
Sammlung Helmut Zambo

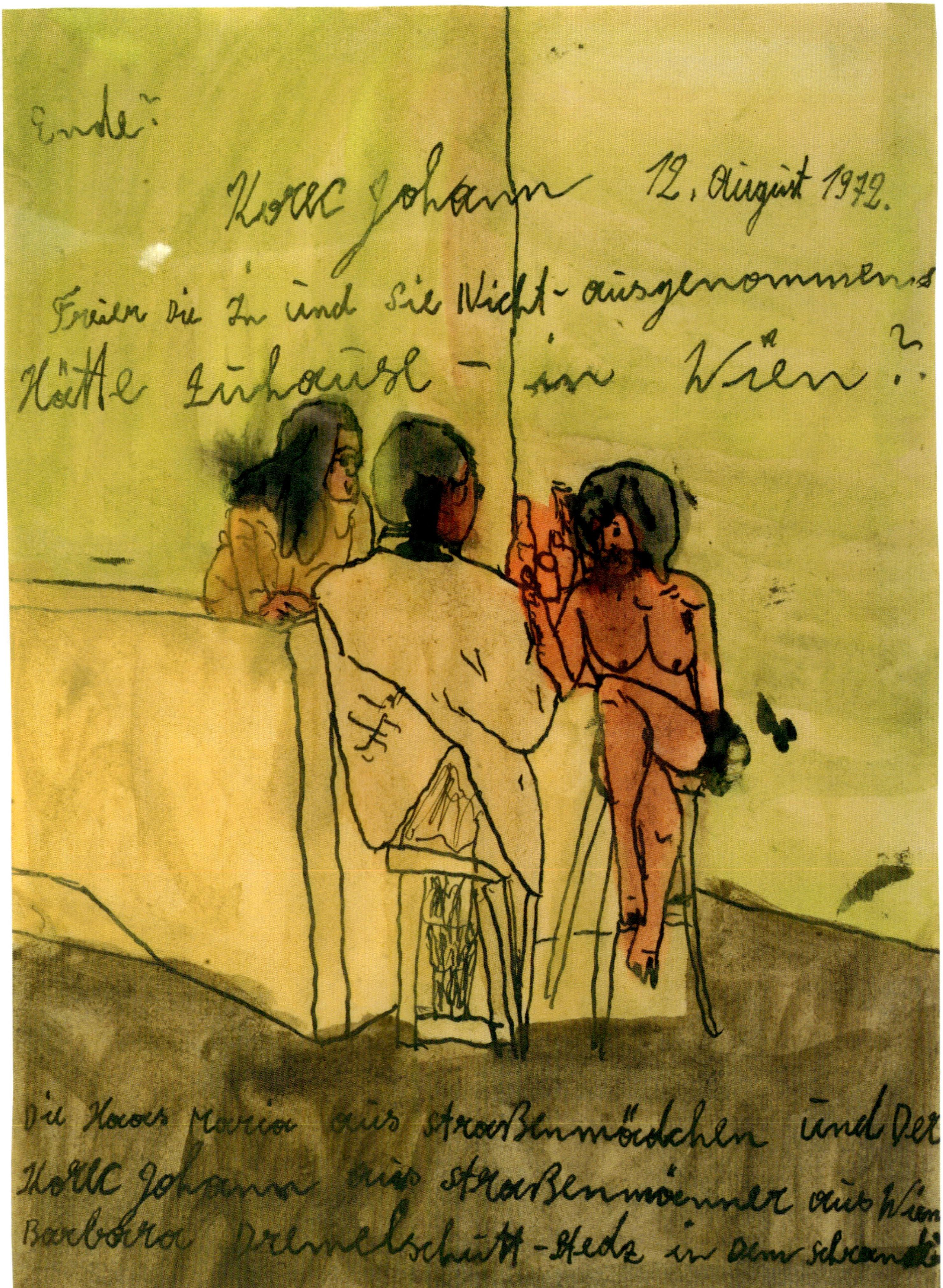
Ende?
Korec Johann 12. August 1972.
Hütte Zuhause - im Wien?

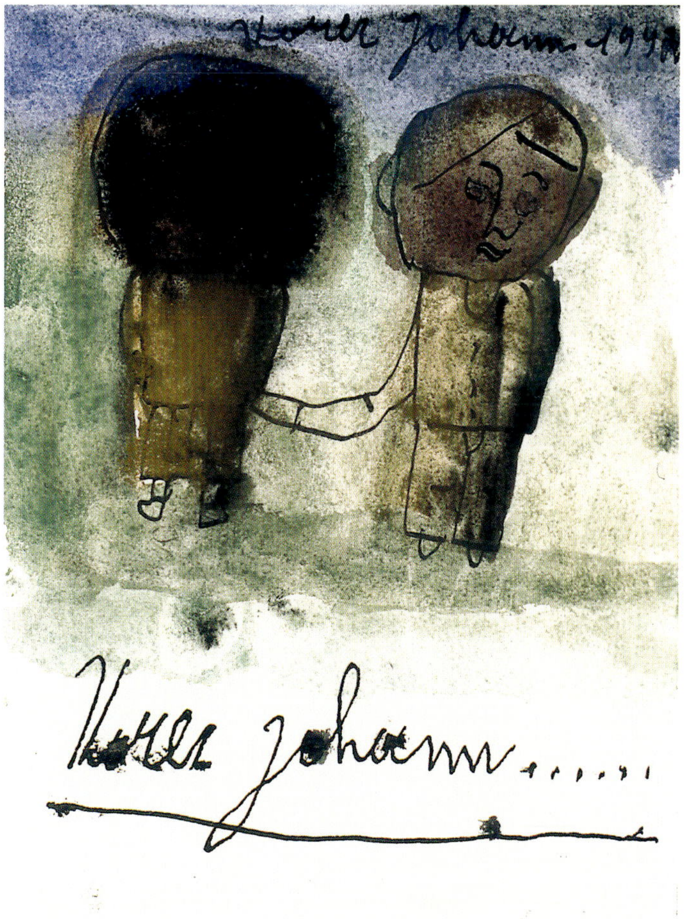

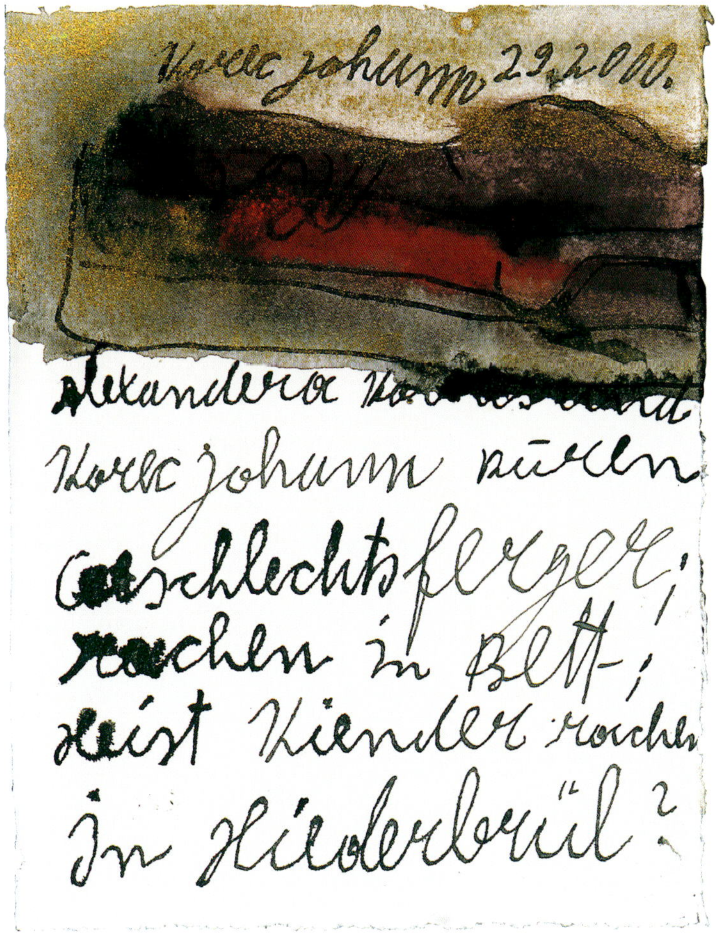

Johann Korec
Ende / End
1972, 29,3 x 23 cm
Tusche, Aquarellfarbe / Indian ink, aquarell
Sammlung Helmut Zambo

Johann Korec
Korec Johann ... / Korec Johann ...
1997, 16,3 x 11,9 cm
Tusche, Aquarellfarbe / Indian ink, aquarell

Johann Korec
Alexandera Korbus ... / Alexandera Korbus ...
2000, 18,9 x 14 cm
Tusche, Aquarellfarbe / Indian ink, aquarell

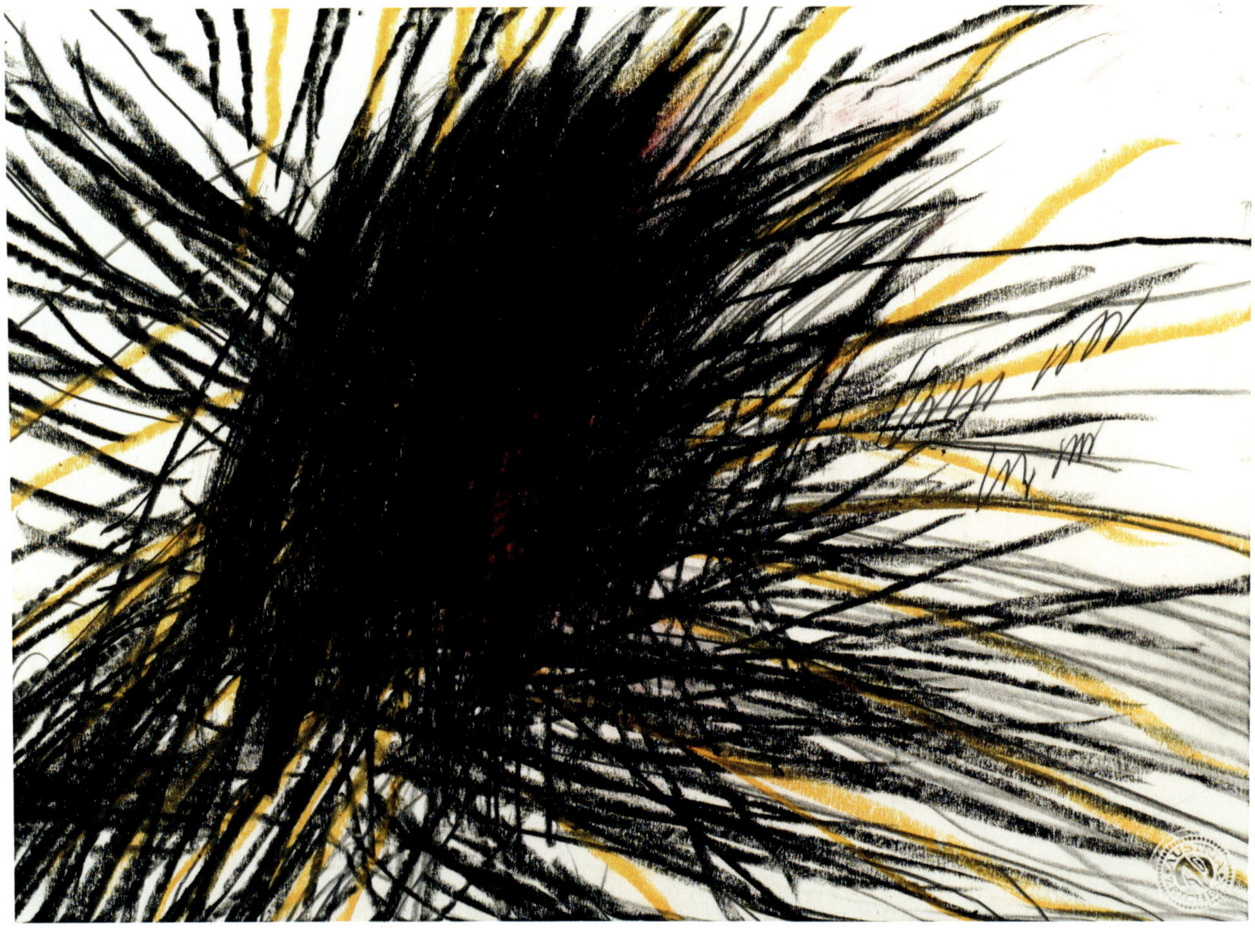

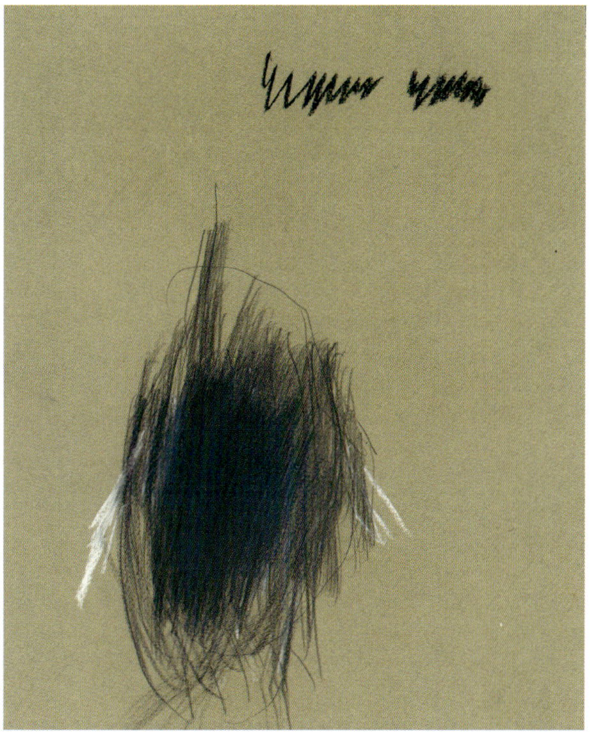

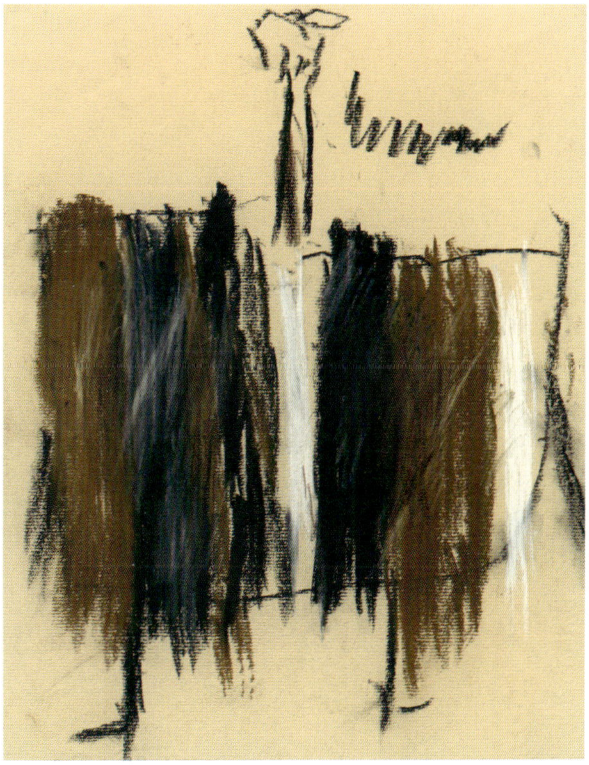

Rudolf Limberger
Die Sonne / The Sun
Undatiert /undated
30 x 40 cm
Bleistift, Wachskreiden/
pencil, crayons
Privatsammlung

Rudolf Limberger
Mensch / Human
Undatiert /undated
32,5 x 25,2 cm
Farbstift, Kohle /
color pencil, charcoal
NÖ Landesmuseum
Sammlung Leo Navratil

Rudolf Limberger
Mensch / Human
Undatiert / undated
32,5 x 25 cm
Kohle, Wachskreiden /
charcoal, crayons
NÖ Landesmuseum
Sammlung Leo Navratil

Rudolf Limberger
Ohne TItel / Untitled
Undatiert / undated
40,1 x 30,1 cm
Bleistift, Wachskreide /
pencil, crayons
NÖ Landesmuseum
Sammlung Leo Navratil

Rudolf Limberger
Ohne TItel / Untitled
Undatiert / undated
40,1 x 30,1 cm
Bleistift, Wachskreide /
pencil, crayons
NÖ Landesmuseum
Sammlung Leo Navratil

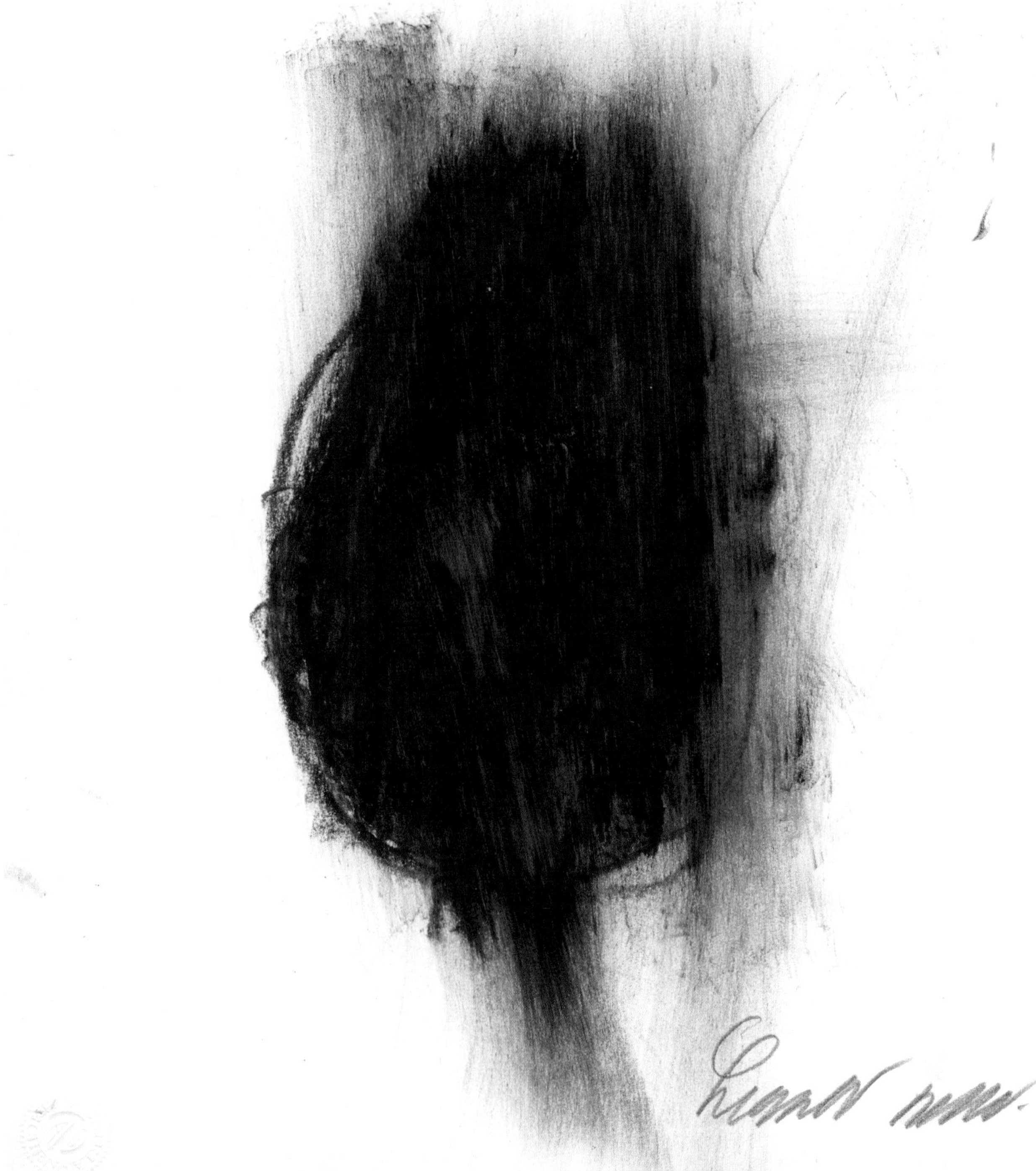

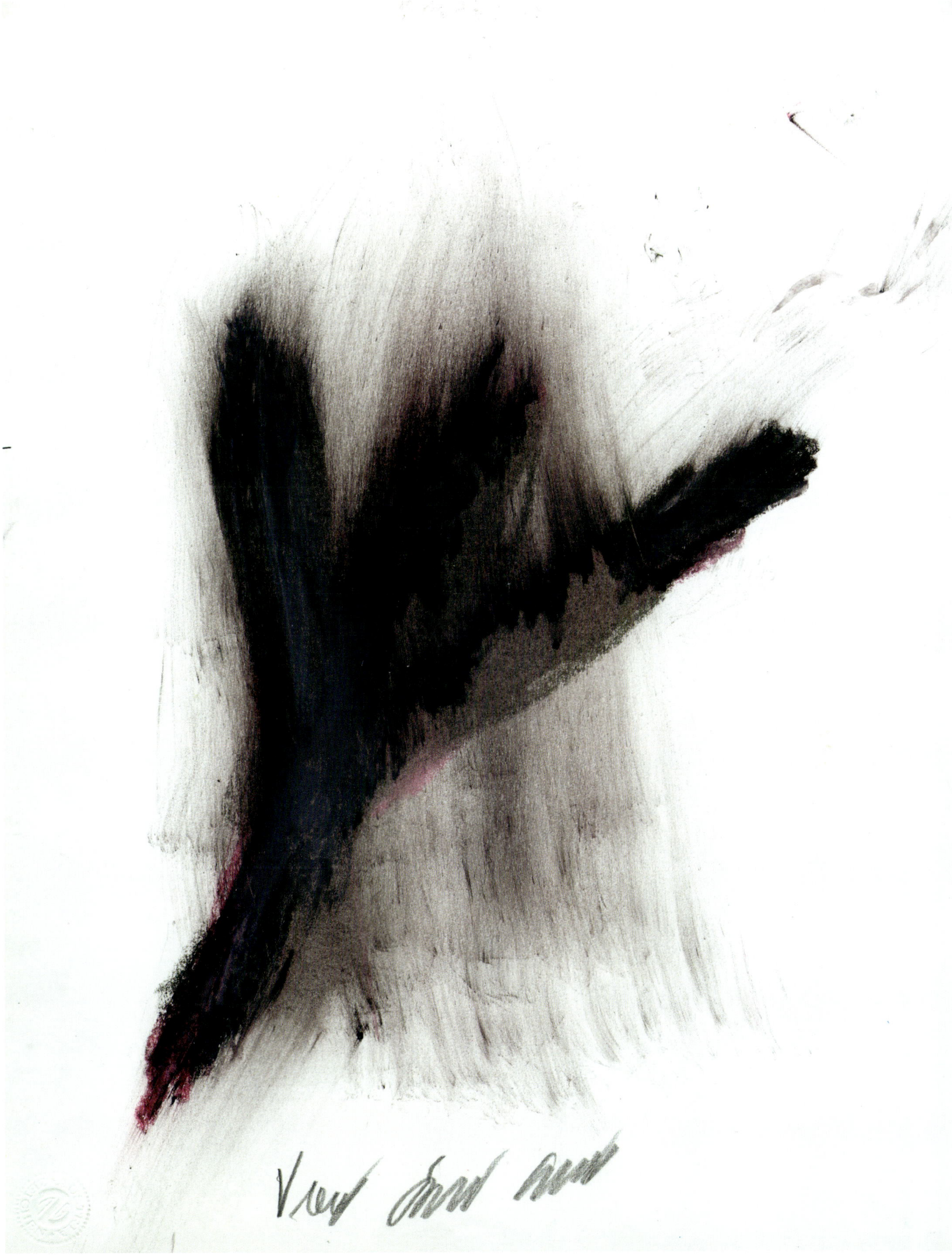

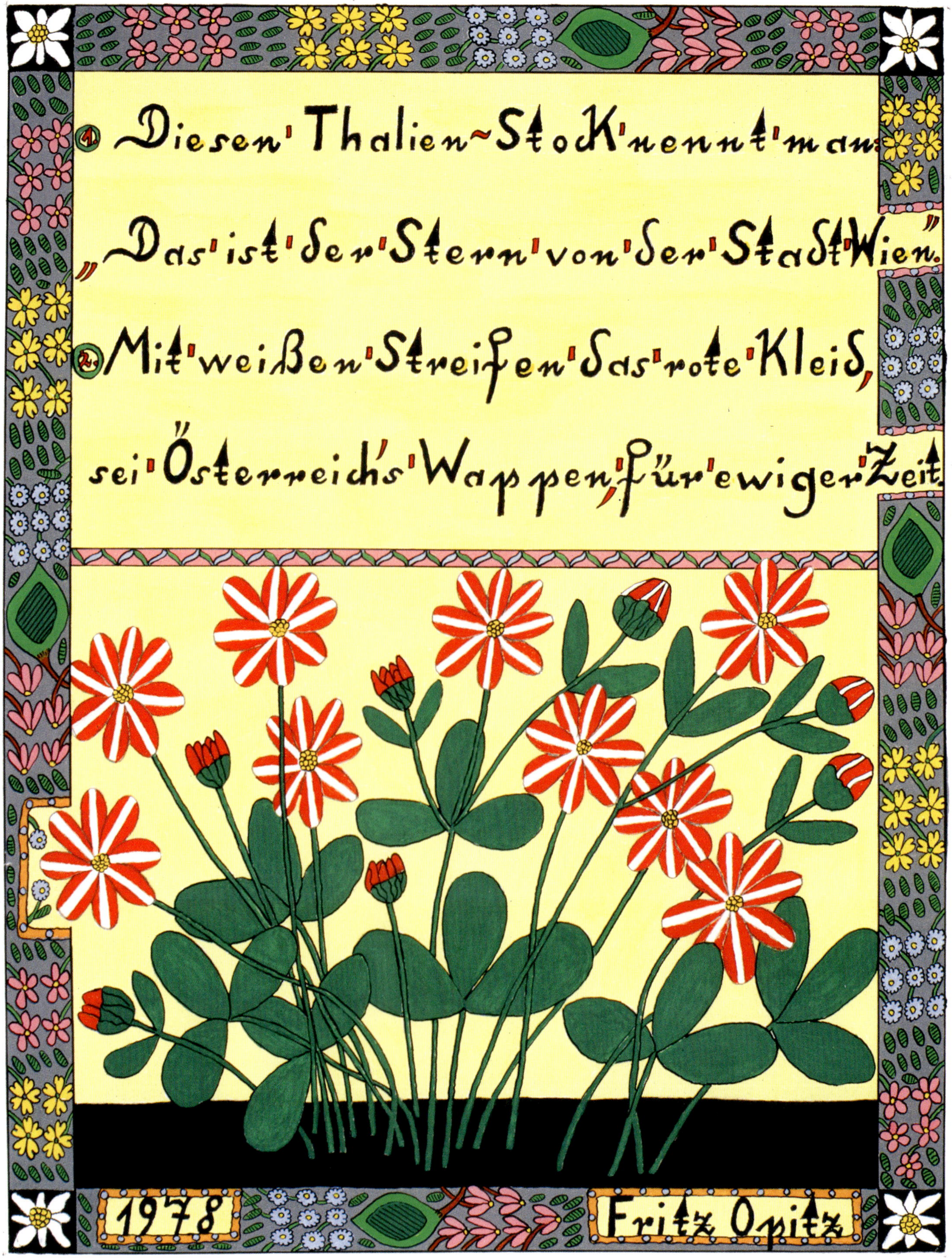
1. Diesen Thalien-Stock nennt man
„Das ist der Stern von der Stadt Wien."
2. Mit weißen Streifen das rote Kleid,
sei Österreich's Wappen für ewiger Zeit.
1978
Fritz Opitz

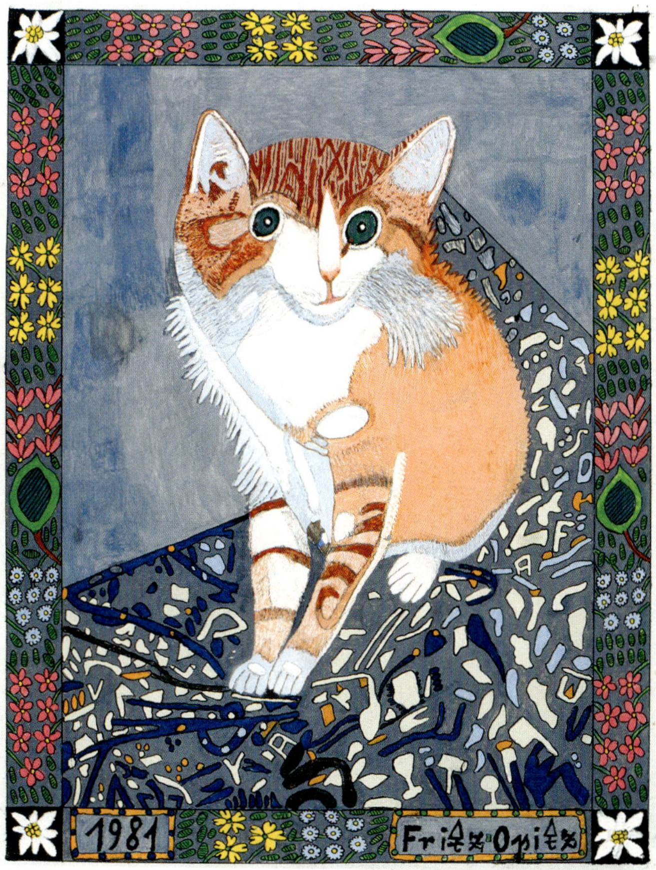

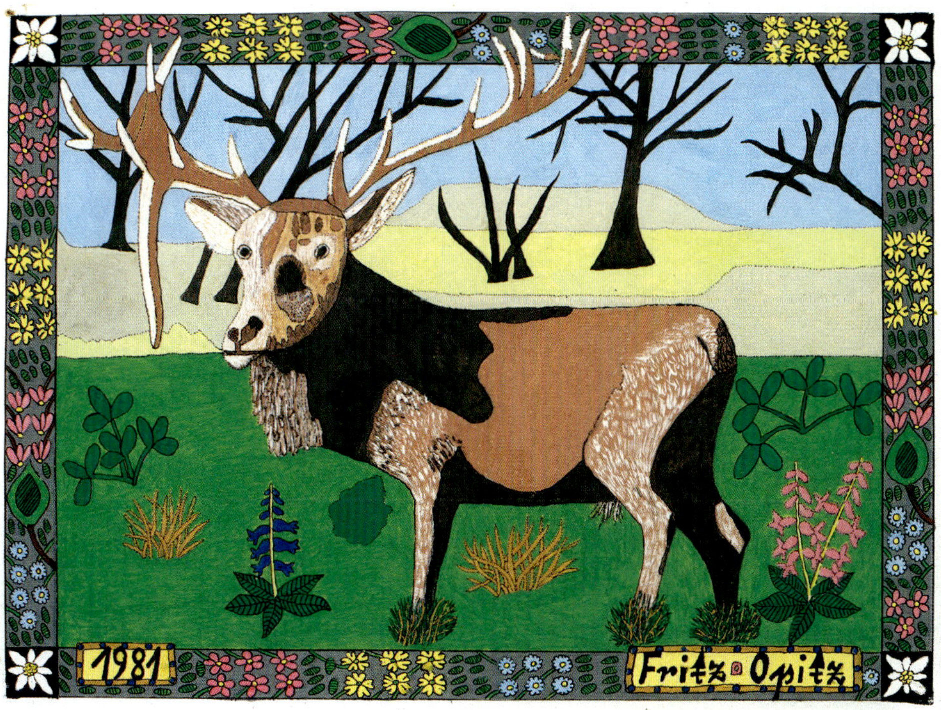

Fritz Opitz
Diesen Thalien-Stock / Dahlias
1978, 40 x 30 cm
Bleistift, Tusche, Deckfarben / pencil, Indian ink, tempera
Privatsammlung

Fritz Opitz
Katze / Cat
1981, 40 x 30 cm
Tusche, Deckfarben / Indian ink, tempera
Privatstiftung - Künstler aus Gugging

Fritz Opitz
Hirsch / Deer
1981, 30 x 40 cm
Tusche, Deckfarben / Indian ink, tempera
Privatsammlung

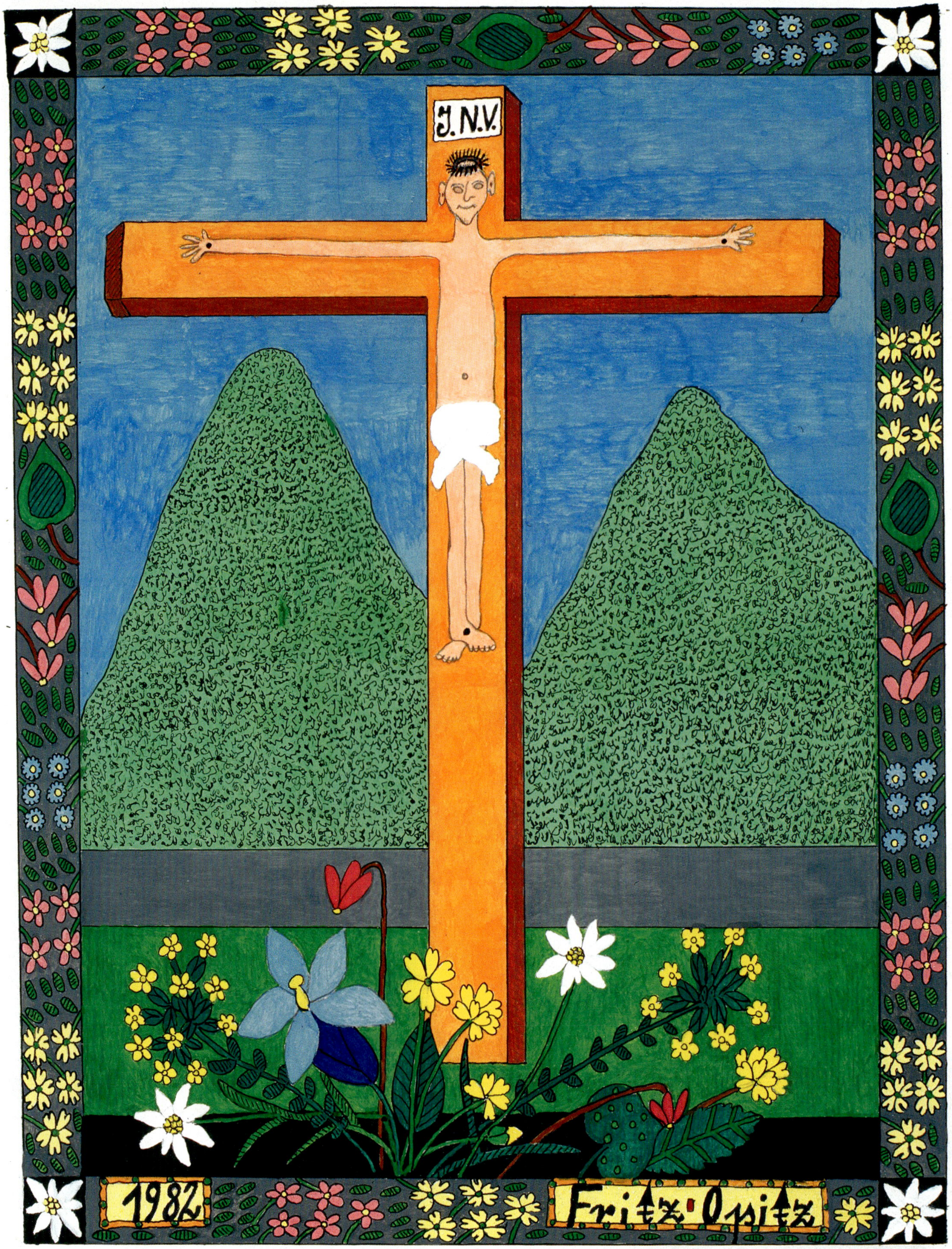

J.N.V.
1982
Fritz Opitz

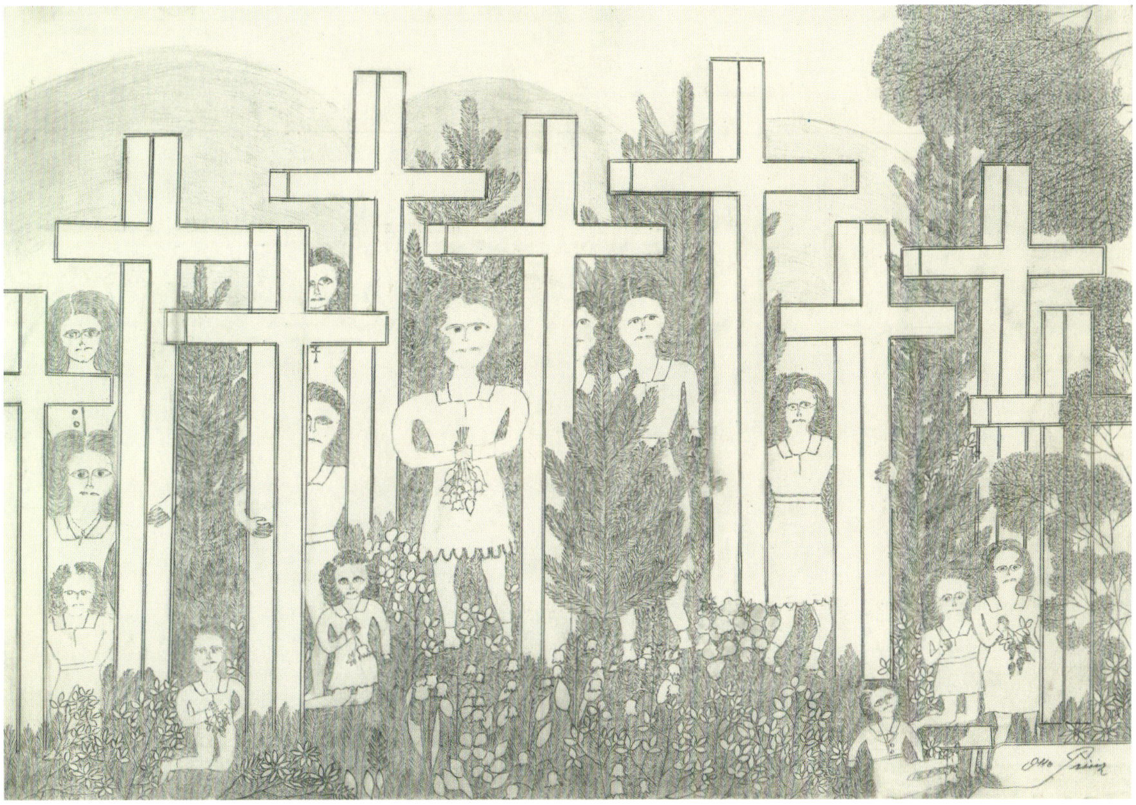

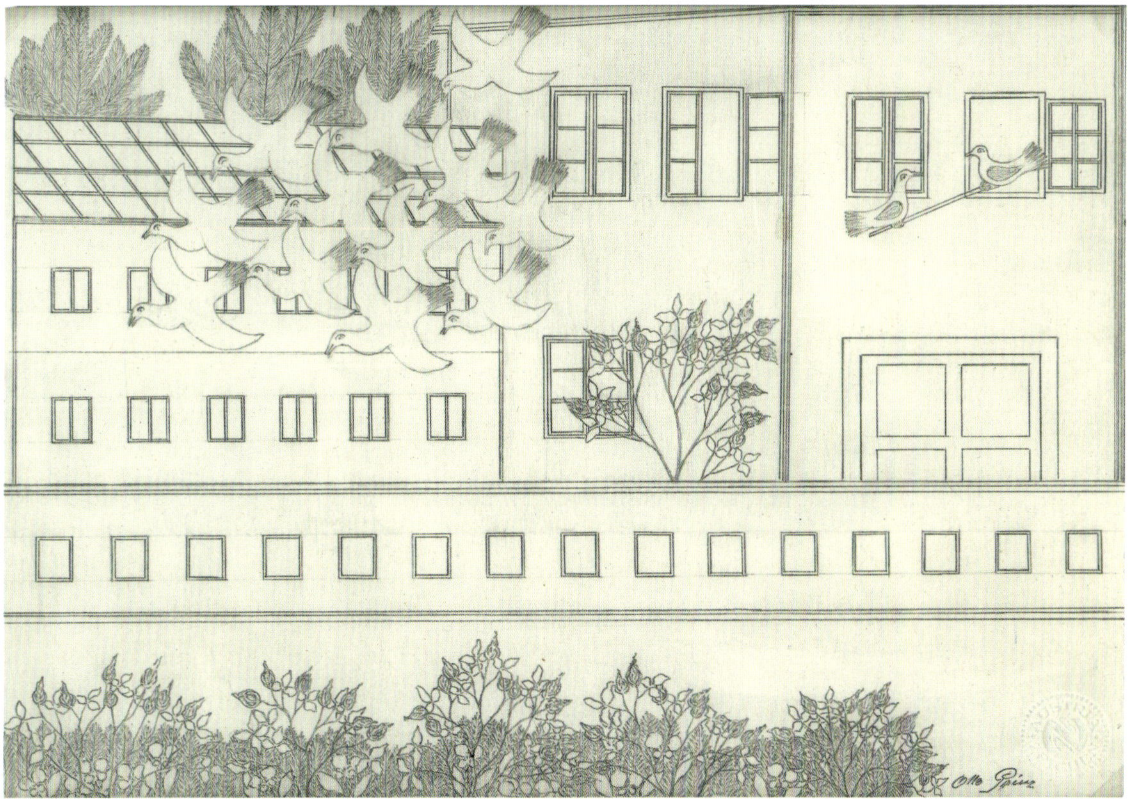

Fritz Opitz
Kreuzigung /
Crucifixion
1982, 40 x 30 cm
Tusche,
Deckfarben, Bleistift /
Indian ink, tempera,
pencil
Privatsammlung

Otto Prinz
Frauen mit Kreuzen /
Women with Crosses
Undatiert / undated
30,8 x 43 cm
Bleistift / pencil
NÖ Landessammlung
Sammlung Leo Navratil

Otto Prinz
Vögel vor einem Haus /
Birds in Front of a
House
Undatiert / undated
42 x 30 cm
Bleistift / pencil
Sammlung Helmut Zambo

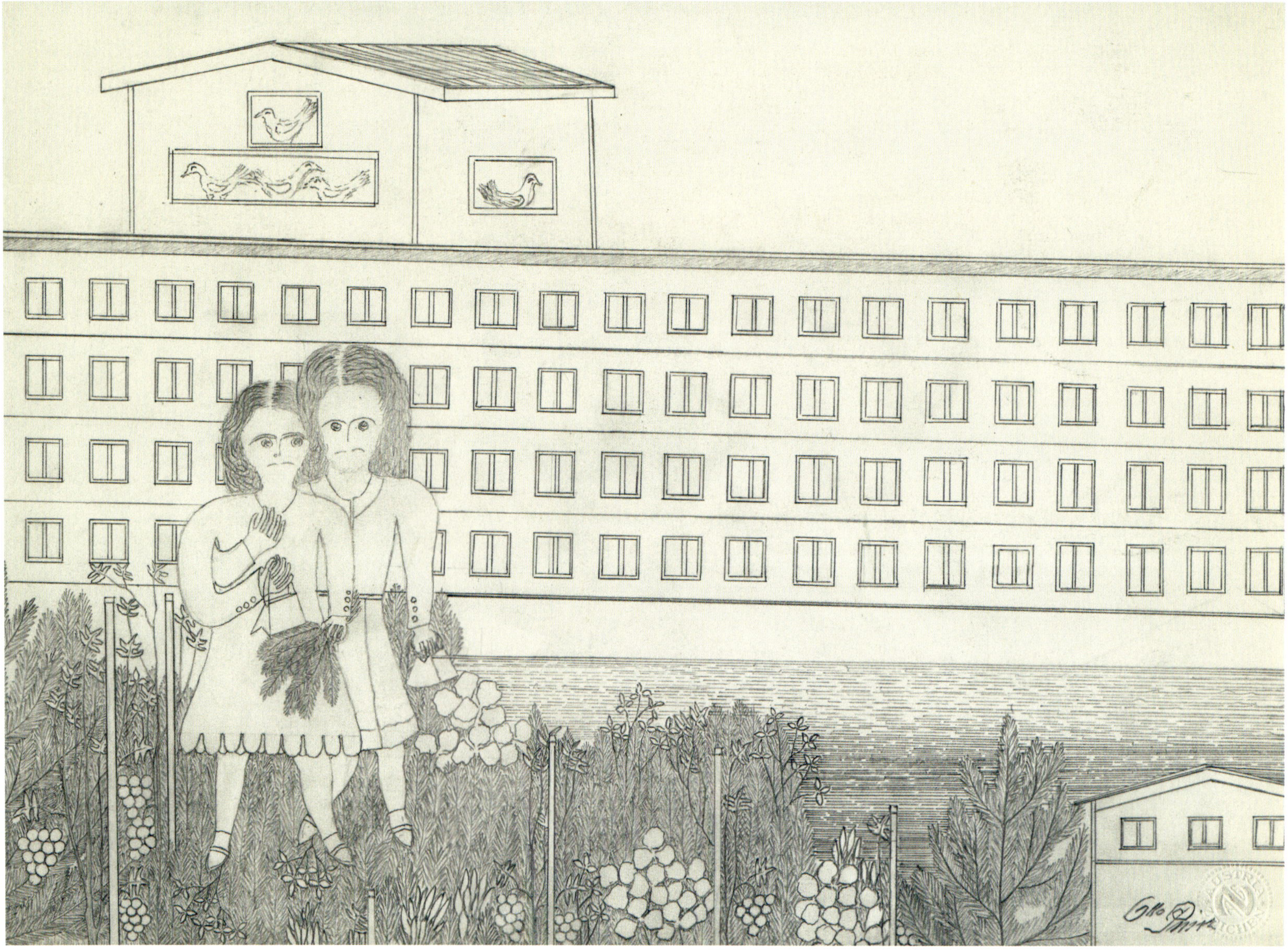

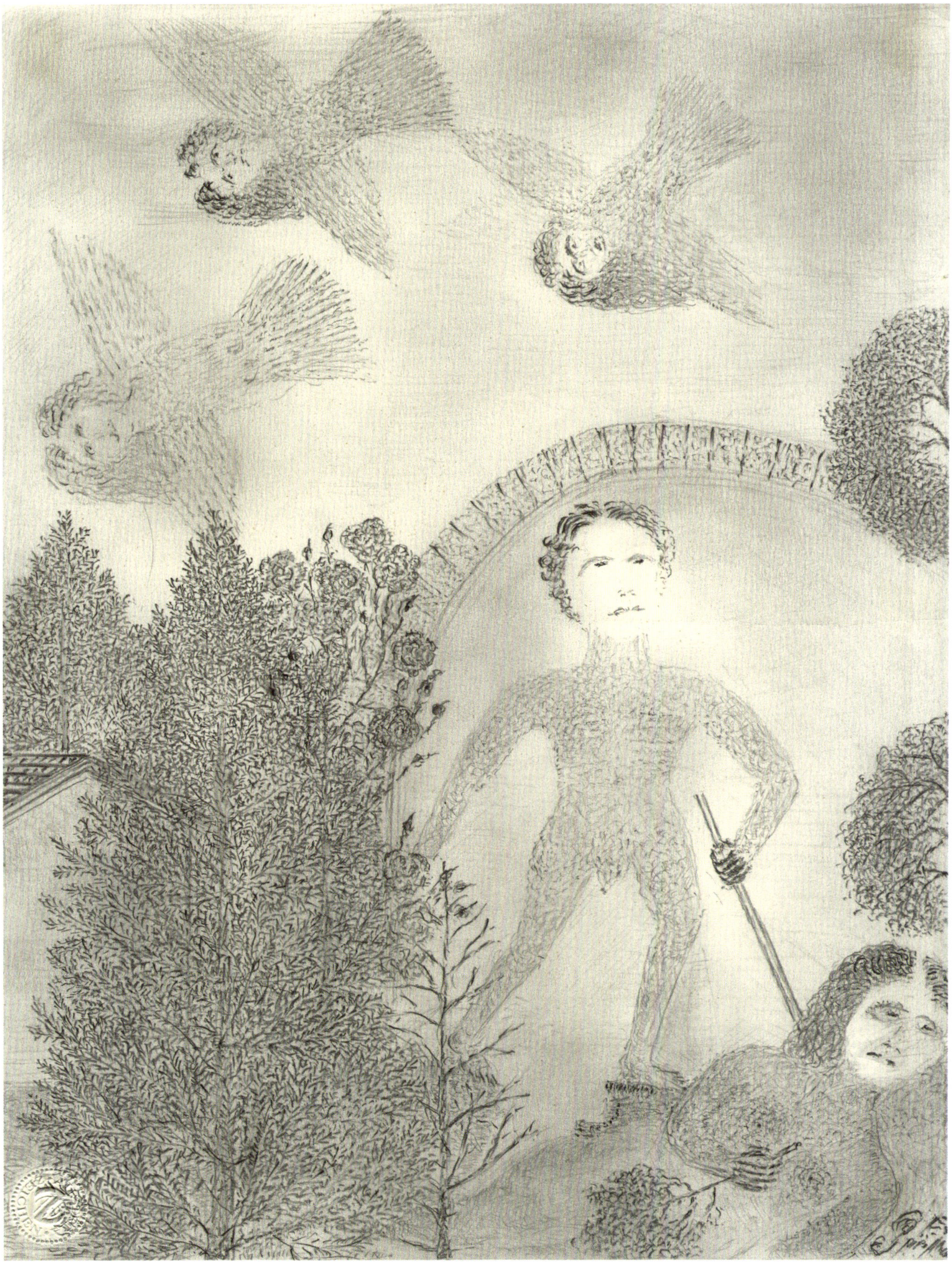

Otto Prinz
Zwei Frauen vor einem Haus /
Two Women in Front of a House
Undatiert / undated
30 x 40 cm
Bleistift / pencil
NÖ Landesmuseum
Sammlung Leo Navratil

Otto Prinz
Ohne Titel / Untitled
Undatiert / undated
40 x 30 cm
Bleistift / pencil
NÖ Landesmuseum
Sammlung Leo Navratil

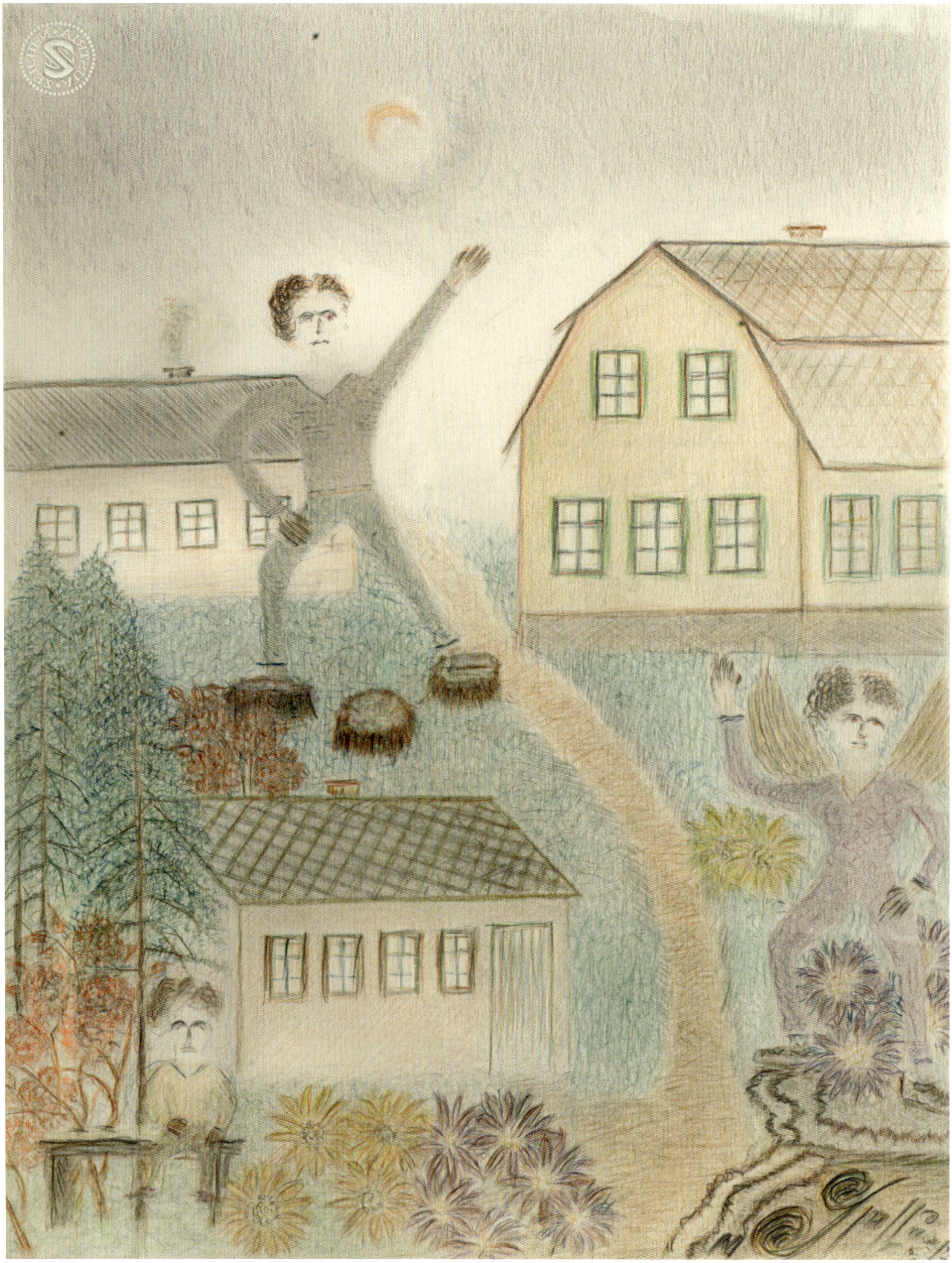

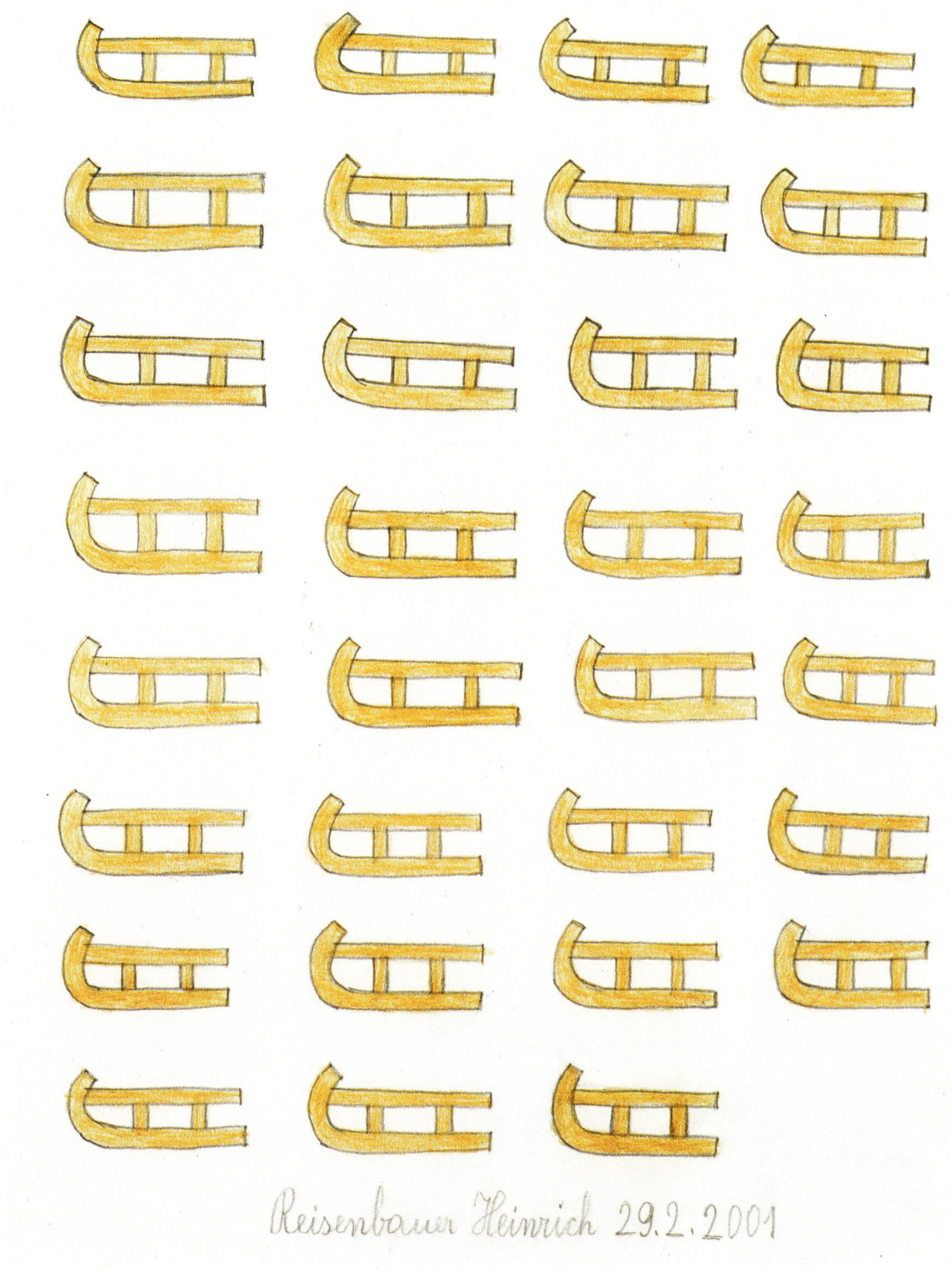

Otto Prinz
Mann, Kind, Engel
und Häuser /
Man, Child, Angel and
Houses
Undatiert / undated
39,8 x 29,8 cm
Bleistift, Farbstifte /
pencil, color pencils
Sammlung Helmut Zambo

Heinrich Reisenbauer
Rodeln / Sleds
2001, 29,7 x 21 cm
Bleistift, Farbstift /
pencil, color pencil
Privatstiftung -
Künstler aus Gugging

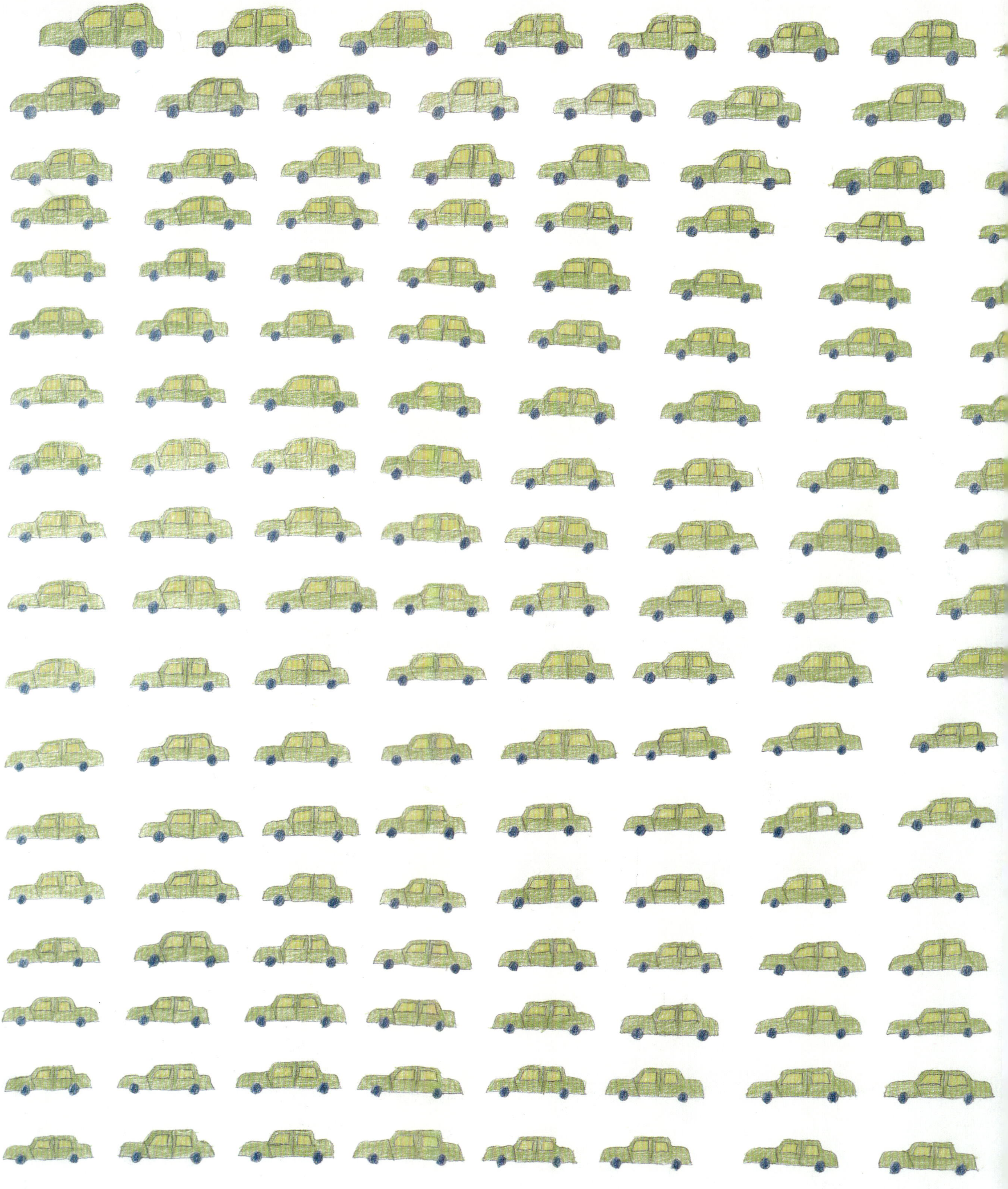

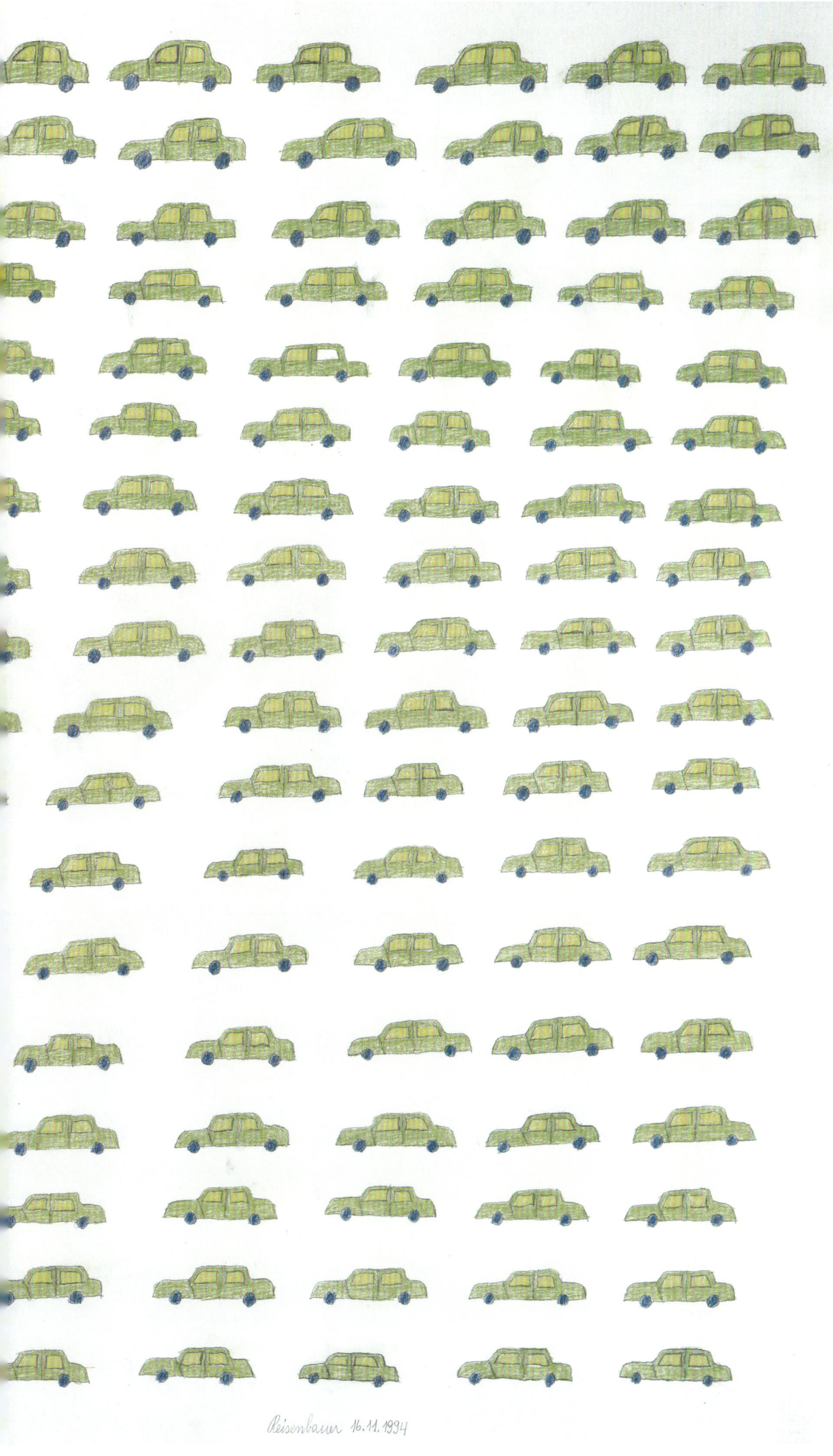

Heinrich Reisenbauer
Autos / Cars
1994, 73 x 101,7 cm
Bleistift, Farbstifte /
pencil, color pencils
Privatsammlung

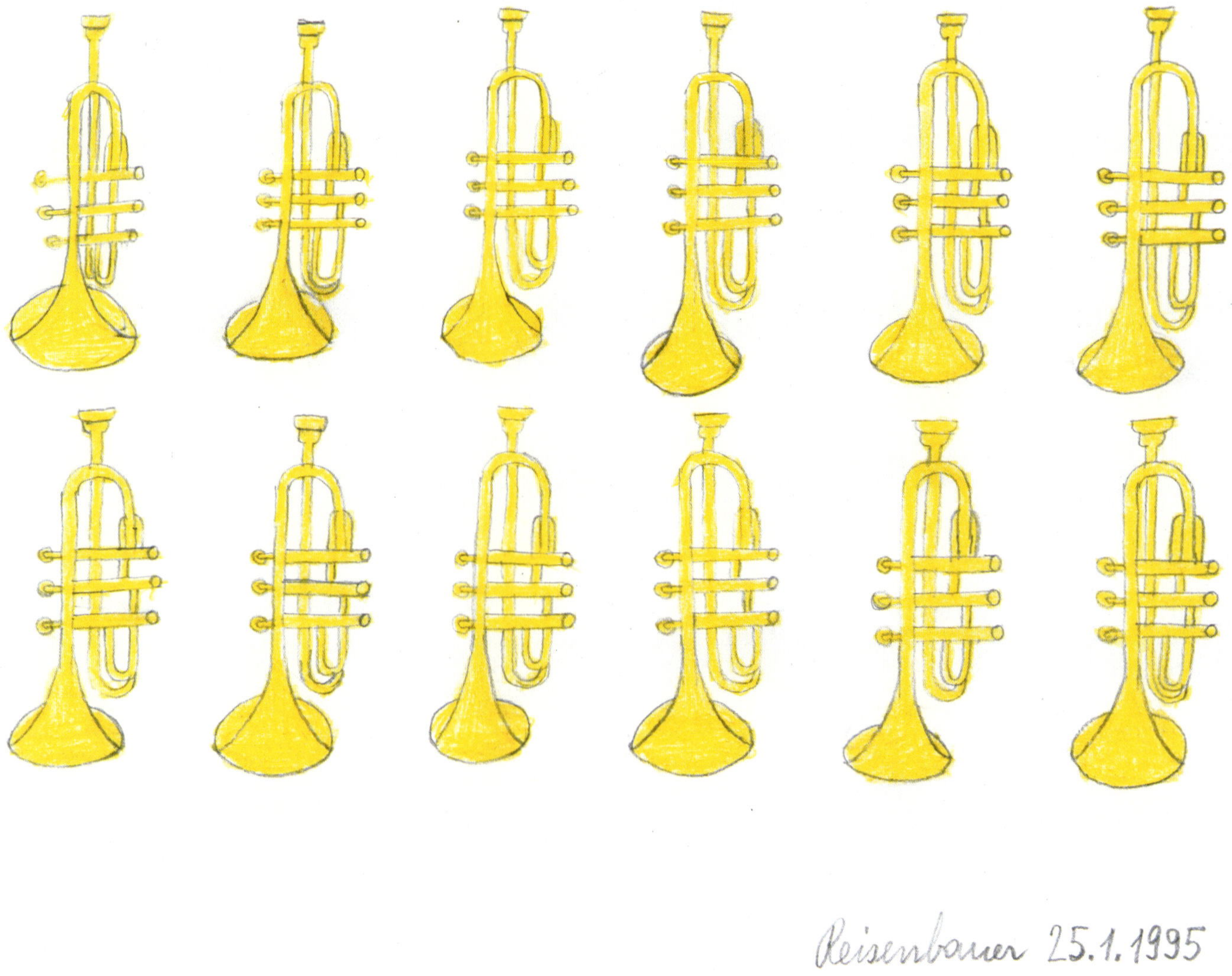
Reisenbauer 25.1.1995

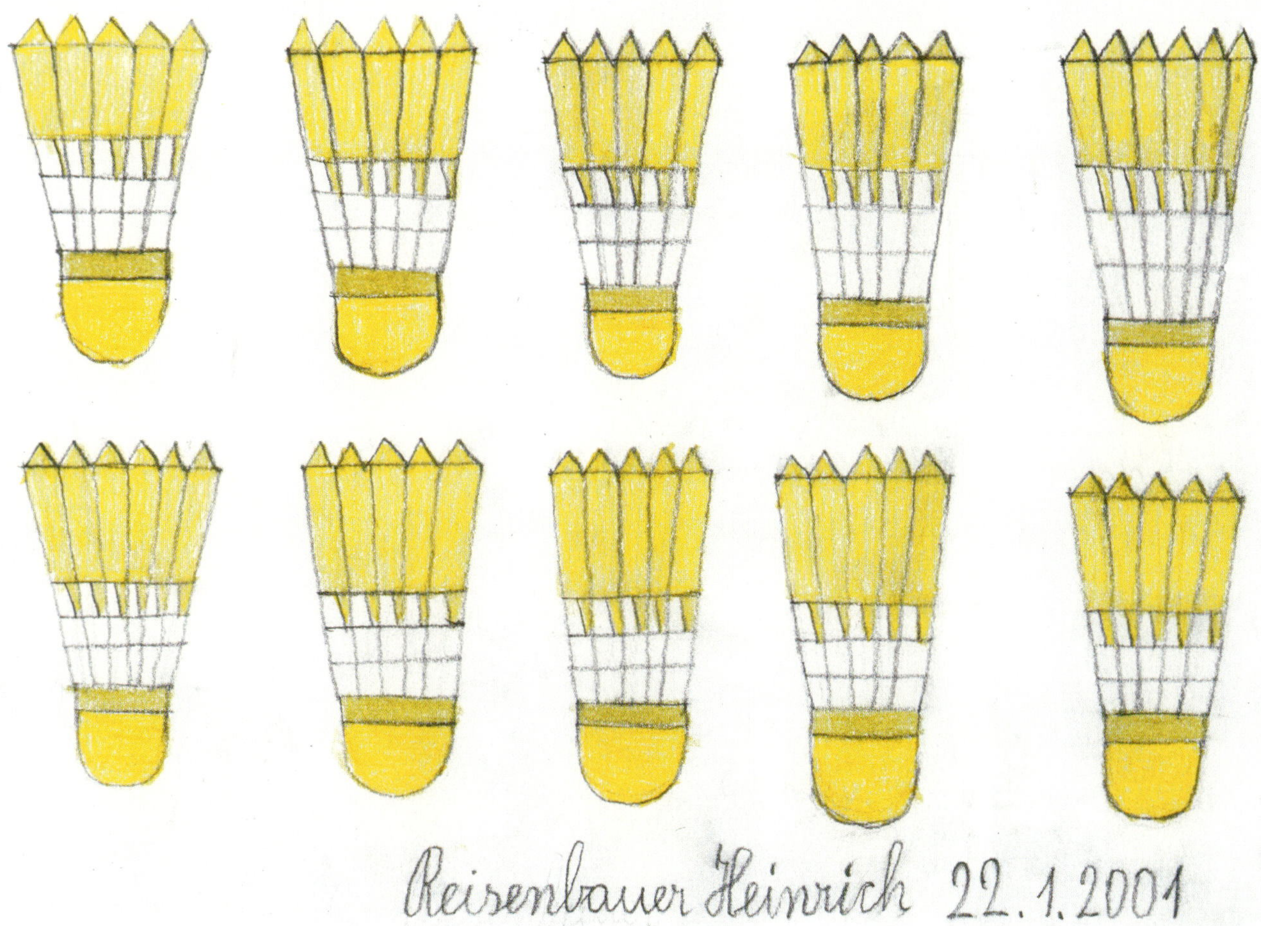

Heinrich Reisenbauer
Trompeten / Trumpets
1995, 21 x 29,7 cm
Bleistift, Farbstift /
pencil, color pencil
Privatstiftung -
Künstler aus Gugging

Heinrich Reisenbauer
Federbälle /
Shuttlecocks
2001, 14,7 x 20,9 cm
Bleistift, Farbstifte /
pencil, color pencils
Privatstiftung -
Künstler aus Gugging

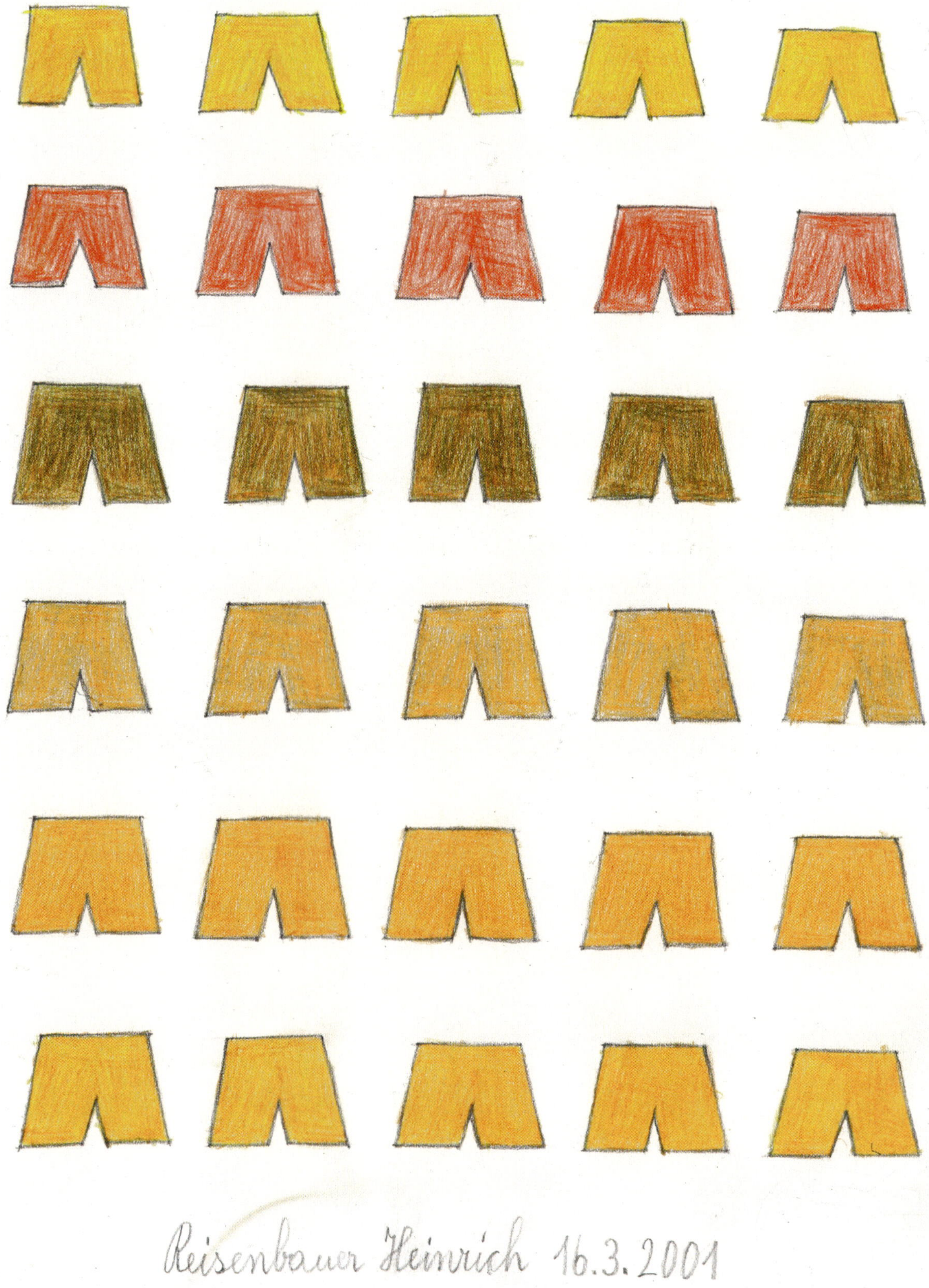
Reisenbauer Heinrich 16.3.2001

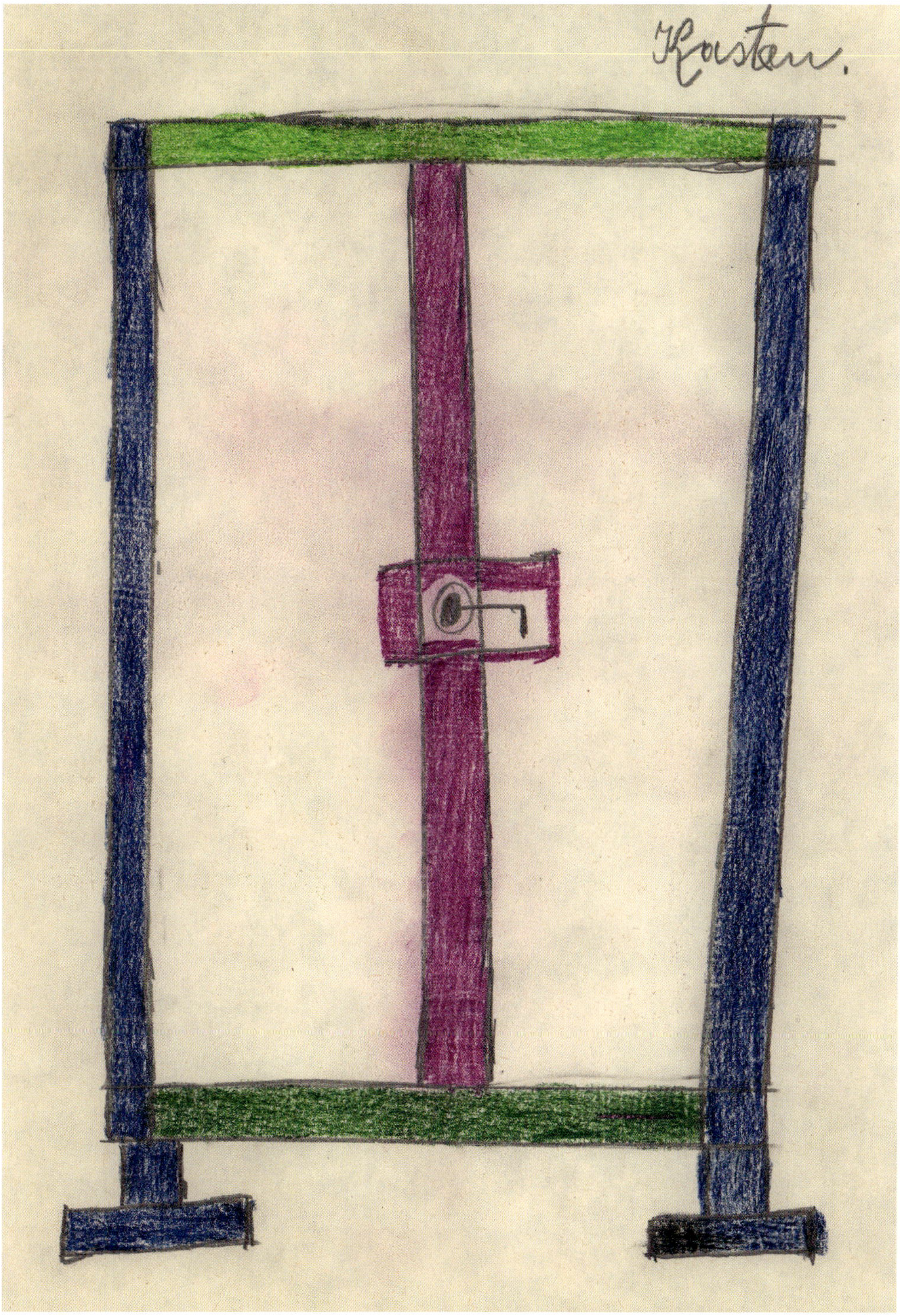

Heinrich Reisenbauer
Badehosen /
Bathing Suits
2001, 29,6 x 21 cm
Bleistift, Farbstifte /
pencil, color pencils
Privatstiftung -
Künstler aus Gugging

Johann Scheiböck
Kasten / Cupboard
1972, 29,6 x 20,5 cm
Bleistift, Farbstifte /
pencil, color pencils
Privatsammlung

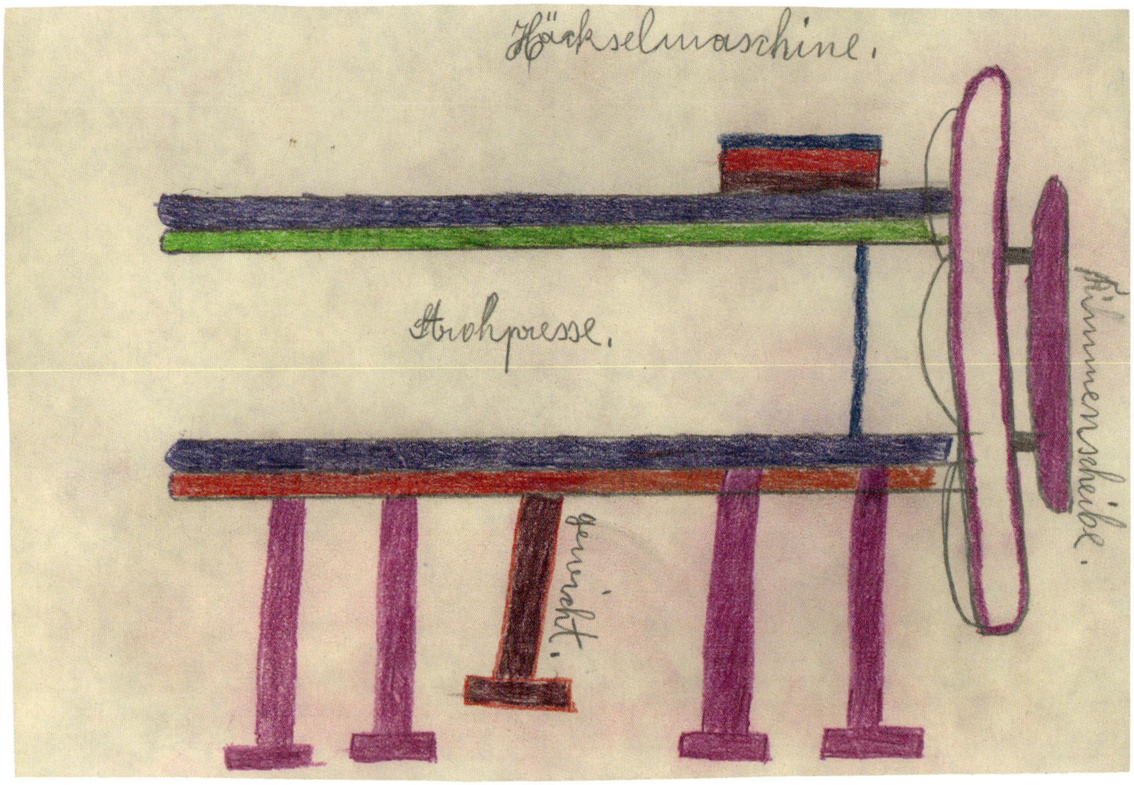
Häckselmaschine.
Strohpresse.

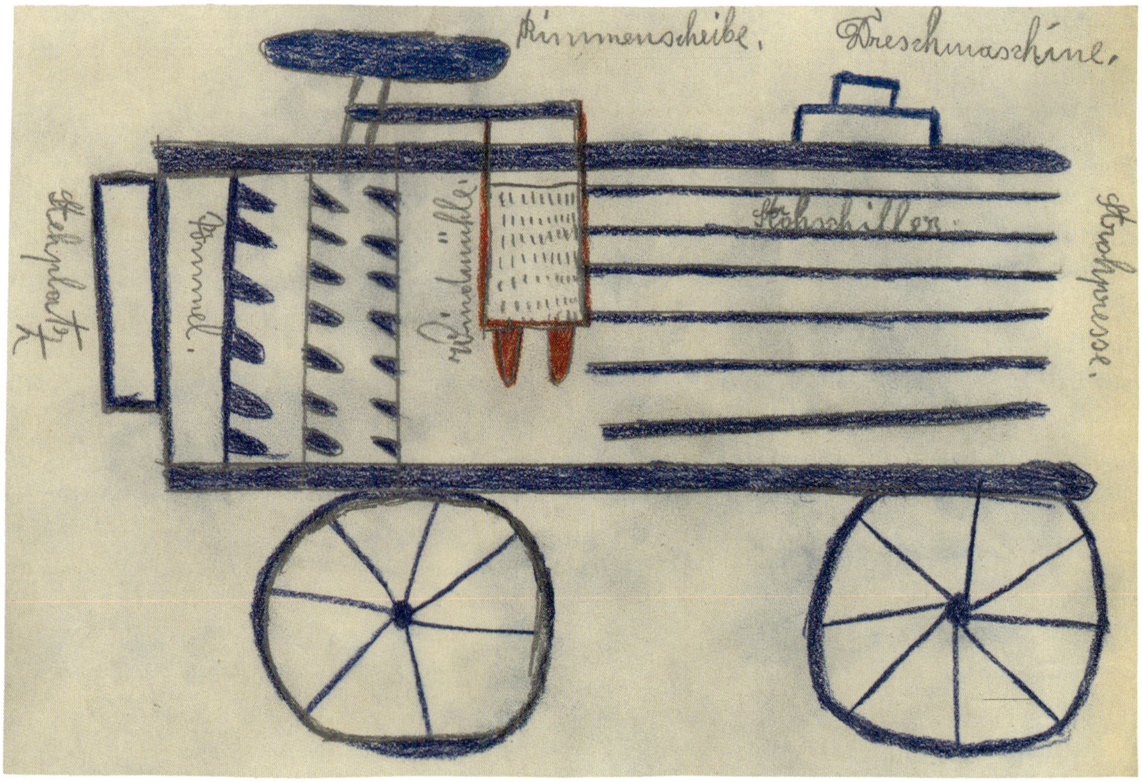
Dreschmaschine.
Strohpresse.

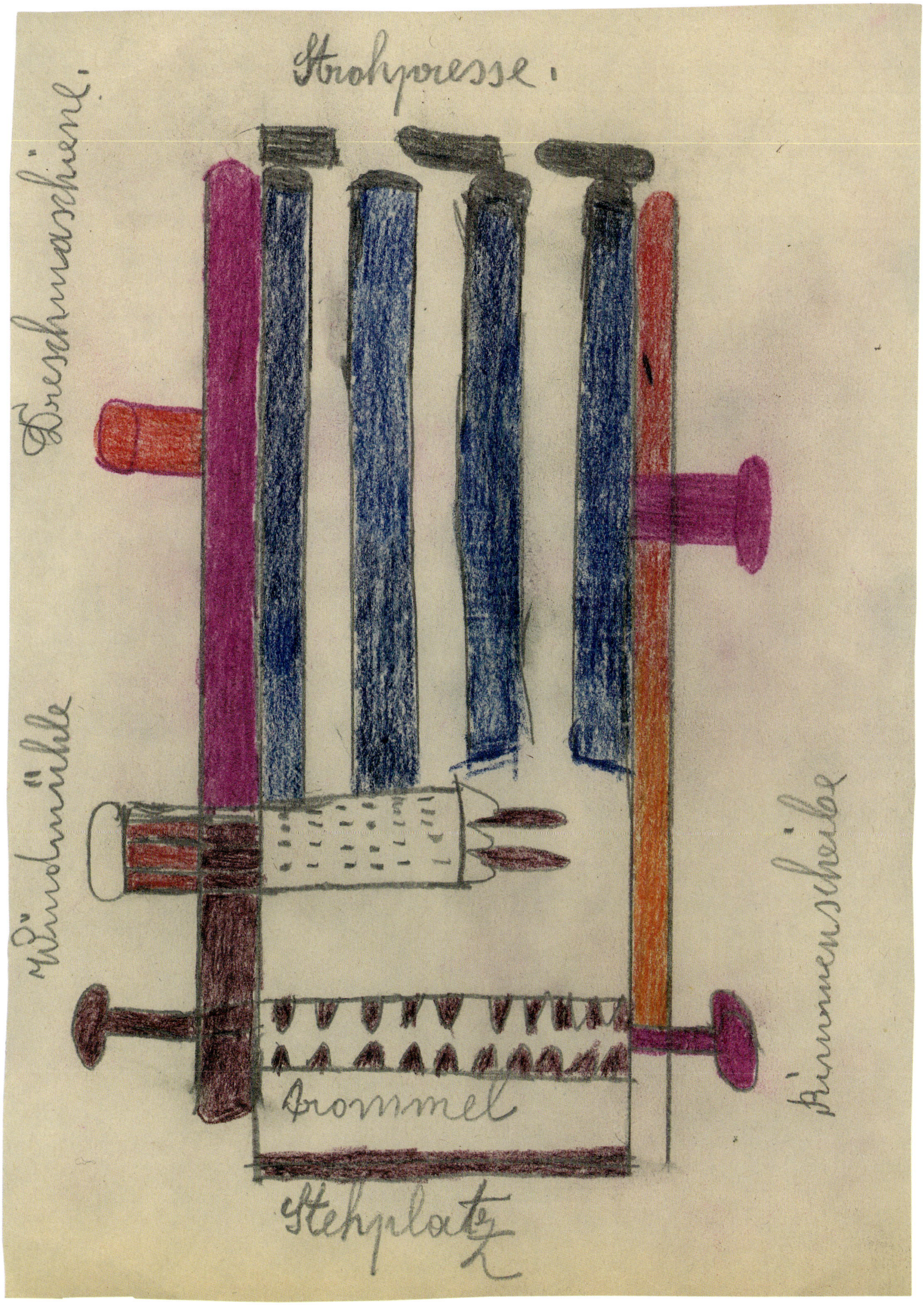

Johann Scheiböck
Häckselmaschine /
Straw Cutter
1972, 20,6 x 29,6 cm
Bleistift, Farbstifte /
pencil, color pencils
Sammlung Arnulf Rainer

Johann Scheiböck
Dreschmaschine /
Tresher
1972, 20,9 x 30,1 cm
Bleistift, Farbstifte /
pencil, color pencils
Sammlung Arnulf Rainer

Johann Scheiböck
Strohpresse /
Straw press
1972, 29,8 x 20,9 cm
Bleistift, Farbstifte /
pencil, color pencils
Sammlung Arnulf Rainer

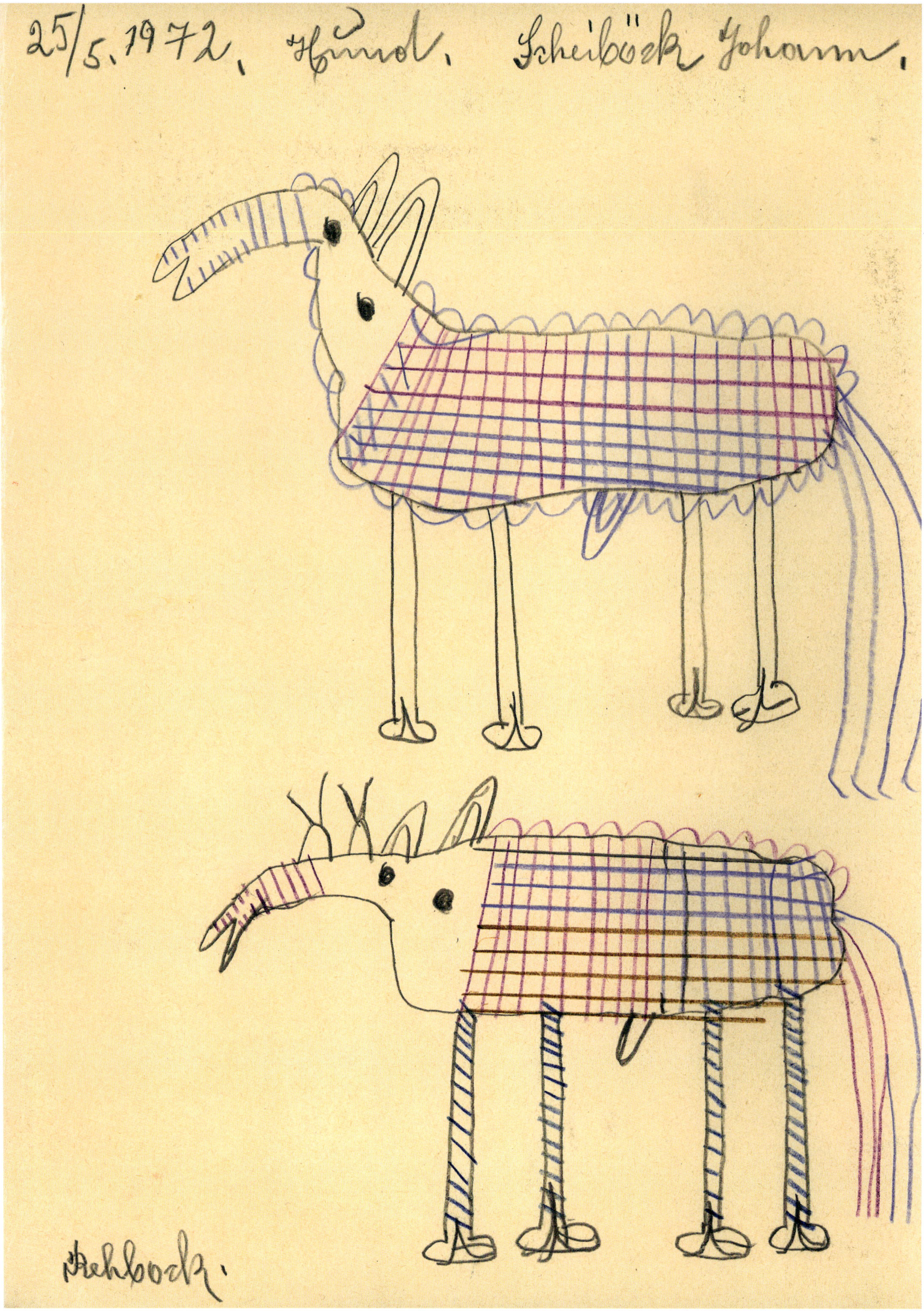
25/5.1972. Hund. Scheiböck Johann.
Rehbock.

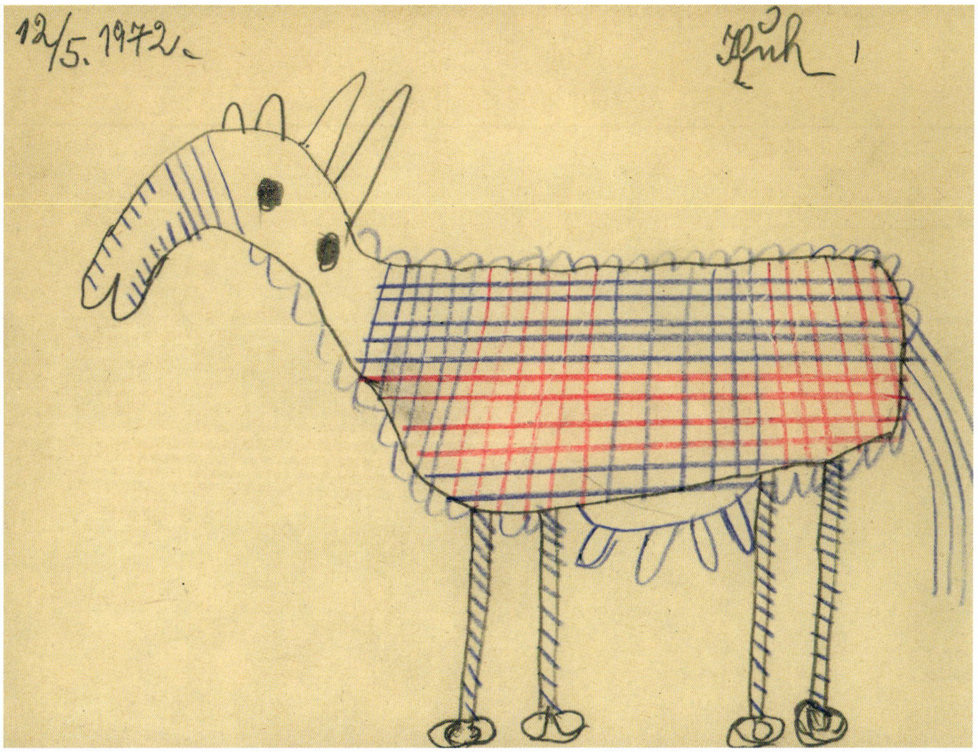

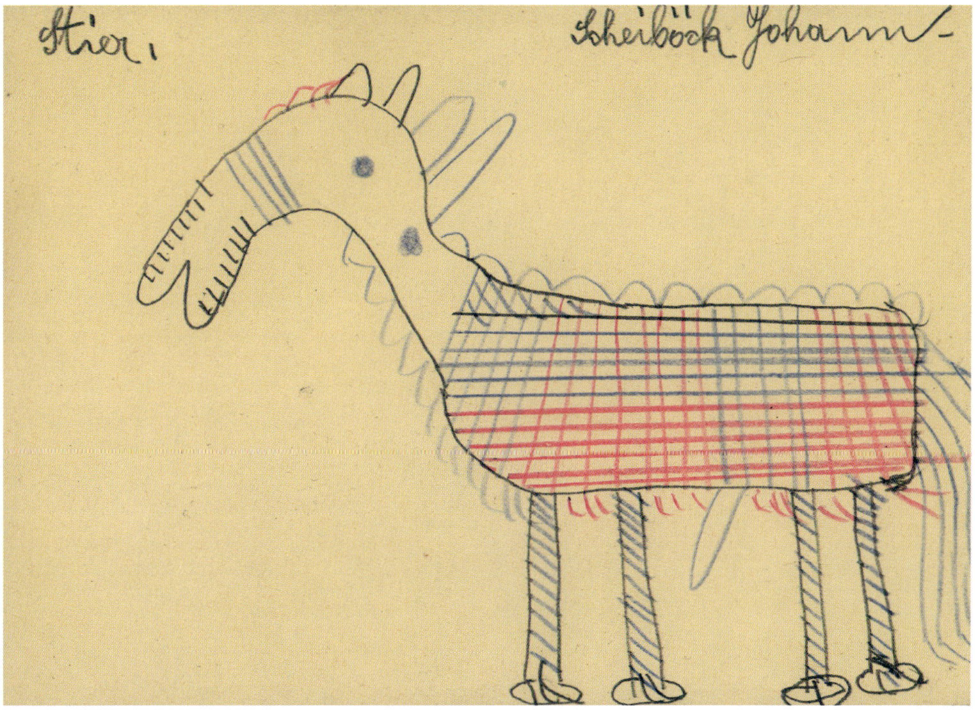

Johann Scheiböck
Hund und Rehbock /
Dog and Roebuck
1972, 29,6 x 21 cm
Bleistift, Farbstifte /
pencil, color pencils
Sammlung Helmut Zambo

Johann Scheiböck
Kuh / Cow
1972, 16 x 21,3 cm
Bleistift, Farbstifte /
Pencil, color pencils
Privatsammlung

Johann Scheiböck
Stier / Bull
1972, 16 x 21,3 cm
Bleistift, Farbstifte /
Pencil, color pencils
Privatsammlung

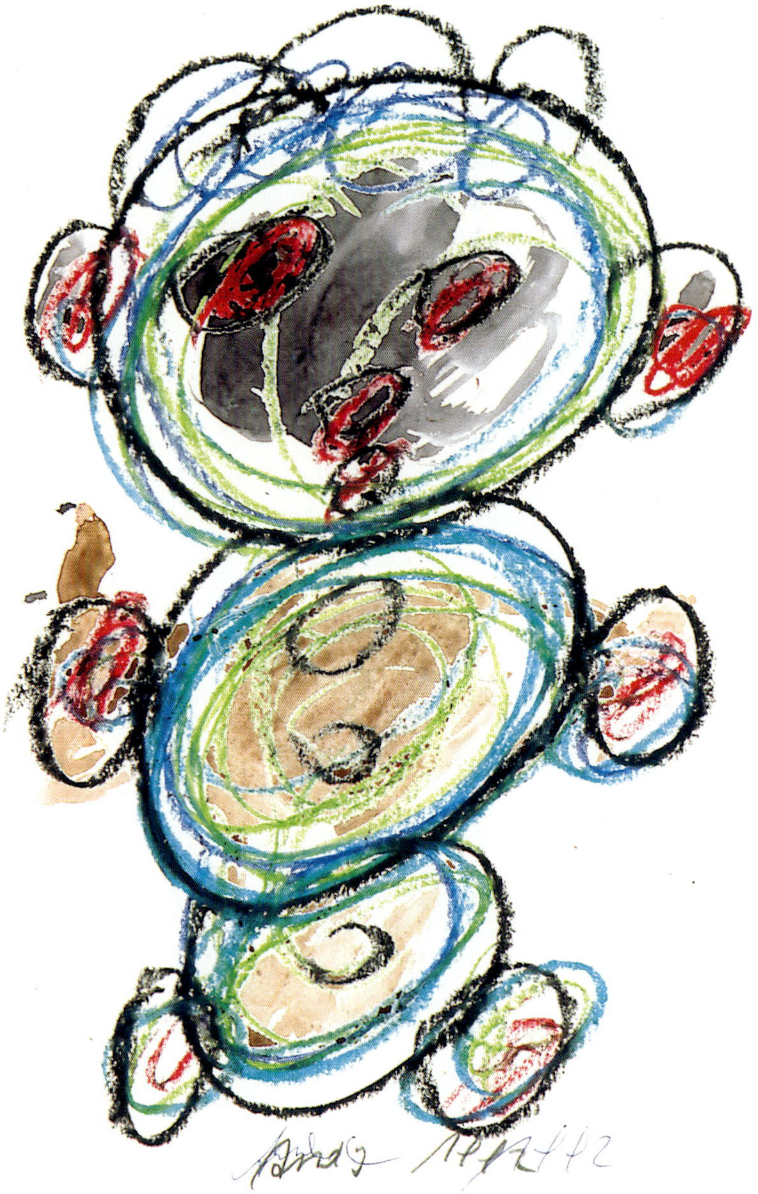

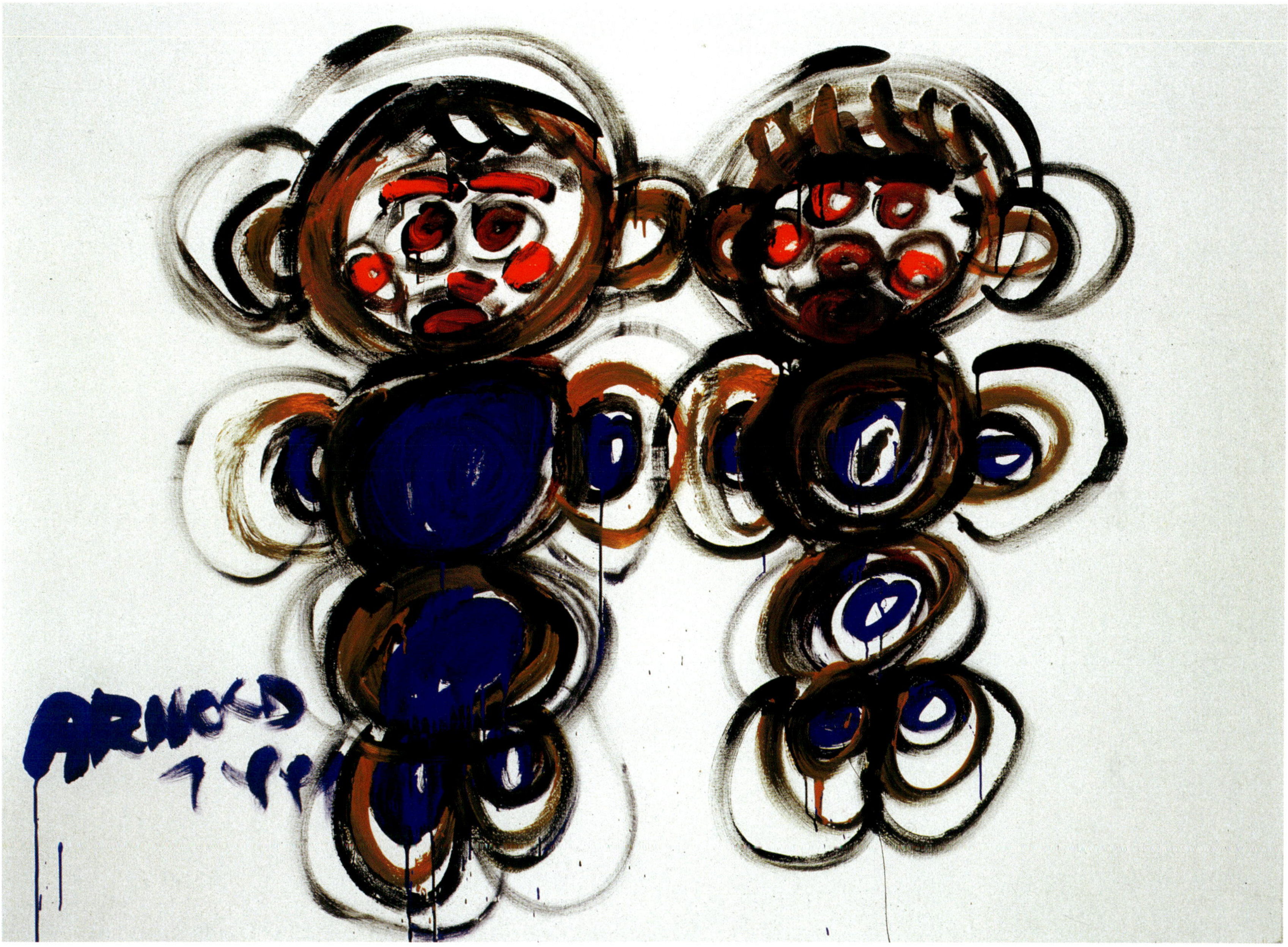

Arnold Schmidt
Figur / Figure
1992, 29,7 x 21 cm
Kohle, Aquarellfarben,
Wachskreide /
charcoal, aquarell,
crayons
Privatsstiftung -
Künstler aus Gugging

Arnold Schmidt
Zwei Figuren /
Two Figures
1991, 120 x 160 cm
Acryl auf Leinwand /
acrylic on canvas
Privatstiftung -
Künstler aus Gugging

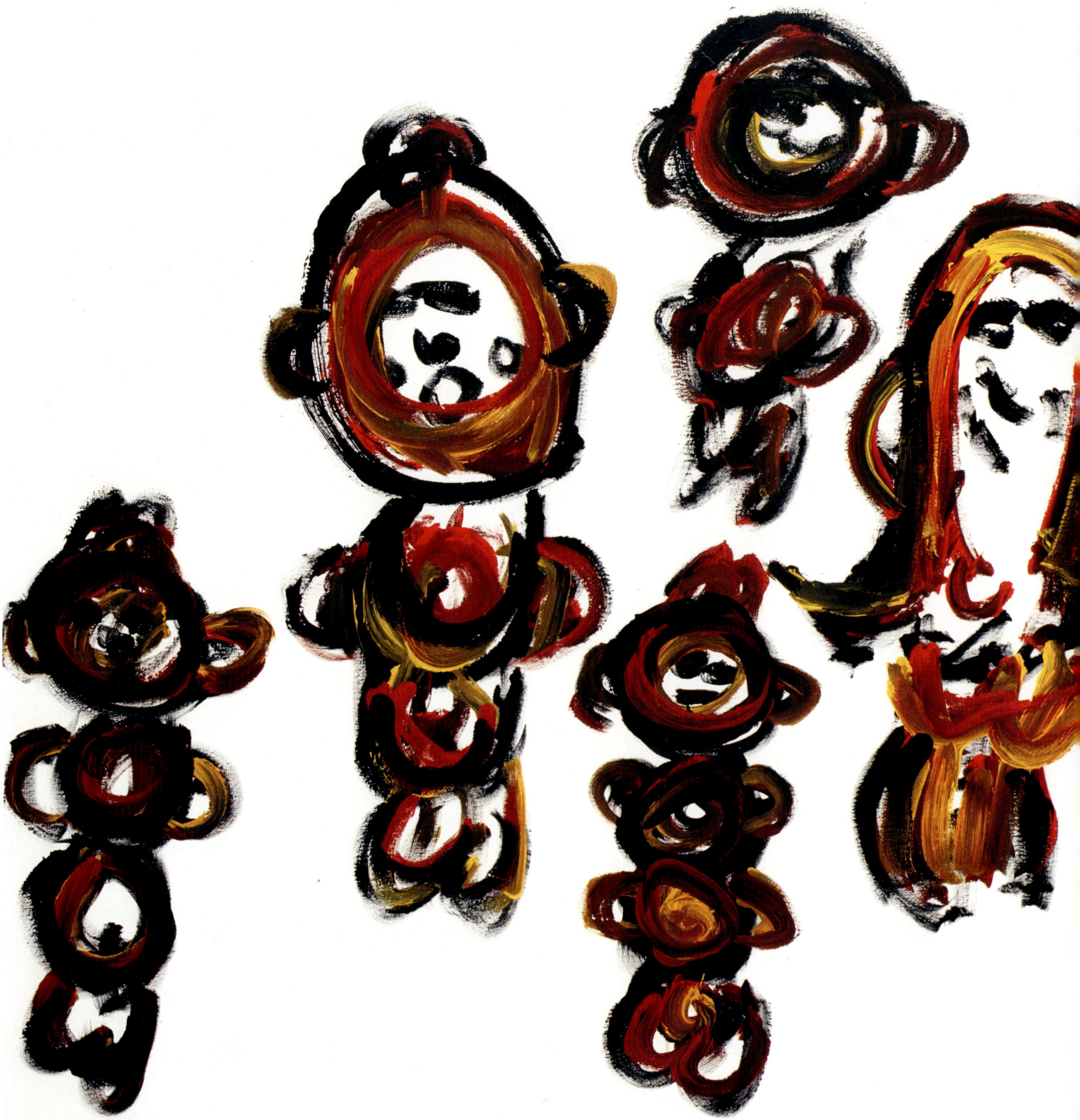

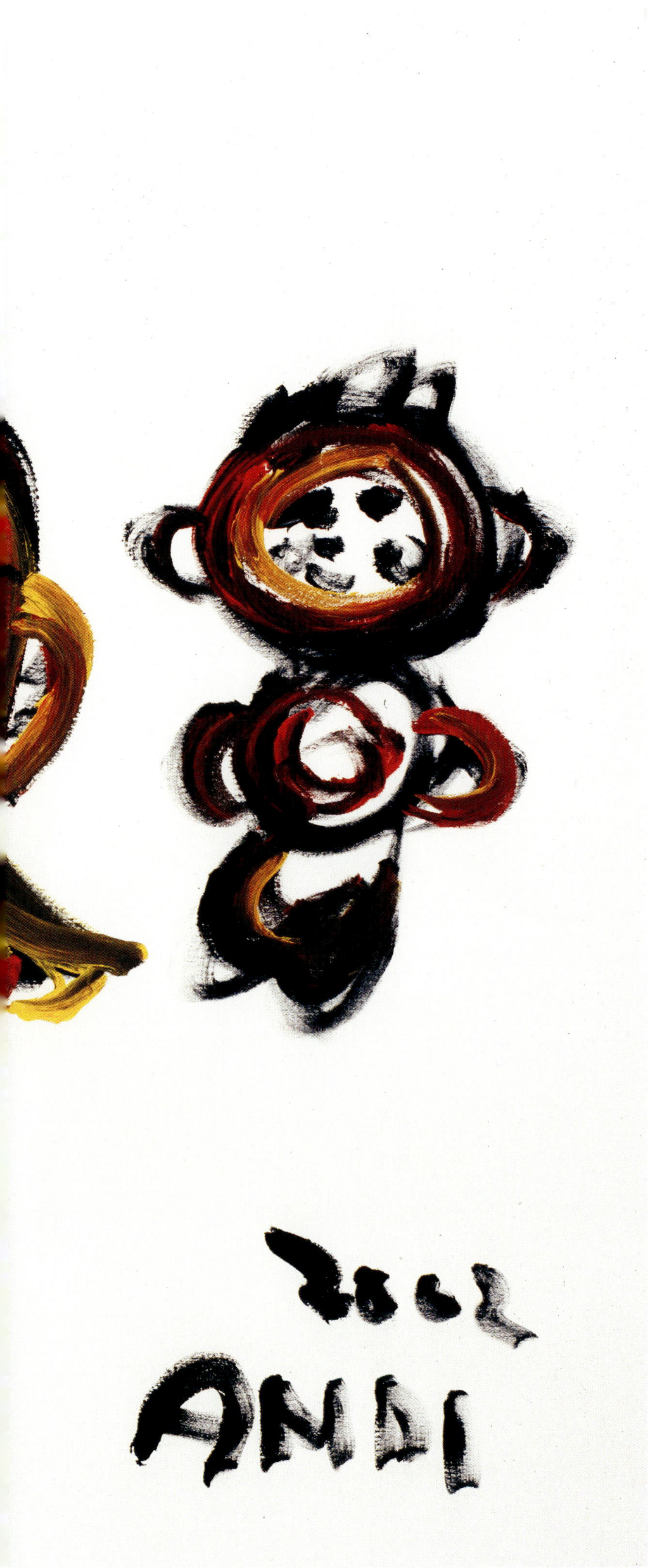

Arnold Schmidt
Viele Menschen /
Many People
2002, 160 x 200 cm
Acryl auf Leinwand /
acrylic on canvas
Privatstiftung -
Künstler aus Gugging

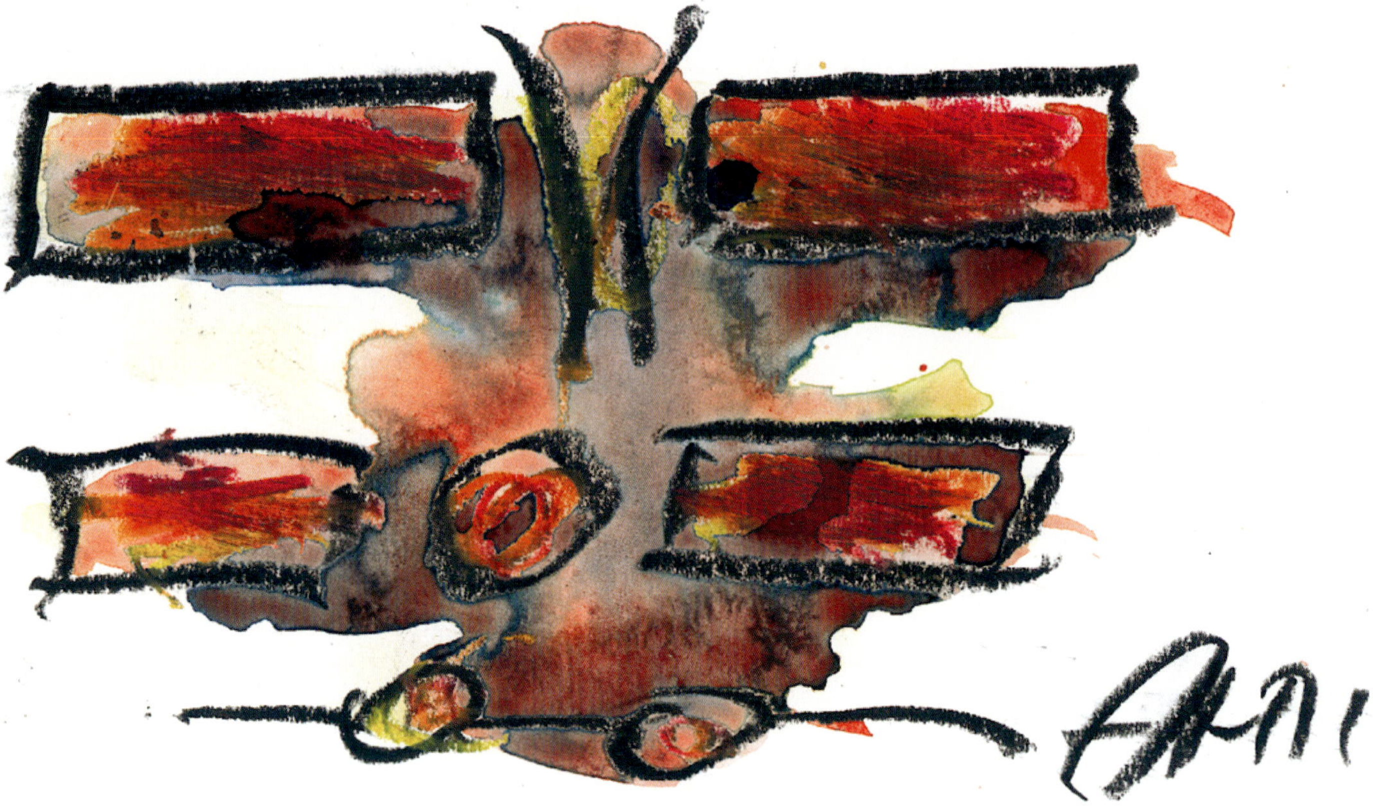

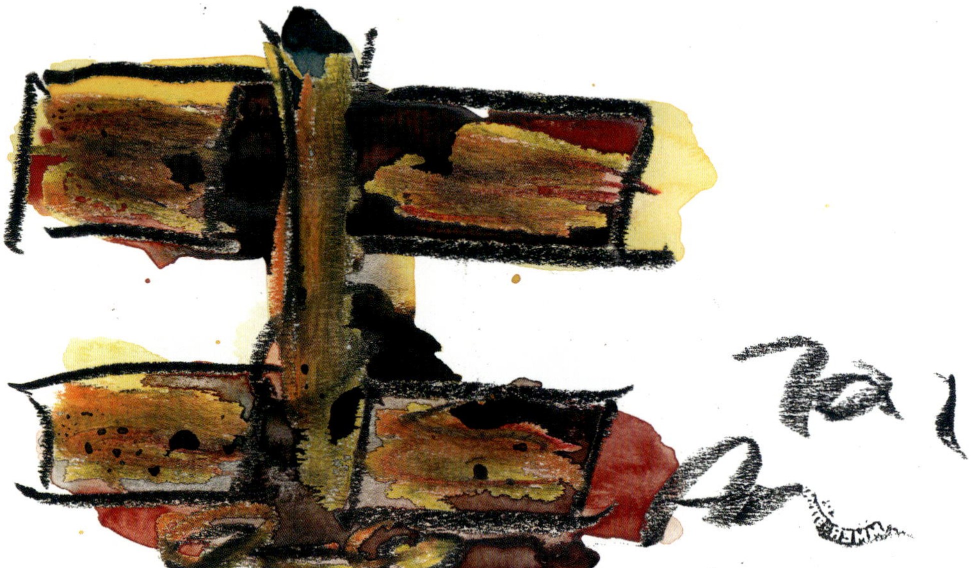

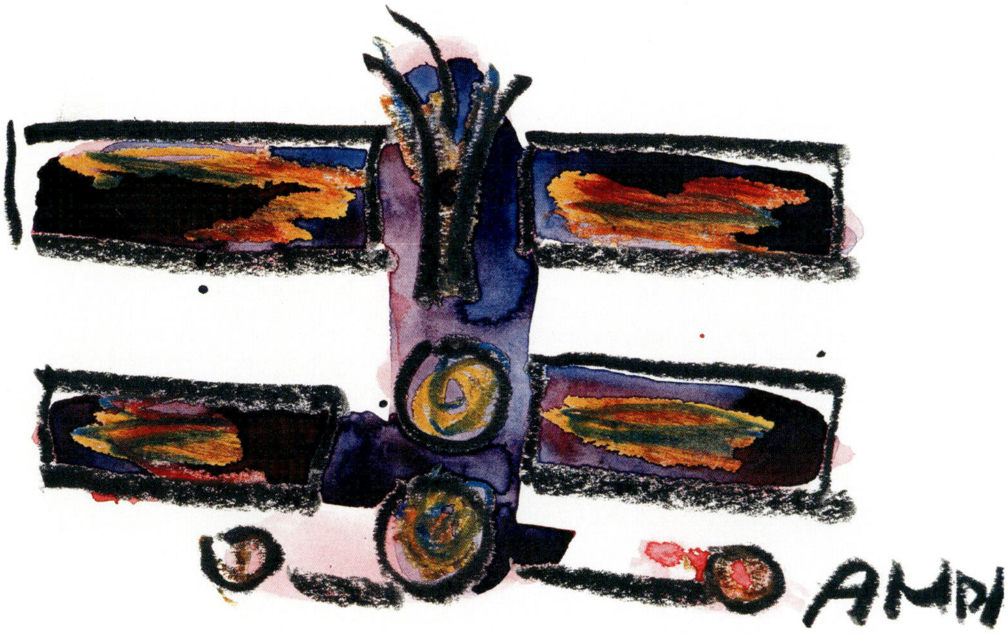

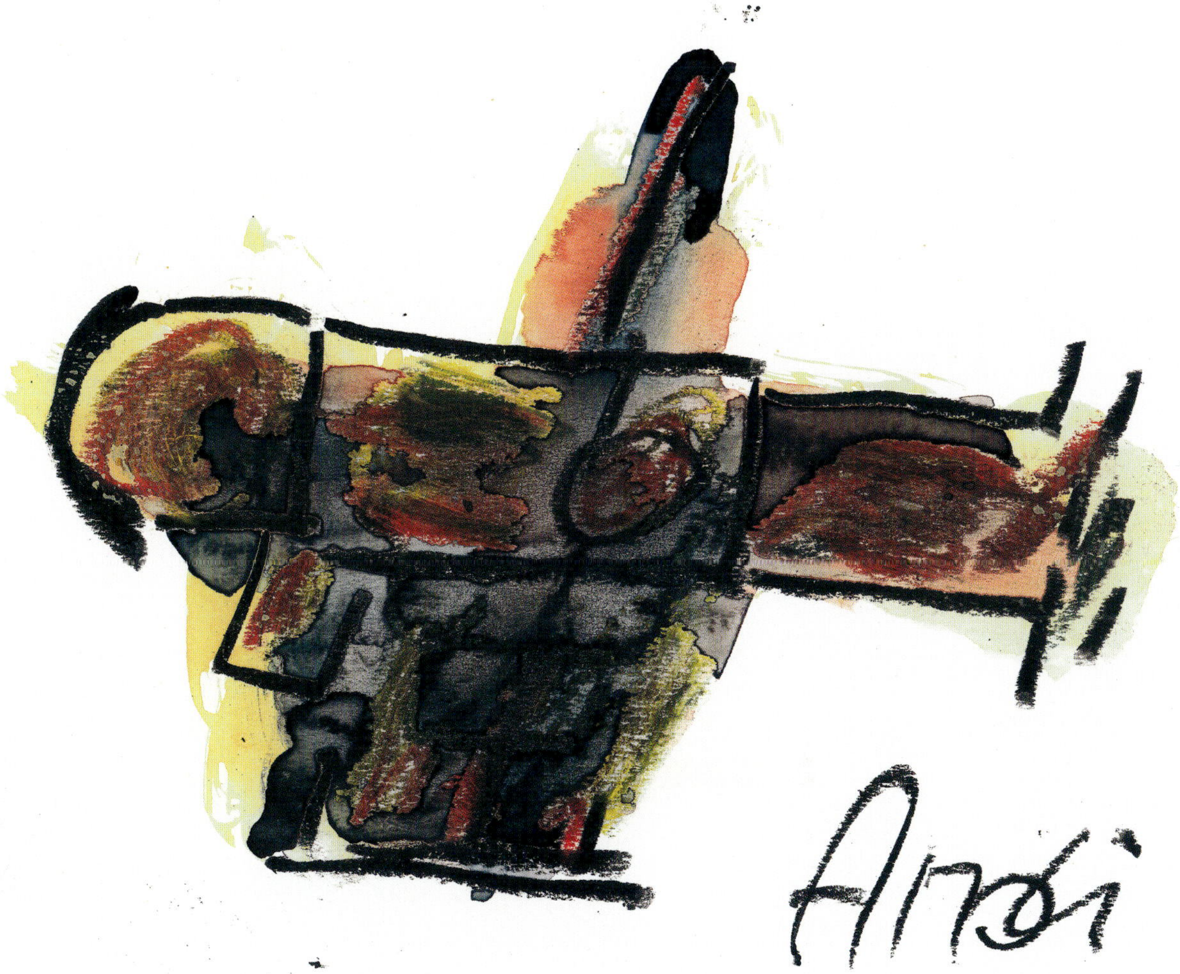

Arnold Schmidt
Flugzeug / Airplane
2003, 14,7 x 20,9 cm
Kohle, Aquarellfarben,
Wachskreide /
charcoal, aquarell,
crayons

Arnold Schmidt
Flugzeug / Airplane
2004, 14,8 x 10,5 cm
Kohle, Aquarellfarben,
Wachskreide /
charcoal, aquarell,
crayons

Arnold Schmidt
Flugzeug / Airplane
2002, 14,7 x 20,9 cm
Kohle, Aquarellfarben,
Wachskreide /
charcoal, aquarell,
crayons

Arnold Schmidt
Hubschrauber /
Helicopter
2005, 14,8 x 20,9 cm
Kohle, Aquarellfarben,
Wachskreide /
charcoal, aquarell,
crayons

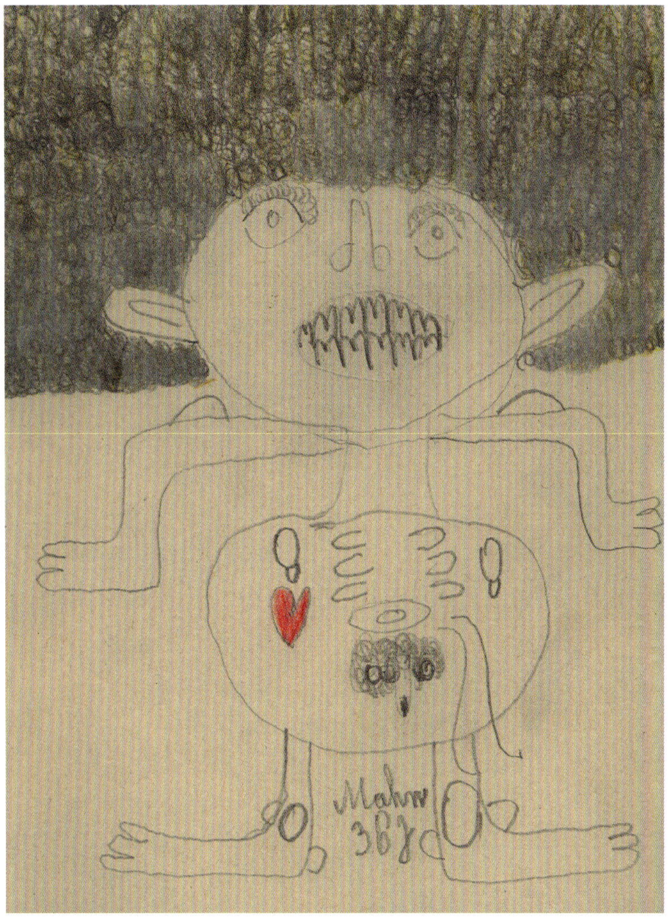
36J

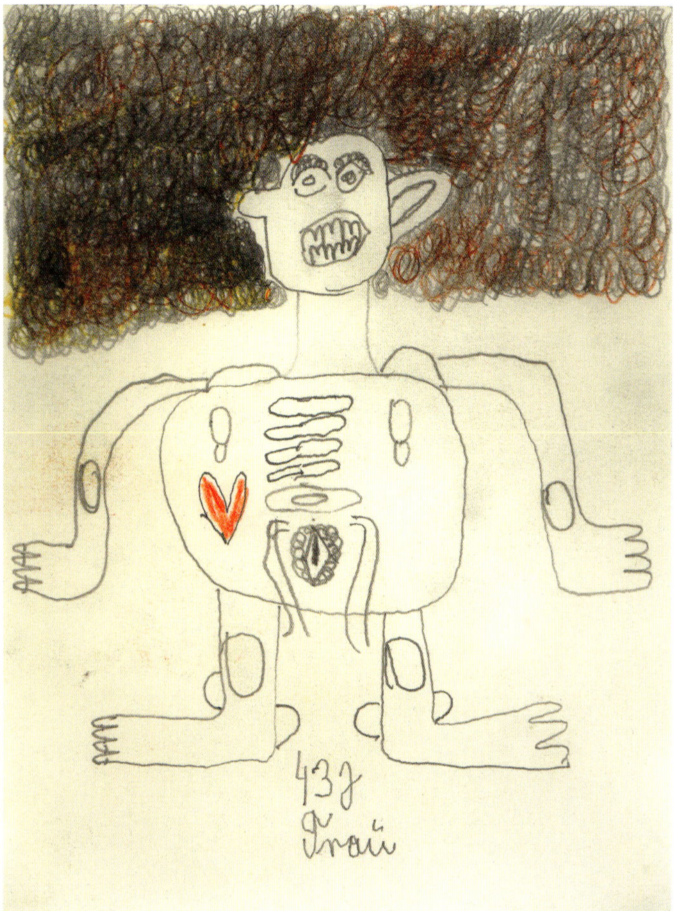
43J

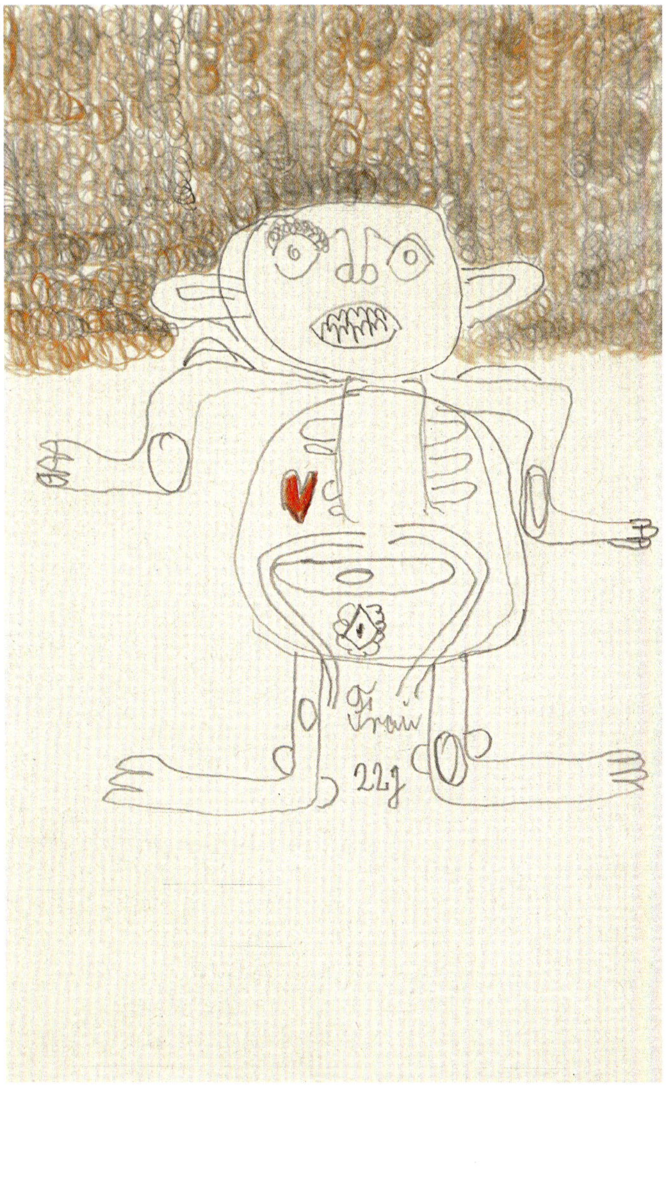
22J

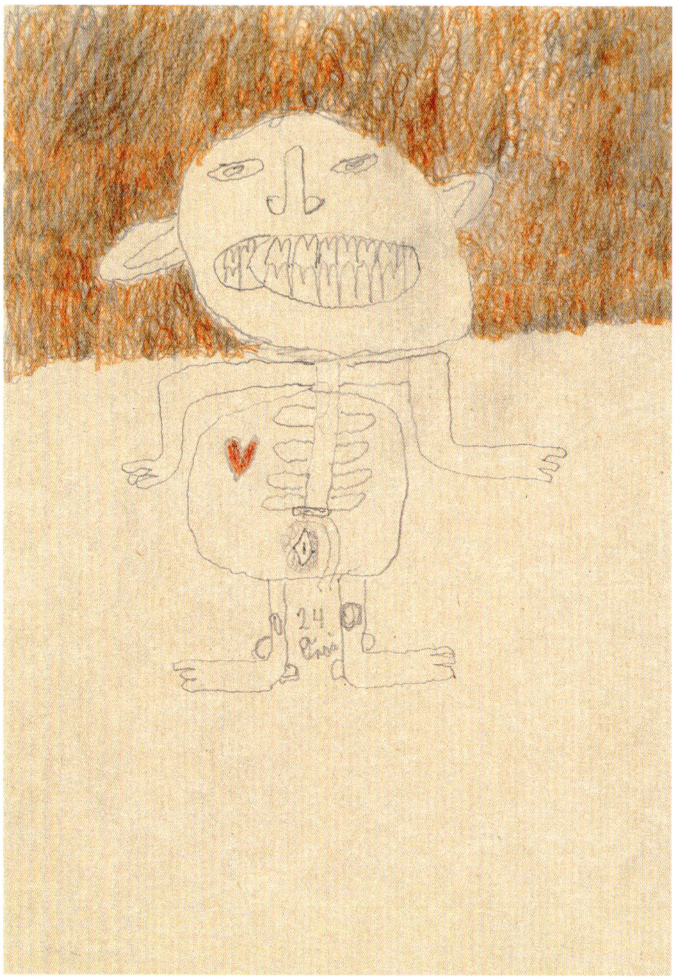
24

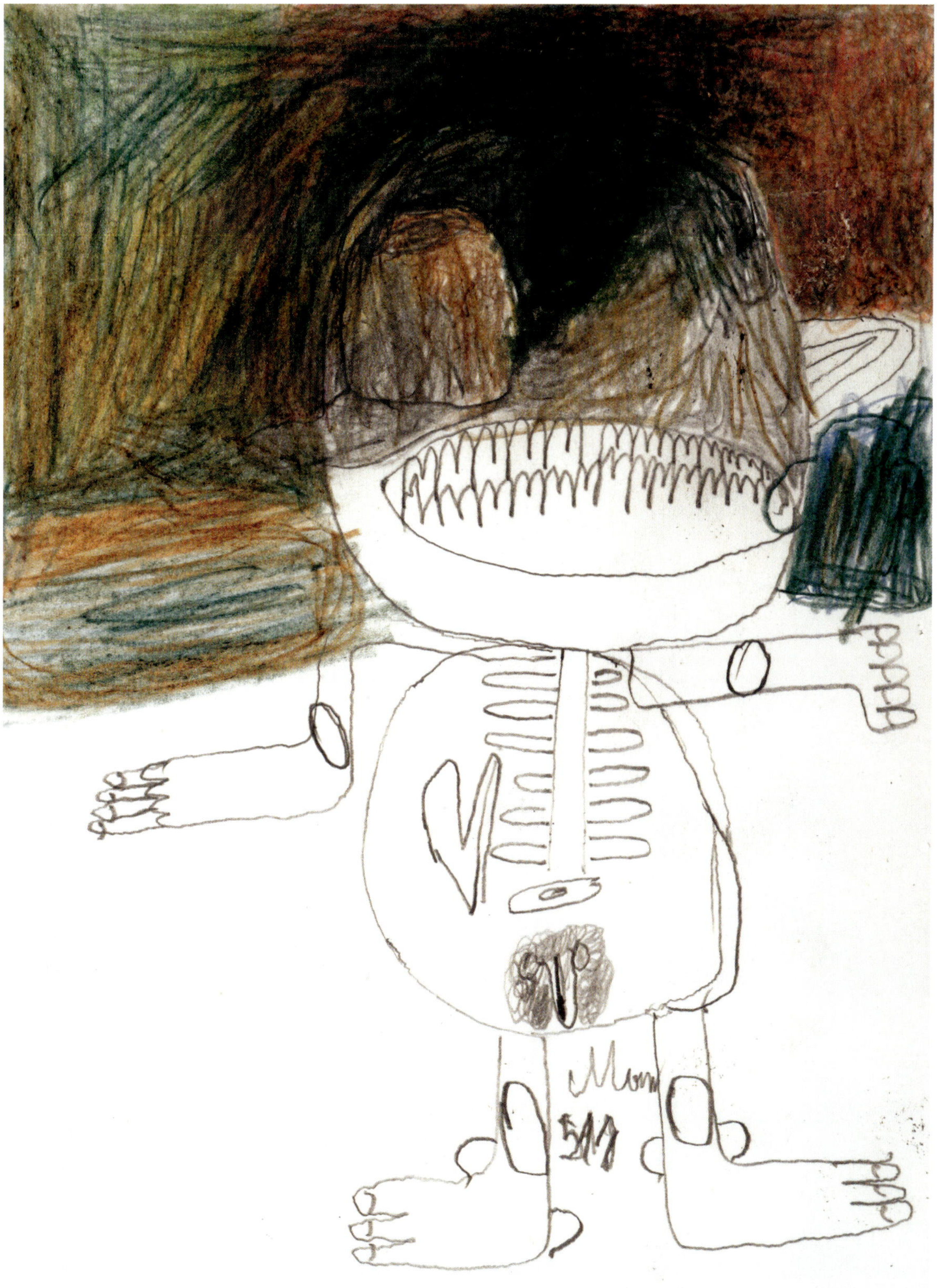

Philipp Schöpke
Mahn 36 J / Man 36 Y
1971, 21,1 x 15,3 cm
Bleistift , Farbstifte /
pencil, color pencils
Privatsammlung

Philipp Schöpke
43 J Frau / 43 Y Woman
1971, 19,7 x 14,8 cm
Bleistift, Farbstifte /
pencil, color pencils
Sammlung Josef Schroll

Philipp Schöpke
Frau 22 J / Woman 22 Y
1971, 24,3 x 15,1 cm
Bleistift, Farbstifte /
pencil, color pencils
Sammlung Josef Schroll

Philipp Schöpke
24 Omi / 24 Granny
1971, 23 x 15,6 cm
Bleistift, Farbstifte /
pencil, color pencils
Sammlung Josef Schroll

Philipp Schöpke
Mann 51 J / Man 51 Y
1972, 20,9 x 14,8 cm
Bleistift, Farbstifte /
pencil, color pencils
Sammlung Josef Schroll

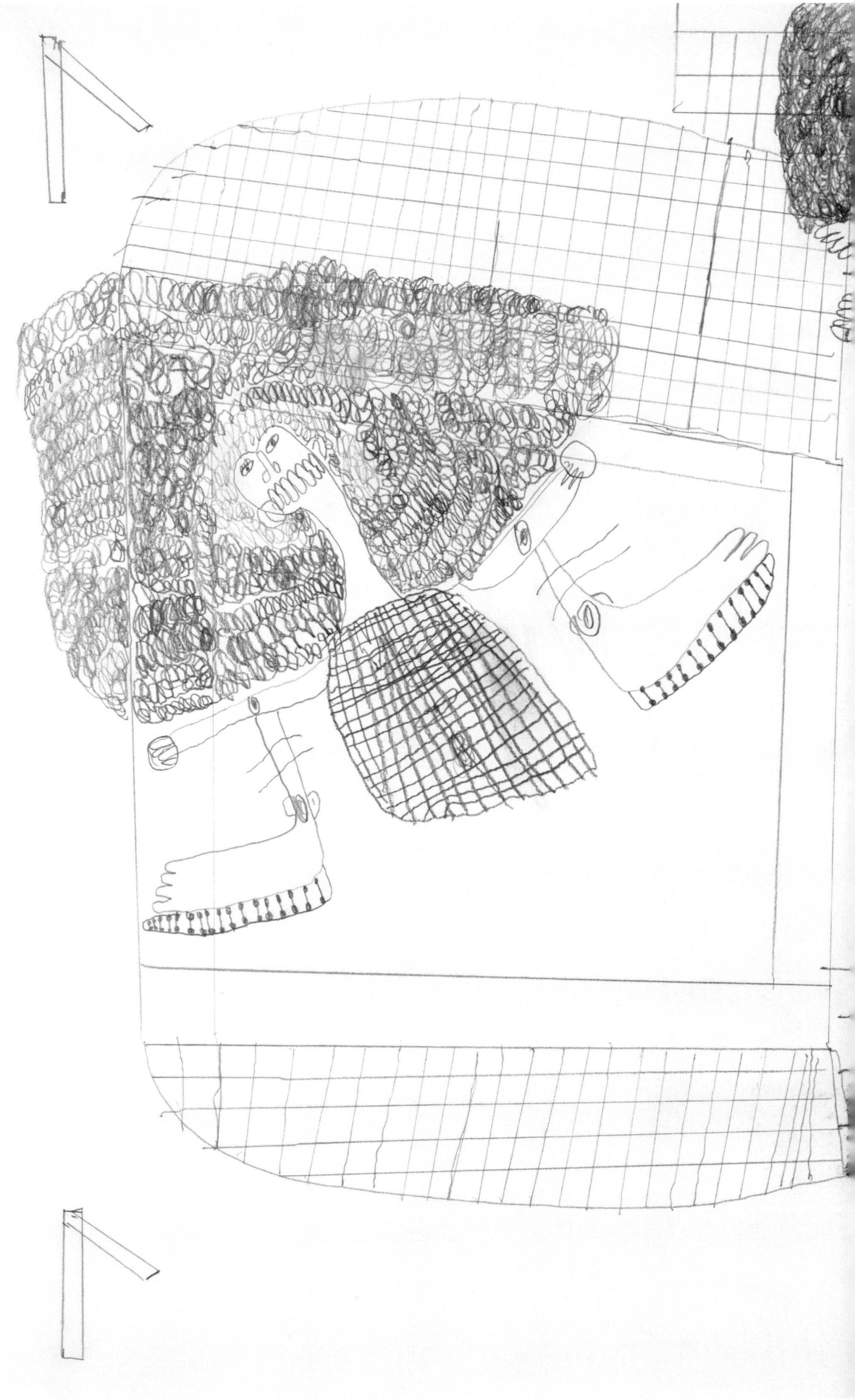

Philipp Schöpke
Fußballspiel /
Football Match
1983, 62,4 x 88 cm
Bleistift / pencil
Privatsammlung

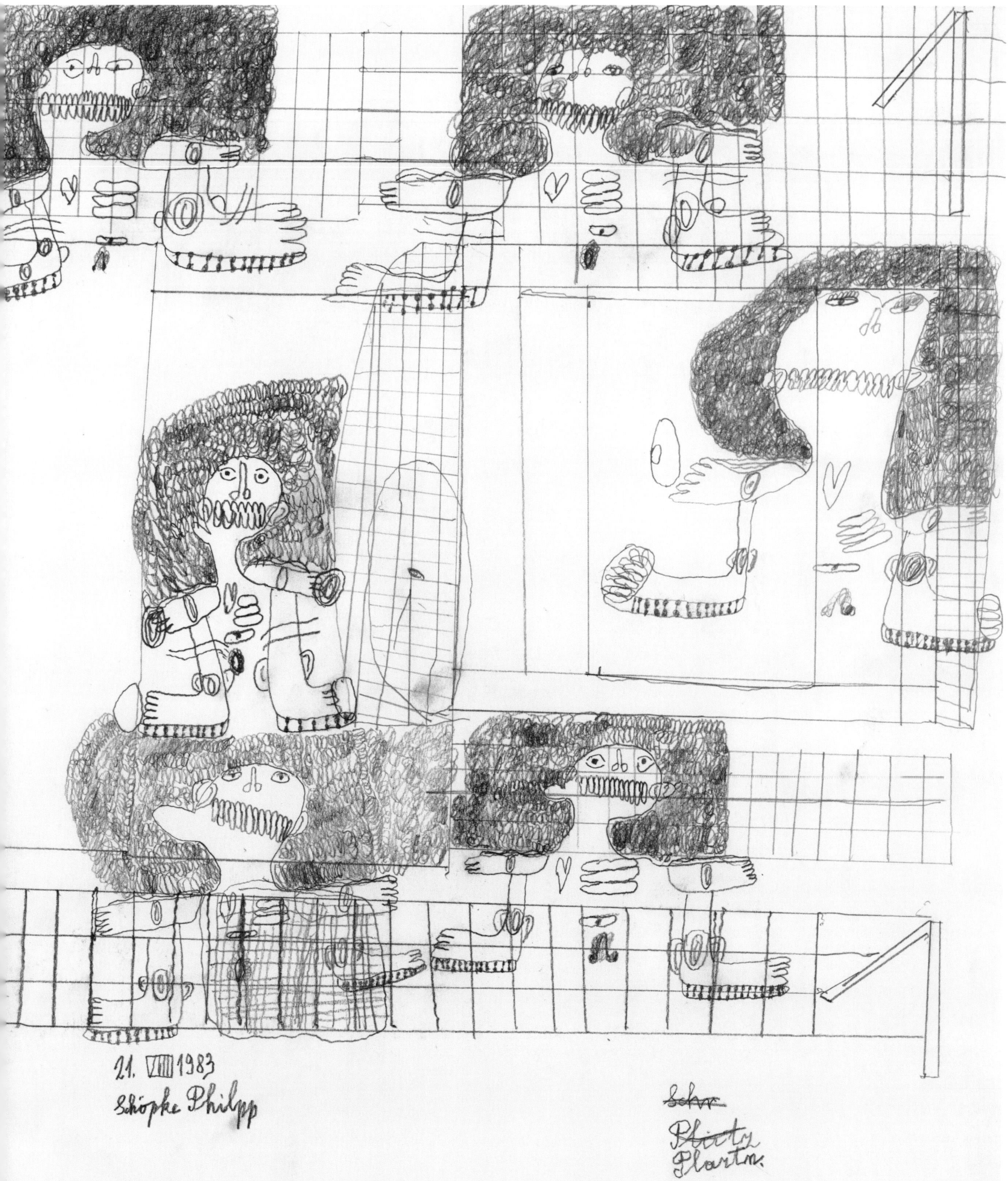
21. VIII 1983
Schöpke Philipp

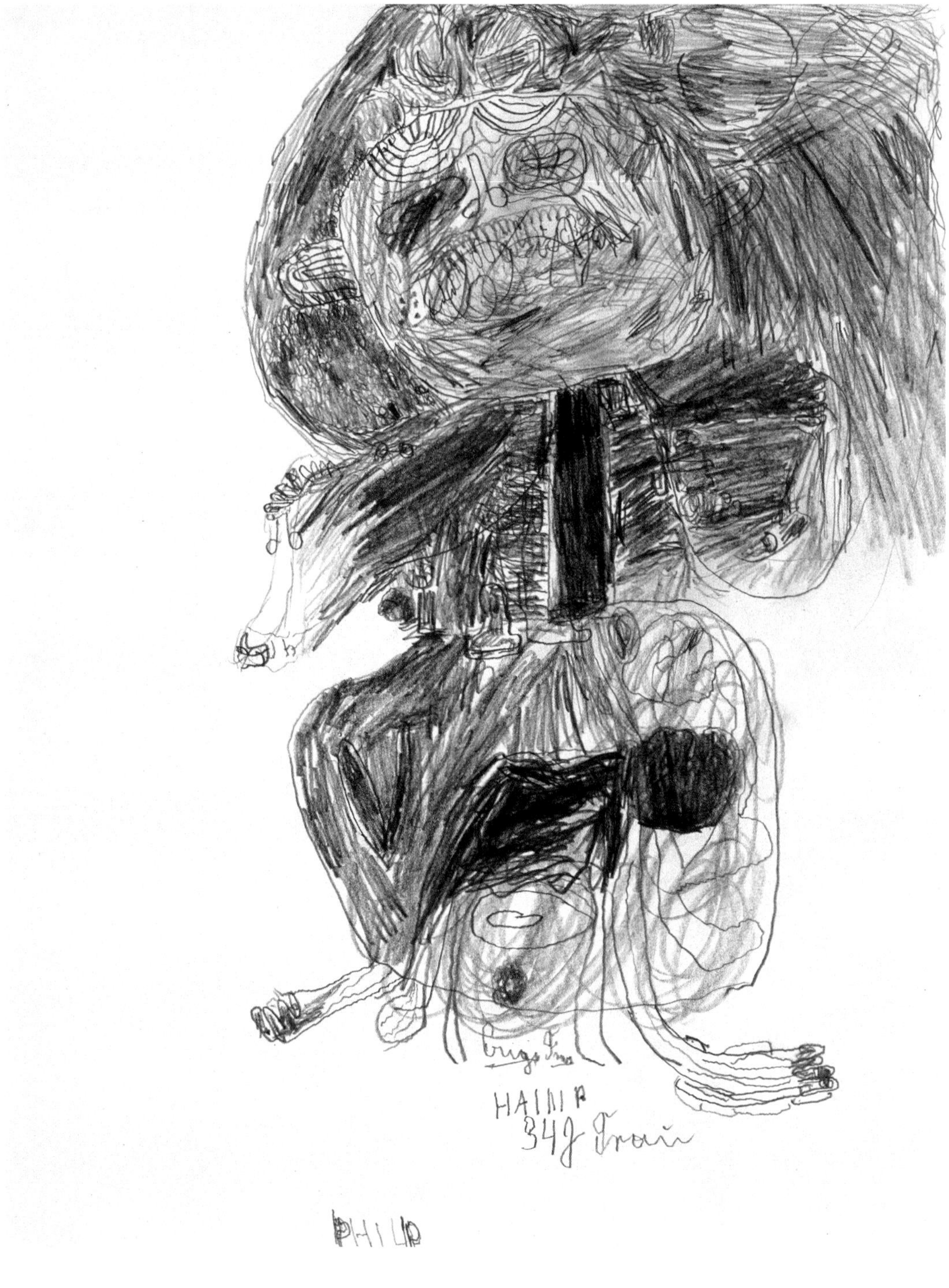
34J Frau

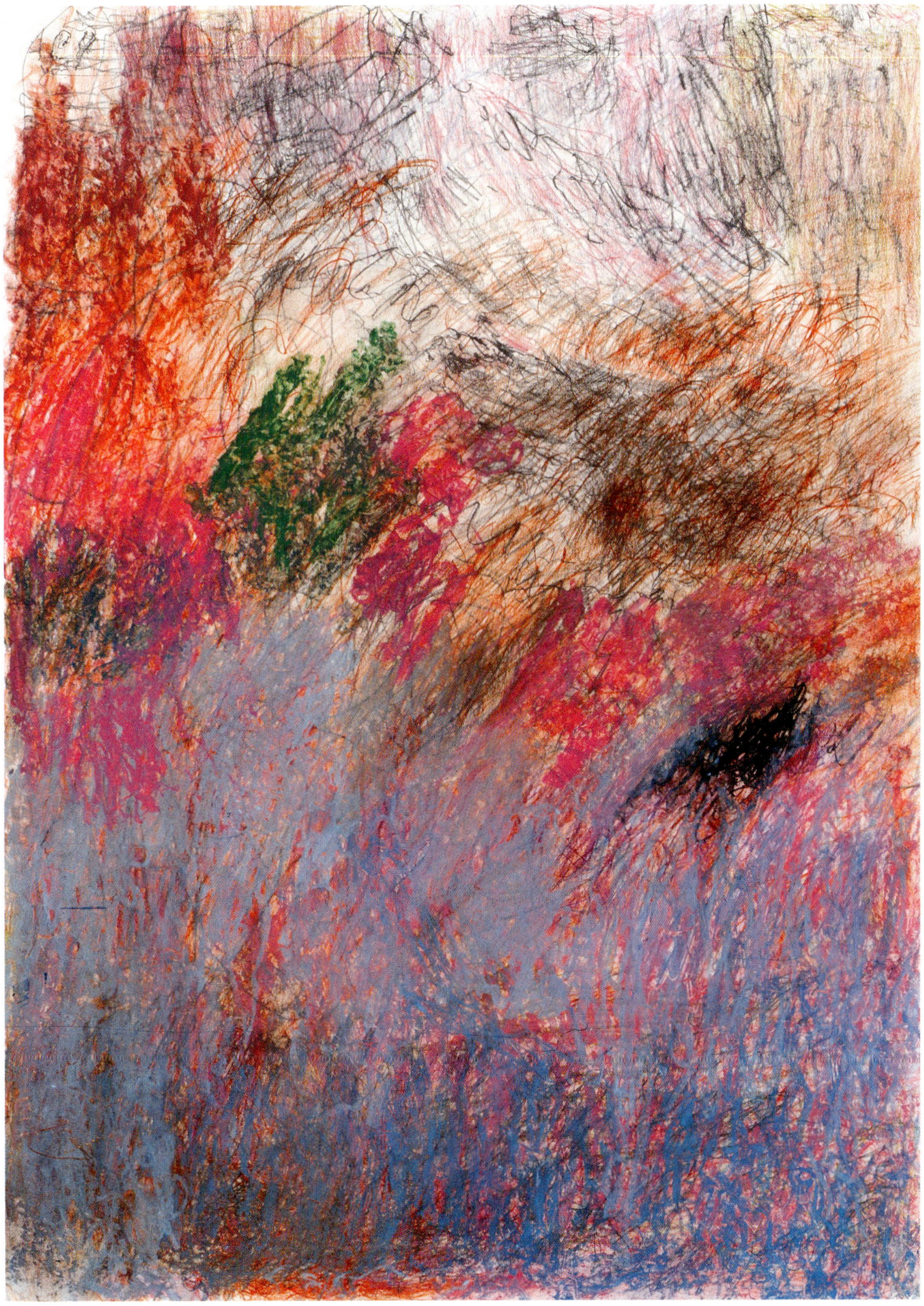

Philipp Schöpke
Frau 34 J / Woman 34 Y
1976, 40 x 30 cm
Bleistift / pencil
Sammlung Arnulf Rainer

Philipp Schöpke
Ohne Titel / Untitled
1997, 44,1 x 62,6 cm
Bleistift, Farbstifte, Wachskreide / pencil, color pencils, crayons
Sammlung Josef Schroll

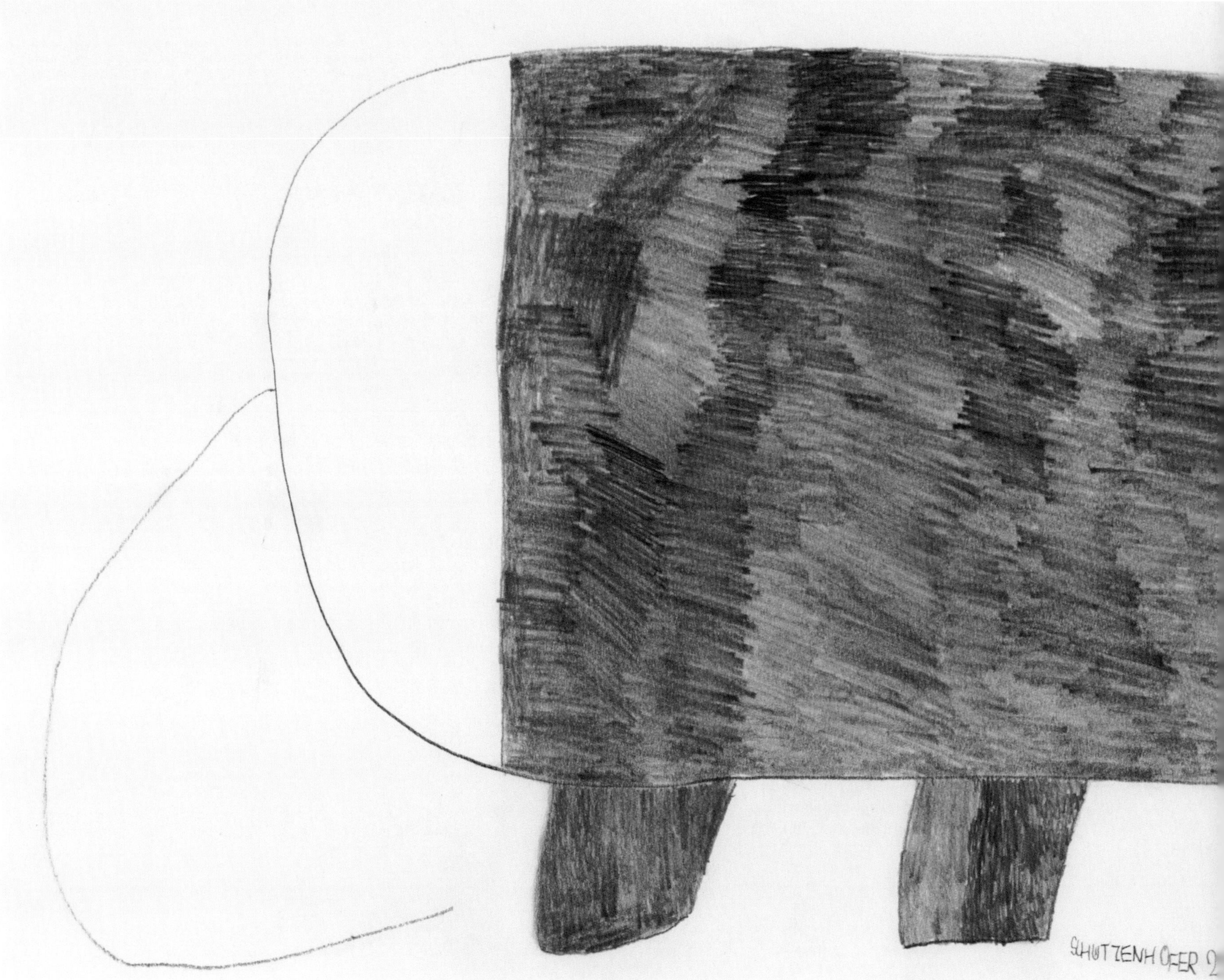
SCHUTZENHOFER 2

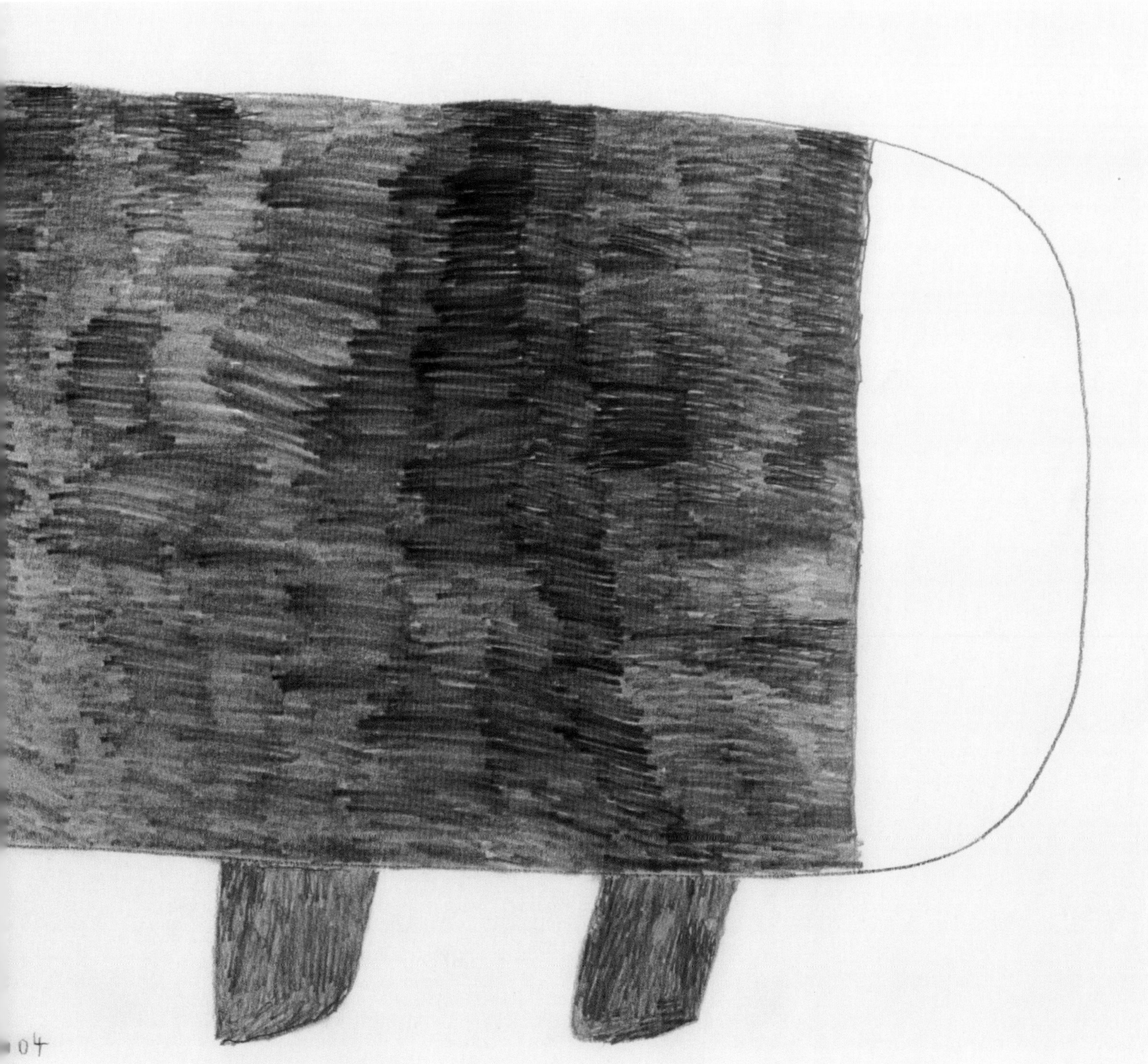

Günther Schützenhöfer
Rodel / Sled
2004, 23,1 x 54,2 cm
Bleistift / pencil

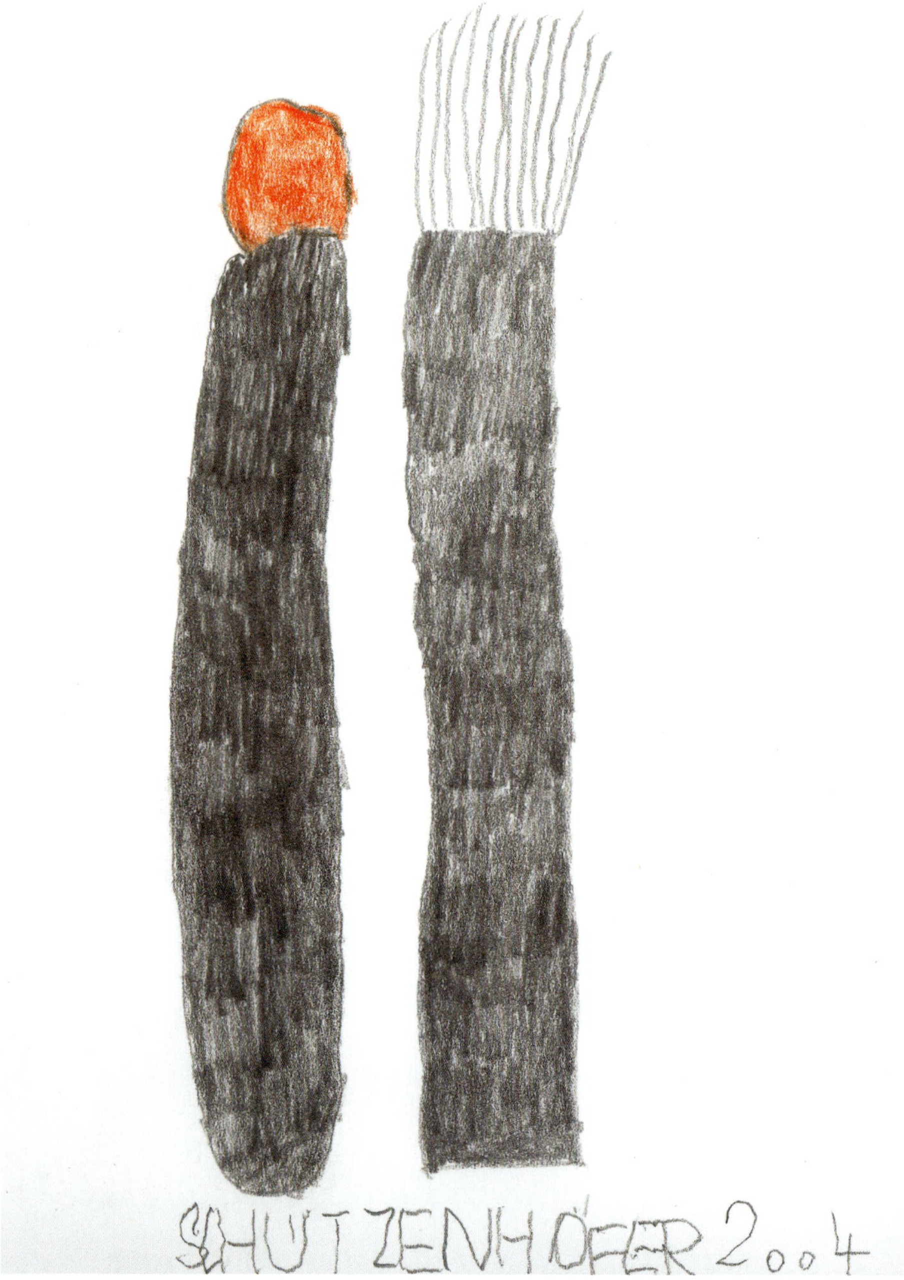
SCHÜTZENHÖFER 2004

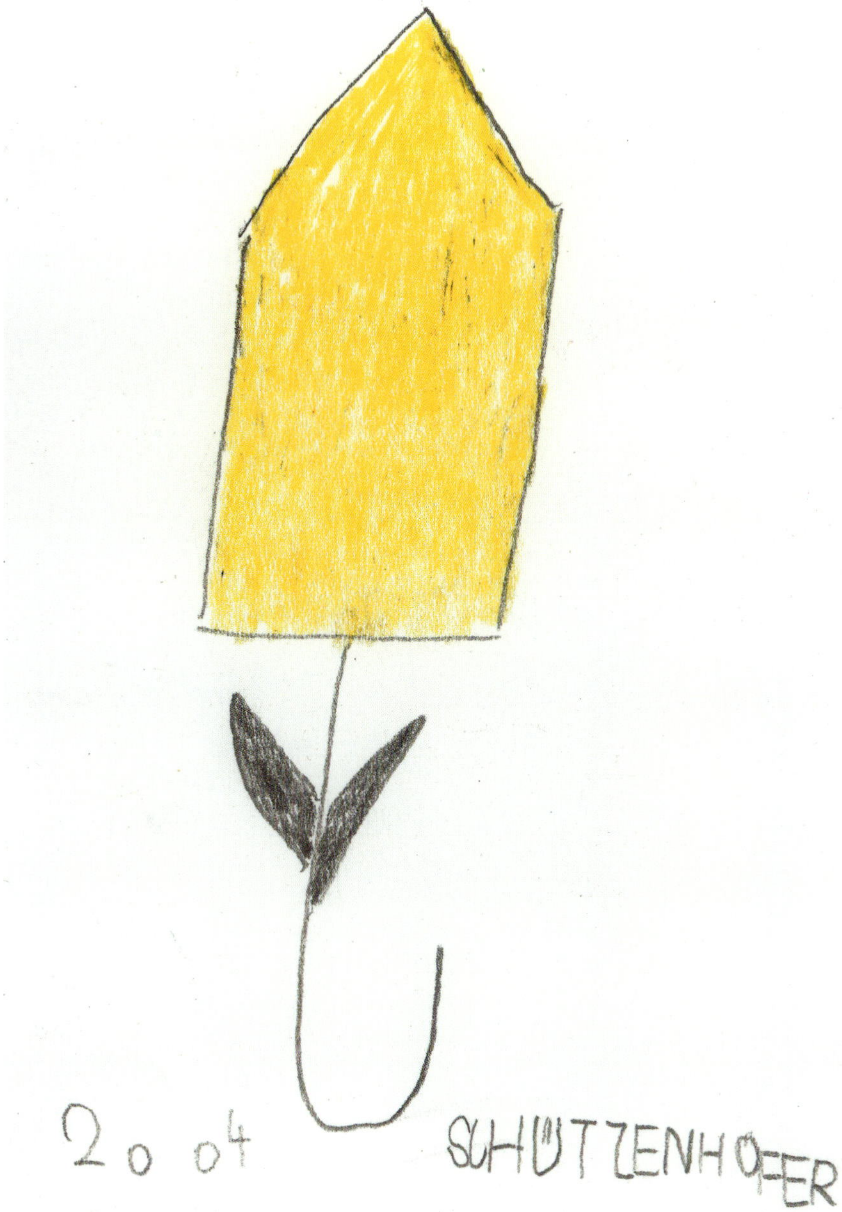

Günther Schützenhöfer
Zahnpasta und Zahnbürste / Toothpaste and Toothbrush
2004, 14,8 x 10,5 cm
Bleistift, Farbstift / pencil, color pencil

Günther Schützenhöfer
Laterne / Latern
2004, 14,8 x 10,5 cm
Bleistift, Farbstift
pencil, color pencil

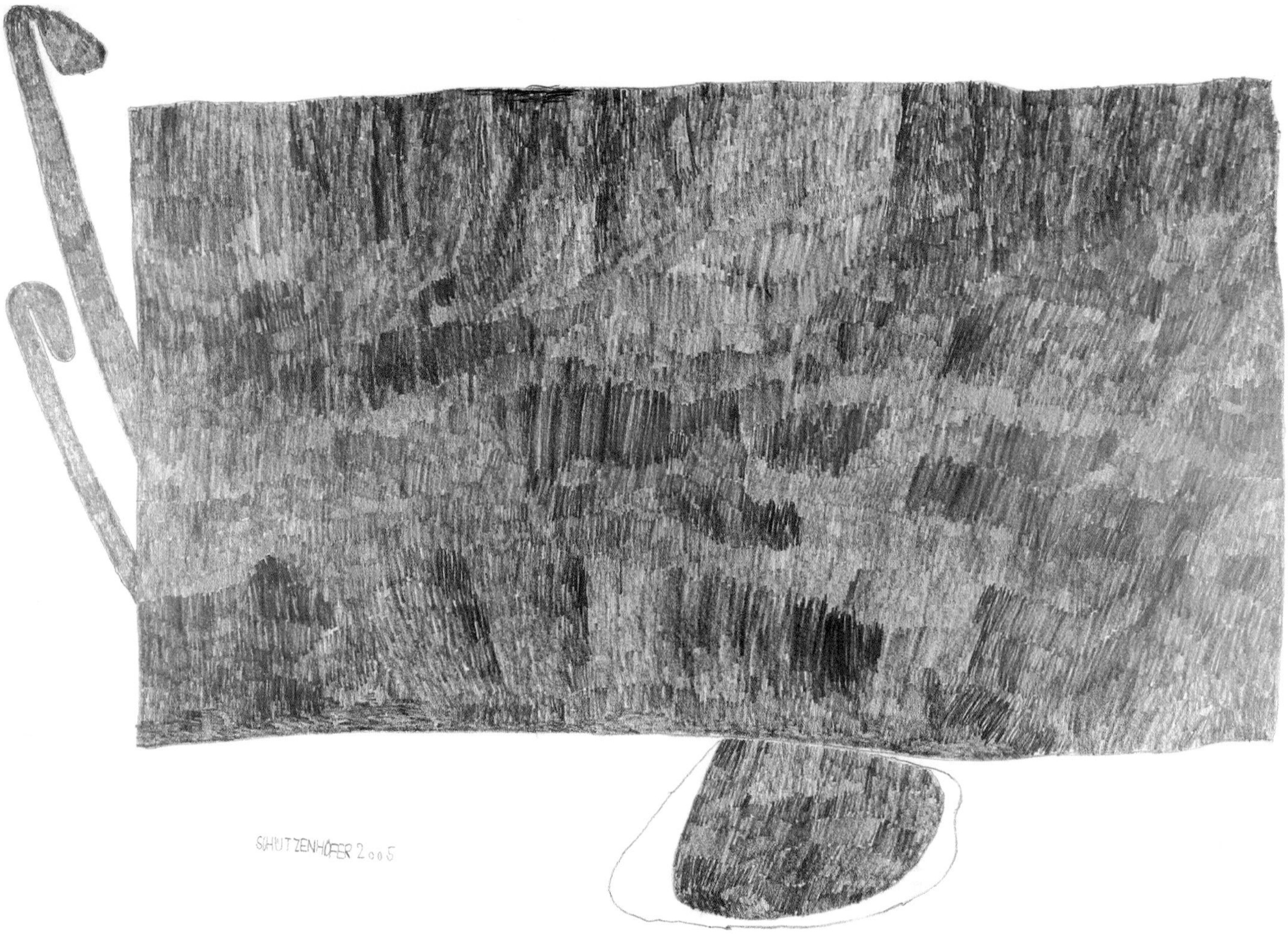
SCHÜTZENHÖFER 2005

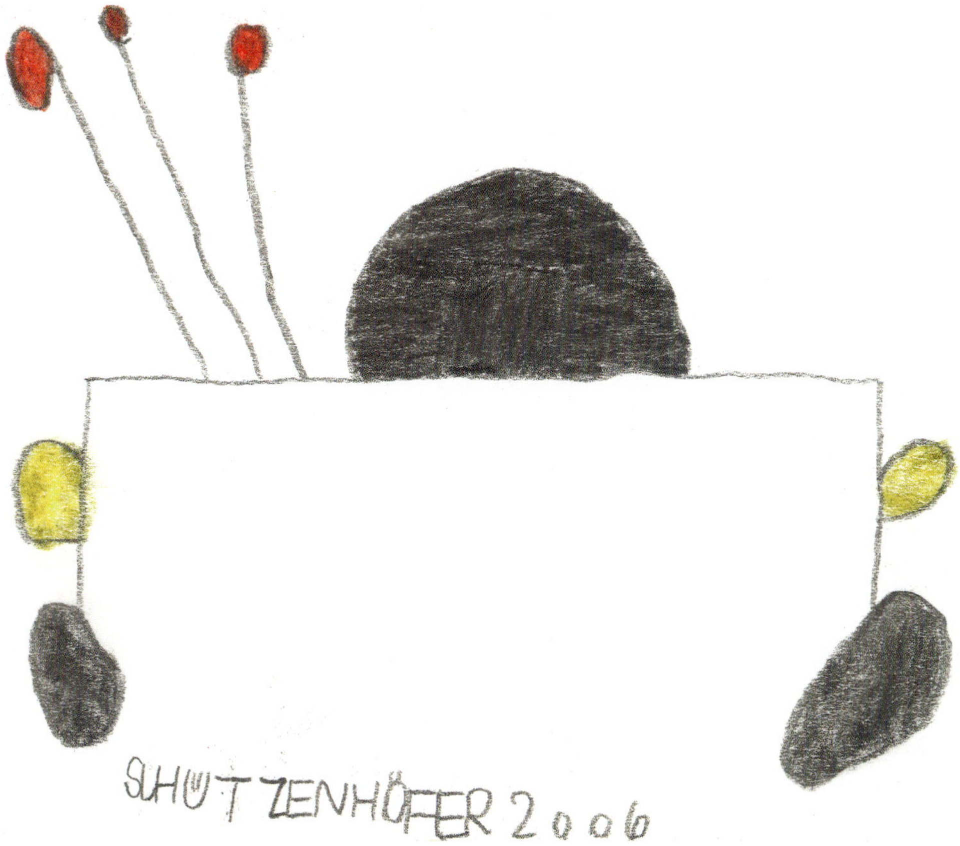

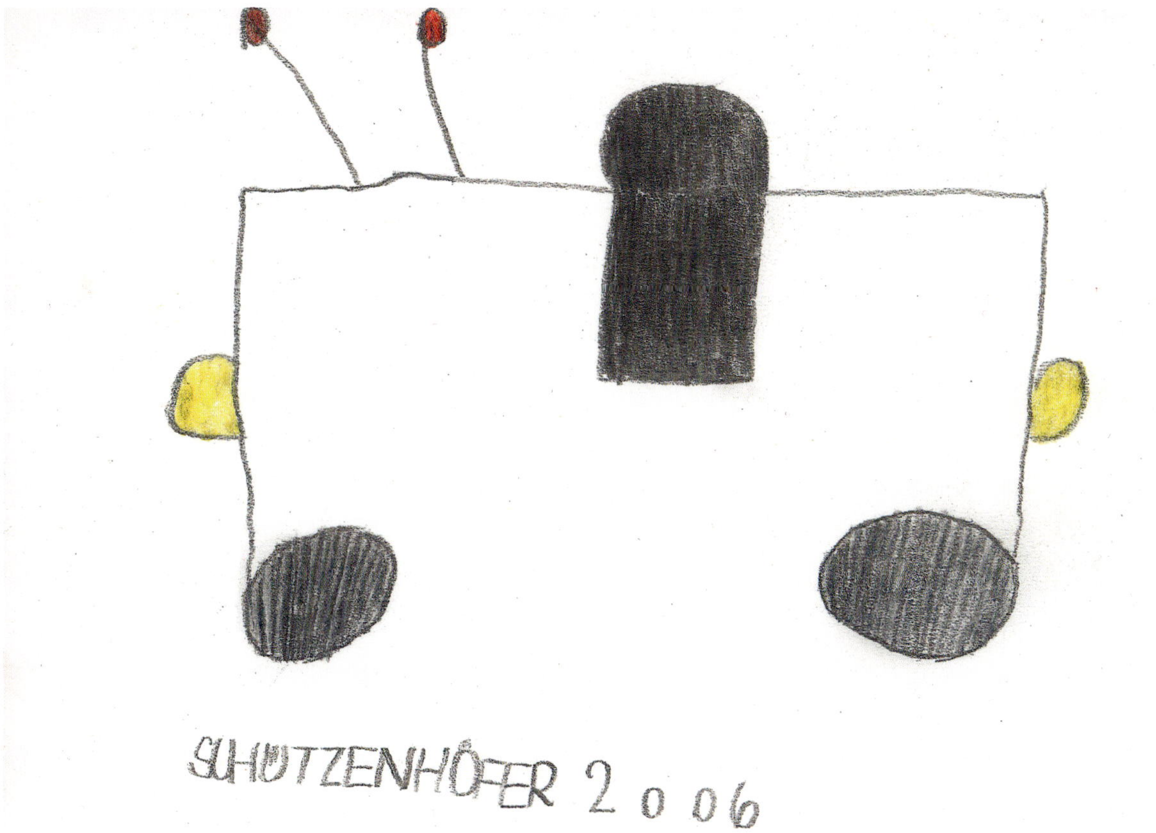

Günther Schützenhöfer
Schubkarren / Wheelbarrow
2005, 44 x 62,4 cm
Bleistift / pencil

Günther Schützenhöfer
Fahrrad / Bicycle
2006, 10,4 x 14,9 cm
Bleistift, Farbstifte / pencil, color pencils

Günther Schützenhöfer
Fahrrad / Bicycle
2006, 10,5 x 14,8 cm
Bleistift, Farbstifte / pencil, color pencils

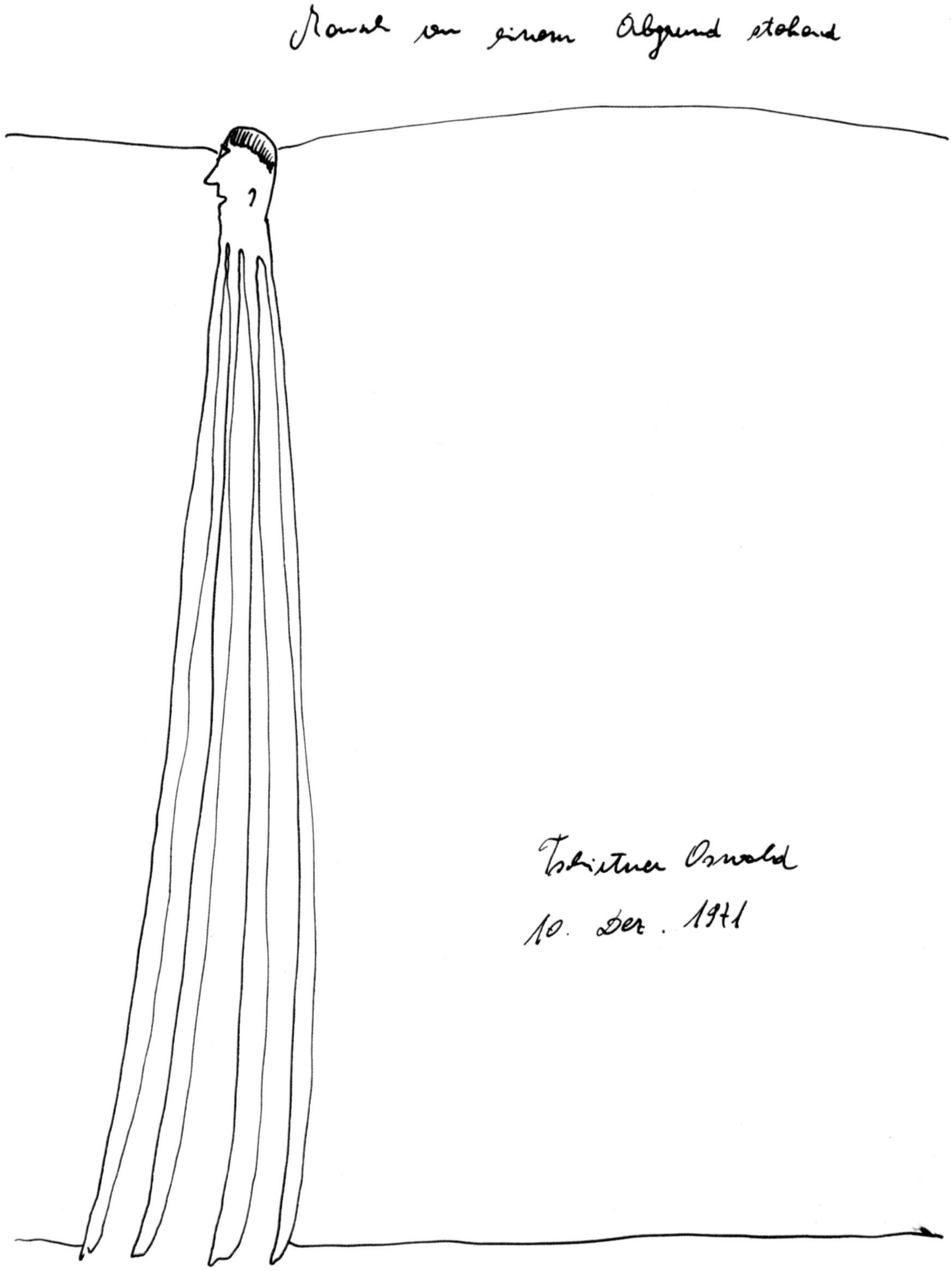
Mensch an einem Abgrund stehend
Tschirtner Oswald
10. Dez. 1971

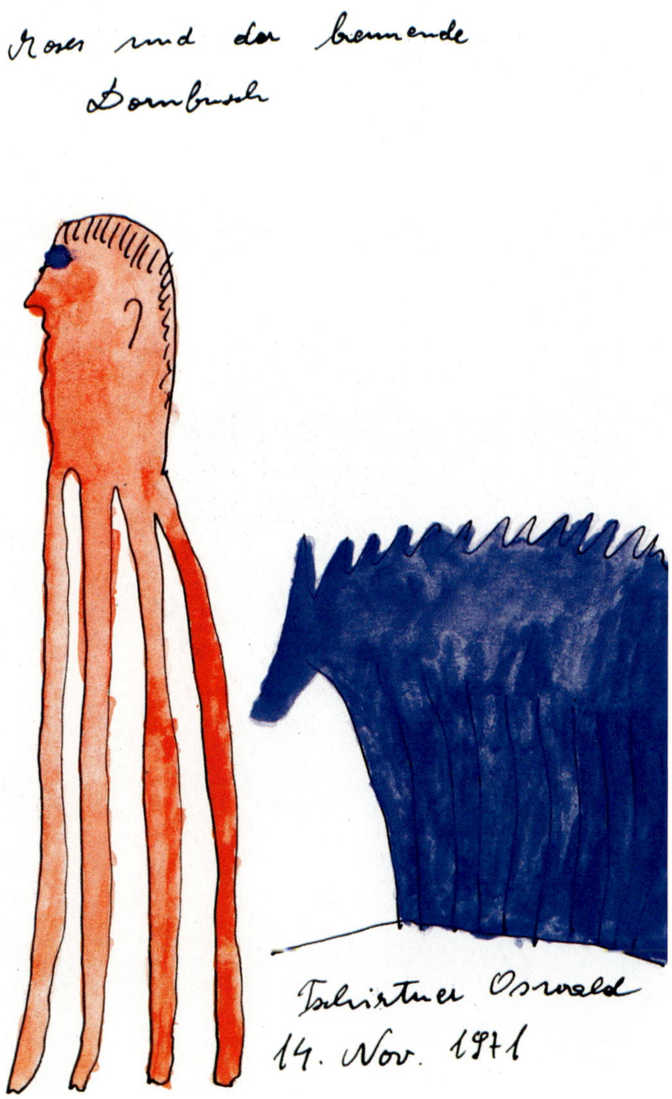

Oswald Tschirtner
Mensch vor einem
Abgrund stehend /
Man standing in Front
of an Abyss
1971, 21 x 14,8 cm
Tusche / Indian ink
Privatstiftung -
Künstler aus Gugging

Oswald Tschirtner
Moses und der
brennende Dornbusch /
Moses and the
Burning Bush
1971, 14,8 x 10,5 cm
Tusche,
Aquarellfarben /
Indian ink, aquarell
Sammlung Hannah Rieger

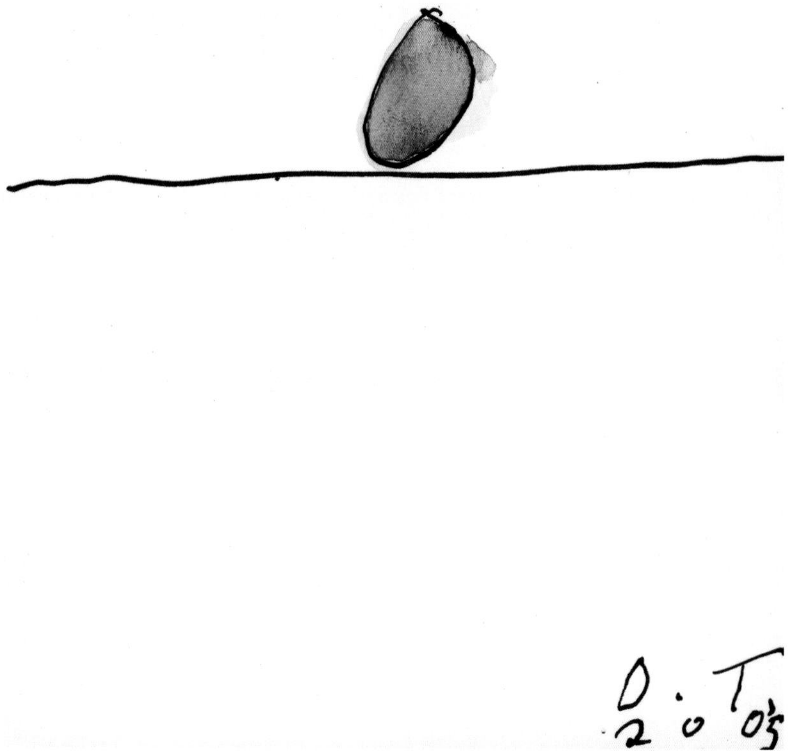

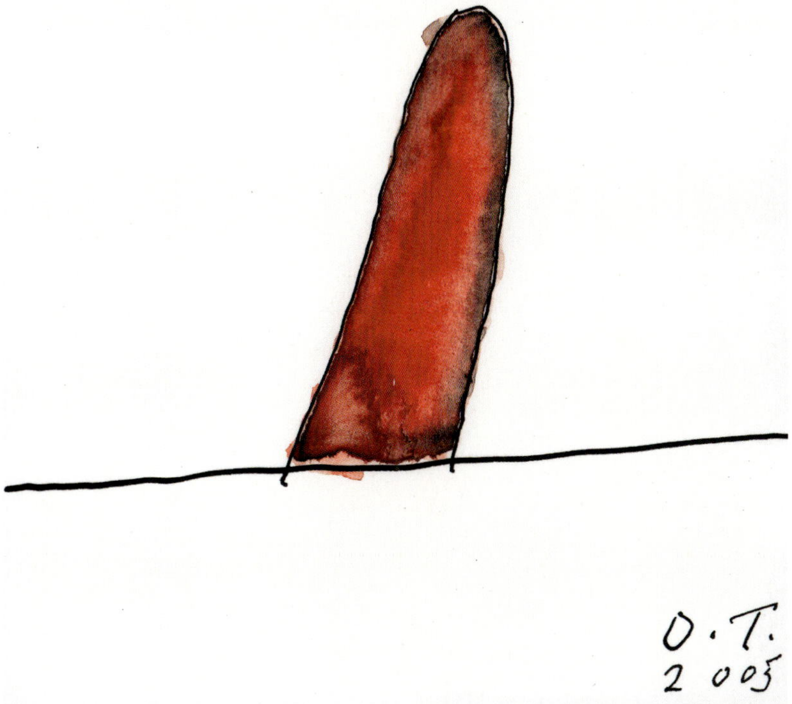

Oswald Tschirtner
Ein Stein / A Stone
2005, 14,9 x 10,5 cm
Tusche,
Aquarellfarben /
Indian ink, aquarell

Oswald Tschirtner
Berg / Mountain
2005, 14,9 x 10,5 cm
Tusche,
Aquarellfarben /
Indian ink, aquarell

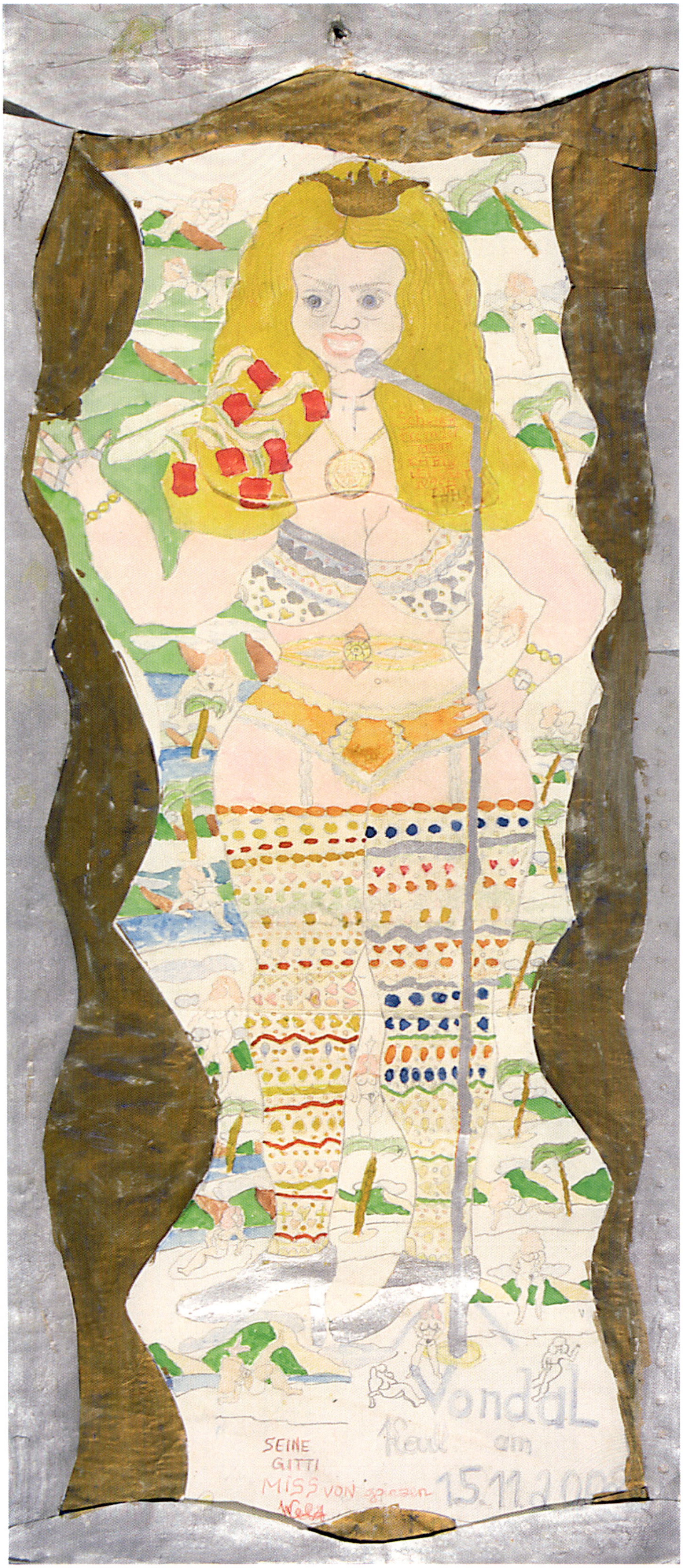
Vondal
Paul am
15.11.200
SEINE
GITTI
MISS VON ganzen
Welt

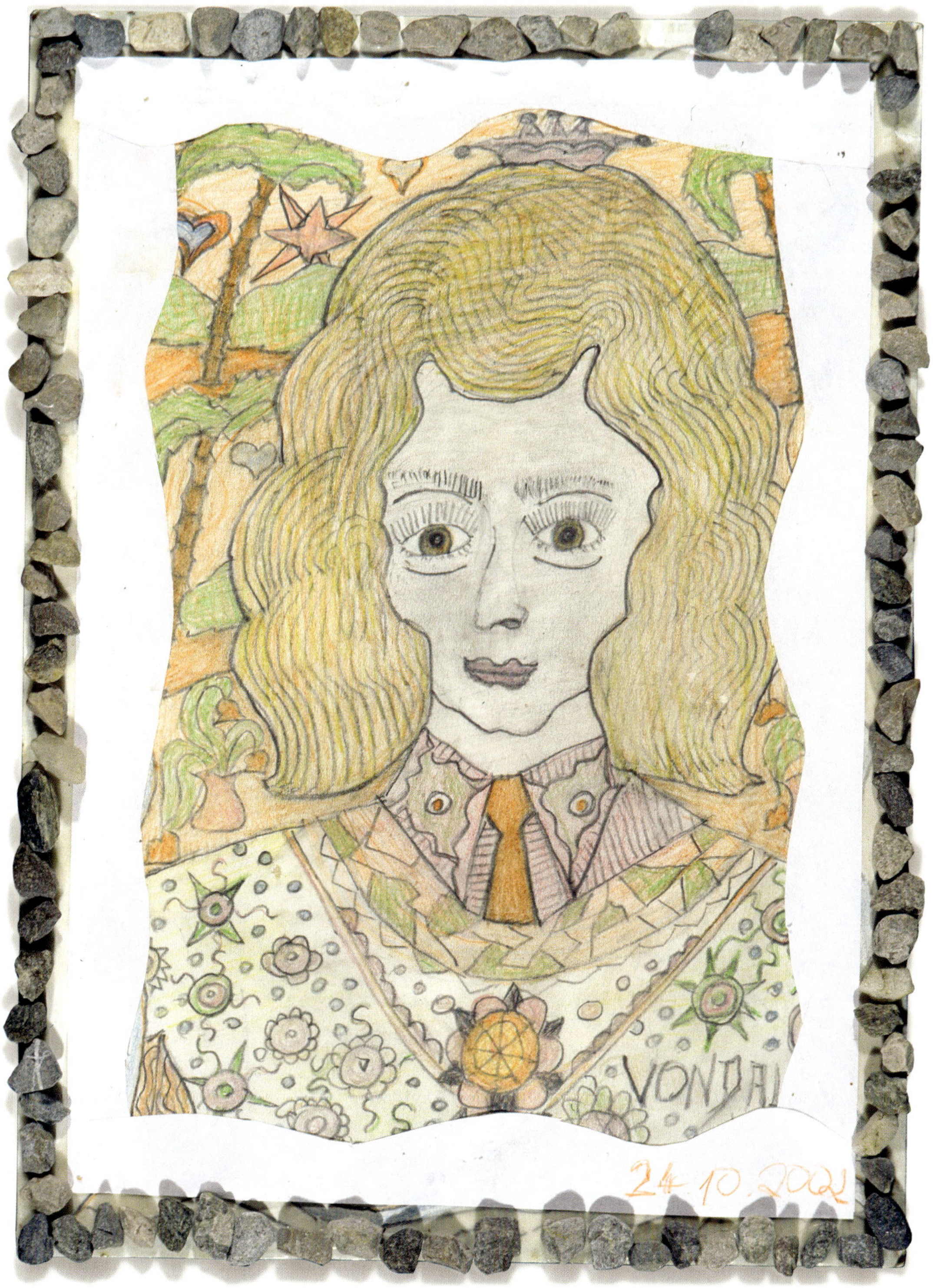

Karl Vondal
Seine Gitti Miss von ganzen Welt /
His Gitti Miss from the Whole World
2002, 99,5 x 43,3 cm
Bleistift, Farbstifte /
pencil, color pencils

Karl Vondal
Frau / Woman
2002, 29,9 x 21,5 cm
Bleistift, Farbstifte /
pencil, color pencils

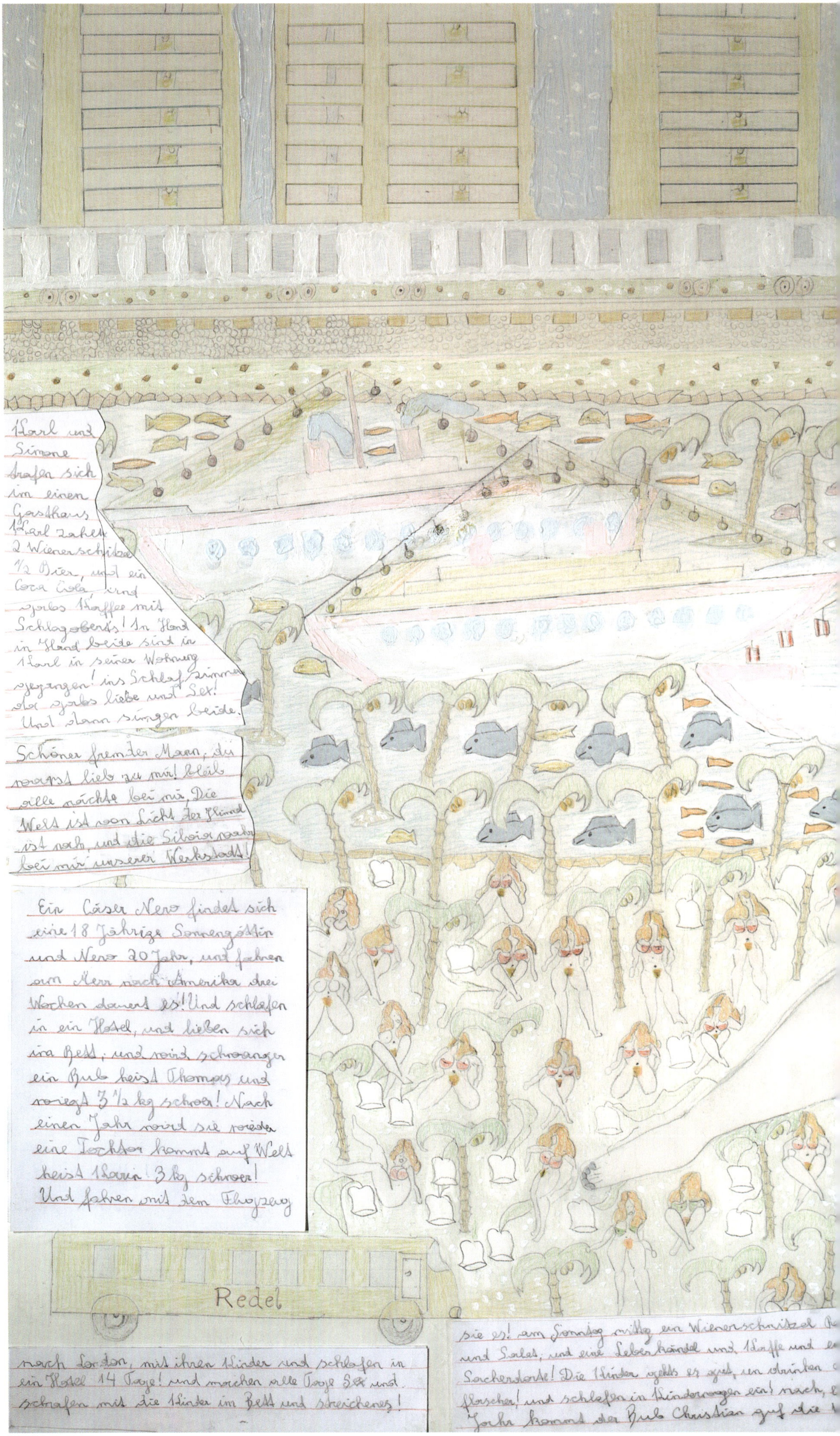

Karl Vondal
Karl und Simone … /
Karl and Simone …
2005, 72,7 x 101,7 cm
Bleistift, Farbstifte /
pencil, color pencils

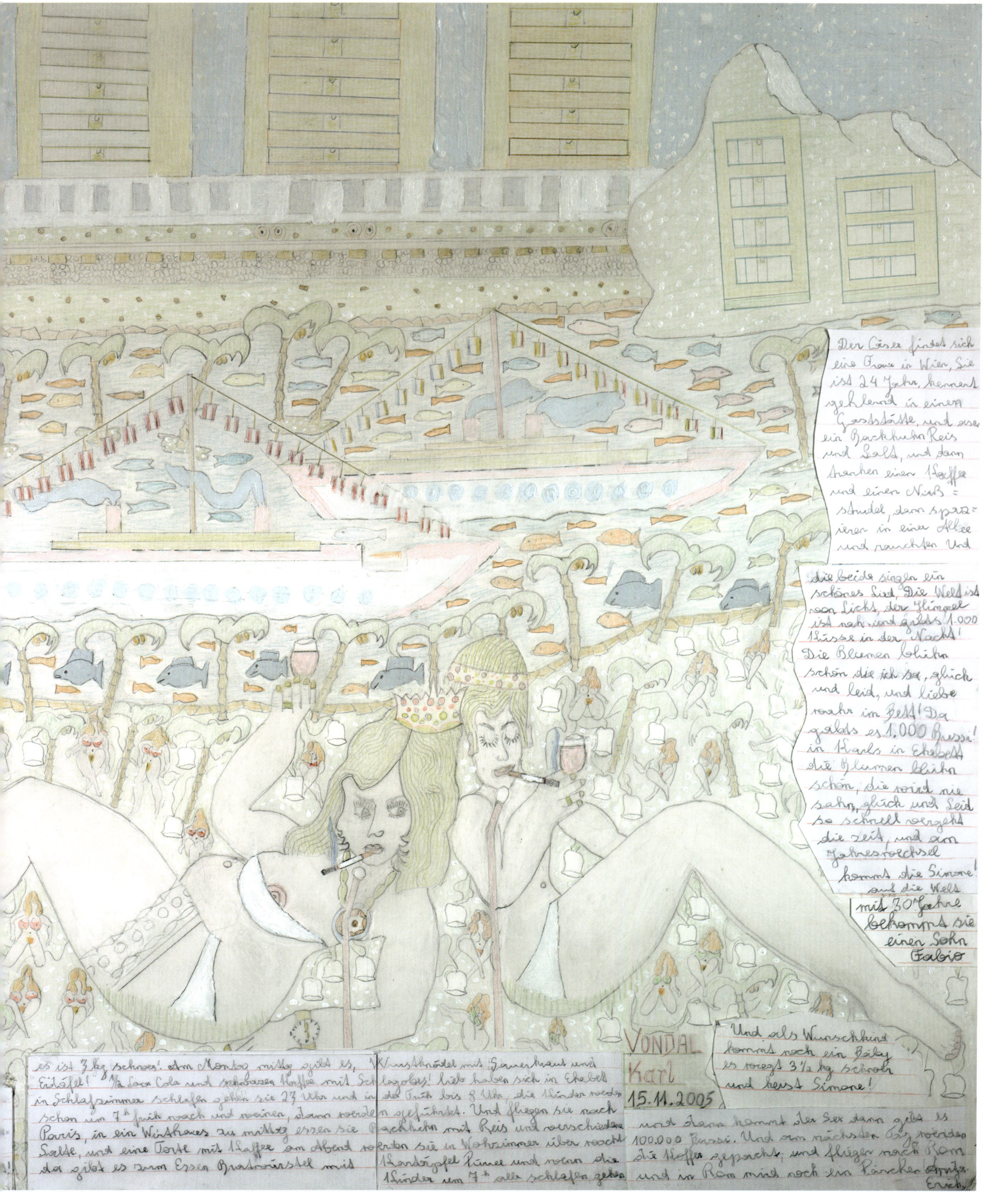
Der Leser findet sich
eine Frau in Wien, Sie
ist 24 Jahr, kennent
gelernt in einem
Gaststätte, und esse
ein Backhuhn Reis
und Salat, und dann
trinken einen Kaffee
und einen Nuß=
strudel, dann spaz=
ieren in einer Allee
und rauchten Und
die beide singen ein
schönes Lied, Die Welt ist
von Licht, der Himmel
ist nah, und gibts 1.000
Küsse in der Nacht!
Die Blumen blühn
schön die ich sa, glück
und leid, und liebe
wahr im Bett! Da
gibts es 1.000 Bussi!
in Karls in Ehebett
die Blumen blühn
schön, die wird nie
sahn, glück und Leid
so schnell vergeht
die zeit, und am
Jahreswechsel
kommt die Simone!
auf die Welt
mit 30 Jahre
bekommt sie
einen Sohn
Fabio
Und als Wunschkind
kommt noch ein Baby
es wiegt 3 1/2 kg schwer
und heist Simone!
VONDAL
Karl
15.11.2005
es ist 3 kg schwer! Am Montag mittag gibt es, W
Eistäfel! 1/2 Coca Cola und schwarzen Kaffee mit Sch
in Schlafzimmer schlafen gehen sie 23 Uhr und in
schon um 7 h früh wach und weinen, dann werde
Paris, in ein Wirthaus zu mittag essen sie B
Salate, und eine Torte mit Kaffee am Abend we
da gibt es zum Essen Bratwürstel mit
Wurstknödel mit Sauerkraut und
lagobers! liebe haben sich in Ehebett
der Früh bis 8 Uhr, die Kinder werden
n gefüttert. Und fliegen sie nach
ackhendl mit Reis und verschiedene
rden sie in Wohnzimmer über nacht
Kartoffel Püree und wenn die
Kinder um 7 h alle schlafen gehen
und dann kommt der Sex dann gibt es
100.000 Bussi. Und am nächsten Tag werden
die Koffer gepackt, und fliegen nach Rom
und in Rom wird noch ein Pärchen Fritz.
Erich.

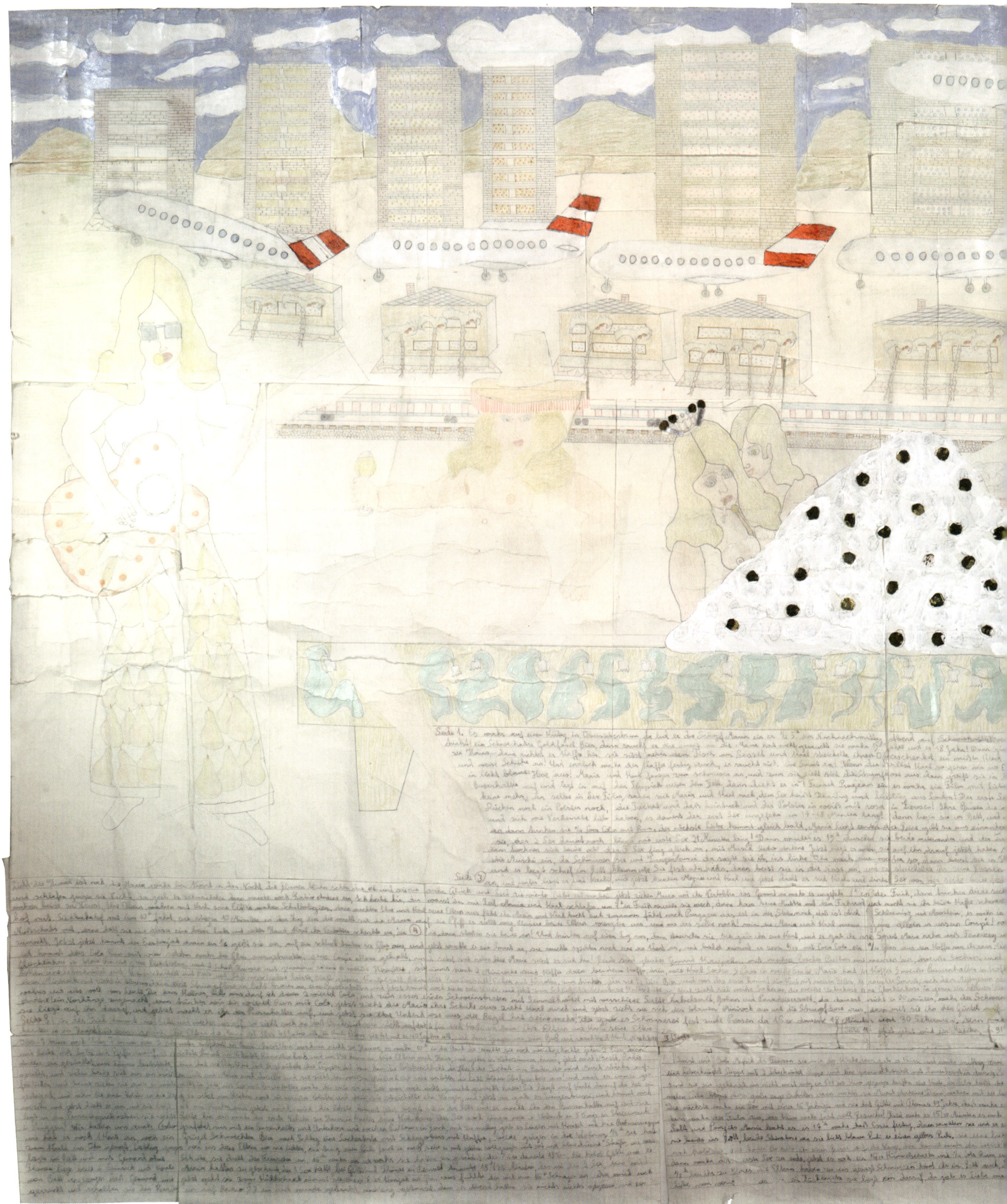

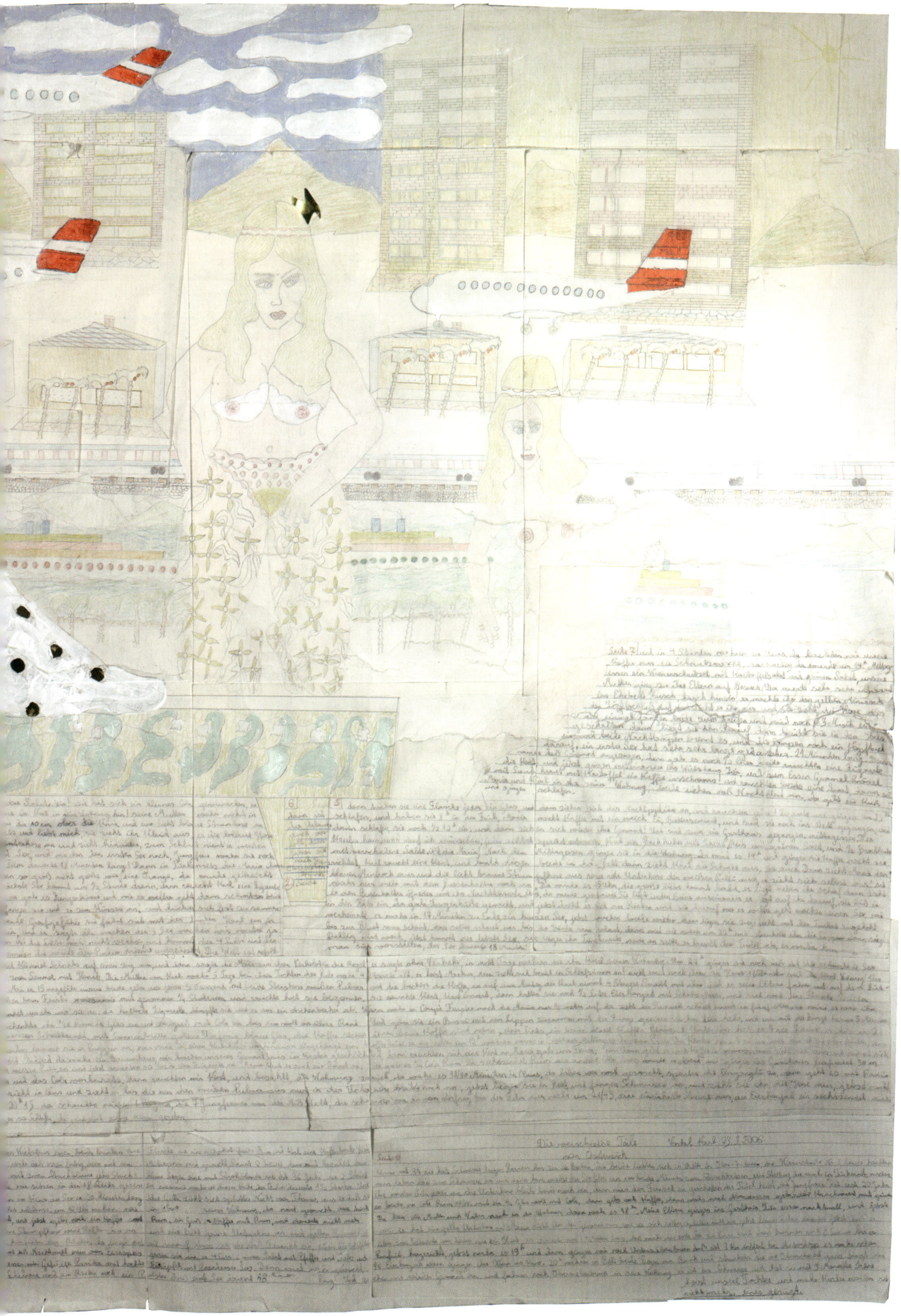

Karl Vondal
Die verschiedne Teile von Österreich / The Different Parts of Austria
2006, 144 x 225 cm
Bleistift, Farbstifte / pencil, color pencils

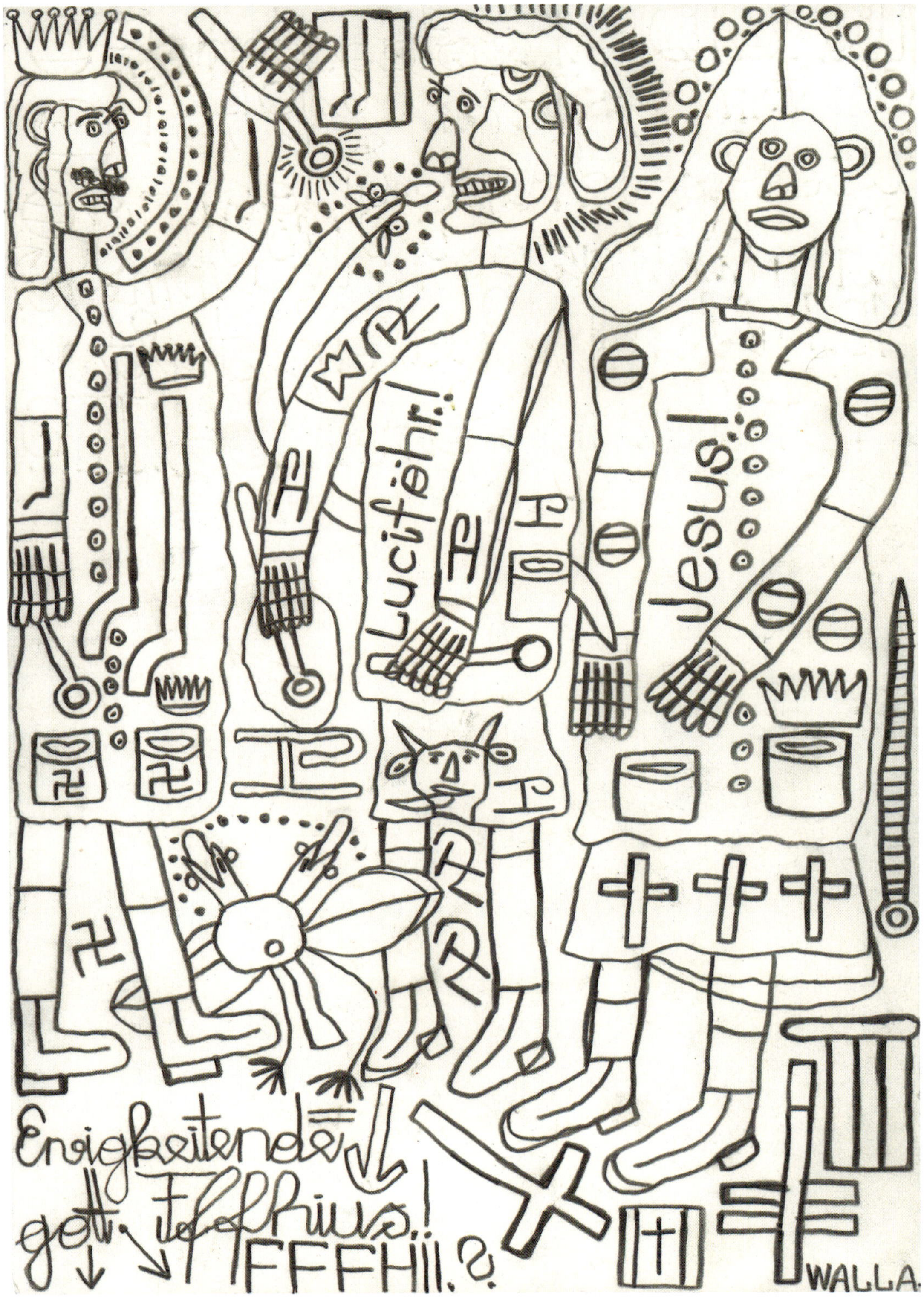
Lucifehr!
Jesus!
Ewigkeitende
WALLA.

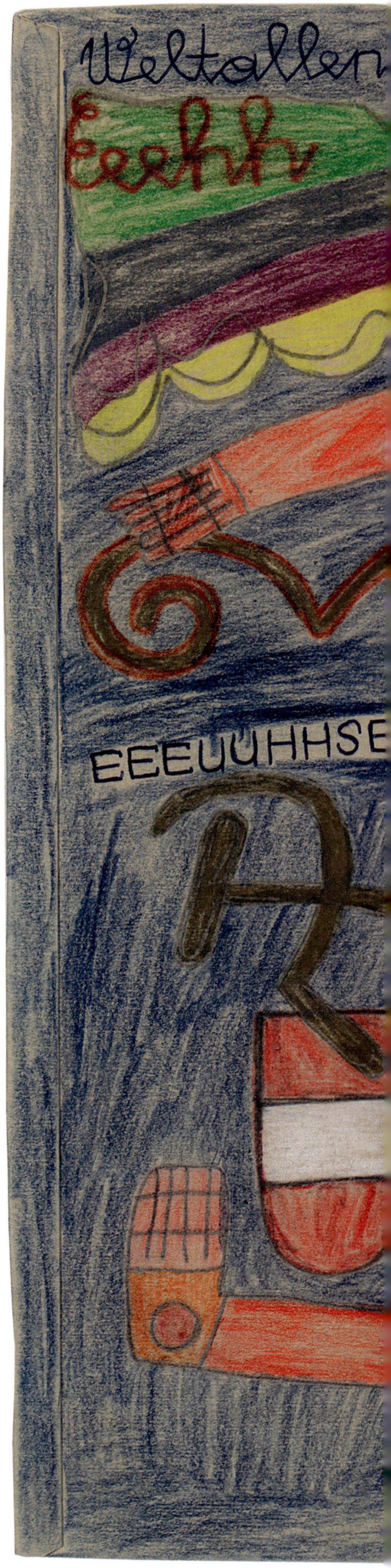
Weltallen
EEEUUHHSE

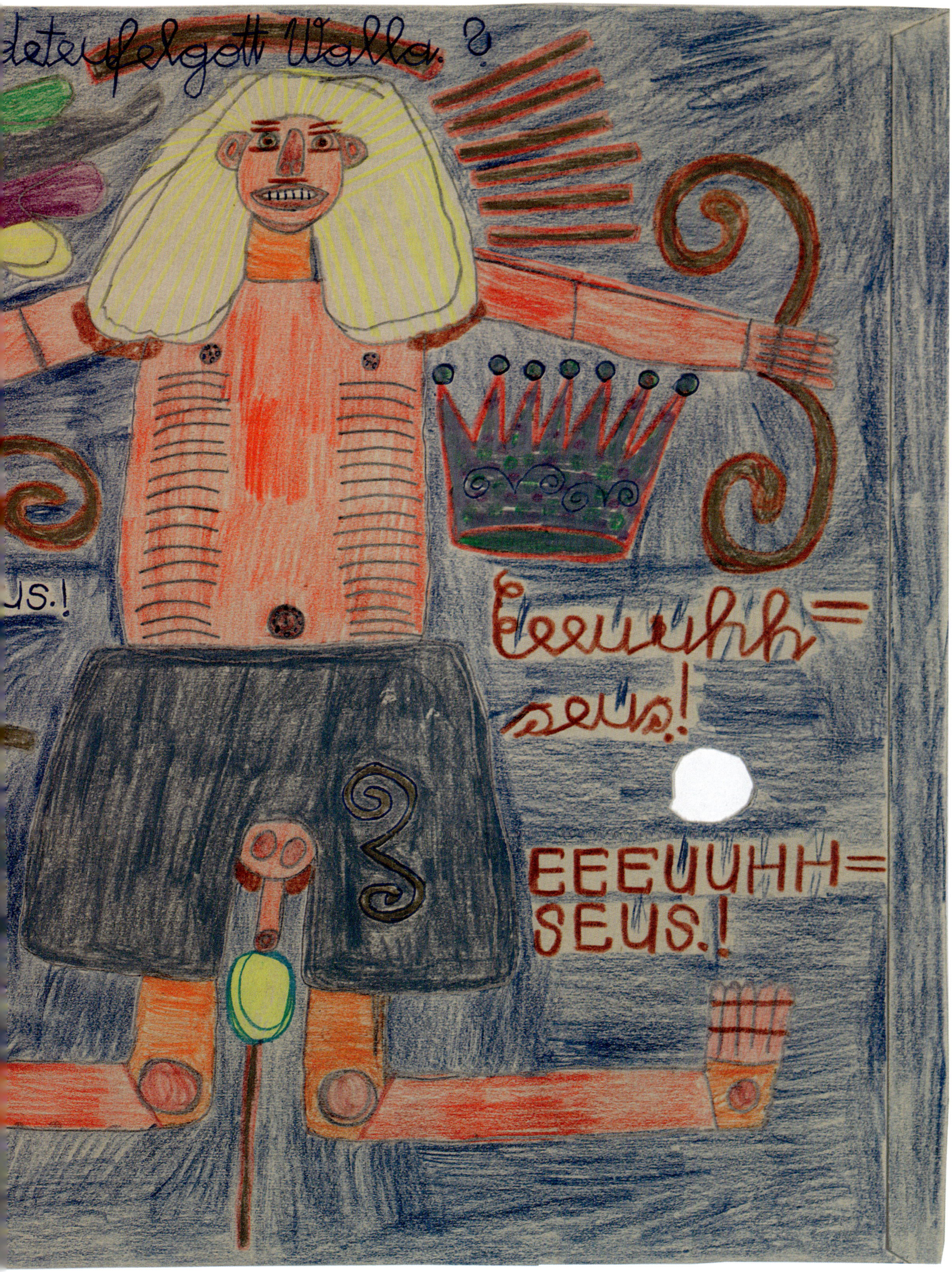

August Walla
Ewigkeitendegott
Fffhius.! /
End-of-eternity-god
Fffhius.!
1973, 20,9 x 14,7 cm
Bleistift / pencil
Sammlung Helmut Zambo

August Walla
Weltallendeteufelgott
Walla.? /
End-of-universe-devil-god Walla.?
Undatiert / undated
31 x 30,4 cm
Kugelschreiber, Bleistift, Farbstifte / ballpen, pencil, color pencils
Privatsammlung

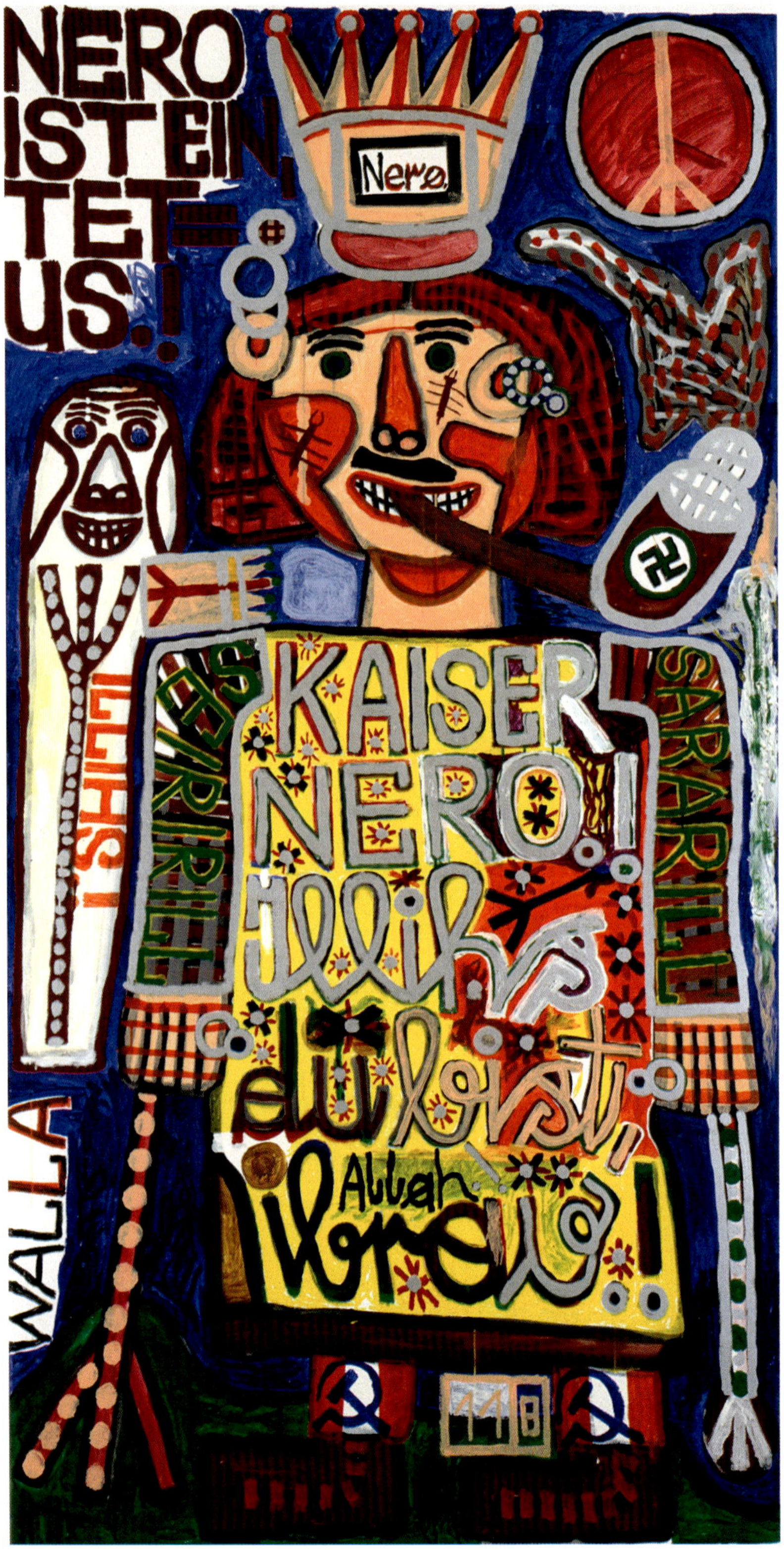
NERO
IST EIN
TET=
US.!
Nero
KAISER
NERO.!
Allah
WALLA

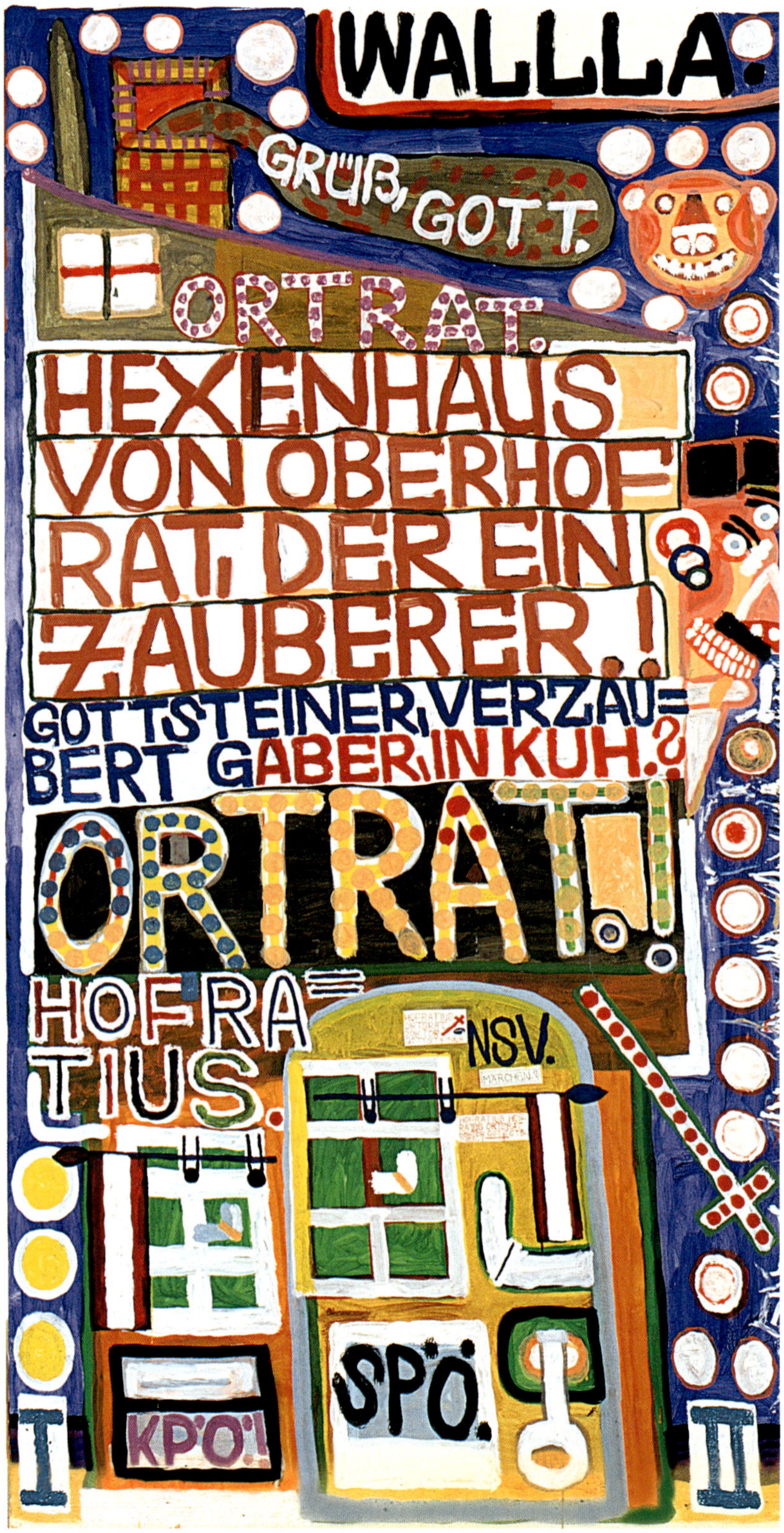
WALLA:
GRÜß, GOTT.
ORTRAT.
HEXENHAUS
VON OBERHOF
RAT, DER EIN
ZAUBERER.!
GOTTSTEINER, VERZAU=
BERT GABER, IN KUH.?
ORTRAT.!
HOFRA=
TIUS
NSV.
SPÖ.
KPÖ!
I
II

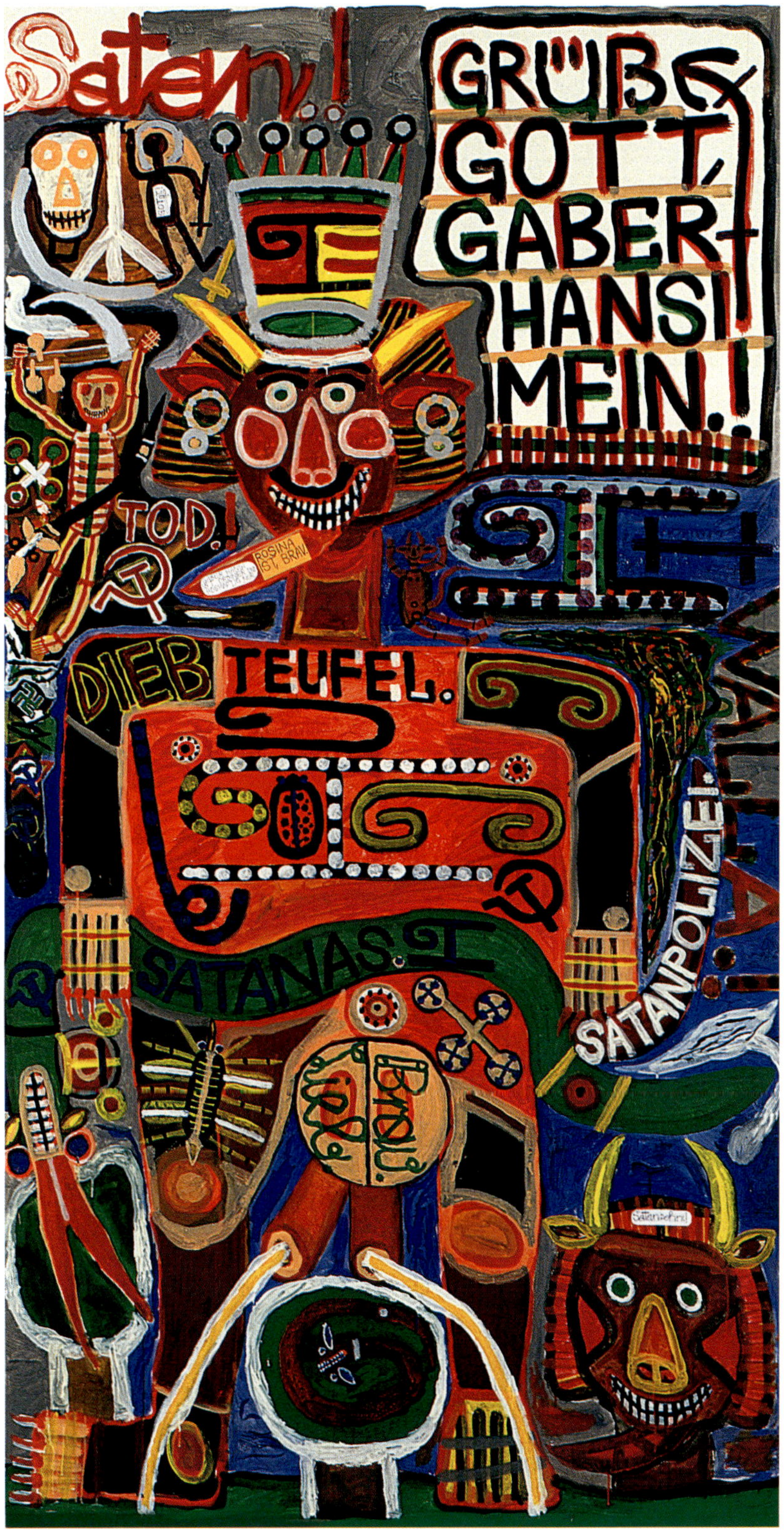

© Sammlung Essl Privatstiftung

August Walla
Kaiser Nero.! /
Emperor Nero.!
1987, 260 x 130 cm
Acryl auf Leinwand /
acrylic on canvas
Sammlung Helmut Zambo

August Walla
Hexenhaus /
House of Witches
1987, 260 x 130 cm
Acryl auf Leinwand /
acrylic on canvas
Sammlung Essl
Privatstiftung

August Walla
Garber Hansi mein /
My Garber Hansi
1987, 260 x 130 cm
Acryl auf Leinwand /
acrylic on canvas
Sammlung Essl
Privatstiftung

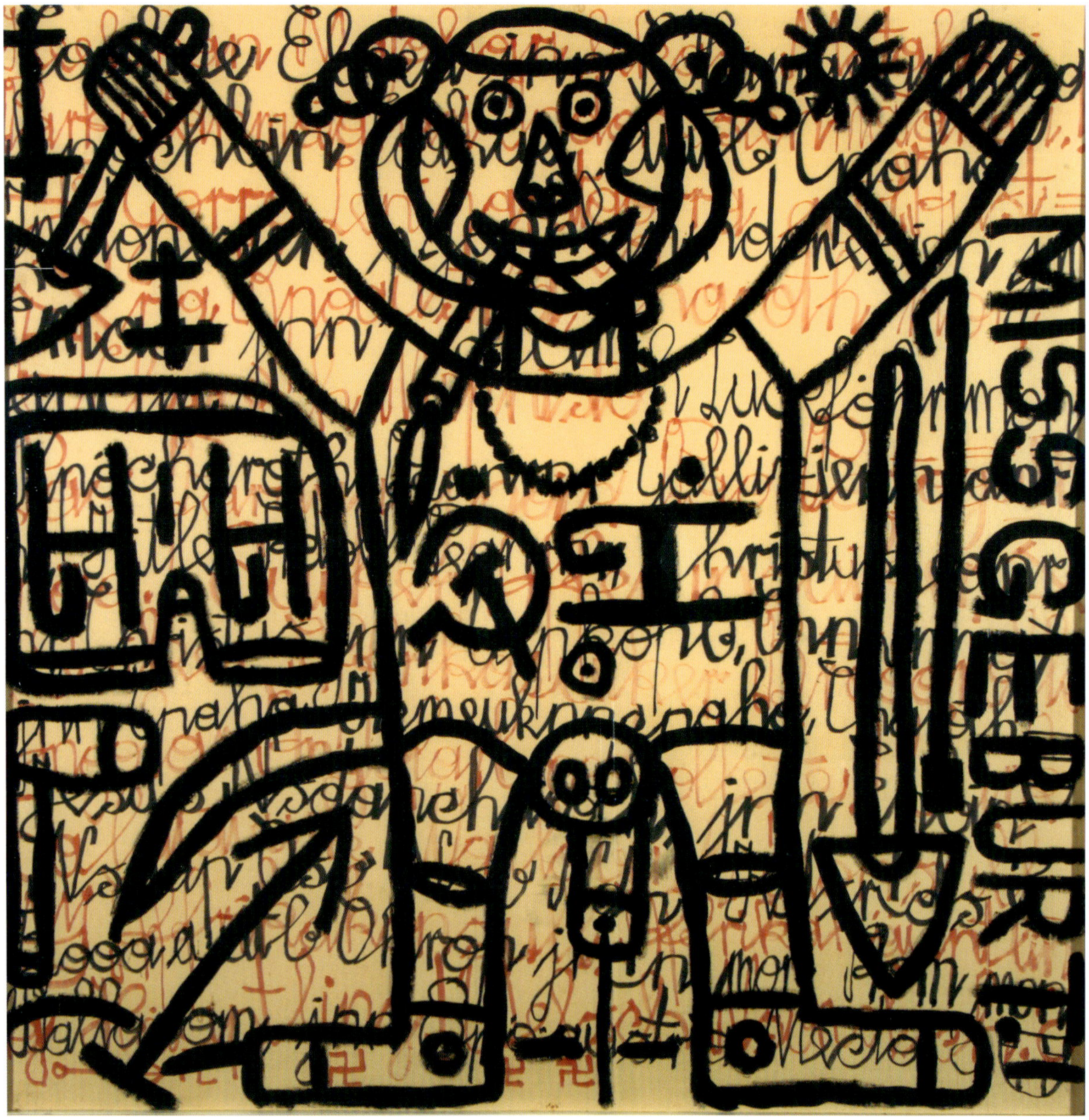
MISSGEBURT!

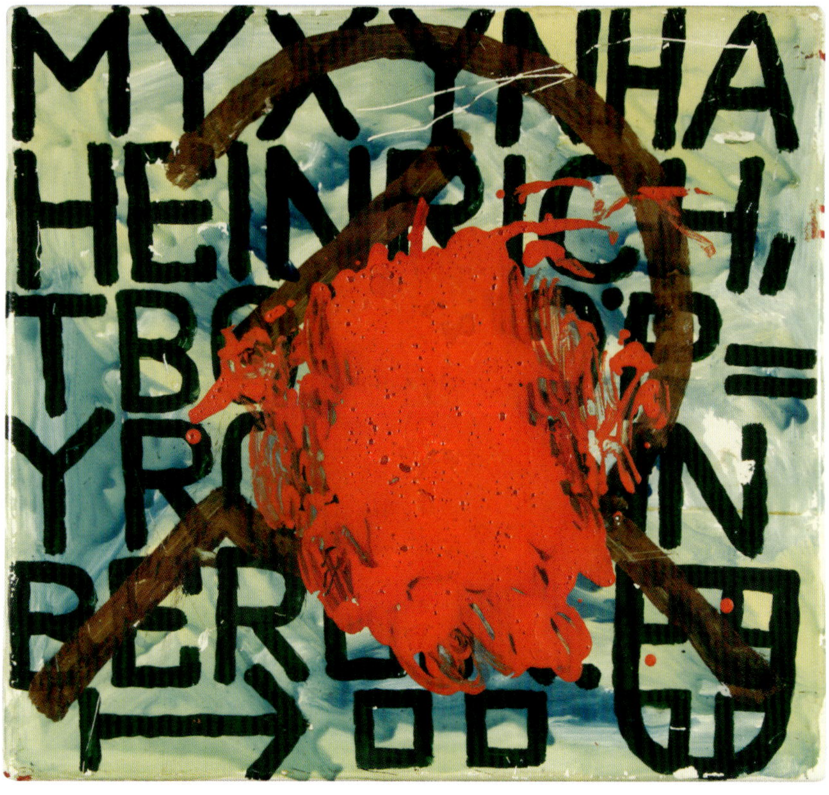
HEINRICH,

August Walla
MISSGEBURT.! /
FREAK.!
Undatiert / undated
122,8 x 120 cm
Filzstifte, Lack /
marker, paint
Sammlung Josef Schroll

August Walla
MYXYNHA
Undatiert / undated
53 x 56 cm
Lacke auf Blech /
paint on tin
Sammlung Helmut Zambo

Erich Zittra
Schrift / Writing
1970, 30 x 40 cm
Bleistift / pencil
Privatsammlung

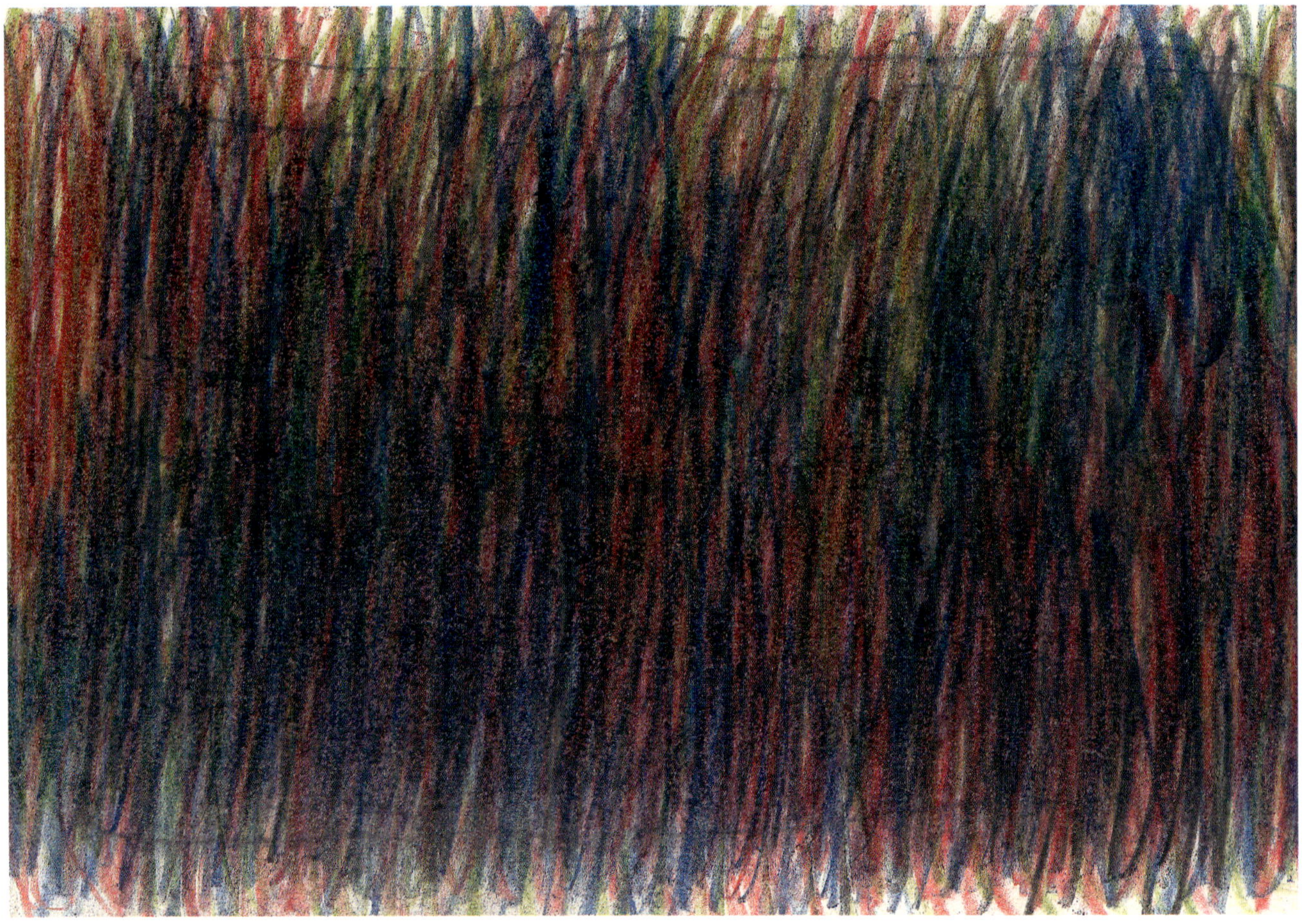

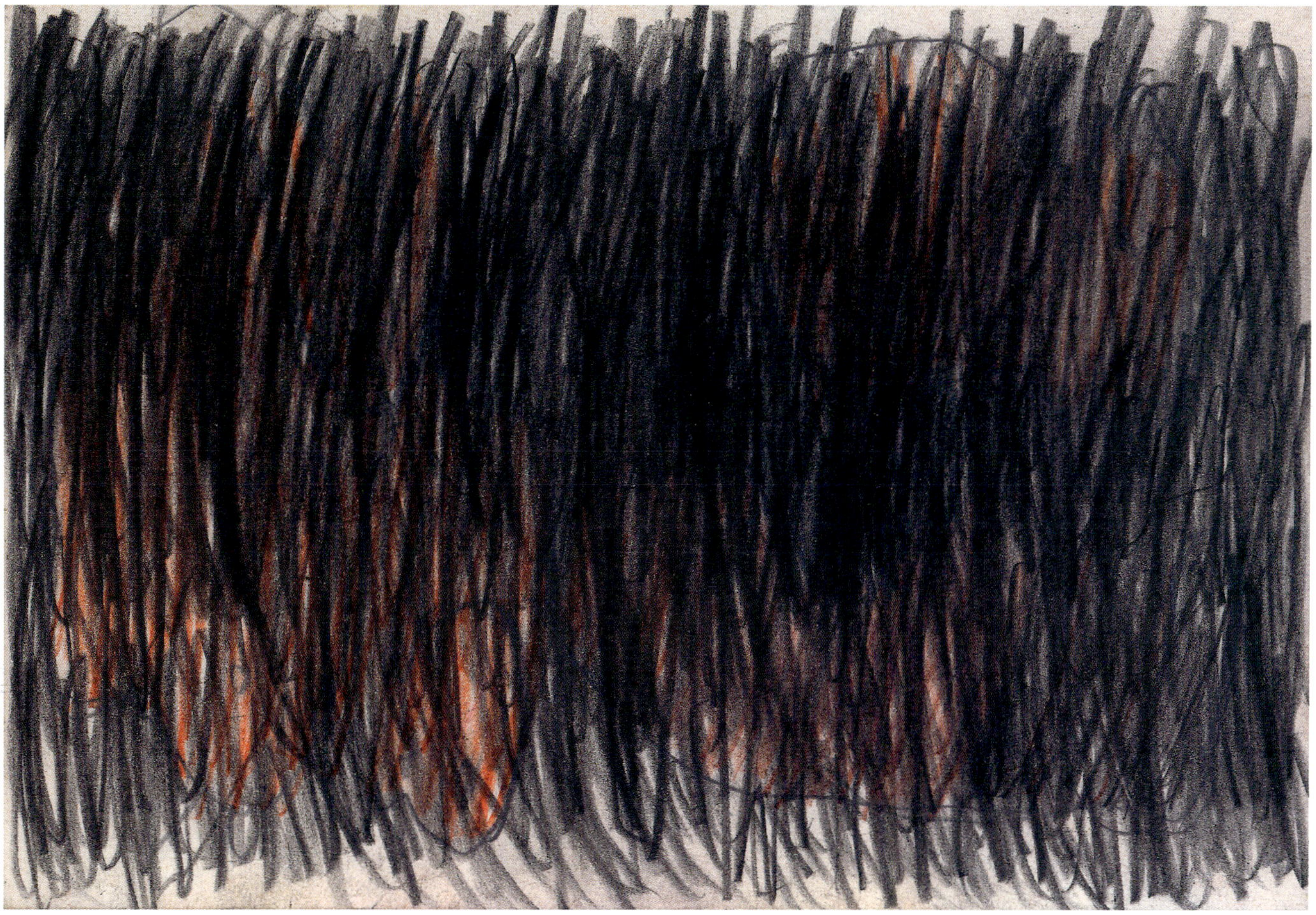

Erich Zittra
Ohne Titel / Untitled
1979, 10,4 x 14,8 cm
Bleistift, Farbstifte /
pencil, color pencils
Privatsammlung

Erich Zittra
Ohne Titel / Untitled
1979, 10,4 x 14,7 cm
Bleistift, Farbstifte /
pencil, color pencils
Privatsammlung

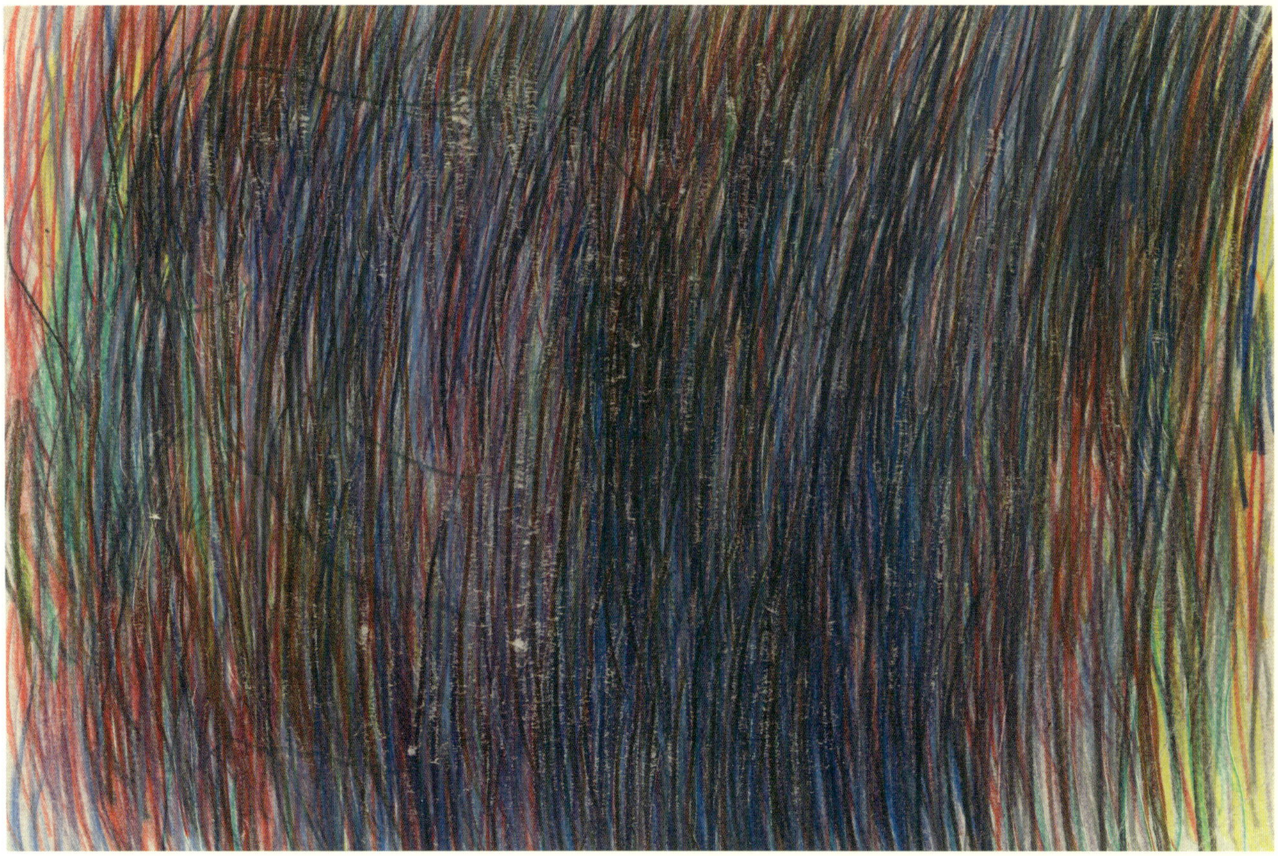

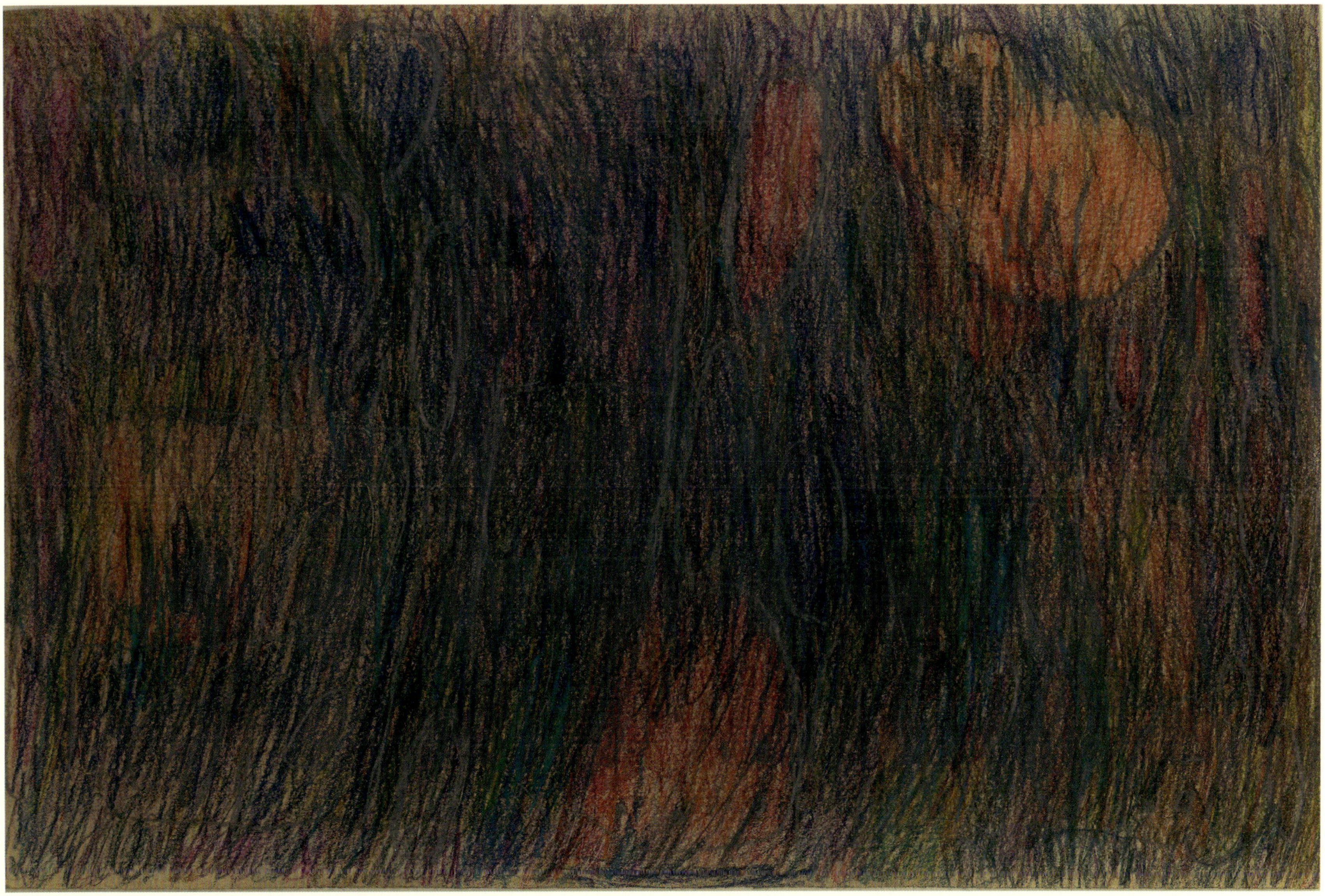

Erich Zittra
Ohne Titel / Untitled
Undatiert / undated
21 x 30 cm
Bleistift, Farbstifte /
pencil, color pencils
Privatsammlung

Erich Zittra
Hasen im Gras /
Bunnies in the Grass
Undatiert / undated
21 x 29,7 cm
Bleistift, Farbstifte /
pencil, color pencils
Sammlung Helmut Zambo

anhang / addendum

Josef Bachler (1914 – 1979) war kein friedlicher Zeitgenosse, fing häufig Streit an und war oft alkoholisiert. Auch seine Zeichnungen sind nicht gerade zimperlich im Strich, sondern fest angedrückt, sie durchtrennen das Weiß des Blattes mit wenigen Linien. Mit einzelnen Strichen ist eine Frau, ein Mann oder ein Tier skizziert, klar, ohne Kompromisse. Es ist mehr als nur eine Skizze, ein *fertiges* Werk, nichts lässt daran zweifeln, dass an der Katze, dem Elefanten oder dem Menschen auch nur irgendetwas fehlen könnte. Schade, dass sein Gesamtwerk nur sehr klein ist, man würde sich mehr solcher Zeichnungen wünschen.

Josef Blahaut (1922 – unbekannt) wurde von befehlenden Stimmen geplagt, die sagten, was er zu tun habe. Überwältigt von diesen Worten *spuckte* er unzählige Buchstaben wieder aus. Buchstaben, mit denen er seine Zeichnungen füllte und mit Köpfen durchmischte. Ein scheinbares Chaos, eine Überflutung, das er, wenn es ihm zuviel wurde, zukritzelte. Er konnte nicht mehr aufhören, versuchte dem inneren Drang zu entrinnen.

Anton Dobay (1906 – 1986) hatte im Alter von 65 Jahren einen Schlaganfall, der ihm einerseits zeitlebens das Sprechen nahm, aber unter der Aufforderung von Dr. Navratil auch das Zeichnen brachte. Täglich zwei Stunden war er konsequent dabei und entwickelte darin seine vorher versteckten Talente. Eindrucksvoll postimpressionistisch, später formal vereinfachend, drückte er dem Zeichenblatt seinen Stempel auf. Intensiv ist in seinen Zeichnungen die Farbe auf das Papier gebracht, in sich überlagernden Schichten türmt sich die Wachskreide – bis sie wieder abbröckelt, sich nicht mehr halten kann.

Johann Fischer (*1919) gefiel sich darin, es den anderen nachzumachen. Ins Mekka der Zeichner von Gugging eingeladen, wollte er nicht nachstehen und tat es ihnen gleich. Ein Tagesplan, eines soliden Handwerkers würdig – vom Frühstück bis zum Abendessen –, verhalf ihm – zusammen mit viel Talent – zu einer kontinuierlichen künstlerischen Entwicklung. Nach Zeichnungen einzelner Gegenstände und oft amüsant ausschauender Tiere, drängte es ihn auch zu ausreichender schriftlicher Kommunikation in seinen Werken: Wie dies und jenes zu verrichten oder zu tun sei, von der Ordnung der Welt, von sozialem Engagement bis zur Stellung der Menschen untereinander, schreibt er in verschrobener Sprache. Die vorher genau gezogenen Striche erinnern an sein früheres Leben als Weinbauer, in dem er die Weinreben in Linien gepflanzt hatte. Noch mit sechsundachtzig Jahren arbeitet Johann Fischer täglich.

Franz Gableck (1910 – 1974) ist der Überschwang in seinen Zeichnungen anzusehen. In gehobener Stimmung vollbrachte er seine wesentlichen Werke. Die Kreide flog behände über das großformatige Papier und er widmete jedes Blatt dem Herrn Primarius. Wunsch und Phantasie trafen einander und gestalteten locker und ohne Hindernisse Kunstwerke von großer Frische und Einfachheit. Nur wenige Blätter umfasst sein viel zu kleines Gesamtwerk, das man sich nur größer wünschen möchte.

Johann Garber (*1947) ist kommunikativ, nimmt gerne Beziehungen auf zu Freunden, aber auch zu Fremden, die gerade vorbeikommen. Sein künstlerisches Werk quillt über von Details, Dekorationen, und seine Zeichnungen sind voll gefüllt bis an die Ränder. Das Hauptthema stellt nur das Grundschema des Inhalts dar, dieses wird aber von einer Fülle von Details oft fast überrollt und ist gelegentlich nicht mehr zu erkennen. In die Landschaft der Darstellungen von Häusern und Kirchen fließen hunderte Figuren ein, aber auch Tiere, Gräser, Sträucher, Wolken und Sterne. Johann Garber baut auch gerne Erlebtes und selbst Gesehenes in seine Bilder mit ein. Mit *Urlaubsbild* kann es dann einfach betitelt sein oder *Hotel Pöder*, aber auch *Sexi-Blatt*. Um seine Werke wirklich gesehen zu haben, braucht man mehrere *Durchgänge* des Betrachtens. Neben diesen sich im Detail ergehenden, mit Feder und Tusche gezeichneten Werken liebt es der Künstler aber auch, einen ganz anderen Stil zu verwenden: Er arbeitet fast plakativ auf unterschiedlichen Objekten, solchen, die er sucht und findet oder kauft. Von geraden Holzstöcken und Schnapsfläschchen bis zu Krickeln (= Geweihen) von Rehen und Gemsen. Eine Wesensveränderung der bearbeiteten Objekte findet statt: Bemalt er Revolver, wirken diese nicht mehr wie eine gefährliche Waffe, sondern fast kitschig und nett, der aggressive Charakter ist verschwunden.

Johann Hauser (1926 – 1996) konnte sehr sympathisch und nett sein, er konnte aber auch schreien und schimpfen, dass sich niemand in seine Nähe traute. Im Grunde war er aber immer gewaltlos und tat keiner Fliege etwas zuleide. Er liebte die Frauen: in natura und in seiner Kunst. Unter den Ersten, die Gugging Weltruhm einbrachten, begeisterten seine Zeichnungen Künstler und Sammler gleichermaßen. Vor dem ersten Strich lange verharrend, explodierte dann seine Farbe auf dem Blatt. Intensiv und mächtig sind seine Bildnisse von schönen und hässlichen Damen, Raketen und Panzern, Schlangen und Schlössern – mit grandioser Fertigkeit des Strichs, der das immer zu dünne Papier durchbohren konnte. Nächtelang entstanden im qualmenden Zigarettenrauch Meisterwerke, die die Zeit überdauern werden.

Rudolf Horacek (1915 – 1986) saß meist abwartend im Raum und lächelte – über sein Gegenüber oder wegen einer Idee – er sagte es nicht. Ebenso stoisch führte er den Bleistift. Fast immer entstand ein Gegenüber, ein Gesicht, eine Maske, die den Betrachter immer ansah. Horacek zerstückelte und füllte danach seine Gesichter wieder, die runden Augen, das immer ovale Gesicht, beschriftete sie mit seinem Namen und *in Mannswörth*. Je nach Geduld wurde das Blatt mehr oder weniger gefüllt, die Anfänge der Zeichnung entweder noch erkennbar oder völlig überlagert von Schraffierungen: Blätter, die den Betrachter zu analysieren scheinen – und nicht umgekehrt.

Franz Kamlander (1920 – 1999). Von einem Bauernhof kommend, hatten es ihm Kühe angetan. In seinem wortlosen Leben – er war taubstumm – hatte er nie die Gehörlosensprache erlernt, entwickelte aber eine eigene Zeichensprache einfacher Art, mit der er sich verständigen konnte. Typische Bewegungen oder Gesten des Gegenübers übernahm er als Symbol für diese Person. Sein spezifisches Talent, Tiere aller Art zu zeichnen, hatte er *schon immer*. Auswendig schuf er nicht nur naturgetreue Abbildungen, sondern oft auch unproportionale animalische Visionen. Diese waren bis auf wenige Ausnahmen, wenn er etwa *Nas-schweine* zu Papier brachte, sehr treffend. Gelbe, rote oder blaue Kühe entsprangen schnell und fließend seinem Stift. Aus der Vielzahl der Bilder wählte er, um einmal auf Wunsch einen großen Rahmen für eine Ausstellung damit zu füllen, zuerst alle vorhandenen, rein schwarzen Kühe aus, und erst als keine mehr vorhanden waren, jene schwarzen, die gelbe Euter hatten. Es war eine Herde entstanden, fast wie auf dem Bauernhof, auf dem er aufgewachsen war.

Franz Kernbeis (*1935) ist wie Franz Kamlander von ländlicher Herkunft und hat einen Zwillingsbruder, der ihm bis heute fast aufs Haar gleicht. Franz Kernbeis hat einfache Vorlieben, pafft gerne seine Zigaretten vor sich hin und liebt Cola. Ebenso einfach erscheinen seine Zeichnungen. Archaisch anmutende Entwürfe, oft in einem Strich durchgezogen, werden flächig so dicht mit Strichen überlagert, dass sie wie gemalt aussehen. Farbschichten überlagern Farbschichten. Man erkennt eine Genialität der Einfachheit in den Zeichnungen von Franz Kernbeis.

Fritz Koller (1929 – 1994) war der dritte Bauernsohn im Bunde der Gugginger Künstler. Gleich aus der Nachbarschaft kommend, nicht von weit entfernten Orten wie die anderen, die aus dem Süden (Kernbeis) oder aus dem Osten (Kamlander) von Niederösterreich stammten. Koller verstand Späße, die er besonders gerne mit seinem Freund und Sammler Heinz Kammerer trieb. Kollers Kunst war die des schnellen Strichs, der oft Figuren zerstückelte, Gegenstände und Bauwerke in ihre Bestandteile zerlegte und diese auf dem Blatt aneinander reihte. Seine Abbildungen von Menschen zeichnete er oft mit gemischtem Profil. Auch Netze von Strichen überzogen oft seine Blätter bis zur völligen Abstraktion. In wenigen Sekunden war oft ein Blatt fertig, schwungvoll souverän.

Johann Korec (*1937) liebt die Liebe und die Frauen. Daher wurden Darstellungen von Liebespaaren – mit oder ohne Geschlechtsakt – seine Lieblingsmotive. Etwas indiskret schreibt er noch dazu, wen er abbildet. Er erhöht basale menschliche Liebes-Bedürfnisse in den Bereich der Kunst und bleibt nicht in der Pornographie hängen. Seine Liebespaare sind salonfähig und brauchen dazu keine raffaelischen göttlichen Titel. Feder, Tusche und Aquarellfarbe verwendet er auf seine Weise. Ein bis ins Mark gehendes Kratzen der gegen den Strich verwendeten, gemarterten Stahlfeder erfüllt während des Zeichnens den Raum. Striche, die anschließend oft in überfließender Farbe ertränkt werden.

Rudolf Limberger (1937 – 1988), auch unter dem Pseudonym *Max* bekannt, verhielt sich meist wirklich etwas kindlich, gelegentlich sich selbst widersprechend oder völlig in sich gekehrt. Um zu zeichnen brauchte er die Anwesenheit seines Psychiaters Leo Navratil. Alleine dieser Tätigkeit nachzugehen, hatte er kein Interesse. Es entstanden Figuren, die unter einem Überschwang von Bleistiftstrichen beim Zeichnen wieder verdeckt wurden. Fast gehackte Linien, die in das Papier eindrangen, entsprangen den Sitzungen über Jahre. Kraftvolle, beeindruckende Werke, die manchen Künstler staunen lassen, wenn sie Ähnliches probieren.

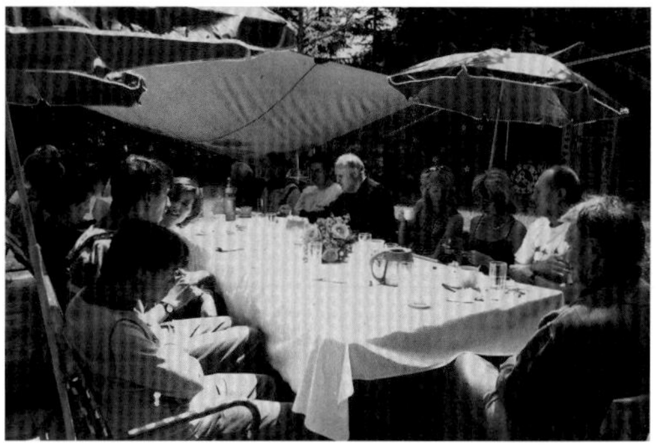

2004
Fest / Party

Fritz Opitz (1911 – 1987) war eine Ausnahme in Gugging. Eigentlich gehören seine Arbeiten nicht in ein Buch über Art Brut Künstler, da seine Werke naiv und volkstümlich sind. Seine Darstellungen sind dem Traditionellen entlehnt, sodass sie naive österreichische Volkskunst darstellen. Aber Opitz lebte im Haus der Künstler und seine Arbeiten sind witzig und originell, und daher sei er hier erwähnt. Fritz Opitz selbst war oft pedantisch, aber auch lästig, er stieß gelegentlich mit seinem spitzen Zeigefinger in die Schultern seiner Kollegen. Er konnte *Die Glocke* zitieren, untermalt von Prosa-Kommentaren, die jedem Zuhörer ein Lächeln abzwangen. Seine gemalten *Haussegenssprüche* ordneten sein Leben, genau, langsam, so wie er sich gerne in endlose Gespräche verwickelte.

Otto Prinz (1906 – 1980) hielt sich zu Höherem berufen, wollte majestätisch sein. Sein Verhalten war auch elegant, ruhig, zurückhaltend. Seine Zeichnungen waren diesem Selbstverständnis angepasst und hatten oft visionären Charakter. Man findet in seinen Bildern Kreuze und schwertbewaffnete Menschen, richtige Heerscharen, die aber nicht wie Kämpfer, sondern eher wie Erschreckte aussehen. Auch engelhafte, im Nebel schwebende Figuren bevölkern oft seine zarten Bleistiftzeichnungen. Es entstanden Werke, die er häufig um ein Butterbrot verkaufte, für die er aber auch nicht mehr annehmen wollte; vielleicht wäre dies nicht majestätisch gewesen.

Heinrich Reisenbauer (*1938) ist ruhig und wandert gerne auf und ab, was ihm von seiner früheren *Gefangenschaft* in der Psychiatrie geblieben ist. Die Freiheit, die er seit Jahren im Haus der Künstler genießt, scheint er gar nicht zu benötigen, denn er nützt sie gar nicht oder nur selten aus. Auch in seinen Zeichnungen ist er kontrolliert, geordnet, pedantisch. In Reih und Glied stehen sein Figuren, Gegenstände oder anderen einfachen Motive. Säuberlich gleich, aber doch nicht identisch, das macht den Reiz seiner Arbeiten aus. Den Radiergummi stets zur Hand, zur Korrektur bereit, falls ein Strich nicht seinen Vorstellungen entpricht. Fast zaghaft berührt sein Stift das Papier. Überwindung kosten ihn die großen Leinwände, die Linien mit schwarzem Filzstift konturiert, da sich hier nichts mehr korrigieren lässt. Unerbittlich ist der Kontrast, aber Heinrich Reisenbauer schafft diesen Sprung ins Absolute der weißen Fläche.

Johann Scheiböck (1905 – unbekannt) führte in seinen frühen Jahren eine Landwirtschaft; zu zeichnen begann er erst während seines Krankenhausaufenthaltes. Seine Hauptthemen sind einfache Geräte aus der Landwirtschaft und Kästen. Weinpressen, Häckselmaschinen und Heuwagen hat er mit prägnantem, sicherem Strich auf das Papier gebracht und danach in starken Farben koloriert. Keine Linie ist zu viel, fast abstrahiert wirken die eindrucksvollen Zeichnungen. Die Einfachheit der Darstellung ist überzeugend. Die meist auf billigem Packpapier gezeichneten Werke beginnen sich schon zu verfärben, was ihrer Qualität aber keinen Abbruch tut.

Arnold Schmidt (*1959) kam 1986 als junger, dynamischer Mann ins Haus der Künstler. Seine Energie ist auch seinen Werken anzusehen: schnell, mit flottem Strich und ungeduldig – am liebsten fertig noch vor dem Beginnen. Menschen und Flugzeuge sind seine malerischen Themen in allen Dimensionen. Doppeldecker aus vergangenen Zeiten, schwungvolle Figuren in kräftigen, strahlenden Farben überzeugen auf der Leinwand. In mehreren Sitzungen überarbeitet er seine größeren Werke.

Philipp Schöpke (1921 – 1998) war ein Schelm, wenn er gut aufgelegt war. Er konnte aber auch verärgert sein, was – zu unserem Glück – selten war. Meist strahlte er vor Heiterkeit und ließ kein Späßchen aus, konnte lachen wie kein anderer und jeden dabei mitreißen. Bei seiner künstlerischen Arbeit war er einmal bedächtig, dann wieder ungeduldig. Seine zähnestrotzenden Menschendarstellungen zeichnete er mit großer Ausdauer. Seine Figuren hatten aber noch eine Eigenheit: Sie waren fast durchsichtig, die Eingeweide und Geschlechtsteile waren zu sehen, die Umrisse verloren sich oft im unteren Teil des Blattes. Sein in den letzten Jahren zunehmender Tremor störte seine Zeichenkunst nicht, mit zittriger Hand fuhr er mit dem Bleistift über das Papier und entwarf *Familien, Seehunde* und *Fußballspiele* – er selbst hatte als großer Fußballfan nie ein in der Umgebung stattfindendes Spiel verpasst.

Günther Schützenhöfer (*1965) ist erst einige Jahre im Haus der Künstler. Erst vor wenigen Jahren entdeckt und eingeladen, entwickelte er seinen eigenen, unverwechselbaren Stil. Dieser wirkt oft humorvoll und treffend. Nach dem Zeichnen der Umrisse füllt Schützenhöfer die entstandenen Flächen mit ruhigen Strichen aus: sehr langsam und bedächtig. Sein Oeuvre umfasst bisher kleine bis mittelgroße Werke. Er arbeitet regelmäßig und steigert langsam die Größe seiner Zeichnungen.

Oswald Tschirtner (*1920) ist in sich gekehrt, nur mit seiner Bibel wirklich verbunden. So wie im Leben verhält er sich auch in seinem künstlerischen Werk. Er hat sich auch auf dem Papier oder der Leinwand mehr der Einsamkeit der Figur, fast dem Minimalismus verschrieben. Tschirtners *Menschen* sind allen Schmuckes entkleidet, sparsam bis auf die Haut, denn weder Gewand noch Geschlecht sind diesen Menschendarstellungen zu entnehmen. Der Kopf verfließt mit dem Körper, Beine sind nicht mehr getrennt, sie vereinen sich – durchaus elegant – zu einem stammartigen Rumpf; die Arme sind die einzigen Formen, die dem Körper anhaften, aber fingerlos bleiben. Wenn Tschirtner die Menschdarstellung verlässt und bei anderen Themen Einkehr hält, wird er noch sparsamer in der Darstellung der Form. Eine *Landschaft* kann als einziger Strich über das Papier wandern, ein Tier ein einziger Punkt sein; umgekehrt kann *Friede* jede Form annehmen. Gelegentlich hat Tschirtner auch seine Zeichnungen koloriert – mit einer Farbe, seltener mit zwei, aber niemals bunt. Der Konzentration der Themenbehandlung und der radikalen Vereinfachung entwächst eine tiefere innere Aussage.

Karl Vondal (*1953) ist noch nicht lange im Haus der Künstler, hat es aber bereits geschafft, völlig eigenständige Werke zu schaffen. Der Zeichner und Bastler, der aus Zündhölzern Villen und Gitarren zusammenleimte, klebt jetzt Papier an Papier, über und über, so groß, wie er diese nur tragen kann. Denn er verlässt ein begonnenes Werk nicht, bis es vollendet ist. Er rollt es zusammen, nimmt es überall hin mit, auch wenn dabei die Ränder leiden: Gebrauchsspuren wie auf Objekten der Stammeskunst. Seine Vorliebe für erotische Frauen und Sexualität hat er mit Johann Korec gemein, der Stil ist jedoch völlig anders. Zarter, weicher Bleistiftstrich formt die Figuren. Paare in märchenhafter Manier, seit neuerer Zeit von dazupassenden Texten umwoben, erfüllen den künstlerisch erotischen Himmel der pikturalen Zweisamkeit. Vondal ist ein Künstler, dem der Ideenreichtum niemals ausgeht und der uns noch ungezählte Male in das Problem der richtigen Präsentation der immer größer werdenden Kompositionen bringen wird.

August Walla (1936 – 2001) war ein Original, stadtbekannt, noch lange bevor ihn jemand als Künstler ernst nahm. Er und seine Mutter *verunsicherten* Klosterneuburg, widersetzten sich vielen bürgerlichen Normen, lebten wie auf einer Mülldeponie, zuerst in den Donauauen und später in einer abbruchreifen Kaserne. Erst als die 88-Jährige sich nicht mehr zurechtfand, kamen Mutter und Sohn ins Haus der Künstler. August Walla war wohl der universellste Künstler der Art Brut Szene, höchstens zu vergleichen mit Adolf Wölfli. Wie dieser schrieb er tausende Seiten, für sich selbst und an andere. Seit seinen jungen Jahren zeichnete er aus innerem Drang und schickte Briefe an Gott und die Welt. Da ihm Papier zu klein wurde, beschriftete er Straßen, Bäume und Häuser, was seinen Beliebtheitsgrad in der Bevölkerung nicht gerade hob. Seine polytheistische Religionsphilosophie füllte seine Hefte und die Wände seines Zimmers. Die gesamte Umgebung des Hauses der Künstler wurde von ihm bemalt und vereinnahmt. Er hatte bereits seinen Stempel der irdischen Welt aufgedrückt, als er viel zu früh in sein *Weltallendeland* einzog.

Erich Zittra (1915 – 1980) begann erst im fortgeschrittenen Alter zu zeichnen. Seine Themen waren Tiere, Häuser und Kirchen. Vor allem Hasen tauchten immer wieder auf. Sie sind in den meisten seiner Werke aber nicht mehr zu erkennen, da er sie mit einer Flut von Strichen in verschiedenen Farben zudeckte, oft so dicht, dass sie eine homogene Fläche ergaben.

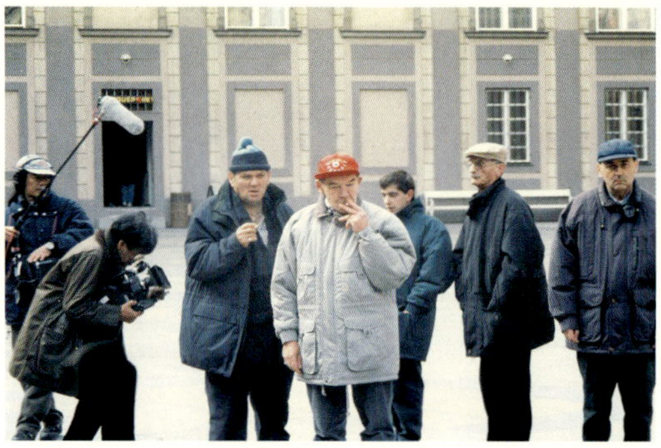

Prag / Prague, 1999

Josef Bachler (1914 – 1979) was not a peaceful man. He liked to pick fights and was often inebriated. The line of his drawing was none too scrupulous, either. He liked to press down on paper and divide the white space with a few strokes. In a few clear-cut lines, he sketched a woman, a man, or an animal without making any compromises. His drawings were more than mere sketches, however. They were finished, leaving no doubt that the cat, elephant or human being was missing anything. It is a pity that his oeuvre is so small. We would like to hope for more drawings of this kind.

Josef Blahaut (1922 – unknown) was plagued by voices that told him what to do. Overwhelmed by the words, he *spit* out innumerable letters that filled his drawings and got mixed up with his *heads*. He created a seeming chaos, an inundation that he covered with scribbles once he had had too much. Even though he couldn't stop himself, he still tried to escape his inner urge.

Anton Dobay (1906 – 1986) had a stroke at the age of 65 that robbed him of his speaking ability for the rest of his life. Urged on by Dr. Navratil, he started to draw. He consistently dedicated two hours a day to develop his previously dormant talents. Dobay left a marvelously post-impressionistic and later on formally simple oeuvre. He introduced intense colors to his drawings, layering so many strokes of wax crayon on the paper that it began to flake off.

Johann Fischer (*1919) likes to imitate other artists. After being invited to visit the mecca of artists at Gugging, he was inspired to follow suit and wanted to be on an equal level with them. By establishing a daily work schedule from the morning to the evening in the manner of a diligent craftsman, this talented artist has consistently developed his skills. After drawing single objects and charming animals, Fischer felt the urge to insert written communication in his work: using a peculiar language, he has jotted down advice on how things should be done and has written about the world order, social involvement and human relationships. His clear-cut lines evoke his former life as a vintner, when he used to plant vines in straight lines. At age 86, Johann Fischer still sits down to work on a daily basis.

Franz Gableck (1910 – 1974). The work of Franz Gableck clearly expresses his exuberance. He completed his best work when he was in good spirits and his chalk would fly swiftly over the large-format paper. He would dedicate every drawing to the senior physician. When his hopes and imagination converged, he would easily create very fresh and simple artwork, without any impediments. His oeuvre consists only of a few works, which leaves us wishing he could have created more.

Johann Garber (*1947) is very communicative and likes to strike up conversations with friends and strangers who pass by the House of Artists. His oeuvre overflows with details and decorations, and his drawings cover the paper to its margins. The artist only provides a basic outline for the content of his subject matter. More often than not, this content is so overrun by detail that it becomes indiscernible. He sets hundreds of figures into a landscape of buildings and churches, but also fills this landscape with animals, grass, bushes, clouds, and stars. Johann Garber also likes to integrate lived experiences and visual memories into his drawings. He might give these works a simple title such as *Vacation Picture, Hotel Pöder,* or *Sexy Picture.* In order to truly appreciate his drawings, viewers have to look at them a few times. In addition to creating detailed drawings with an ink pen, the artist also likes to work in a very different style. He compellingly reworks various objects that he either looks for and finds, or buys, such as straight wooden sticks, liquor bottles and deer antlers. Garber then proceeds to change the objects' characteristics. When he paints a revolver, it doesn't look like a dangerous weapon anymore, but turns into a nice and almost kitschy object, devoid of any aggression.

Johann Hauser (1926 – 1996) could be very likeable and nice at times, but would also yell and curse so that nobody dared to come near him. Deep down, he was not aggressive, however, and couldn't harm a soul. He loved women and liked to depict them on paper. One of the first artists to bring world fame to Gugging, Hauser found an enthusiastic response among artists and collectors. He would wait for a long time before jotting down the first line, but then colors would explode on paper. His depictions of beautiful and ugly ladies, rockets, tanks, snakes, and palaces were intense and powerful. The artist had a superbly skilled stroke that could pierce the thin paper sheets. His masterworks, which were created in a room full of cigarette smoke night after night, will endure.

Rudolf Horacek (1915 – 1986) could usually be found sitting in the room, waiting and smiling about the person next to him or about an idea. He would never communicate his thoughts, however. His stroke on paper is equally stoic. He created a vis-à-vis, a face, or a mask that always looked at the viewer. Horacek cut up and filled his faces, their round eyes, and their consistent oval shape again and again. He always gave his figures a name and wrote *in Mannswörth* (the place of his birth) on the paper. Depending on his patience, he filled the paper to a greater or lesser extent. Sometimes you can make out the beginning lines, sometimes they are completely covered with hatches. His work seems to analyze the viewer, not the other way round.

Franz Kamlander (1920 – 1999). Having grown up on a farm, Kamlander loved cows. During his wordless life – he was hearing and speech impaired – he never learned sign language, but developed his own simple language that enabled him to communicate. He would translate a person's typical movements and gestures into symbols. He *always had* a special talent for drawing animals of any kind. Kamlander not only drew pictures true to nature from memory, but also created disproportionate animalistic visions. Apart from a few exceptions such as his *nose-pigs,* these visions were very piercing. Yellow, red, or blue cows leapt effortlessly from his pencil. When he was once asked to fill a big frame for an exhibition, he first chose only black cows and then black cows with yellow udders from a wide variety of drawings. He had thus created herds like the ones he had seen on his farm as a child.

Franz Kernbeis (*1935). Like Franz Kamlander, Kernbeis was raised in a farming community. He has a twin brother, and to this day, the two of them look like two peas in a pod. Franz Kernbeis delights in simple things: he likes to puff cigars and drink coca cola. His archaic drawings are just as simple. They are often drawn in one line and covered by such dense strokes that they look as if they had been painted. Layers of color cover other layers of color. Franz Kernbeis's ingenuousness becomes apparent in the simplicity of his drawings.

Fritz Koller (1929 – 1994) was the third farmer's son among the Gugging Artists. He was born in a neighboring village, not in a remote Lower Austrian town in the South like Kernbeis or the East like Kamlander. Koller was a jokester and particularly liked to play around with his friend and collector Heinz Kammerer. A quick line characterizes Koller's art. After frequently dissecting figures and disassembling objects and buildings into their parts, he lined them up on paper. His depictions of human beings often bear a mixed profile. Networks of lines frequently cover his drawings. Some of them became completely abstract. With his superbly sweeping stroke, he frequently finished a drawing within seconds.

Johann Korec (*1937) loves love and women. This is why he focuses on depicting couples and sometimes shows them during intercourse. Never one to be discreet, he also writes down the names of the persons depicted on paper. Korec raises the fundamental human desire for love into the realm of art without ever becoming pornographic. His lovers are presentable in public and don't require divine Raphaelesque titles. Korec uses pen, ink, and watercolors in his own particular style. While he is drawing, the sounds of a wildly scratching steel pen working against the grain fill the room. These strokes are subsequently drowned in an overflow of color.

Rudolf Limberger (1937 – 1988), also known under the pseudonym *Max,* mostly behaved in a very childish manner. He would sometimes contradict himself or turn completely inward. In order for him to draw, psychiatrist Leo Navratil needed to be present in the room. Otherwise, he was not interested in any artistic activity. He created figures that are covered by an abundance of pencil strokes. His lines are almost chopped apart. Created during many years of drawing sessions, these lines penetrate the paper. Limberger's works are powerful and impressive and astonish artists who try out similar methods.

Fritz Opitz (1911 – 1987) was the exception in Gugging. His work doesn't actually belong in a book about Art Brut. Drawing from traditional sources, it belongs to the realm of naïve Austrian folk art. Opitz lived in the House of Artists, however, and his work is funny and original. That is why it deserves to be mentioned in this context. Opitz could be very pedantic and annoying at times. He would sometimes ram his pointed index finger into his colleagues' shoulders. He could recite Schiller's poem *The Bell* by heart and embellish it with prose commentaries, which made every listener smile. In his painted *house blessings,* he organized his life in a precise and slow manner, just like the way in which he liked to get involved in endless conversations.

Otto Prinz (1906 – 1980) believed he had a higher calling and wanted to appear majestic. His behavior was elegant, calm, and reserved. His drawings were a direct result of this self-image and often had a visionary ring to them. He would include crosses and men with swords

in his drawings, thus constituting entire legions that didn't look like warriors, but rather like scared hordes. His subtle pencil drawings frequently include angel-like figures that float in the fog. Prinz would sell his drawings for a song, not wanting to accept more. Maybe he believed that his acceptance of a higher fee wouldn't have been befitting a prince?

Philipp Schöpke (1921 – 1998) was a prankster when he was in a good mood. He would also get annoyed, which fortunately was not often the case. He mostly was beaming with joy and never left a trick undone. He could laugh like nobody else, infecting others with his happiness. His artistic work was sometimes marked by thoughtfulness, other times by impatience. He would persistently draw toothy human beings. One other thing was peculiar about his figures: They were almost transparent and viewers could see their innards and private parts. Their contours often got lost in the lower part of the picture. The tremor of the latter years of his life didn't interfere with his art. Tremblingly, he would draw his pen over the paper to create *families, seals,* and *soccer games.* Schöpke himself was an ardent soccer fan that never missed a neighborhood game.

Heinrich Reisenbauer (*1938) is a calm person who likes to walk up and down in his room, a reminder of his *internment* in a psychiatric ward. Apparently, it is only on rare occasions that he wants to make use of the freedom he has enjoyed in the House of Artists for years. In his drawings, he is very controlled, organized, and pedantic. His figures, objects, and other simple motifs stand in single file. They are neatly similar, but never identical. That is what makes his work so enjoyable. Reisenbauer always has his eraser in hand and is constantly ready to correct a line if it doesn't meet his expectations. His pencil touches the paper almost hesitantly. It is hard for him to contour a line with a black felt tip pen on a big canvas because he feels that nothing can be corrected. Contrasts are merciless for him. In the end, Heinrich Reisenbauer succeeds in diving into the absolute white space.

Johann Scheiböck (1905 – unknown) was a farmer in his younger years. He didn't start drawing until he was hospitalized. His main motifs are simple farming tools and cupboards. He delineated straw cutters and hay wagons with an assured stroke and then colored them in strong tones. No line is excessive. His impressive drawings almost seem abstract and convince viewers with their simplicity. Most of Scheiböck's work was executed on cheap packaging paper, which is starting to fade away. This degeneration process doesn't diminish the quality of Scheiböck's oeuvre, however.

Arnold Schmidt (*1959) came to the House of Artists as a young, dynamic man in 1986. His energy becomes manifest in his work: his strokes are quick and impatient, revealing that the artist would like to be done in no time. Human beings and airplanes in all dimensions are his favorite subjects. Double-deckers from the past and sweeping figures in powerfully bright colors are a convincing presence on canvas. He reworks his bigger canvases in several sessions.

Günther Schützenhöfer (*1965) has only been at the House of Artists for a few years. After he was discovered, he was invited to come and stay in Gugging. Since then, he has developed his own distinctive, humorous and striking style. After drawing contours, Schützenhöfer fills his surfaces with very slow, calm, and deliberate strokes. His oeuvre presently consists of smaller and medium-size works. He regularly sits down to work, with his drawings slowly increasing in size.

Oswald Tschirtner (*1920) is a very introverted person and only truly relates to his bible. His work is similar to his life. On paper or on canvas, he likes 'to focus on the loneliness of his figures, which he depicts in an almost minimalist fashion. Tschirtner's *human beings* are devoid of any ornament. They are sparse to the skin. Neither their clothing nor their sex can be discerned. Their heads fuse with their bodies. Their legs are not separate, but elegantly join to form a single, trunk-like rump. Their arms are the only forms that extend from the body, but they are devoid of fingers. When Tschirtner leaves behind the human figure and takes up other subjects, his depictions become even sparser. A *landscape* may wander over the paper in a single line, an animal may be a single dot. Conversely, *peace* may take on any form. At times, Tschirtner colors his drawings with a single color, and on a few occasions, two, but never more. A deep inner meaning emerges from this concentrated subject matter and radical simplification.

Karl Vondal (*1953). Even though he hasn't been at the House of Artists for a very long time, Vondal has succeeded in creating an independent oeuvre. A former hobbyist who glued together mansions and guitars with matchsticks, he now glues paper on paper, over and over again, to create pieces that are small enough that he can still carry them around with him. Vondal never leaves a work behind until it is fully completed. He rolls it up and takes it everywhere even if the edges suffer. Signs of use become apparent, just like on objects of native art. He shares a preference for sensual women and sexuality with Johann Korec, but depicts the subject quite differently. Gentle and soft strokes give shape to his figures. More recently, fairy-tale couples are framed with texts that go well with the images. These couples epitomize his erotic heaven of pictorial togetherness. Vondal is an artist who never runs short of ideas. As Vondal's compositions steadily grow, we will increasingly face the challenge of presenting his work in the right format.

August Walla (1936 – 2001) was a character who was known all over town long before anyone took him seriously as an artist. He and his mother *unsettled* Klosterneuburg by opposing many bourgeois norms. Their accommodations on the banks of the Danube and later in dilapidated barracks resembled a dump. It was not until his 88-year-old mother could no longer get a grip on life that the two of them joined the House of Artists. August Walla probably was the most universally trained artist in the field of Art Brut. Comparisons to Adolf Wölfli are in order. Like Wölfli, he wrote thousands of pages for himself and others. Since his early years, he followed an inner urge to draw and send letters to the entire world and his brother. Since paper became too small for him, he wrote on pavements, trees and buildings, which didn't make him any more popular with his fellow citizens. He filled his booklets and the walls of his room with his polytheistic religious beliefs. The whole area around the House of Artists was his playing field. Even though he passed on to his *All World's Land* far too early, Walla left a strong mark on the earthly world.

Erich Zittra (1915 – 1980) didn't start drawing until an advanced age. He liked to depict animals, buildings, and churches. Rabbits, in particular, keep reappearing in his drawings. Often they are no longer discernible, however, because an avalanche of strokes in different colors, so dense that they form a homogenous surface, covers them.

2006
Galerie Latal, Zürich, CH (K. Vondal)
Galerie Objet trouvé, Paris, F (Gruppe)
Stadtmuseum Klosterneuburg, A (A. Walla)

2005
Galerie 3, Klagenfurt, A (Gruppe)
Gallery Yukiko Koide, Tokyo, J (O. Tschirtner)
Galerie Hilt AG, Basel, CH (Gruppe)
Sigmund Freud Museum, Wien, A (Gruppe)

2004
Slovakische Nationalgalerie, Bratislava, SK (Gruppe)
Galerie Latal, Zürich, CH (F. Kernbeis, H. Reisenbauer)

2003
Galerie Latal, Zürich, CH
(G. Schützenhöfer, Ph. Schöpke)
Intuit, Chicago, USA (Gruppe)
Kunstverein Horn, A (Gruppe)
Galerie Altnöder, Salzburg, A (Gruppe)
Judy A. Saslow Gallery, Chicago, USA (Gruppe)
Galerie Latal, Zürich, CH (Gruppe)

2002
Galerie 3, Klagenfurt, A (Gruppe)
Biblioteca Pubblica Comunale, Borgo Valsugana, I (Gruppe)
Galerie Hamer, Amsterdam, NL (F. Kernbeis)
Galerie Pimmingstorfer, Peuerbach, A (Gruppe)
Galerie am Steinweg, Passau, A (Gruppe)
Freilichtmuseum Gerersdorf, A (Gruppe)

2001
Kunsthaus Nürnberg, D (Gruppe)
Kunstverein Hof, D (Gruppe)
Kunsthalle Krems, A (J. Hauser)
Galerie Maringer, St. Pölten, A (Gruppe)
Musée de l'Art Différencié, Liège, B (H. Reisenbauer)
Galerie St. Etienne, New York, USA (Gruppe)
Galerie Steinek, Wien, A
(J. Korec, H. Reisenbauer, A. Walla)
Galerie Altnöder, Salzburg, A (J. Fischer, F. Kernbeis)
Galerie Altnöder, Salzburg, A (J. Garber, A. Walla)
Galerie Dagmar Chobot, Wien, A (J. Hauser)
Kaiman Art and New Trends, Genua, A (J. Korec)
Galerie 422, Gmunden, A (Gruppe)

2000
Galerie 422, Gmunden, A (Gruppe)
Galerie Latal, Zürich, CH (J. Korec, A. Walla)
Galerie Hilt AG, Basel, CH (Gruppe)
Galerie Susanne Zander, Köln, D (A. Walla)
Galerie Ute Stebich, Lenox, USA (Gruppe)
Galerie Dagmar Chobot, Wien, A (A.Schmidt)
Kulturzentrum Kapfenberg, A (Gruppe)
Kaiman Art and New Trends, Ivrea, I (Gruppe)
Kaiman Art and New Trends, Rom, I (Gruppe)

1999
Galerie am Steinweg, Passau, D (Gruppe)
Galerie Latal, Zürich, CH (J. Garber, A. Walla)
Galerie Hammer & Herzer, Weiden, D (Gruppe)
Galerie Oliver Bittel, München, D (Gruppe)
Galerie Pimmingstorfer, Peuerbach, A (Gruppe)
Galerie 3, Klagenfurt, A (Gruppe)
Le Creahm – Centre d'Art différencié, Liège, B (Gruppe)
Sammlung Essl Privatstiftung
Klosterneuburg/Wien, A (Gruppe)
Galerie Pimmingstorfer-Schloss Peuerbach, A (Gruppe)
Galerie Altnöder, Salzburg, A (Gruppe)
Galerie Susanne Zander, Köln, D (J. Korec)
Kaiman Art and New Trends, Genua, I (Gruppe)
Art Center Dazibao, Montréal, CDN (A. Walla)
St. Marien-Krankenhaus, Dresden, D (Gruppe)
Museum de Stadshof, Zwolle, NL (O. Tschirtner)

1998
Colléction de l'Art Brut, Lausanne, CH (O. Tschirtner)
Salzburger Landessammlungen Rupertinum,
Salzburg, A (O. Tschirtner)
Castello Visconteo, Museo CiviciPavia, I (Gruppe)
Galerie Lange-Wasserwerk, Siegburg, D (Gruppe)
Galerie Hamer, Amsterdam, NL (Gruppe)
Galerie Heike Curtze, Wien, A
(J. Korec, A. Schmidt, A. Walla)
Museum Heimathaus Münsterland, Telgte, D (Gruppe)
Galerie du Fleuve, Paris, F (Gruppe)
Galerie Pabst, München, D (Gruppe)
Schlumper Galerie, Hamburg, D (Gruppe)
Anderwelt, Artstetten, NÖ, A (Gruppe)
Tschechische Nationalgalerie Prag, CZ (Gruppe)
Galerie Oliver Bittel, München, D (Gruppe)
Galerie Susanne Zander, Köln, D (Gruppe)
Galerie Lange – Wasserwerk, Siegburg, D (Gruppe)
Galerie Altnöder, Salzburg, A (Gruppe)

1997
Autonomes Culturcentrum Weimar, D (Gruppe)
Städtische Galerie Göppingen, D (Gruppe)
Galerie Jäger, Hochheim, D (Gruppe)
Museum moderner Kunst, Passau, D (Gruppe)
Galerie Raphael Rigassi, Bern, CH (O. Tschirtner)
Galerie Lange – Wasserwerk, Siegburg, D (Gruppe)
Galerie Latal, Zürich, CH (Gruppe)
Galerie Heike Curtze, Berlin, D (Gruppe)

1996
Hunt Gallery, Webster University, St. Louis, USA (Gruppe)
Kunstwerkstatt Tulln, A (Gruppe)
Museumsverein Landeck, A (Gruppe)
Haus an der Teutoburger Straße
Soz.psychiatr. Zentrum, München, D (Gruppe)
Galerie Janet Fleisher, Philadelphia, USA (Gruppe)
Galerie Mangisch, Zürich, CH (Gruppe)
Galerie Raphael Rigassi, Bern, CH (Gruppe)

1995
Galerie Altnöder, Salzburg, A (J. Korec)
Galerie Susanne Zander, Köln, D (A. Walla)
Galerie Dagmar Chobot, Wien, A (J. Korec)
Galerie Andreas Binder, München, D (Gruppe)
Galerie Susanne Zander, Köln, D (F. Kamlander)
Galerie Susanne Zander, Köln, D (Gruppe)
Galerie Hamer, Amsterdam, NL (Gruppe)
Galerie Würthle, Wien, A (Gruppe)
Galerie Latal, Zürich, CH (J. Garber, J. Korec, A. Schmidt)

1994
Museum de Stadshof, Zwolle, NL Gruppe)
Galerie Raphael Rigassi, Bern, CH (Gruppe)
Galerie Latal, Zürich, CH (J. Fischer, O. Tschirtner)

1993
Fondatione Galleria Gottardo, Lugano, CH (Gruppe)
Amos Anderson Museum, Helsinki, FIN (Gruppe)
Autonomes Culturcentrum Weimar, D (Gruppe)

1992
Galerie Heike Curtze, Düsseldorf, D
(F. Kernbeis, J. Hauser, A. Walla)
Galerie Susanne Zander, Köln, D (H. Reisenbauer)
Phyllis Kind Gallery, Chicago, USA (Gruppe)
Southern Exposure Gallery, San Francisco, USA (Gruppe)
Galerie Faber, Wien, A (A. Walla)
Galerie Latal, Zürich, CH (Gruppe)
Galerie Altnöder, Salzburg, A (O. Tschirtner)
Galerie Susanne Zander, Köln, D (J. Korec)

1991
Phyllis Kind Gallery, New York, USA (Gruppe)
Galerie Altnöder, Salzburg, A (Gruppe)
Galerie Steinek, Wien, A (A. Schmidt)
Galerie Susanne Zander, Köln, D (J. Hauser)
Galerie Charlotte, München, D (F. Kamlander)
Austrian Culture Institute, New York, USA (Gruppe)
Moore College of Art, Philadelphia, USA (Gruppe)
Galerie Dagmar Chobot, Wien, A (Gruppe)
Galerie Susanne Zander, Köln, D (F. Kamlander)
Kunstamt Wedding, Berlin, D
(J. Fischer, F. Kernbeis, H. Reisenbauer)

1990
Galerie Dagmar Chobot, Wien, A (A. Walla)
Kunstmuseum des Kantons Thurgau,
Kartause Ittingen, CH (Gruppe)
Colléction de l'art brut, Lausanne, CH (Gruppe)
Hochschule für angewandte Kunst –
Heiligenkreuzerhof, Wien, A (Gruppe)
Galerie Steinek, Wien, A (A. Schmidt)
Galerie Susanne Zander, Köln, D (J. Fischer)
Galerie Susanne Zander, Köln, D (Gruppe)

1989
Galerie Susanne Zander, Köln, D (J. Fischer, A. Walla)
Kunstamt Wedding, Berlin, D (A. Walla)
Museum Bochum, D (A. Walla)
Heidelberger Kunstverein, D (A. Walla)
Stadtmuseum Oldenburg, D (Gruppe)

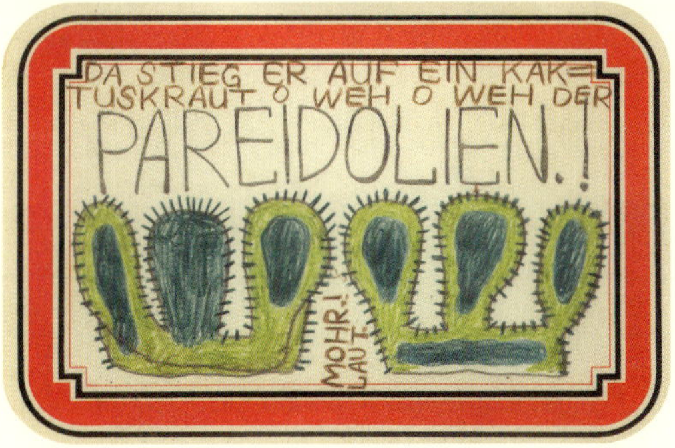

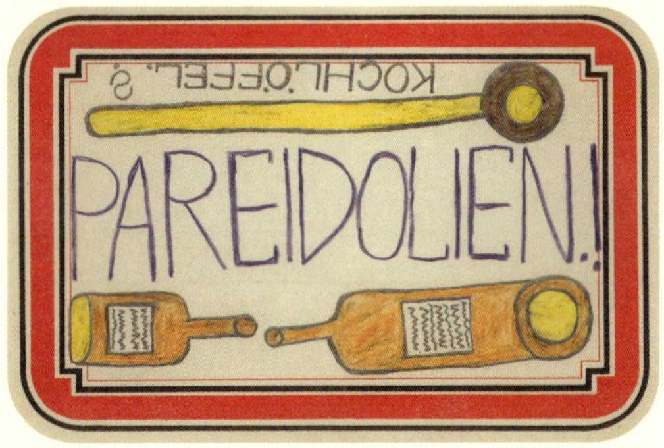

August Walla, Pareidolien,
1970, 12,8 x 19cm,
Bleistift, Farbstifte / pencil,
color pencil

1988
Massachusetts College of Art, Boston, USA (Gruppe)
Collection de l'art brut, Lausanne, CH (A. Walla)
Aargauer Kunsthaus, CH (A. Walla)
Museum moderner Kunst, Wien, A (A. Walla)
Galerie Heike Curtze, Wien, A (A. Walla)

1987
L'Aracine, Neuilly-sur-Marne, F (Gruppe)
Galerie Heike Curtze, Wien, A
(F. Kernbeis, Ph. Schöpke, O. Tschirtner)
Galerie Dagmar Chobot, Wien, A
(J. Fischer, J. Hauser, J. Korec)

1985
Galerie Messine, Paris, F
(Ph. Schöpke, O. Tschirtner, A. Walla)
Aargauer Kunsthaus, Aarau, CH (Gruppe)
Neue Galerie – Staatl und. Städt. Kunstsammlungen, Kassel, D (Gruppe)

1984
Collection de l'art brut, Lausanne, CH (A. Walla)
Galerie Heike Curtze, Düsseldorf, D (Gruppe)
Kunstamt Wedding, Berlin, D (Gruppe)

1983
Salzburger Landessammlungen Rupertinum, A (Gruppe)
Museum moderner Kunst, Wien, A (Gruppe)
Galerie Heike Curtze, Düsseldorf, D (Gruppe)
Galerie Heike Curtze, Wien, A (Ph. Schöpke)

1982
Galerie Heike Curtze, Wien, A (F. Koller)
Galerie Heike Curtze, Wien, A (J. Garber)

1981
Neue Galerie der Stadt Linz, A (Gruppe)
Collection de l'art brut, Lausanne, CH (A. Walla)
Kunstmuseum Düsseldorf, D (Gruppe)
Kunsthalle Tübingen, D (Gruppe)
Heidelberger Kunstverein, D (Gruppe)

1980
Collection de l'art brut, Lausanne, CH (A. Walla)
Neue Galerie der Stadt Linz Wolfgang-Gurlitt-Museum, A (Gruppe)
Kulturamt Wedding, Berlin, D (Gruppe)
Galerie Heike Curtze, Wien, A (O. Tschirtner)
Neue Galerie der Stadt Linz Wolfgang-Gurlitt-Museum, A (J. Hauser)
Museum moderner Kunst, Wien, A
(J. Hauser, O. Tschirtner)
Josef-Haubrich-Kunsthalle, Köln, D (J. Hauser)
Kunsthalle Bremen, D (Gruppe)

1979
Kulturhaus der Stadt Graz, A (J. Hauser)
Städtische Galerie im Lenbachhaus, München, D
(J. Hauser)
Hayward Gallery, London, GB (J. Hauser)
Neue Galerie der Stadt Linz Wolfgang-Gurlitt-Museum, A
(J. Hauser, O. Tschirtner)

1978
Staatliche Kunsthalle Baden-Baden, D
(J. Hauser, O. Tschirtner)

1976
Neue Galerie der Stadt Linz Wolfgang Gurlitt-Museum, A (Gruppe)

1975
Kunsthaus Zürich, CH (J. Hauser)
Kulturhaus der Stadt Graz, A (Gruppe)
Bregenzer Künstlerhaus, Theater am Kornmarkt, A (Gruppe)

1974
Haus der Kunst, München, D (J. Hauser)

1972
Galerie nächst St. Stephan, Wien, A (Gruppe)

1971
Kunsthalle Helsinki, FIN (Gruppe)

1970
Galerie nächst St. Stephan, Wien, A (Gruppe)

beteiligung bei internationalen ausstellungen / participation at international exhibitions

2006
Art en Marge, Brüssel, B (A. Walla)
Sammlung Essl Privatstiftung Klosterneuburg/Wien, A (J. Hauser, F. Kamlander, A. Walla)

2005
La Maison Rouge, Paris, F (J. Fischer, F. Kernbeis)
Museum of Contemporary Art Kiasma, Helsinki, FIN (J. Fischer, O. Tschirtner)
Kunstpalast Düsseldorf, D (J. Hauser)
Österr. Galerie Belvedere, Wien, A (O. Tschirtner)
Gemeentemuseum den Haag, NL (J. Fischer, F. Kernbeis)
Collection de l'art brut, Lausanne, CH (J. Fischer, J. Hauser, Ph. Schöpke)

2003
Salzburger Landessammlungen Rupertinum, *Art Brut um und in Salzburg*, A (Gruppe)

2000
American Visionary Art Museum, *We are not alone*, Baltimore, USA (J. Garber, A. Walla)
Museum Charlotte Zander, *Outsider Art*, Bönnigheim, D (Gruppe)
Deutsches Hygienemuseum, Dresden, D (A. Walla)
Setagaya Art Museum, Tokyo, J (Gruppe)

1999
Ivan Dougherty Gallery, *L'Art Brut, de la dandestinité à la consécration*, Sydney, AUS (A. Walla)
Musée d'ethnographie Genève, *L'Art Brut, de la dandestinité à la consécration*, Genf, CH (A. Walla)
Schillermuseum, *L'Art Brut, de la dandestinité à la consécration*, Weimar, D (A. Walla)
Le Botanique, *L'Art Brut, de la dandestinité à la consécration*, Brüssel, B (A. Walla)
American Visionary Art Museum, Baltimore, USA (J. Garber, A. Walla)

1998
Garonne Art Festival – Le Bazacle, *l'Intracabe Frontière*, Toulouse, F (Gruppe)
Palais des beaux Arts de Bruxelles, *Austria im Rosennetz*, Brüssel, B (J. Hauser, A. Walla)
Appartamento del Doge di Palazzo Ducale, *Figure dell'anima*, Genua, I (Gruppe)

1997
Kunsthaus Zürich, *Austria im Rosennetz*, CH (J. Hauser, A. Walla)

1996
Les Halles Saint-Pierre et le Musée d'art naif Max, *Art Brut et compagnie*, Paris, F (J. Hauser, A. Walla)
Künstlerhaus Wien, *Malerei in Österreich 1945-1995/Sammlung Essl*, Wien, A (Gruppe)
Kunstverein Davos, *Art-Brut Woche*, Davos, CH (Gruppe)
Otsu City Museum of History, Nishinomiya City, J (Gruppe)
Museum für angewandte Kunst, *Austria im Rosennetz*, Wien, A (J. Hauser, A. Walla)
Setagaya Art Museum, *From the Collection: Naivety in Art - A Decade of Exploration*, Tokyo, J (J. Hauser, O. Tschirtner, A. Walla)

1995
Le Creahm Centre d'Art différencié, *The Nude*, Liège, B (J. Garber)
Foires Internationales de Luxembourg, *Neue Qualitäten*, L (J. Garber)

1993
County Museum of Art, *Parallel Visions*, Los Angeles, USA (J. Hauser, A. Walla)
Reina Sofia, *Parallel Visions*, Madrid, E (J. Hauser, A. Walla)
Kunsthalle Basel, Parallel Visions, Basel, CH (J. Hauser, A. Walla)
Setagaya Art Museum, *Parallel Visions*, Tokyo, J (J. Hauser, A. Walla)
Refettorio delle Stelline, *La Normalita' dell'Arte*, Mailand, I (Gruppe)

1992
Neue Galerie am Landesmuseum Joanneum, Identität: Differenz, Tribüne Trigon. *Eine Topographie der Moderne 1940-1990*, Graz, A (Gruppe)

1991
Malmö Konsthall, *Särlingar. Art Brut. Outsider Art*, Malmö, S (Gruppe)

1990
Parson School of Design, *Portraits from the Outside*, New York, USA (Gruppe)
DuMont-Kunsthalle, *Von einer Welt zur anderen*, Köln, D (Gruppe)
Basel landschaftlicher Kunstverein – Schloss Ebenrain, *L'Art brut*, Sissach/Basel, CH (Gruppe)

1989
Clemens-Sels-Museum, *Kunst, wo man sie nicht vermutet*, Neuss, D (Gruppe)

1988
Kunsthaus St. Alban, *Outsiders. An Exhibition of Art Brut*, Basel, CH (J. Hauser, O. Tschirtner, A. Walla)
Atrium Gallery, University of Connecticut, *Outsider Art from Europe: A selection of Works on Paper*, Storrs, USA (Gruppe)
Northern Illionois University Art Gallery, *Outsider Art from Europe: A selection of Works on Paper*, Chicago,USA (Gruppe)
North Hall Gallery, College of Art, Massachusetts, USA (Gruppe)

1986
Rosa Esman Gallery, *European Outsiders*, New York, USA (Gruppe)

1984
Phyllis Kind Gallery, *Austrian Art Brut*, Chicago, USA (Gruppe)

in öffentlichen sammlungen / in public collections

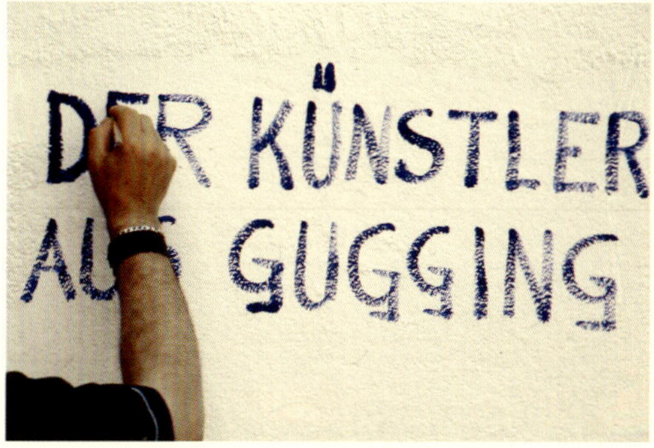

Museum moderner Kunst, Wien, A
Grafische Sammlungen der Albertina, Wien, A
Neue Galerie der Stadt Linz, A
Salzburger Landessammlungen Rupertinum, A
Niederösterreichische Landessammlung, St. Pölten, A
Städtische Galerie im Lenbachhaus, München, D
Neues Museum Weserburg, Bremen, D
Collection de l'art brut, Lausanne, CH
Musee d'Art moderne, Villeneuve d'Ascq, F
Museum de Stadshof, Zwolle, NL
Museum of modern Art, Philadelphia, USA
Malmö Konsthall, S
Setagaya Museum, Tokyo, J
Museum Charlotte Zander Schloß Bönnigheim, D
Outsider Archive, London, GB
Petullo Collection, Milwaukee, USA
Outsider Art Museum, Moskau, RUS

literaturliste / bibliography

Bader, Alfred und Navratil, Leo, *Zwischen Wahn und Wirklichkeit.* Kunst-Psychose-Kreativität, C.J. Bucher Luzern u. Frankfurt/Main, 1976
Brugger, Ingried; Gorsen, Peter u. Schröder, Albrecht/Kunstforum Wien, *Kunst & Wahn,* Dumont Buchverlag, Wien-Köln, 1997
Bütler, Heinz, *Zur Besserung der Person* Film, Fotos, Zeichnungen, ... Zytglogge Verlag, Bern, 1982

Chobot, Manfred, *August Walla.* Schrift – Zeichen, Wien, 1990

Dichter, Claudia und Feilacher, Johann/Dr. Feilacher KEG, *Miteinander – Gegeneinander,* Arnulf Rainer u. die Künstler aus G., Haus der Künstler, Gugging, 1995
Dichter, Claudia/Zander Ch., *Outsider Art.,* Collection Charlotte Zander, Bönnigheim, 1999

Feilacher, Johann/Galerie Heike Curtze, *Philipp Schöpke,* Galerie Heike Curtze, Wien, 1983
Feilacher, Johann/Galerie Heike Curtze, *Drei Zeichner aus Gugging,* Kernbeis, Schöpke, Tschirtner, Galerie Heike Curtze, Wien, 1987
Feilacher, Johann, *Künstler aus Gugging.* Zur Art Brut der Gegenwart., Bibliotheks-u.Informationssystem, Oldenburg, 1989
Feilacher, Johann/Kulturabteilung des Landes NÖ und Haus der Künstler *Sonneastro.* Die Künstler aus Gugging, Wien, 1990
Feilacher, Johann/Austrian Cultural Institute, *The Artists of Gugging.* Die Künstler aus Gugging, New York-Gugging, 1991
Feilacher, Johann u. Zander, Susanne/Haus der Künstler, *August Walla.,* Interieurs Köln, 1992
Feilacher, Johann/Cultur Centrum Wolkenstein, *Bestände 21.,* Schräge Vögel, Stainach, 1992
Feilacher, Johann/Patocchi Luca, *gugging la casa degli artisti,* Fond. Per cultura della Lugano, 1993
Feilacher, Johann/Dr. Feilacher KEG, *Guggging.* Die Künstler aus Gugging, Repro Druck Gugler, Melk/Gugging, 1993
Feilacher, Johann, *Sterne aus Gugging,* Autonomes Cultur Centrum e.V., Weimardruck GmbH, Weimar, 1993
Feilacher, Johann/Galerie, Rigassi, *Künstler aus Gugging,* Art Brut der Gegenwart, Galerie Rigassi Benteli – Wird Verlags AG, Bern, 1994
Feilacher, Johann/Galerie Heike Curtze und Haus der Künstler, *Tigerlachen – Löwentreiben.,* Wien, 1994
Feilacher, Johann, *Das rote Zebra,* Zeichnungen von Oswald Tschirtner, Wienand, Köln, 1997
Feilacher, Johann, *Menschen mit Heiligenschein,* Zeichnungen von Oswald Tschirtner, Wienand, Köln, 1997
Feilacher, Johann/ Städt. Galerie Göppingen, *Die Künstler aus Gugging,* Werner Meyer, Städt. Galerie Göppingen, 1997
Feilacher, Johann/Edition Feilacher, Johann, *Sovären,* Das Haus der Künstler in Gugging, Edition Braus, Heidelberg, 2004

Heller, André, *Luna Luna,* Wilhelm Heyne Verlag GmbH, München, 1987
Herbeck Ernst/Navratil, Leo, *Alexanders poetische Texte,* Taschenbuchverlag, München, 1977
Herbeck, Ernst u. Tschirtner, Oswald/Navratil, Leo, *Bebende Herzen im Leibe der Hunde,* Rogner & Bernhard GmbH, München, 1979
Herbeck, Ernst, *Alexander,* Ausgewählte Texte 1961-1981, Residenzverlag, Salzburg/Wien, 1982
Herbeck, Ernst/Navratil, Leo, *Im Herbst da reiht der Feenwind.,* Gesammelte Texte 1960-1991, Residenzverlag, Salzburg/Wien, 1992

Jägers, Achim, *Von Gugging aus ...,* VIP-Verlag, Innsbruck, 1998

Le Guillou, Thomas/Galerie Messine, *Philipp Schöpke, August Walla, Oswald Tschirtner,* 1985

Mach, Edmund, *Buchstaben Florenz.,* Texte 1965-1979, Medusa Verlag, Wien-Berlin, 1982
Mach, Edmund/Chobot, Manfred, *Triumph des Schockens,* Grasl Verlag, Baden bei Wien, 1995
Maizels, John, *Raw Creation,* Outsider Art and beyond., Phaidon Press Ltd., London, 1996

Navratil, Leo, *Schizophrenie und Kunst.,* Ein Beitrag zur Psych. des Gestaltens, Taschenbuchverlag München, 1965
Navratil, Leo, *a + b leuchten im Klee.,* Psychopathologische Texte, Carl Hanser München, 1971
Navratil, Leo, *Schizophrenie und Sprache,* Schizophrenie und Kunst, Taschenbuchverlag, München, 1976
Navratil, Leo, *Johann Hauser,* Kunst aus Manie und Depression, Rogner & Bernhard, München, 1978
Navratil, Leo/Galerie Heike Curtze, *Fritz Koller,* Zeichnungen, Wien-Düsseldorf, 1981
Navratil, Leo/Galerie Heike Curtze, *Johann Garber,* Zeichnungen, Wien-Düsseldorf, 1982
Navratil, Leo, *Die Künstler aus Gugging,* Medusa Verlag Wien-Berlin, 1983
Navratil, Leo, *Schizophrenie und Dichtkunst,* Taschenbuchverlag, München, 1986
Navratil, Leo, *August Walla,* Sein Leben & seine Kunst, Delphi Nördlingen, 1988
Navratil, Leo, *Bilder nach Bildern,* Residenzverlag Salzburg-Wien, 1993
Navratil, Leo, *Art Brut und Psychiatrie,* Brandstätter Verlag, Wien, 1997
Navratil, Leo, *Die Künstler und ihre Werke,* Brandstätter Verlag, Wien, 1997

Oshima, Seiji/Setagaya Museum, *From the Collection Naivety in Art,* A Decade of Exploration, Tokyo, 1996

Peiry, Lucienne, *L'art brut,* Flammarion Paris, 1997
Pijaudier-Cabot, Joelle und Faupin, Savine/Musée d'Art Moderne, *Art Brut.* Collection de L'Aracine Lille, 1997

Ronte, Dieter, *Oswald Tschirtner,* Museum moderner Kunst, Wien, 1980

Sammlung Essl, *Carom!,* Kunst aus Gugging in d. Sammlung Essl, Edition Sammlung Essl, Klosterneuburg, 1999
Schmidt, Arnold, *Arnold Schmidt: 111,* aufgeschrieben von Otmar Schmid, minimal Verlag, Wien, 1991
Schmied, Wieland/Sammlung Essl, *Malerei in Österreich 1945-1995,* Die Sammlung Essl, Prestel Verlag, München, 1996
Schreiner, Gerard A., *European Outsiders,* Basel-New York, 1986

Thévoz, Michel/Editions d'Art Albert Skira S.A., *L'Art Brut,* Skira Flammarion Genève, 1980
Thévoz, Michel/Roulin Geneviève, *Gugging,* Publications de la collection de l'art Lausanne, 1983
Thévoz, Michel, *Art Brut,* Kunst jenseits der Kunst, AT Verlag Aarau, 1990
Tuchmann, Maurice u. Eliel, Carol S., *Parallel Visions,* Modern Artists and Outsider Art, Princeton University Press, 1992
Tosatti, Bianca, *Figure dell'Anima,* Arte irregolare in Europa, Edizioni Gabriele Mazzotta, Milano, 1997
Tosatti, Bianca u. Rovasino, *Gigliola Lanormalità dell´arte.,* Utet Periodici Scientifici SRL, Milano, 1993

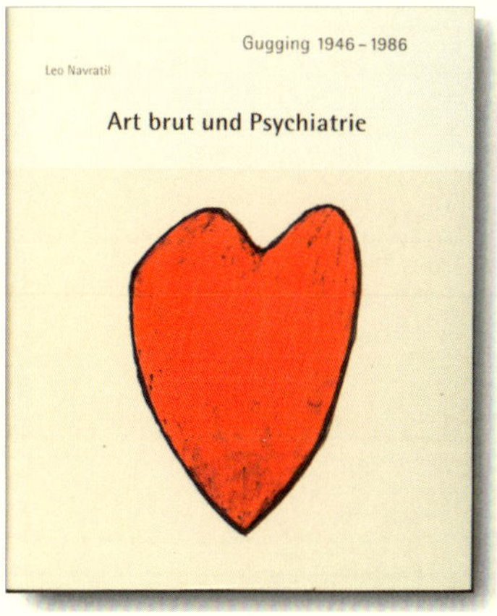
Gugging 1946 – 1986
Leo Navratil
Art brut und Psychiatrie

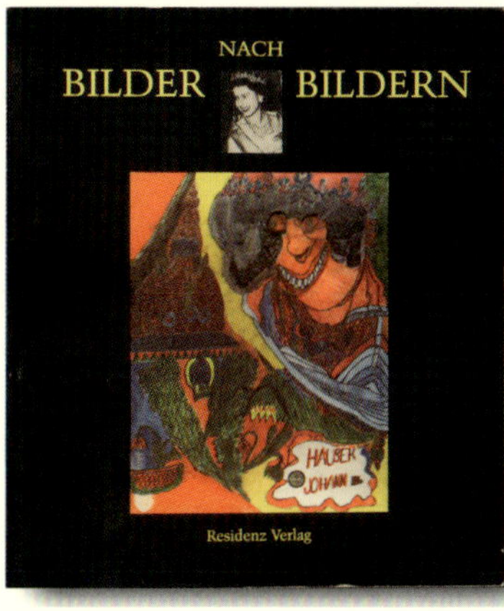
NACH
BILDER BILDERN
HALBER JOHANN
Residenz Verlag

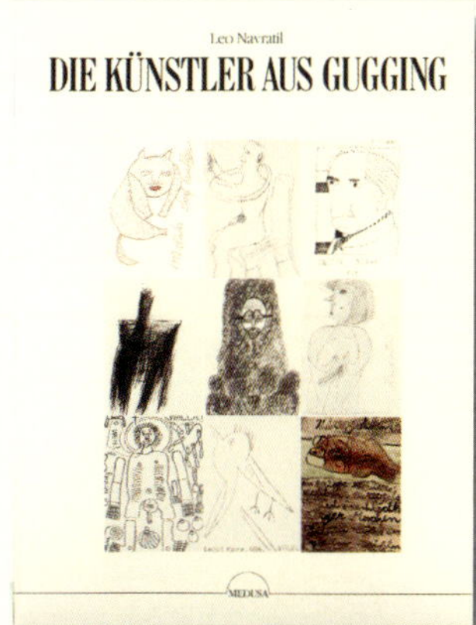
Leo Navratil
DIE KÜNSTLER AUS GUGGING

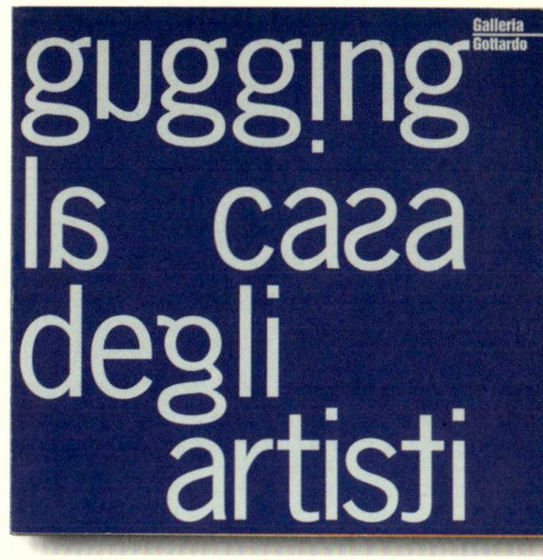
Galleria Gottardo
gugging
la casa
degli
artisti

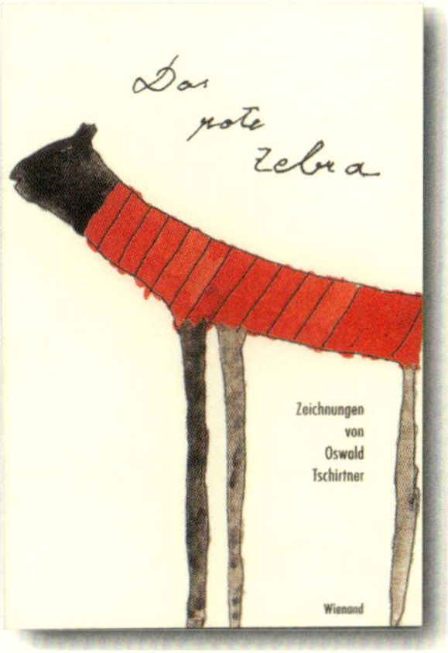
Das rote Zebra
Zeichnungen von Oswald Tschirtner
Wienand

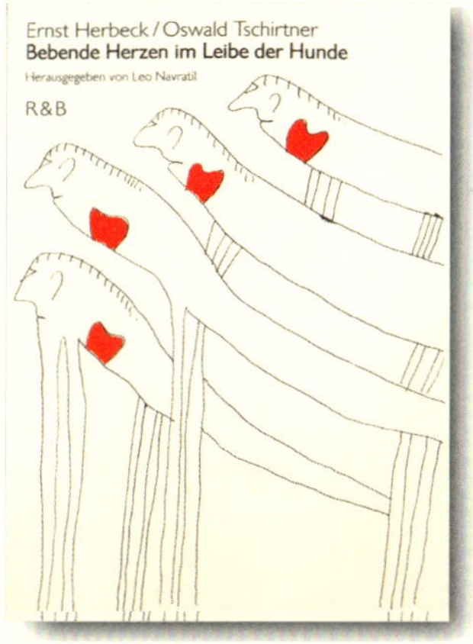
Ernst Herbeck / Oswald Tschirtner
Bebende Herzen im Leibe der Hunde
Herausgegeben von Leo Navratil
R&B

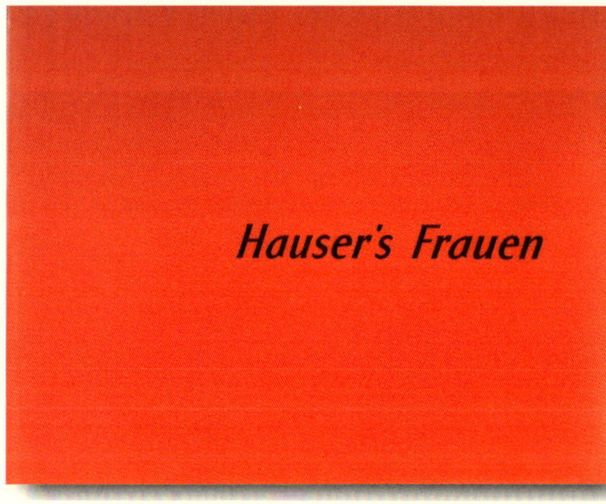
Hauser's Frauen

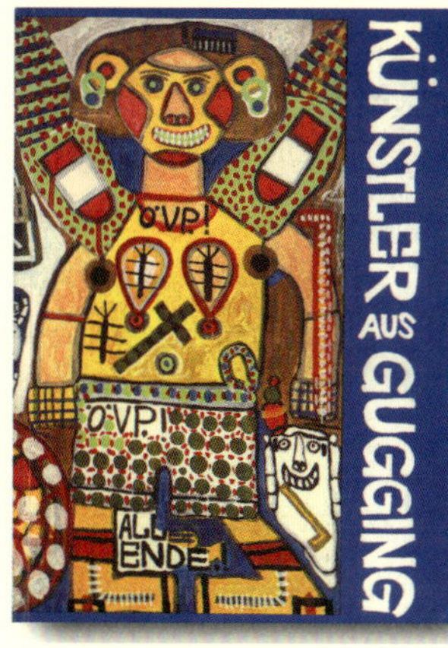
KÜNSTLER AUS GUGGING
ÖVP!
Ö.V.P.
ALL ENDE

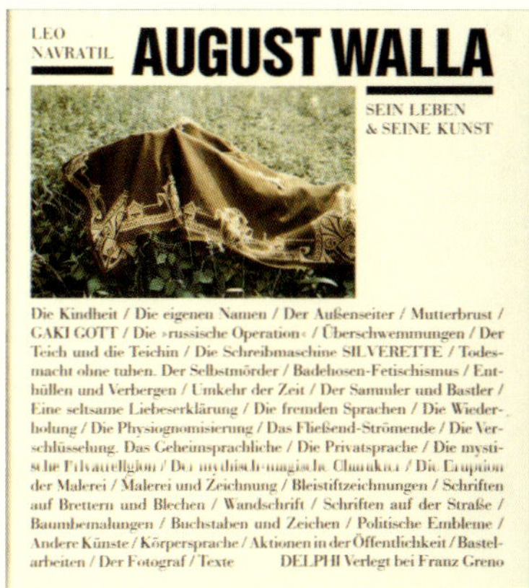
LEO NAVRATIL
AUGUST WALLA
SEIN LEBEN & SEINE KUNST
Die Kindheit / Die eigenen Namen / Der Außenseiter / Mutterbrust / GAKI GOTT / Die »russische Operation« / Überschwemmungen / Der Teich und die Teichin / Die Schreibmaschine SILVERETTE / Todesmacht ohne tuben. Der Selbstmörder / Badehosen-Fetischismus / Enthüllen und Verbergen / Umkehr der Zeit / Der Sammler und Bastler / Eine seltsame Liebeserklärung / Die fremden Sprachen / Die Wiederholung / Die Physiognomisierung / Das Fließend-Strömende / Die Verschlüsselung. Das Geheimsprachliche / Die Privatsprache / Die mystische Privatreligion / Der mythisch-magische Charakter / Die Eruption der Malerei / Malerei und Zeichnung / Bleistiftzeichnungen / Schriften auf Brettern und Blechen / Wandschrift / Schriften auf der Straße / Baumbemalungen / Buchstaben und Zeichen / Politische Embleme / Andere Künste / Körpersprache / Aktionen in der Öffentlichkeit / Bastelarbeiten / Der Fotograf / Texte
DELPHI Verlegt bei Franz Greno

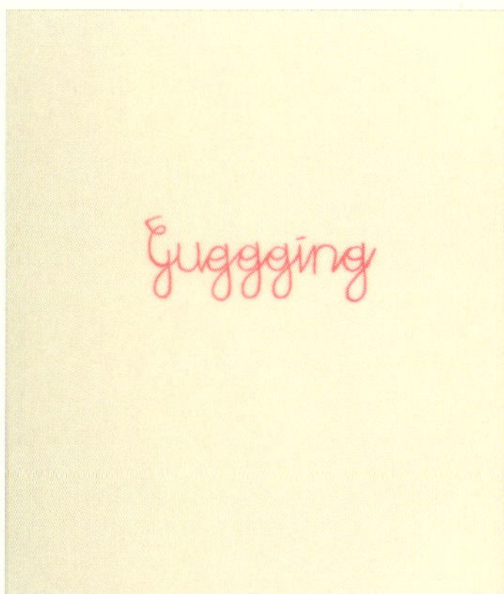
Gugging

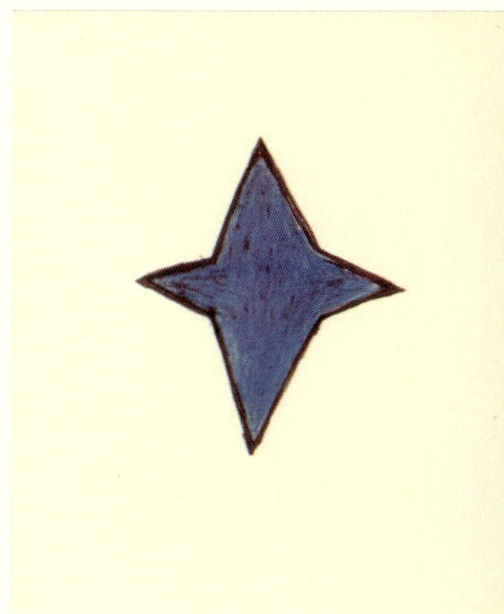

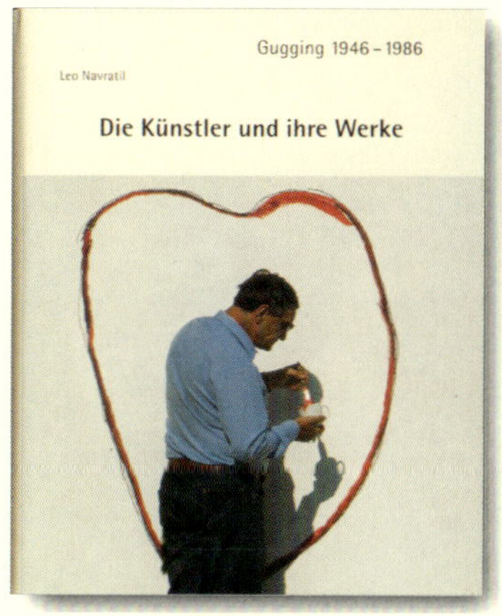
Gugging 1946 – 1986
Leo Navratil
Die Künstler und ihre Werke

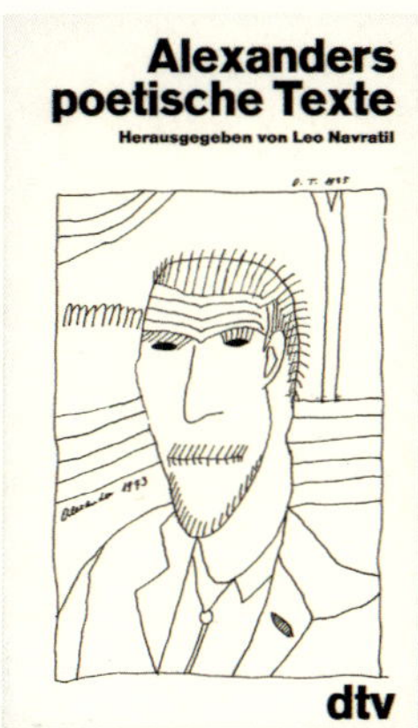
Alexanders poetische Texte
Herausgegeben von Leo Navratil
dtv

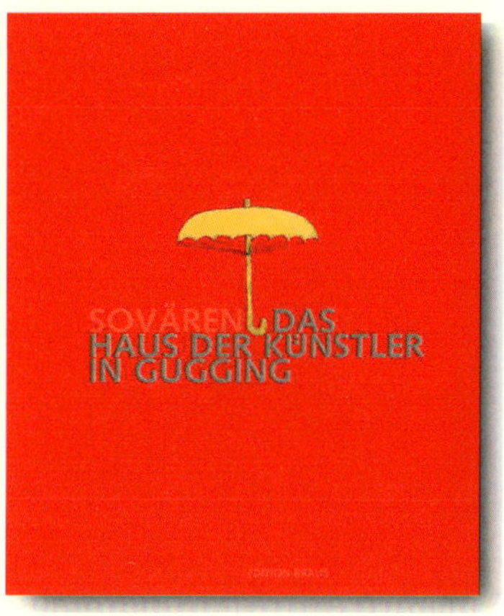
SOVÄREN DAS
HAUS DER KÜNSTLER
IN GUGGING

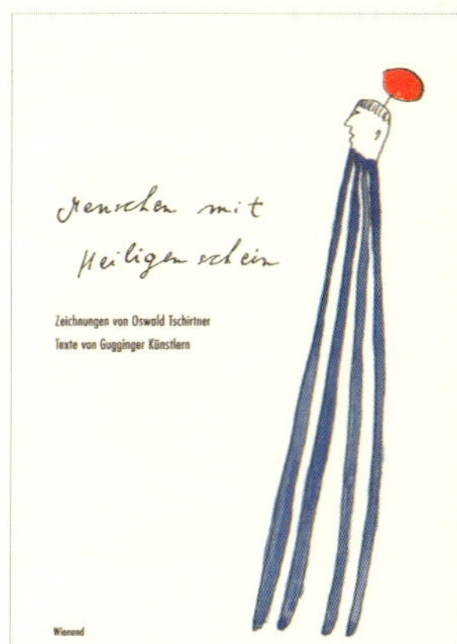
Menschen mit Heiligenschein
Zeichnungen von Oswald Tschirtner
Texte von Gugginger Künstlern
Wienand

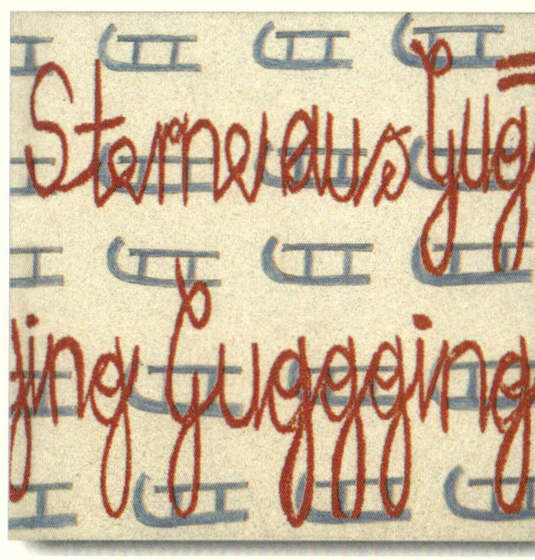
Sterne aus Gugging
Gugging

schlussgedanken / final thoughts

Ein Projekt wie der Aufbau des Art/Brut Center Gugging bedarf der Arbeit und Unterstützung vieler Menschen. Von den Anfängen bis heute sind viele Jahre vergangen und unzählige Helfer haben das Haus der Künstler temporär oder langfristig durch Aufbringen von Zeit, Arbeit, moralischen Zuspruch, Öffentlichkeitsarbeit oder auch nur durch Besuche so weit gefördert, dass die Künstler aus Gugging zu dem werden konnten, was sie jetzt sind und darstellen. Allen diesen Menschen sei gedankt. Unserer Erfahrung nach haben sie alle aber auch etwas mit nach Hause genommen, sodass man von einer Symbiose sprechen kann - und nicht von einseitigem Geben oder Nehmen. Erst das macht ein reifes und langfristig haltendes System aus. Wir sind sicher, dass es in Zukunft so sein wird und dass auch jeder Leser dieses Buches, wenn er einmal nach Gugging kommt, dies so empfinden wird.

A project like the creation of the Art/Brut Center Gugging relies on the work and support of many people. Many years have passed since the beginnings of this project, and numerous helpers have supported the House of Artists temporarily as well as long term. They have invested time, work, moral assistance, and efforts in public relations, or they simply paid us visits. Through their encouragement the Gugging Artists managed to become and represent what they are today. Thank you to all those people. From our experience we know that they have also been able to take something home with them, so that one can speak of a symbiosis rather than a one-sided act of giving or taking. This symbiosis is what constitutes a mature system, which can survive over time. We are certain that this will be the case in the future and that each and every reader of this book will feel the same once he comes to visit Gugging.

Umschlagbild / front cover
Rudolf Horacek, Horacek Rudolf in Mannswörth, 1984
186,8 x 140,2 cm, Acryl auf Holz / acrylic on wood

Impressum / credits

Herausgeber / editor
Johann Feilacher

Gestaltung / layout
Günter Eder, Roman Breier
grafisches Büro, Robert Schrotthofer

Übersetzung / translation
Susan Schwarz, Karin Hanta

Lektorat / editing
Rolf Röthlisberger

Druck / print
Grasl Druck & Neue Medien, Bad Vöslau

ISBN 3-902510-91-9

Die Deutsche Bibliothek – CIP-Einheitsaufnahme
Ein Titelsatz für diese Publikation ist bei Der Deutschen Bibliothek erhältlich.

1. Auflage

Christian Brandstätter Verlag
GesmbH & CoKG
A-1080 Wien, Wickenburggasse 26
Telephon (+43-1) 512 15 43-0
Telefax (+43-1) 512 15 43-231
E-Mail: info@cbv.at
www.cbv.at